INTERPRETING

THE FREE

EXERCISE

OF RELIGION

INTERPRETING

The Constitution

THE FREE

and American

EXERCISE

Pluralism

OF RELIGION

Bette Novit Evans

THE UNIVERSITY OF NORTH CAROLINA PRESS

CHAPEL HILL AND LONDON

Manufactured in the
United States of America
The paper in this book meets the
guidelines for permanence and
durability of the Committee on
Production Guidelines for Book
Longevity of the Council on Library
Resources.
Library of Congress Cataloging-in-
Publication Data
Evans, Bette Novit.
Interpreting the free exercise of
religion : the Constitution and
American pluralism / Bette Novit
Evans.
p. cm.
Includes index.
ISBN 0-8078-2399-6 (cloth: alk.
paper). — ISBN 0-8078-4674-0 (pbk.:
alk. paper) 1. Freedom of religion—
United States. 2. Church and State—
United States. I. Title.
BR516.E9 1998
323.44'2'0973—dc21 97-8408
CIP

01 00 99 98 97 5 4 3 2 1

*To my amazingly
complex and
wonderfully loving
family for whom
pluralism isn't
a "normative
vision," but a
simple fact of life.
And with special
love to my sons,
Micah and Jeremy.*

CONTENTS

ACKNOWLEDGMENTS

During the several years this work was in preparation, I received support from Creighton University and from my colleagues and students here. I prepared an early draft of this manuscript while I was a fellow at the Creighton's Center for Health Policy and Ethics. Later stages of this project were supported by a summer research grant of the graduate school and by the sabbatical program of the College of Arts and Sciences. I am grateful to both. In addition, I would like to thank Mary Caviness of The University of North Carolina Press, whose careful eye saved me from many potentially embarrassing mistakes. Above all, I have benefited from generous insights of colleagues in the Faculty Research Group of the Center for Religion and Society at this university. Their encouragement and kindness, expertise and intelligence transcend collegiality and reflect genuine friendship.

INTRODUCTION

One of the achievements of the American constitutional system we most justly celebrate is the First Amendment guarantee of religious freedom. The very first words of the Bill of Rights announce this protection: "Congress shall make no law respecting an establishment of religion or prohibiting the free exercise thereof."[1] Traditionally, we have understood these words to encompass two separate guarantees. The Establishment Clause protects us against state-sponsored or -imposed religious obligations, and the Free Exercise Clause protects the liberty of individual and group religious expressions from state penalties. Judges, activists, and scholars have long argued about whether the two clauses encompass a single principle of religious liberty, or whether they protect essentially different kinds of interests: are they fundamentally consistent or ultimately contradictory? In either case, together they provide the context in which each one separately makes sense. This book is about the guarantee of free exercise of religion, but only in the sense that it is the foreground of a photograph—distinguishable only because of the constitutional context in which it is situated.

Taken alone, the two religion clauses are merely "words on paper" or, in James Madison's words, "parchment guarantees." A constitution involves social practice; the words in practice mean what they have come to mean in the context of social life. Government officials at all levels, religious leaders, community leaders, and ordinary citizens are engaging in this social practice when they make decisions based on their understanding of what the constitution requires and permits. Most of the time their interpretations remain unchallenged, but occasionally, disputes about their understandings reach the judicial system. At that point, judges engage in the social practice of rendering authoritative interpretations. But, of course, this practice itself is situated in the context of our political institutions as a whole and, beyond that, the wider cultural context. The purpose of this book is to elaborate comprehensively and systematically what the "Free Exercise of Religion" has come to mean in contemporary practice in the last years of the twentieth century.[2]

No words speak for themselves. The meaning of the Free Exercise Clause cannot be found in any attempt to identify literal definitions of the individual words; it means both a little bit less and a great deal more. Clearly, the clause does not protect every conceivable exercise of religion; no one doubts that government could prohibit human sacrifices even if they were sincere religious practices. Many of the most contentious Free Exercise problems concern the limits of the guarantee. Even more controversy arises because the clause means *more* than it says — and we disagree about how much more. Although the words of the First Amendment forbid government to "*prohibit the free exercise*" of religion, the clause may also be violated when government penalizes a religious practice, denies persons benefits because of their religious obligations, and in other ways "burdens" unnecessarily religious free exercise. Just as the range of religions and religious practices is almost unbounded, so are the ways people may perceive their religious exercise to be burdened by the actions of government. Finally, while the first words of the First Amendment state that "*Congress* shall make no law," this prohibition, like the Bill of Rights generally, is understood to apply to any governmental actor, federal or state.[3]

In recent decades, this guarantee has been rendered increasingly problematic by the confluence of at least three social trends: increased religious diversity, the expansion of religious institutional activities beyond worship services, and the increased scope of governmental regulations. The first makes it more difficult to identify religious exercises; the latter two increase the areas of intersection between religious institutions and government and hence the opportunities for conflict. More and more, people seek protection under the First Amendment for activities that would not previously have been considered religious, demanding exemptions from governmental policies in order to accommodate beliefs and activities that stretch our traditional understanding of the First Amendment. Adherents to nontraditional faiths seek religious protection for nontheistic beliefs and forms of worship, and adherents of traditional religions seek to include church-related financial and social activities under the religious exercise umbrella. To cite only a few examples, under the Free Exercise Clause, Native Americans have sought to forestall the destruction of sacred places, workers fired for refusing to work on their sabbaths have won unemployment compensation, believers have sought to be permitted to dress in ways associated with their faiths, schoolchildren have sought exemptions from reading religiously objectionable materials in textbooks, and religious institutions have sought exemptions from labor laws and taxation. The virtual boundlessness of religious free exercise claims makes principled protection extremely difficult. To ignore these expanding boundaries would limit the guarantee to the kinds of religions that dominated American life during its formative period. But to offer First Amendment exemptions to anyone who claims a religious motivation would render the protection totally unbounded, unprincipled, and potentially vacuous.

The dominant understanding of the Free Exercise Clause has evolved continually, reflecting changes in the cultural, social, and political context in which constitutional understanding is situated. In 1878 the Supreme Court ruled that it protected only beliefs, not the actions stemming from them, and had no trouble sanctioning penalties against religiously motivated polygamy.[4] Furthermore, until the Bill of Rights was incorporated into the Fourteenth Amendment during the decades surrounding the 1930s, its guarantees only offered protections against acts of the national government, not the states. During the 1930s and 1940s, the religion clauses were applied to the states, and they began to provide some genuine protection to religious minorities, due largely to the effective legal advocacy by the Jehovah's Witness legal organization.[5] The civil rights and liberties era of the 1960s was reflected in a number of landmark developments concerning religious liberty, best exemplified by *Sherbert v Verner* in 1963. In this case, the Supreme Court ruled that only compelling state interests could justify governmental burdens upon religious freedom; absent such interest, the state is constitutionally obligated to exempt from secular regulations religiously inspired behavior with which they conflict.[6] The same era also saw major developments in Establishment Clause cases, with the still controversial rulings prohibiting Bible reading and prayers in the public schools.[7] Guarantees for nontraditional and minority religions were further increased in the 1970s. In *Wisconsin v Yoder* the Court extended the approach it used in *Sherbert*, affirming that "only those interests of the highest order and those not otherwise served can overbalance legitimate claims to the free exercise of religion."[8] Furthermore, in several cases stemming from conscientious objection to military service during the Vietnam War, the Court extended religious protection to those whose faiths did not rest on belief in a Supreme Being, hence making the First Amendment more congruent with contemporary theological developments and the increased religious diversity of American life.[9] The 1980s saw a resurgence of traditional religion, including the development of sophisticated political action groups to represent their interests. In addition, traditional religious institutions became increasingly involved in social service and institutional activities beyond worship services. During the 1980s, courts began to pay closer attention to the institutional rights of religious bodies.[10] At the same time, these groups criticized the "wall of separation" approach to the Establishment Clause that had characterized the previous generation's understanding, and they sought a renewed accommodation between government and religion.[11] In 1988 the Williamsburg Charter, a broad-based and sophisticated restatement of the American commitment to religious liberty, was signed in celebration and reaffirmation of the bicentennial of the Bill of Rights.[12]

First Amendment watchers and many religious leaders were shocked in 1990 when the Supreme Court made a significant step to reverse the expansive trends of the past decades. In *Employment Division, Department of Human Resources of Oregon v Smith*, a majority rejected both the compelling state interest approach and the constitutional requirement of religious exemptions.[13] Just as *Sherbert* and *Yoder* exemplify the landmark cases of their eras, *Smith* seemed to exemplify the conservative Court's approach to Free Exercise. In 1993 Congress passed and the president signed a law repudiating the constricted approach of the *Smith* majority. While this book was in press, in June 1997, the Supreme Court struck down the Religious Freedom Restoration Act as overstepping congressional power to enforce constitutional rights.[14]

An adequate account of any constitutional principle should make sense of the body of precedent and offer guidance for future adjudication. An account of the religion clauses must be grounded in an understanding of religious experience for Americans, and it should situate the interpretation within a satisfying normative vision of the polity.[15] To do so it must encompass two different kinds of religious experience. One kind understands religion as deeply personal spirituality; it captures the traditional value we place on unfettered conscience, and it situates the religious clause within the context of constitutional values of privacy and autonomy. The other kind understands religion as a "binding vision," the creator of shared meanings and of the social bonds that enable people to situate themselves within a community.[16]

These two understandings of religion are often complementary but occasionally painfully contradictory; in either case, any adequate account of the religion clauses must encompass insights from both views.

Whereas Free Exercise language (and constitutional language in general) a generation ago was dominated by the ideology of individual rights, recent years have witnessed a powerful resurgence of communitarian thinking. This trend has impacted substantially on Free Exercise law—especially in the arguments for recognizing rights of religious institutions. Some of the best scholarly literature on religious freedom reflects these insights. My own approach is inevitably influenced by this intellectual trend, but I have attempted to incorporate it without sacrificing enduring values from the individualist tradition.

Regrettably, I think, communitarian insights have been almost exclusively associated with advocates of accommodation for conservative religious agendas.[17] For example, one of the most perceptive scholars of religious freedom, Frederick Mark Gedicks, has recently interpreted religion clause jurisprudence as a debate between two discourses: religious communitarians and secular individualists. His distinction makes explicit the assumptions of many of the contemporary communitarian scholars. In this view, religious communitarianism "presupposes a faith that relies primarily on tradition and authority, and only secondarily on reason, to articulate and defend . . . values and practices. . . . Religious communitarianism permits and even demands that government exercise its power to influence citizens to adopt the foundational morality of conservative religion to guide their choices in private life." In contrast, secular individualism "considers religion to be an irrational and regressive antisocial force that must be strictly confined to private life in order to avoid social division, violence, and anarchy."[18]

While my work often contrasts communitarian and individualist premises, it explicitly *rejects* Gedicks's dichotomy. I see no reason why communitarianism should be definitionally connected with conservative religion. Gedicks ignores the communitarian commitments to social justice emanating from the religious left; my own progressive Judaism is communitarian in its insistence on a religious obligation to "repair the world." The social commitments of United Methodists illustrate a similar kind of liberal communitarianism. Likewise, there is no logical necessity for individualism to be secular; the Baptist tradition of "soul liberty" exemplifies a Protestant commitment to faith and piety grounded in individual responsibility. Hence, while I often cite approvingly from the "religious communitarian" scholars, my incorporation of their excellent insights does not imply an acceptance of this dichotomy.

Some Free Exercise claims are made by individuals; some are made by more or less organized groups. Those making collective claims tend to reduce them to claims about individual conscience because this is the issue to which we have always been most sensitive. The distinction I have drawn between the conscience claims of an individual believer and the institutional claims of a religious organization and the identity claims of groups is one that courts have hesitated to make. Because the institution's or group's well-being is so closely tied to the well-being of its members, the courts have often treated the claims of institutions as standing in place of the conscience claims of individual members. But reducing group practice and institutional and identity claims to individual ones obscures the uniqueness of collective activity and devalues religious group activities not strictly required by religious conscience. To conceive of religion totally in terms of the individual believer is to fail to appreciate the fact that religion is not a purely individual experience but a social one. For many Americans, religion is experienced more as a commitment to a people, a congregation, or an institution than as personal spirituality. To focus on individual conscience gives a somewhat protestant theological tinge to the characterization of religious experience and hence underemphasizes its institutional and social elements.[19]

A survey of contemporary Free Exercise cases reveals a mosaic of individual and communitarian guarantees. People who raise Free Exercise claims seem to be responding to several different kinds of perceived threats — (1) threats to individual religious belief, (2) threats to religious practices both of individuals and of groups, (3) threats to the autonomy of religious institutions, and/or (4) threats to religious identity. Therefore, the Free Exercise Clause can best be understood as an umbrella for these four overlapping kinds of protections.

Separating and analyzing these claims can provide some insights about the nature of religious experience in America. Doing so brings to our attention the fact that theological beliefs are not the whole of religion; that secular and religious practices are not, even in principle, separable; that religious institutions are themselves sacred for some people; and that religious identities are central to the meaning by which many people understand their lives.

These claims are often preceded by a threshold one. A *religious* belief, practice, institution, or identity must be at stake in order for one of the religion clauses to be invoked. Often, the threshold argument is the most controversial issue in a Free Exercise claim. Before we undertake the substantive issues, we will consider in detail the constitutional implications of various understandings of religion itself; subsequent chapters pick up this argument when it is necessary to consider threshold definitions of religious beliefs, practices, institutions, and identities.

Once past the threshold, a claimant must argue that a religious belief, practice, identity, or institution has been burdened. No clear constitutional doctrine is yet available for identifying the kinds and magnitude of burdens that raise constitutional problems. Once a burden has been shown, courts must still consider whether the burden is justified by some greater interest. These kinds of arguments are intensely controversial, especially since *Smith*. Those most sensitive to religious rights argue that once a threat to religion is shown, the state must demonstrate a compelling state interest that cannot be achieved in any less burdensome way. Those more amenable to state interests argue that government need not meet such a demanding standard in order to justify inadvertent burdens on religion. As long as a governmental policy neither coerces religious belief nor singles out religion intentionally for unfavorable treatment, they argue, it should be considered constitutional. As we shall see, many controversies turn on just how important a governmental interest must be in order to justify burdening religious interests. By passing the 1993 Religious Freedom Restoration Act, Congress attempted to adopt the "compelling state interests" standard for federal jurisdictions.

This argument overlaps a dispute about whether or not the Constitution requires exemptions for religiously mandated behavior. Advocates of exemptions argue that the Free Exercise Clause requires government to exempt religiously motivated behavior from governmental regulations that burden it—at least when there is no "compelling state interest" in enforcement. Opponents of this view deny that the Constitution requires such exemptions; some argue that legislatively granted exemptions are constitutional; others believe that legislatively granted exemptions violate the Establishment Clause.

An earlier generation phrased these conflicts as a simple polarity between accommodation of religion and separation of church and state. Those favoring separation of church and state took their imagery from Thomas Jefferson's famous call for a "wall of separation" between church and state. This argument envisions religious and governmental functions as operating in separate spheres. Perhaps the strongest statement of this view is Philip Kurland's argument that the government should be religion blind—recognizing no religious classifications.[20] Those favoring accommodation argue for a benevolent governmental stance toward religion, and they understand the intent, history, and guiding vision of the religion clauses to recognize that "we are a religious people whose institutions presume a Supreme Being."[21] It will be clear that these relatively straightforward positions become hopelessly entangled when both government and religious institutions are multifunctional.

The purpose of this book is to provide a comprehensive account of contemporary Free Exercise jurisprudence, set in the context of American religion and politics. I must first be clear about what the book is not. This book does not recount the history of Free Exercise interpretation nor the "classic" cases that brought us to where we are. Those stories have been told often and well; I have assumed the reader's familiarity with them. My focus begins within the past couple of decades and proceeds directly to constitutional doctrines, issues, and problems. In the interest of being comprehensive and systematic, I have sacrificed the narratives that give drama and personality to constitutional law. Therefore, this is a book more about problems and principles than about cases. So, for example, the *Smith* case is discussed in numerous contexts but never stands alone as a topic in its own right.

A great deal of literature, largely in legal periodicals, has been written on these controversies. Law review articles are so specialized that they are often inaccessible to scholars other than academic lawyers. Yet, many reflect sophisticated integration of philosophic, social, and political thought with broad-ranging implications for public policy, which should be made available to a wider range of scholars and decision makers. I have attempted to integrate this branch of scholarship with works from sociology, political science, philosophy, and religious studies wherever appropriate. Indeed, a subsidiary "agenda" of this work is to cross-fertilize disciplines that have grown apart and bring to bear lawyers' insights on problems that are *all* of our problems.

I begin my efforts to understand the Free Exercise Clause by looking at what people complain about when they believe that they have been deprived of religious freedom. This approach requires neither that we accept the validity of every complaint nor that we accept judicial opinions as authoritative doctrine; we search both for patterns illustrating a composite understanding of religious freedom. We look at judicial decisions as evidence of how authoritative spokesmen of our political system wrestle with the issues. Because judges (at least appellate judges) feel constrained to articulate reasoned and principled explanations for their decisions, they allow us to observe conscious reflection on political philosophy in the concrete disputes that create public policy.

The sequence of chapters suggests the structure of my argument. The first chapter approaches the broadest question: What is the Free Exercise Clause about? Attempts to answer this question remind us that the Free Exercise and Establishment Clauses are parts of a single sentence. All of our explanations of Free Exercise implicate the Establishment Clause as well, although the latter remains in the background. After a brief note on my approach to constitutional interpretation, I survey four of the best accounts of the guarantee and explore their strengths and weaknesses. Then I propose one—the pluralist account—that encompasses the strongest features of all of them and the fewest of their disadvantages. In the remainder of the book, these approaches will provide the backdrop for analyzing and evaluating the various kinds of Free Exercise claims.

Chapter 2 examines the threshold to the Free Exercise Clause—the claim that a religion is at stake. When this issue becomes controversial, courts are forced to confront the difficult task of defining a religion. Some approaches to a definition focus on the content of belief, some on its functions for the believer, and some on the social practices associated with religious belief. This chapter surveys these approaches to religious definition and their implications for general principles of religious freedom.

Chapter 3 examines legal controversies arising from claims that a religious *belief* has been burdened. While there have been relatively few such cases, some serious controversies remain about official coercion of religious beliefs. Chapter 4 explores the concept of a "religious exercise": How do we recognize a practice as a religious one? This chapter identifies three broad kinds of religious practices by individuals and surveys a wide range of cases and problems in which they have been controversial. Chapter 5 turns our attention to religious groups and considers whether the First Amendment implies a right of autonomy for religious institutions or whether the guarantee of free religious exercise is for individuals only. This chapter surveys the growing body of case law on religious institutional rights. Chapter 6 develops an issue that is not ordinarily viewed as a separate Free Exercise problem—perceived burdens on religious *identities*. Chapter 7 explores what it means "to *prohibit*" an exercise of religion. This chapter surveys several forms of burdens to religious exercise and relates them to the general accounts of religious freedom offered earlier. Chapter 8 engages the continuing debate about how to balance religious interests against other social values. This chapter summarizes the major arguments concerning accommodation of religion, religious exemptions, and the compelling state interests test and discusses their implications for the political process. Chapter 9 concludes by returning to the pluralist interpretation of Free Exercise, situates it within political and religious thought, and illustrates the guidance it would offer in characteristic religious freedom controversies.

The ultimate project of this book is both analytical and normative; I hope that classifying the points of controversy produces a satisfactory conceptualization of the guarantee. Ultimately, my effort is something like a response to Ronald Dworkin's admonition to find the principles that give the best account of the body of precedents.[22] This task begins in the next chapter as I examine four of the most well considered accounts (or guiding principles) of the religious liberty guarantee. It concludes with a fifth account, which I propose as the most comprehensive, and convincing, as well as most sensitive to both the individual and communitarian conceptions of religion. The arguments developed in Chapter 1 will provide the context for understanding the specific Free Exercise claims and problems I address throughout the remainder of the book.

1

THE SEARCH FOR PRINCIPLES

CONSTITUTIONAL INTERPRETATION:
SOME PRELIMINARIES ON METHOD

Religious liberty is not reducible to a single core value but encompasses a family of related values. Some of these are the conscience claims of individuals seeking protection occasionally for beliefs, more often for religiously mandated practices. Others are the claims of religious groups representing their interests in preserving the bonds of religious institutions and collective identity. Any satisfying account of the free exercise of religion guarantee must encompass two very different understandings of religion. One understanding views religion as deeply personal spirituality; it emphasizes theology, faith, private conscience, and personal moral obligation. The other understanding views religion as a set of practices, institutions, symbols, and identities that create and sustain a sense of belonging to a community.

A great deal has been written about the "purpose" of the religion clauses, understood as the intentions of those who wrote and ratified the First Amendment. Numerous works of superb scholarship have been written in contribution to this debate; it is not my purpose to contribute to it.[1] Steven Smith has recently added to the debate by arguing that the founding intent had *nothing* of substance to say about religious freedom because the First Amendment was a directive about federalism.[2] My own position in the debate over originalist constitutional interpretation is straightforward; I do not hold the understandings of the original drafters or ratifiers to be authoritative.[3] To hold such a position is not to deny the importance of their understandings; the founding generation's understandings are important, but not because of *whose* they were but because the insights they contain remain very good ones. Moreover, their concerns shaped the world in which ours developed; we live in a world that their insights helped create. It should be said at the outset, however, that those who look to founding intent for authoritative interpretation will not find my approach convincing.

I understand the search for the authors' purpose in writing the Constitution is different from the search for their motivations. Ronald Dworkin describes the role of purpose in interpretation thus:

> Interpretation of works of art and social practices . . . is indeed essentially concerned with purpose not cause. But the purposes in play are not (fundamentally) those of some author but of the interpreter. Roughly, constructive interpretation is a matter of imposing a purpose on an object or practice in order to make of it the best possible example of the form or genre to which it is taken to belong. It does not follow . . . that an interpreter can make of a practice or work of art anything he would have wanted it to be. . . . For the history or shape of a practice or object constrains the available interpretations of it. . . . Creative interpretation . . . is a matter of interaction between purpose and object.
>
> A participant interpreting a social practice . . . proposes value for the practice by describing some scheme of interests or goals or principles the practice can be taken to serve or express or exemplify.[4]

Overall, my goal is to construct principles that give the most satisfying account of the body of precedents. (I will use the terms "account" and "principle" interchangeably in this context.) "In law, as in literature, interpretation attempts to show which way of reading the text reveals it as the best work of art."[5] But even this apparently straightforward assertion raises a serious problem; it assumes that *there is a text* to be interpreted.[6] Literary theorists debate the very existence of a canonical text in literature, and in law this uncertainty poses an undeniable problem. To what exactly do we refer in invoking the religion clauses? Does it mean only the sixteen relevant words of the First Amendment, or does it extend beyond the four corners of the document? I understand a constitutional text—in this case the Free Exercise Clause—to include not only the words of the clause but also the entire religion clause, the First Amendment, the Bill of Rights, and the Constitution in which it is embedded, as well as the whole "body" of precedents by which it has been understood. This "body" of precedent itself is not canonical. Judges, lawyers, and scholars disagree over which cases are relevant precedents as well as how they are to be read.

The enterprise to which this book is devoted has been brought into serious question. Steven Smith, in his provocative *Foreordained Failure*, argues persuasively that the search for religious freedom principles is inherently contradictory. No neutral understanding of the religion clauses is possible because every understanding inescapably entails a theory of religion. Smith's argument is summarized in the following paragraph:

> The problem, simply put, is that theories of religious freedom seek to reconcile or to mediate among competing religious and secular positions within a society, but these competing positions disagree about the very background beliefs on which a theory of religious freedom must rest. One religion will maintain beliefs about theology, government, and human nature that may support a particular version of religious freedom. A different religion or secular viewpoint will support different background beliefs that logically generate different views of theories of religious freedom. In adopting a theory of religious freedom that is consistent with some background beliefs, but not others, therefore, government (or the judge or legal scholar) must adopt, or privilege, one of the competing secular or religious positions. Yet, this adopting or preferring of one religious or secular position over its competitors is precisely what modern theories of religious freedom seek to avoid. Hence, theories of religious freedom can function only by implicitly betraying their own objective.[7]

I find no way to avoid Smith's challenge. Indeed, the pluralist principle I advocate at the end of this chapter and through the remainder of the book is anything but religiously neutral. It explicitly prefers a society of fragmented identities and multiple identities, thus undermining those religions that insist on a unity of meanings. In Smith's view, the impossibility of finding religiously neutral principles should make scholars and judges more modest in their intellectual endeavors. I am inclined to "muddle through" in search of a principle that comes as close as possible to encompassing the American religious experience.[8] Ultimately, a religiously pluralistic society may not be any *better* than one that shares a religious heritage. What is crystal clear, however, is that only a religiously plural system is compatible with American cultural reality, with our system of government, and perhaps (as Franklin Gamwell suggests), with modernity.[9]

This limitation needs to be stated more explicitly. Any search for "the best" account of a legal text can only mean the understanding most persuasive *to us*, given who we are and the current concerns we bring to it at the end of the twentieth century. To understand our text is to understand our interpretive community. While I cannot fault Smith's logic, I am more willing than he to "bite the bullet" and advocate a principle that seems best to suit America entering the twenty-first century.

> Ultimately, the task of evaluating Free Exercise principles will involve doing political theory, and addressing fundamental questions about the polity and human condition. As Robert Cover has observed, doing constitutional interpretation requires that we expand our perspectives far beyond "law" in the narrow sense, and look to the normative order, the narratives, the collective life of a culture to inquired about the shared life which gives law its meaning: "No set of legal institutions or prescriptions exists apart from the narratives that locate it and give it meaning. For every constitution there is an epic, for every decalogue a scripture. Once understood in the context of the narratives that give it meaning, law becomes not merely a system of rules to be observed, but a world in which we live. In this normative world, law and narrative are inseparably related."[10]

For Cover, to know law is to know the communities that generate it—and communities are always plural, overlapping, and interdependent. Hence, I will argue, to understand American First Amendment law is to understand the law of a polity with plural, overlapping, and interdependent communities.

This chapter considers several of the most powerful accounts of religious freedom and their corresponding principles of Free Exercise jurisprudence. As Steven Smith has so rightly observed, no principle is "neutral." Each principle implicitly advances some vision of the good polity and hence holds some goals as ultimate while viewing others as instrumental. A good principle, as I will often have occasion to repeat, must be understood as one good for the kind of political community we are.

In addition, a good account must explain why the Constitution singles out religion for special protection. Many instances of religious liberty could be subsumed under protections of speech, the freedom of association, or the equal protection of law. Is religious liberty simply a specific case of Fifth or Fourteenth Amendment liberty? Is it simply another example of the value of equal respect? Since the Constitution views religion as either particularly valuable or particularly vulnerable, or both, a fuller account of the guarantee must develop that assertion.

The broad questions are: what is the point of the Free Exercise guarantee; and what is the most satisfying account of the body of interpretation?

A methodological question immediately follows them. How shall we proceed to search for one? I shall survey some of the most fruitful attempts so far to interpret the Free Exercise Clause and then engage in some "reflective equilibrium," a philosophical method best known through John Rawls's *A Theory of Justice*. Reflective equilibrium involves comparing each proposed normative principle with the body of precedents to examine the guidance each would have offered courts in deciding them. Here is Rawls's own description of the method:

> In searching for the most favored description of this situation we work from both ends. We begin by describing it so that it represents generally shared and preferably weak conditions. We then see if those conditions are strong enough to yield a significant set of principles. If not, we look for further premises equally reasonable. But if so, and these principles match our considered convictions of justice, then so far well and good. But presumably there will be discrepancies. In this case we have a choice. We can either modify the account of the initial situation or we can revise our existing judgments, for even the judgments we take provisionally as fixed points are liable to revision. By going back and forth, sometimes altering the conditions of the contractual circumstances and others withdrawing our judgments and conforming them to principle, I assume that eventually we shall find a description of the initial situation that both expresses reasonable conditions and yields principles which match our considered judgments duly pruned and adjusted. This is the state of affairs I refer to as reflective equilibrium. It is an equilibrium because at last our principles and judgments coincide; and it is reflective since we know to what principles our judgments conform and the premises of their derivation. But this equilibrium is not necessarily stable. It is liable to be upset by further examination. . . . Yet for the time being we have done what we can to render coherent and to justify our convictions.[11]

We juxtapose on one hand a proposed explanatory account and on the other hand previous court decisions—"experience," in Rawls's terms. When we find discrepancies between the guidance suggested by the principle and the outcomes of cases, we must then decide which ought to have prevailed. Perhaps we will decide that a whole line of precedents was decided incorrectly and that courts would have done better had they been guided by the principle. But the discontinuity may lead us to consider the proposed principle simply inadequate. A very large discrepancy between a proposed principle and the body of precedents should make us at least suspicious of the adequacy of the principle. Lest there be any doubt, "reflective equilibrium" is anything but a scientific or systematic approach; it is selective, intuitive, and, at best, suggestive. However, I believe that the intuitions and suggestions it provides may be fruitful ones.

The advantage of this method is that it does not require that we take either the proposed principle or existing decisions as an authoritative and fixed standard by which to evaluate the other. We can constantly adjust our evaluations, using insights from a decision to criticize or modify the principle, or reject the principle entirely. Conversely, a principle may give us criteria for criticizing or appreciating decisions in ways that were not apparent before.

The following sections examine four familiar and appealing accounts of the Free Exercise Clause and explore the guidance that each would offer on recent controversies. The chapter concludes with a fifth account that seems to offer the most inclusive and satisfying approach.

FOUR PARTIAL ACCOUNTS

The First Account: Protecting the Freedom of Religious Choice
Perhaps the most common interpretation of the First Amendment religious clauses is that they protect free religious choice. Supreme Court opinions contain many statements of this view. Justice John Paul Stevens's opinion in *Wallace v Jaffree*, overturning Alabama's moment of silence law as an Establishment Clause violation, provides an eloquent statement of the value of religious choice:

> Just as the right to speak and the right to refrain from speaking are complementary components of a broader concept of individual freedom of mind, so also the individual's freedom to choose his own creed is the counterpart of his right to refrain from accepting the creed established by the majority. . . . [T]he individual freedom of conscience protected by the First Amendment embraces the right to select any religious faith or none at all. This conclusion derives support not only from the interest in respecting the individual's freedom of conscience, but also from the conviction that religious beliefs worthy of respect are the product of free and voluntary choice by the faithful.[12]

Supreme Court decisions are replete with similar language. Justice Roberts, writing for the majority in *Cantwell v Connecticut*, phrased the idea in these words: "Freedom of conscience and freedom to adhere to such religious organization or form of worship as the individual may choose cannot be restricted by law."[13] In *Abington Township School District v Schempp* Justice Clark justified the banning of public school Bible readings by referring to "the right of every person to freely choose his own course" in religion.[14] In *Sherbert v Verner*, affirming Ms. Sherbert's refusal to work on her Sabbath, the Court said that she should not be "forced to choose" between her livelihood and her religion.[15]

The principle of free religious choice is rooted in classical liberalism, derived both from the Kantian notion of autonomy and the Lockian notion of natural rights. The liberal vision values, above all, human autonomy. The classic American statement of this position is from John Rawls's *A Theory of Justice* and is worth quoting at length.

> Thus a moral person is a subject with ends he has chosen, and his fundamental preference is for conditions that enable him to frame a mode of life that expresses his nature as a free and equal rational being as fully as circumstances permit. . . .
>
> [Persons] think of themselves as beings who can and do choose their final ends (always plural in number). Just as one person is to decide upon his plan of life in the light of full information (no restrictions being imposed in this case), so a plurality of persons are to settle the terms of their cooperation in a situation that gives all fair representation as moral beings. The parties' aim in the original position is to establish just and favorable conditions for each to fashion his own unity. Their fundamental interest in liberty and in the means to make fair use of it is the expression of their seeing themselves as primarily moral persons with an equal right to choose their mode of life.[16]

In a similar vein, philosopher David Richards develops a theory of the "primacy of religious toleration" as an outgrowth of the fundamental right of each individual to equal respect as a rational creature.[17]

Sociological observations of the patterns of American religious experience can either support or challenge interpretations based on choice. The remarkable persistence of denominational affiliation generally suggests that ascription explains religious behavior better than choice.[18] However, sociologist Andrew Greeley offers just the opposite explanation for the same phenomenon—one that is quite consistent with the notion of choice. Greeley suggests that "[a] 'rational choice' theory does much to explain the persistence of religion in the United States. . . . I suggest that the reason for this is the calculus of benefits, the choice of ones own religion seems to most Americans, finally, to confer the most benefits. The choice of the religion of ones parents may suggest a certain propensity to choose the familiar because so much has been invested in the familiar."[19]

Many sociologists have described American religiosity in consumer terms; Americans not only go "church shopping," they also seem to select elements from various proffered belief systems to construct their own religious worldviews. Thomas Luckmann describes this process: "The autonomous consumer selects certain religious themes from the available assortment and builds them into a somewhat precarious private system of 'ultimate' significance. Individual religiosity is thus no longer a replica or approximation of an 'official model.'"[20]

Recently, Roger Finke and Rodney Stark have used marketing metaphors to describe the competition of churches for members.[21] A typical sentence illustrates their approach: "[T]he primary impact of religious pluralism is to provide a broad spectrum of specialized religious firms competing to attract and hold a segment of the market."[22]

The principle of free choice suggests a unified understanding of the two religion clauses; the danger to be avoided is *coercion*. Hence, this principle is consistent with the recent direction in Establishment Clause jurisprudence, which evaluates governmental symbolic support of religious activities, such as public prayers, by looking for evidence of coercion of nonparticipants. This issue formed the crux of judicial disagreement in *Lee v Weisman*, which declared unconstitutional the practice of school officials inviting clergy to offer invocations and benedictions during graduation ceremonies. Justice Kennedy, writing for the majority, emphasized the implicit coercion of students to participate in a religious exercise.[23]

The fear of coercion reflects the value we place on the *freedom* of religious belief and profession. This understanding counsels a broad threshold to Free Exercise protection and the widest latitude possible for individuals to define their own religions. As we shall see in the next chapter, functional definitions, which focus on whatever is of "ultimate concern" to the individual, serve this goal particularly well. Definitions that emphasize personal belief rather than social practices are most consistent with this principle.

Formulating the religion clauses as a protection against religious coercion is an appealing principle, but as we shall see, coercion turns out to be hard to identify or even to define clearly. The "cult deprogramming" cases discussed in Chapter 3 illustrate the difficulty of distinguishing freely chosen beliefs from coerced ones; indeed, they call into question whether the concept of a free religious choice is a meaningful one at all. During the 1970s and 1980s, "anti-cult" activists developed several legal strategies to combat religious movements that, they believed, gained new adherents by coercive methods. One strategy relied on the argument that the First Amendment protects *freedom* of religion; it does not protect religion that has been coerced or groups who recruit membership by deception or coercion. Hence, these advocates posit a "coercion exception" to the First Amendment.[24] However, the notion of a "freely chosen" religion is a tenuous concept at best. Religions are seldom "chosen"; they are ascribed. Few members even of mainstream religions "choose" their religions. To distinguish "brainwashed" conversions from legitimate ones is to ask judges to make just the kind of theological judgments the First Amendment traditionally prohibits. These disputes force us to confront both the vision of free religious choice and its difficulties. Moreover, as we shall discover frequently in Chapter 7, there are many serious burdens to religious freedom that do not involve coercion at all.

Critics argue that the "free choice" principle misunderstands both the nature of the human individual and of religion. The view of the autonomous self, as articulated by Rawls, is profoundly individualist. The principle rests on a view of human nature that critic Michael Sandel has aptly termed the "unincumbered self." "The Kantian self is a choosing self, independent of the desires and ends it may have at any moment. As Rawls writes, 'The self is prior to the ends which are affirmed by it; even a dominant end must be chosen from among numerous possibilities.' "[25]

Among many articulate critics of this view, Sandel's has become classic:

Communitarian critics of rights-based liberalism say we cannot conceive ourselves as independent in this way, as bearers of selves wholly detached from our aims and attachments. They say that certain of our roles are partly constitutive of the persons we are—as citizens of a country, or partisans of a cause. But if we are partly defined by the communities we inhabit, then we must be implicated in the purposes and ends characteristic of those communities. . . . Open-ended though it may be, the story of my life is always embedded in the story of those communities from which I derive my identity—whether family or city, tribe or nation, party or cause. On the communitarian view, these stories make a moral difference, not only a psychological one. They situate us in the world, and give our lives their moral particularity.[26]

In short, the principle of free religious choice rests on a philosophical premise that is, at least, controversial. Moreover, the profoundly individualist assumptions of this principle entail a number of problems. First, it may turn out to offer ambiguous guidance, as Justice Douglas's partial dissent in *Wisconsin v Yoder* illustrates. In that case, the majority exempted Amish children from compulsory high school attendance and affirmed the right of Amish parents to direct the religious life of their children. But Justice Douglas was concerned that parents' choices might foreclose choices by the children themselves. He therefore would have required some evidence of the religious and educational choices of the affected children. Many contemporary Free Exercise cases pose conflicts among the choices of individuals. This problem arises particularly when the choices of religious *groups* conflict with those of affected individuals.[27] Communitarian interpretations of religious liberty advocate protecting rights of religious *groups* to define their own internal policies and membership rules; however, these arguments may fail to appreciate the impact of such internal choices on dissenters and nongroup members.[28]

This ambiguity, according to many observers, suggests a profound misunderstanding of religion. Emphasis on individual choice fails to capture the communal aspects of religion; at best, the strong individualism of this view implies a particular view of a religion. Classical liberalism developed in a protestant world that emphasized individual spiritual responsibility and understood a church as a voluntary association, an understanding that is foreign to traditional Catholicism, Judaism, and Islam, at the very least. Consequently, this account does adequately protect religious institutions—particularly ones that do not themselves foster choice. Strongly collective or strongly hierarchical religions would not fare well under this interpretation. It fails to appreciate the communal and institutional character of religion in practice—an insight that will be significant in our third and fourth interpretations. As Mark Tushnet argues, it is precisely the collectivist orientation that sets religious liberty apart from individual liberties:

A major problem with the liberal tradition's treatment of religion . . . is that it cannot account for the separate identification of religion in the first amendment without recognizing nonindividualist values that are implicit in religious activities. When the liberal tradition takes religion seriously, the result subverts the individualist premises of the very theory into which religion is supposed to fit. Yet, by distinguishing between religion and other forms of belief, the first amendment itself contains a nonindividualist principle. It thus signals that the Constitution is not an entirely individualist document.[29]

For this reason, Free Exercise problems that pit individual claimants against religious groups or institutions challenge the philosophical premises of individualist Protestantism and liberal individualism. Moreover, many critics point out that this account is on weak grounds morally and theologically, as well as constitutionally. From the perspective of constitutional text, it arguably renders the religion clauses of the First Amendment redundant. To posit *choice* as the ultimate Free Exercise value fails to distinguish religious choice from any other choice—and hence, it reduces the religious guarantee to a simple subset of the protection of "liberty" in the Fifth and Fourteenth Amendments. From a theological and moral perspective, it fails to appreciate the obligatory nature of religious commands for those who follow them and hence trivializes religion. To treat religion as a choice is to treat religious choice as equivalent to consumer choice. In Douglas Laycock's striking critique of the jurisprudence of *Goldman v Weinberger*, "[a] soldier who believes he must cover his head before an omnipresent God is constitutionally indistinguishable from a solider who wants to wear a Budweiser gimme cap."[30] Stephen Carter, in *The Culture of Disbelief*, eloquently attacks the way our emphasis on choices has trivialized religion itself. This criticism becomes the point of departure for our second account.

In contemporary American culture, the religions are more and more treated as just passing beliefs . . . rather than as the fundamentals upon which the devout build their lives. . . . And if religions *are* fundamental, well, too bad—at least if they're the *wrong* fundamentals—if they're inconvenient, give them up. If you can't remarry because you have the wrong religious belief, well hey, believe something else! If you can't take your exam because of a Holy Day, get a new Holy Day! If the government decides to destroy your sacred land, just make some other lands sacred! If you must go to work on your sabbath, it's no big deal! It's just a day off! Pick a different one! If you can't have a blood transfusion because you think God forbids it, no problem! Get a new God! And through all of this trivializing rhetoric runs the subtle but unmistakable message: pray if you like, worship if you must, but whatever you do, do not on any account take your religion seriously.[31]

In spite of its shortcomings, the strengths of this account remain considerable; protecting freedom of religious choice is no small accomplishment! When we focus on burdens to religious exercise in Chapter 7 we will have occasion to appreciate many of the ways that laws can, indeed, foreclose individual choice—sometimes by criminal and civil penalties, sometimes by the denial of benefits, and sometimes by totally foreclosing the possibilities of the religious practice in its entirety. Thus, while the emphasis on choice may not be adequate as a comprehensive understanding of religious freedom, any alternative that addresses these inadequacies must encompass the individual liberty protection offered by this view.

The Second Account: Protecting the Sanctity of Individual Religious Conscience

One of the founding documents of American religious freedom is James Madison's justly famous "A Memorial and Remonstrance on the Religious Rights of Man." Madison eloquently argues that the obligations an individual owes to "his Creator" are superior to the obligations of citizenship:

> Because we hold it for a "fundamental and undeniable truth" that religion, or the duty which we owe to our Creator, and the manner of discharging it, can be directed only by reason and conviction and not by force or violence. That religion, then of every man, must be let to the conviction and conscience of every man; and it is the right of every man to exercise it as these may dictate. This right is, in its nature, an unalienable right. It is unalienable, because the opinions of men, depending only on the evidence contemplated in their own minds, cannot follow the dictates of other men; it is unalienable also, because what is here a right toward men, is a duty towards the creator. It is the duty of every man to render the creator such homage, and *such only*, as he believes to be acceptable to him, this duty is precedent, both in order of time and degree of obligation, to the claims of civil society. Before any man can be considered as a member of civil society, he must be considered as a subject of the governor of the universe, and if a member of civil society, who enters into any subordinate association, must also do it with a reservation of his duty to the general authority, much more must every man who becomes a member of any particular civil society do it *with the saving his allegiance to the universal sovereign.*[32]

To the extent that religious precepts are thought to emanate from powers or realities that transcend the human, these precepts are more authoritative than those of human authorities. Several intellectual trends that converged during the founding period of American constitutionalism emphasized the moral sanctity of the individual conscience. The Lockians, the participants in the Great Awakening, and the Deists all assumed a Deity who had created ways for the human mind to comprehend His moral commandments. For philosophers such as Locke, God endowed human beings with reason suffi-cient to understand divine commandments. For Reform Calvinist thinkers, Scripture provides the knowledge necessary for the individual to live accord-ing to God's commands. The differences among these positions is significant, but all insist that spiritual enlightenment and moral behavior are matters of individual conscience, which can only be corrupted by the interference of the public magistrate.[33] Particularly influential in the battle for religious liberty were the American Baptists, whose doctrine of "soul liberty" holds that the only faith acceptable to God must be an uncoerced act of faith: "The idea of soul liberty derives from the doctrine of salvation through grace: the only way that unregenerate man can come to faith and salvation is through the intervention of God. It is worse than useless—it is blasphemous—for an outside party, the government for example, to presume to supplant the free act of God."[34]

The American Deists, such as Thomas Jefferson, reached the same con-clusion. Significantly, Jefferson began his famous Bill for Establishing Reli-gious Freedom with a statement of the same theological position: "Whereas Almighty God hath created the mind free; that all attempts to influence it by temporal punishments or burthens, or by civil incapacities, tend only to beget habits of hypocrisy and meanness, and are a departure from the plan of the Holy author of our religion, who being Lord both of body and mind, yet chooses not to propagate it by coercion on either."[35]

Our history is replete with heroic acts of religiously inspired conscience that challenged governmental authority in the name of higher law. The abo-lition movement derived much of its leadership from Christian activists, as did the civil rights movement. Indeed, one of the most eloquent statements of a right of conscientious objection is the justly famous *Letter from a Bir-mingham Jail* addressed by Dr. Martin Luther King to his fellow ministers. During the 1980s, members of the Sanctuary Movement were willing to violate U.S. immigration law because they believed that the commands of religious conscience outweighed their obligations to secular law.[36]

These conflicts have often reached our courts, with very mixed results. Judge Augustus Hand, writing in 1943 about conscientious objection to mili-tary service, captured the power of religious duty in these terms: "Religious belief arises from a sense of the inadequacy of reason as a means of relating the individual to his fellow-men and to his universe. . . . It is a belief find-ing expression in a conscience which categorically requires the believer to disregard elementary self interest and to accept martyrdom in preference to transgressing its tenets."[37]

These statements summarize our second account of religious liberty, one based on the freedom of *conscience*. Like the preceding account, this one conceives of religious freedom as an individual right. But unlike the one that emphasizes choices, this principle rests on the insight that religion is powerful precisely *because it is not a choice*, but a command—an obligation that the believer does not choose.

One of the most eloquent statements of this conviction is found in the amicus curia brief submitted by the Mennonite Church on behalf of Bob Jones University and quoted by Robert Cover.

> Our faith and understanding of scripture enjoin respect and obedience to the secular governments under which we live. We recognize them as institutions established by God for order in society. For that reason alone, without the added distress of punitive action for failure to do so, we always exercise ourselves to be completely law abiding. Our religious beliefs, however, are very deeply held. When these beliefs collide with the demands of society, our highest allegiance must be toward God, and we must say with men of God of the past, "we must obey God rather than men," and *these are the crises from which we would be spared*.[38]

Michael Sandel has argued forcefully that understanding religious liberty as freedom of choice badly mistakes the nature of religion; for believers, its commands are not choices, but obligations.

> But despite its liberating promise, or perhaps because of it, this broader mission depreciates the claims of those for whom religion is not an expression of autonomy but a matter of conviction unrelated to a choice. Protecting religion as a "lifestyle," as one among the values that an independent self may have, may miss the role that religion plays in the lives of those for whom the observance of religious duties is a constitutive end, essential to their good and indispensable to their identity. Treating persons as "self-originating sources of valid claims" may thus fail to respect persons bound by duties derived from sources other than themselves.[39]

In this view, violations of the Free Exercise Clause are found when the state coerces individuals in ways that conflict with religious commitments. The point of the guarantee, in this view, is to protect people from agonizing conflicts between obligations to the state and to religious commands. Because the commands of government come with strong moral presumptions in their favor, as well as physical force to gain compliance, it is entirely appropriate for government to avoid forcing sincere persons into such painful conflicting obligations. This account is consistent with interpretations that take *obligations* as the defining characteristics of religion. The source of these obligations, whether a Supreme Being or some functional equivalent, is less important than its motivating force.

The focus on religious conscience sheds a different light on some of the cases we considered in the preceding section. In *Sherbert v Verner* Adelle Sherbert had been denied unemployment compensation when she refused to work on her Sabbath.[40] In a landmark decision, the Supreme Court majority ruled that she had a right to state compensation. Justice Harlan dissented, arguing that the unemployment compensation statutes made assistance available only to those who were unemployed *involuntarily*; they were intended to protect people from job loss for reasons beyond their control, such as plant closings and layoffs. Ms. Sherbert, he argued, clearly *chose* not to work. Harlan's dissent suggests a failure to take seriously the notion of religious obligation. Ms. Sherbert refused to work because she believed keeping the Sabbath to be *obligatory*—not a matter of choice.

Consider again *Goldman v Weinberger*, in which the Supreme Court upheld the Air Force's refusal to permit an Orthodox Jewish officer to wear his yarmulke with his military uniform.[41] Justice Rehnquist, writing for the majority, totally blurred the distinction between a religious obligation and a personal choice. His opinion is replete with terms such as "the subordination of the desires and interests of the individual" and "subordination of personal preferences and identities," hence treating the wearing of a yarmulke as a lifestyle choice. Captain Goldman did not *choose* to wear a yarmulke; he felt religiously obligated to do so. Indeed, if religious practices were matters of choice, there would be far less powerful reasons for protecting them; it is their obligatory character that makes the protection of these acts seem so compelling. An appreciation of the obligatory character of religious commands would surely have led to decision more respectful of conscience and obligation.

The same case reveals some dangers in this appealing approach. A judge scrupulously applying the conscience principle might have asked Captain Goldman whether he believed covering his head to be a command of God, or whether it was an act of cultural identity. Such an inquiry is a problematic one indeed. Such a question would require a judge to delve into individual theology; moreover, it is also a question that even many thoughtful, conscientious religious persons could not answer for themselves. If the judge were satisfied that Captain Goldman, as an Orthodox Jew, believed that wearing a head covering was religiously required, she would likely order the Air Force to accommodate that need—at least unless the Air Force could show a compelling interest in refusing to do so.

In general, this view would be sympathetic toward a broad range of conscience claims that conflict with the commands of the state, such as those most dramatically raised by conscientious objectors to military service. However, while this approach strengthens First Amendment protection in some kinds of cases, it significantly limits the kinds of activities and motivations that would merit that protection. These limitations are made quite explicit by Steven Gey, who advocates a narrow guarantee that encompasses *only* those commands that are believed to emanate from a source beyond human control and that are immutable and absolutely authoritative. Quite explicitly, this formulation would remove constitutional protection to the "sociological, psychological, and institutional epiphenomena of religion." In his reasoning, "[r]eligious principles that are neither immutable nor absolutely authoritative would not lead to a conflict between secular and religious obligations because, by definition, mutable and non-absolute religious obligations can be modified or ignored by the adherent in order to comply with secular duties."[42]

This kind of reasoning has found its way into several recent Supreme Court opinions—and has indeed resulted in a narrow scope of constitutional protection. The decision in *Lyng v Northwest Indian Cemetery Protective Association* permitted the federal government to build a road through public lands held sacred by Native Americans and long used for their religious ceremonies. Justice Sandra Day O'Connor, writing for the majority, found no First Amendment violation because desecration of sacred lands required no individual Native American to undertake an act that violated his or her religious conscience.[43] Similarly, in *Jimmy Swaggart Ministries v Board of Equalization of California*[44] the majority found no violation in requiring a religious institution to pay state sales taxes on the sale of religious materials. Justice O'Connor, writing for the majority in that case, reasoned that the ministry's religious freedom was not violated by the application of a state sales tax to religious materials because no religious conscience was violated by paying the tax.

As Douglas Laycock has pointed out in his criticism of this opinion, this approach takes a remarkably narrow view of religious exercise. It supposes that religion is no more than a list of "thou shalt not" rules. As long as government does not compel a person to violate one of these rules, religion is not harmed. His words are worth quoting:

This position implies a wholly negative view of religion. It assumes that religions lay down certain binding rules, and that the exercise of religion consists only of obeying the rules. It is as though all of religious experience were reduced to the Book of Leviticus. . . .

In the view of religion as obeying the rules, all the affirmative, communal, and spiritual aspects of religion are assumed away, placed outside the protection of the Free Exercise clause. Practices that merely grow out of religious experience, or out of the traditions and interactions of a religious community, are institutionally unprotected unless they are mandated by binding doctrine. . . .

It is probably the case that most religious practice is religiously motivated but not religiously mandated. Most religions have some unambiguous requirements, and in some religions, compliance with a distinctive set of rules is one of the central and defining characteristics of the faith. But for many believers, the attempt to distinguish what is required from what grows organically out of the religious experience is an utterly alien question, perhaps a nonsensical and unanswerable question, certainly a question that reflects failure to comprehend much of their faith.[45]

This view clearly rejects accommodation for the activities of religious groups that are social, cultural, or in other ways, optional. Many important Free Exercise issues are not really about conscience at all. The more diffuse burdens on religion—those associated with institutions, identities, and cultural life—seem inadequately protected by this principle. Religious exercises that are not imperative would lose their justification for protection.

In evaluating this principle, we must bear in mind that conscience is an individual phenomenon, and the strengths and weaknesses of this approach stem from its individualist understanding of religious commitment. Michael McConnell, discussing the origins of the Free Exercise Clause, makes much of the distinction between the "freedom of conscience" proposed in James Madison's original draft and the free exercise of "religion" that was ultimately adopted. The word "exercise," he notes, connotes activities—a far broader protection than the focus on mental states implied by the word "conscience." Furthermore, the word "religion" comprehends religion as a collective phenomenon:

[An] important difference between the terms "conscience" and "religion" is that "conscience" emphasizes individual judgment, while "religion" also encompasses the corporate or institutional aspects of religious beliefs. In the great battle cry of the Protestant Reformation—"God alone is Lord of the conscience"—the individual conscience was used in contradistinction to the teachings of the institutional church. "Religion," by contrast, connotes a community of believers. The most widely accepted derivation of the word "religion" is from the Latin "religare"—to bind. Religion binds believers together; conscience refers to the inner faculty of judgment. Thus, the "free exercise of religion" suggests that the government may not interfere with the activities of religious bodies, even when the interference has no direct relation to a claim of conscience.[46]

Reducing "religion" to "conscience" would likely suggest accommodation for some individual religious acts, but it would be less solicitous of collective or institutional religious behavior, except where it stems from authoritative structures or sources. And as we shall see in Chapter 5, determining the "conscience" of an institution or group is a precarious undertaking indeed.

In spite of its strengths in protecting some important individual rights, this principle fails to encompass the nonobligatory religious practices and the communal aspects of religious life, such as religious institutions or the identity interests of religious persons. To the extent that religion is about identity and social binding, this principle fails to offer adequate protection for the full range of religious experiences.

The Third Account: Protecting the State from Religious Controversy

As these words are written, religious divisions have led to massive bloodshed in India, Ireland, the Balkans, and the Middle East. Human history has been filled with brutalities undertaken in the name of religion. Countless peacemakers have called for the depoliticizing of religion in the pursuit of simple peace. The Williamsburg Charter describes the "Religious Liberty provisions" as "articles of peace concerned with the constitutional constraints and the shared prior understanding within which the American people can engage their differences in a civil manner and thus provide for both religious liberty and stable public government."[47]

John Locke, whose *Letter Concerning Toleration*[48] so heavily influenced the American thinking on the subject, was writing in reaction to a century of religious warfare in England. For Locke, religious toleration was essential to protect the peace of civil society; government could be spared needless conflict by avoiding religious controversies. In America, sheer necessity reinforced Locke's insight. Even before becoming a nation, the American colonies were extraordinarily religiously heterogeneous. Moreover, the intense religiosity that characterized much of American culture charged that diversity with tension. Hence, the separation of religious from political conflict was a natural solution to a potential danger. The core idea of this account is that church and state ought to be separated, both structurally and functionally, so that religious conflicts do not spill over and cause civic ones.[49] Many of the earliest controversies in the newly independent states involved established religions, taxes for the support of churches, and compulsory tithes.[50] The potential for religious conflict was an important element in the arguments for avoiding *national* religious establishments. Fear of sectarian conflict motivated state legislatures as well. As late as 1978, Tennessee still retained a once-common statute prohibiting members of the clergy from holding elective office. When the law was challenged, Tennessee defended it, arguing that it would "prevent those most intensely involved in religion from injecting sectarian goals and policies into the lawmaking process, and thus . . . avoid fomenting religious strife."[51]

This account provides some insight into the common idea Americans associate with religious liberty—the "separation of *church* and state." The term "church" suggests an institutional view of religion, understanding religion as an organized group phenomenon.[52] Private faith, individual theology, and individual acts of conscience are not its concern. Whereas the first two principles understood religion as an individual phenomenon, this one focuses on the groups or institutions by which religious persons organize themselves. It also understands religion as a source of social power, and potentially dangerous power, at that.[53]

The danger of sectarian discord has been a frequent element in Establishment Clause jurisprudence. We find its influence in one of the Court's most enduring efforts to provide a systematic Establishment Clause doctrine, the *Lemon* test: "First, the statute must have a secular legislative purpose; second, its principal or primary effect must be one that neither advances nor inhibits religion; finally, the statute must not foster an excessive government entanglement with religion."[54] The third prong of this test, avoiding excessive entanglement, expresses the danger of involving government in the institutional affairs of religious institutions and the danger of allowing sectarian conflict to spill over into the political arena: "Political division along religious lines was one of the principal evils against which the First Amendment was intended to protect. . . . The political divisiveness of such conflict is a threat to the normal political process."[55]

From time to time, members of the Supreme Court have reiterated this concern—particularly when making decisions involving the allocation of public funds to religious institutions. When the majority approved state funding for transportation to parochial as well as public schools in *Everson v Board of Education*, Justice Rutledge dissented, fearing that any financial benefits to religions would initiate an unseemly competition among sects for state monies.[56] In *Meek v Pittinger*, the majority rejected a Pennsylvania program to loan textbooks and teaching materials and to provide ancillary services to private schools, in part because of the program's potential to foment political divisiveness.[57] One of the strongest statements of this concern is Justice Black's dissenting opinion on the potential divisiveness of state aid to education in *Board of Education v Allen*: "[S]tate aid to religion . . . generates discord, disharmony, hatred, and strife among our people."[58]

However, many judges and commentators believe that the fear of religious discord has been exaggerated and that it suggests a faulty justification for invoking either one of the religion clauses. Justice Powell, concurring in *Wolman v Walters*, was quite explicit: "Whatever may have been the horrors of religious wars in early modern Europe, and the tragedy of religious intolerance in the American colonies, religious divisions are not among our most serious political problems."[59] The "political divisiveness" test has had its share of critics.[60] Many observers fear that allowing political divisiveness to influence Establishment Clause interpretation would deprive some people of religious liberty because of the reaction of others. The mere filing of a religious freedom challenge to a state action could itself generate political conflict, possibly creating a self-fulfilling prophecy of Establishment Clause violation. In 1988 in *Bowen v Kendrick* the majority ruled that evidence of political divisiveness alone cannot invalidate an otherwise lawful government program.[61]

In spite of the decline (and perhaps demise) of the political divisiveness test under the Establishment Clause, the fear of religious conflict continues to inform our broad understanding of religious liberty. A focus on political conflict directs one's attention to the *institutional* functions of religious groups, but the guidance it offers is not always clear. Preventing intergroup conflict might suggest leaving a wide clearing around powerful religious institutions, as the Court chose to do in *Corporation of the Presiding Bishop of the Church of Jesus Christ of Latter-Day Saints v Amos*[62] and *NLRB v Catholic Bishop of Chicago*.[63] In both cases, the Supreme Court refused to enforce labor laws (the Civil Rights Act in the former case and the National Labor Relations Act in the latter case) upon powerful religious institutions in fear that doing so would impact ultimately on the religious decision-making authority of the institution.[64]

The fear of religious controversy underlies arguments on both sides of the "accommodation" and "religious exemptions" controversy. Arguments from this perspective are not phrased in terms of "rights" but of political wisdom. Their point of departure recognizes religions, as Madison recognized factions, as enduring elements of the political environment in which government must operate. Consequently, this approach would likely disappoint those who read the Free Exercise Clause as mandating a *right* to exemptions, or to the affirmative accommodation of religious practices. A blanket refusal to recognize rights to exemptions from generally applicable laws is potentially less divisive than granting exceptions—especially when it would be virtually impossible to grant all of them. Such reasoning might well explain Justice Scalia's much criticized passage in *Smith*: "It may fairly be said that leaving accommodation to the political process will place at a relative disadvantage those religious practices that are not widely engaged in; but the unavoidable consequences of democratic government must be preferred to a system in which each conscience is a law unto itself."[65]

In Justice Scalia's view, the Establishment Clause permits accommodation by legislative decision, but the Free Exercise Clause does not require accommodation as a matter of constitutional right.[66] Just the opposite conclusion is reached by Ira Lupu. In his view, both constitutional doctrine and civic peace counsel a strong right to Free Exercise exemptions, but no additional ones. His reading of the Establishment Clause forbids discretionary accommodation largely because of the favoritism, prejudice, and political jealousies involved in the legislative process and because it encourages religions to act as interest groups.[67]

This view makes religious toleration (to use a rather quaint word) an instrumental or prudential value; it takes the health of the polity as the primary goal and uses religious policy to accomplish secular ends. Thus, it divests the First Amendment religious guarantee of its status as a principle and invites instead an ad hoc approach, granting exemptions to politically favored groups or to groups whose requested accommodation would not be controversial. Doing so, however, turns the Free Exercise Clause from the realm of a *right* back to an element of the pluralist bargaining process. It is surely no accident, as Kathleen Sullivan has noted, that "not a single religious exemption claim has ever reached the Supreme Court from a mainstream Christian religious practitioner."[68]

An understanding of the Free Exercise Clause that looks first to the health of the polity as a whole cannot easily encompass the strong concept of an individual right against the polity. While an individual-rights approach might offer an *insufficient* understanding of the clause, it has been too important in our traditions and our values to ignore. This instrumental understanding of the clause would offer virtually no support for the accommodation of unpopular religious minorities, who have traditionally been the beneficiaries of its protections. In any balancing of the relative weight of state interests against religious ones, the instrumental approach keeps its thumbs on the scale on the side of the state. Any protection of religious minorities from neutral legislation must come from the political process, not the Constitution.

This approach reflects the same cool acceptance of religious identity groups as Madison expressed toward "factions." These lesser identifications —religious, regional, economic, geographic, or whatever—are legitimate but slightly suspect. Part of the genius of American pluralism is that it does not seek to destroy them but recognizes their durability and legitimacy. Nevertheless, to the extent that they pull members of the political community away from loyalty to the nation as a whole, they are tolerated, not celebrated. It is worth noting that Rousseau, writing approximately contemporaneously with Madison, reached an opposite conclusion in his instrumental approach to religion; enforced "civil religion" was necessary for political harmony, since people could not be expected ever to live in peace with those they considered damned.[69] Indeed, most of the wisdom of humankind up to that point would have agreed with Rousseau: the unity of religion was almost universally considered a sine qua non of civil peace. Summarizing the historical record, Sidney Mead concludes: "For more than fourteen hundred years . . . it was a universal assumption that the stability of the social order and the safety of the state demanded the religious solidarity of all the people in one church. Every responsible thinker, every ecclesiastic, every ruler and statesman who gave the matter any attention, held this as an axiom. There was no political or social philosophy which did not build upon this assumption."[70]

Where does this leave the First Amendment? If group conflict is the organizing principle of our political life, why is this particular form of group conflict particularly to be avoided? If religious protections are to be sought through the electoral process, why is religion mentioned in the Bill of Rights at all? Without additional theory that justifies the special nature of religion, we lack a reason for exempting religious politics from the interplay that characterizes the rest of political life.

The Fourth Account: Limiting the Role and Power of Government

Religious liberty is a powerful barrier against a tyrannical state. Once again, John Locke provides a natural starting place. For Locke and his American followers, the separation of church and state was not only a protection against religious conflict but also a hedge against the accumulation of power. A division between the functions of the state and of the church limited the power of both institutions. For Locke, the separation between religious and civic functions seemed a fairly simple one. Religion should stick to the business of saving souls, and government's own functions should be limited by natural rights. Locke's *Letter Concerning Toleration* of 1689 distinguishes between the ends of religion (the salvation of souls) and those of government, whose functions are limited to "life, liberty, health, and indolency of body, and the possession of outward things." Locke, of course, recognized that some matters belong to the jurisdiction of both the "magistrate and conscience" and thereby create "a great danger, lest one of these jurisdictions intrench upon the other." Yet, the areas of conflict appeared to Locke to be relatively insignificant. "I esteem it above all things necessary to distinguish exactly the business of civil government from that of religion, and to settle the just bonds that lie between the one and the other." The proper division between the realms of government and religion comes down to this: "[A]ll the power of civil government relates only to men's civil interests, is confined to the care of the things of this world, and hath nothing to do with the world to come," while "churches have [no] jurisdiction in worldly matters."[71]

To make this argument is to stake out a position about both the nature of religion and the nature of government. It implies both that government lacks overriding moral purposes and that those it has are subordinate to religious morality. While carving out a protected sphere of religious belief into which the state may not tread, it also implicitly carves out the realms of secular interests into which religion is not invited. Thus, Locke was concerned with not only limiting the powers of government but also limiting the purview of religion. "The end of a religious society is the public worship of God, and by means thereof the acquisition of eternal life. All discipline ought therefore to tend to this end, and all ecclesiastical laws to be thereunto confined."[72] Ralph Hancock makes clear the diminution of religion implied in Locke's *Letter Concerning Toleration*:

Locke's rhetoric may however obfuscate his real intentions. For the effectual truth of Locke's insistence on the absolute incommensurability of civil and religious concerns is that only civil (that is, material) interests are public interests. Although Locke may repeat the pious maxim that "there is nothing in this world that is of any consideration in comparison with eternity" (46) the practical upshot of his argument is that there is nothing in "eternity" worthy of any consideration by government; on close inspection, Locke's elevation of religious affairs to another world may look more like a relegation. Men must cooperate in securing the goods of this world, but every man is left to himself where any higher goods are concerned. Thus, Locke calls Christianity's bluff: you claim to be of another world—so leave this one to us![73]

In the interests of limiting power, *both* governmental and religious institutions find their functions circumscribed. Locke's neat separation is bought at the expense of denigrating both the functions of religion and of the state. Contemporary critics argue that the banishment of religious purposes and symbols from public life has left us with a "naked public square," thus impoverishing our civic and cultural lives.[74]

Locke's solution to tyrannical power was to authorize only a government of limited powers constrained by individual natural rights. Contemporary pluralists emphasize instead the fragmentation of power through multiple autonomous institutions. Hence, American institutions are characterized by fragmentation of power among the branches of governments, between central and local institutions, between the public and private sectors in the market economy, in the free press, and among voluntary associations. Alexis de Tocqueville very early in our history appreciated the importance of private associations in American life.[75] They offer alternative ways for groups of people to achieve their ends and to pursue alternative policies; they perform community functions in ways analogous to those performed by governments. The paradigm of these private alternatives are private schools. Recently Stephen Carter has emphasized the importance of religion among the kinds of voluntary associations that Tocqueville saw as the strength of the American republic:

> Religions are in effect independent centers of power, with bona fide claims on the allegiance of their members, claims that exist alongside, are not identical to, and will sometimes trump the claims to obedience that the state makes. A religion speaks to its members in a voice different from that of the state, and when the voice moves the faithful to action, a religion may act as a counterweight to the authority of the state. . . .
>
> First, [religions] can serve as the sources of moral understanding without which any majoritarian system can deteriorate into simple tyranny, and, second, they can mediate between the citizen and the apparatus of government, providing an independent moral voice. Indeed, from Tocqueville's day to contemporary theories of pluralism, the need for independent mediating institutions has been a staple of political science.[76]

The debate about mediating institutions raises serious Establishment Clause questions as well as Free Exercise ones. In general, these theorists hold that smaller and voluntary associations (such as churches) are to be preferred to large, public ones for accomplishing public functions. But they differ on whether religious institutions should seek governmental subsidies to help in performing mediating functions. Berger and Neuhaus have argued forcefully that government should both subsidize these institutions but scrupulously respect their autonomy; Dean Kelley responds that subsidies almost inevitably carry with them regulation and supervision.[77] This issue arose very concretely in the Establishment Clause case of *Bowen v Kendrick*, in which the Supreme Court upheld federal grants of funds to Catholic organizations as part of the adolescent pregnancy prevention program.[78]

Not only do voluntary associations provide private alternatives to governmental functions, they also offer competing conceptions of public policy, which challenge the government's agenda. The religious pacifist and civil rights movement, the Catholic Bishop's Letter on the Economy, and religious activism on both sides of the abortion controversy illustrate some ways independent religious institutions foster alternative conceptions of public policy and attempt to influence public policy toward those ends. Robert Cover calls these efforts "redemptive constitutionalism" and waxes almost poetic in defending the autonomy of religious groups who seek to change the world:

> Liberty of association is not exhausted by a model of insular autonomy. People associate not only to transform themselves, but also to change the social world in which they live. Associations, then, are a sword as well as a shield. . . . Despite the interactive quality that characterizes transformational associations, however, such groups necessarily have an inner life and some social boundary; otherwise, it would make no sense to think of them as distinct entities. It is this social organization, not the datum of identity of interest, that requires the idea of liberty of association. Commonality of interests and objectives may lead to regularities in social, political, or economic behavior among numbers of individuals. Such regularities, however, cannot be accommodated within a framework of individual rights. When groups generate their own articulate normative order concerning the world as they would transform it, as well as the mode of transformation and their own place within the world, the situation is different—a new *nomos*, with its attendant claims to autonomy and respect, is created. Insofar as the vision and objectives of such a group are integrative, however, the structure of its *nomos* differs from that of the insular sectarian model.[79]

The two Sanctuary Movement cases, *United States v Aguilar*[80] and *Presbyterian Church USA v United States*,[81] illustrate Cover's "redemptive constitutionalism." The religiously inspired Sanctuary Movement sought to transform immigration policy by the moral force of its civil disobedience. These cases, discussed at length in Chapter 5, illustrate a sharp tension between the advantages of institutional challenges to governmental power and the dangers of these institutions substituting their own religious agendas for those of the rest of the polity.

When we look carefully at "transformative agendas," we discover some subtle but important differences in the way religious groups pursue their visions. Four education cases, *Bob Jones University v United States*,[82] *Wisconsin v Yoder*,[83] *Smith v Board of School Commissioners of Mobile County*,[84] and *Board of Education of Kiryas Joel Village School District v Grumet*,[85] illustrate the problem of insular religious groups pursuing private alternatives to the public agenda. Bob Jones University was perhaps the classic example of a private association seeking to pursue a private alternative to the policy of racial integration; the constitutional question it raised was whether it could do so while receiving the public subsidy of a tax exemption. In *Wisconsin v Yoder* the Amish, an insular religious group, sought a change in *public* school policy, requesting exemptions from state educational requirements to accommodate their religious needs. In *Smith*, parents wanted a change in the public school curriculum *for all students* in order to make public instruction more congruent with their religious vision. And the Kiryas Joel case involved a public school district whose boundaries were drawn on religious lines to meet the religious needs of an insular religious community (the Satmar Chasidim). Superficially, these constitutional issues seem similar in that they all grow out of the desires of religious communities to pursue educational policies in conflict with those of the prevailing state model. However, our fourth account illuminates some important differences among them. Oddly, *Bob Jones* seems to have the strongest case under this account because it seeks a private alternative to state policy. In both *Yoder* and *Kiryas Joel*, petitioners demanded changes in public school policy, but only as limited exceptions to meet the needs of insular communities. The weakest case under this model is *Smith v Mobile County*, in which the claimant sought not an exemption but a change in the entire policy to meet the religious needs of a noninsular group. In general, the principle of limiting government would not offer encouragement to those who seek to impose their own religious agenda on public policy because doing so is not *limiting* the power of government, but capturing it.

Common to all of these issues is an understanding of religion as a source of social power, a view often neglected by religious sociologists.[86] Overall, this view would offer strong protection for religious institutional autonomy and identity claims because both are sources of collective power. However, it seems to offer inadequate protection for the vision of religion protected in first two accounts—the individual rights of autonomous choice and the sanctity of private conscience. Moreover, this view may give insufficient weight to the needs for national standards of behavior or for unified policy.

A FIFTH ACCOUNT: FOSTERING
INDEPENDENT SOURCES OF MEANING

I propose that the most satisfying account of the Free Exercise Clause is the pluralist principle, which understands the clause as a way of protecting independent sources of meaning and full and equal citizenship within the polity. To appreciate this argument, we must expand the inquiry and consider what a religion is and why it is worth protecting. This inquiry, in turn, leads us back to some reflections about the human condition.[87]

One of the distinctive features of the human condition is the need for meaning; unlike other animals who are equipped with instincts adequate for most situations, humans must create meaning. Of course, individuals do not do this de novo but within the language and culture in which they find themselves. Language is the most obvious source of meaning; it gives us the basic categories in which we think—time and space, names, logic, and relationships. Families, local communities, identity groups, educational and economic institutions, government, voluntary associations, and countless other forms of interaction are meaning-creating and meaning-sustaining sources. Science, history, art, and literature offer important ways of knowing or bodies of knowledge that help situate us in a comprehensible world. Among these sources of meaning, religion has always been particularly important because it situates the person within the cosmos, addresses ultimate questions (Where do I fit in the universe? Why do bad things happen? How do I understand death?), and helps make sense of "marginal situations," when our everyday understandings are most sharply called into question.[88]

The profound need for meaning implies two dangers. One is the absence of sources of meaning, and the other is an imposed unity of meaning systems. The first produces abject misery for the individual and anomie for the society as a whole. The second is more problematic: many believe that a unified meanings system is a positive good. Totalitarianism is appealing precisely because it offers a unified system of meanings. But when single institutions have a monopoly on social meanings, the result is an Orwellian nightmare; recall that in Orwell's story the state acquired power to specify the meaning of words.[89]

This need for meaning may help explain why the First Amendment privileges *religious* meanings over other kinds. One of the defining characteristics of religion, as we shall see in the following chapter, is that it provides comprehensive systems of meaning that address the ultimate questions of human life and help organize other kinds of meaning.[90] Peter Berger writes:

> The cosmos posited by religion thus both transcends and includes man. The sacred cosmos is confronted by man as an immensely powerful reality other than himself. Yet this reality addresses itself to him and locates his life in an ultimately meaningful order. . . . Put differently, religion is the audacious attempt to conceive of the entire universe as being humanly significant. . . .
>
> [T]he historically crucial part of religion in the process of legitimation is explicable in terms of the unique capacity of religion to "locate" human phenomena within a cosmic frame of references. All legitimation serves to maintain reality — reality, that is, as defined in a particular human collectivity. Religious legitimation purports to relate the humanly defined reality to ultimate, universal, and sacred reality. The inherently precarious and transitory construction of human activity are thus given the semblance of ultimate security and permanence. Put differently, the humanly constructed *nomoi* are given a cosmic status.[91]

Religions are often distinguished from other sources of meaning by the fact that they offer *comprehensive answers to "ultimate questions."* Theologian Franklin Gamwell defines religion as "the primary form of culture in terms of which the comprehensive question is asked and answered."[92] For Gamwell, religious freedom is the single constitutional issue of modern government; precisely because religious questions are the comprehensive ones, the way they are treated can be no less than constitutional. The entire purpose of a constitution is to maintain a system in which free discourse on ultimate questions is possible. Even if one does not adopt Gamwell's inclusive view of constitutionalism, this understanding of religion explains why religion deserves its preeminent place at the head of the Bill of Rights. It also makes sense of the context of the words in the First Amendment, which link freedom of religion, speech, press, and assembly, all of which are ways of assuring that government does not monopolize the role of definer of meanings and values.[93]

This insight does the most justice to the language and history of the debate over the adoption of the First Amendment. Whereas the Enlightenment Deists such as Thomas Jefferson found strong secular reasons for protecting religious liberty, evangelical religious leaders found *religious* ones. Their concern was not the health of the polity, but the protection of religion from contamination by political expediency. When Roger Williams described religion as "the garden in the wilderness," his concern was to protect religion as a haven of morality and truth. If religion becomes enmeshed with the state, secular concerns (we might say lowest-common-denominator ones) would infect the haven created by religion.[94] The point is not to protect the state but to protect religion. Mark Howe, in his now-classic *The Garden and the Wilderness*, emphasizes the *religious* purposes of church-state separation: "A frank acknowledgment that, in making the wall of separation a Constitutional barrier, the faith of Roger Williams played a more important part than the doubts of Jefferson . . . might suggest that the First Amendment was designed not merely to codify a political principle but to implant a somewhat special principle of theology in the Constitution—a principle, by no means uncontested, which asserts that a church dependent on governmental favor cannot be true to its better self."[95]

The logic of both Enlightenment and religious arguments converges on a pluralism that is deeply entrenched in our traditions. Whatever else our differences, Americans have tended to agree that autonomous families, private economic power, private education, and geographical, ethnic, and religious diversity are sources of enriched meanings for us. We value and protect religion, in this view, because it is a profoundly important source of meaning. It does not matter whether religions are acquired by free choice or by ascription, since the value to be preserved is not simply "freedom," it is something far more basic—the opportunity for a meaningful life.

How are meaningful lives to be attained in a society of large and impersonal institutions? Peter Berger and Richard John Neuhaus, whose work we considered in the preceding section, offer one influential answer.[96] They diagnose the major problem of American society as the large gap between "megastructures" (government and large corporations, for example) and the private world: "The essence of the modern crisis for the individual is the discontinuity between public megastructures, experienced as overwhelming and alienating, and the private world, experienced as anomic, so 'grossly under-institutionalized' that home is poorly equipped to provide a foundation for public identity. This identity crisis has a political dimension as well, 'because megastructures (notably the state) come to be devoid of personal meaning and are therefore viewed as unreal or even malignant.' "[97]

In this gloomy situation, Americans are desperately in need of "mediating institutions" that buffer individuals from potentially tyrannical bureaucracies, whether public or private. Mediating structures are "those institutions standing between the individual in his private life and the large institutions of public life. The mediation takes place in the gap between the megastructures of the public sphere . . . and the private, 'home' sphere, the modern American's primary refuge from the public world."[98] Among the social functions performed by religious groups, an essential function is to serve "as value generating and value maintaining agencies in society."[99]

We are now in a position to appreciate and to confront Robert Cover's powerful challenge to the special role of the state in creating meanings. The most controversial part of Cover's "Nomos and Narrative" asserts that each community has equal claim to interpret meaning—even public meanings—for its members, hence the state has no particular claim to authority in the interpretation of the laws of its society:

> I am asserting that within the domain of constitutional meaning, the understanding of the Mennonites assumes a status equal (or superior) to that accorded to the understanding of the Justices of the Supreme Court. In this realm of meaning—if not in the domain of social control—the Mennonite community creates law as fully as does the judge. First, the Mennonites inhabit an ongoing *nomos*—that must be marked off by a normative boundary with a religious community's resistance and autonomy. Each group must accommodate in its own normative world the objective reality of the other. . . . [F]rom a position that starts as neutral— that is, nonstatist—in its understanding of law, the interpretations offered by judges are not superior.[100]

He continues:

> Groups assume different constitutional positions in order to create boundaries between the outside world and the community in which real law grows—in order to maintain the jurisgenerative capacity of the community's distinct law. We ought not lightly to assume a statist perspective here, for the *nomos* of officialdom is also "particular"—as particular as that of the Amish. And it, too, reaches out for validation and seeks to ex-

tend its legitimacy by gaining acceptance from the normative world that lies outside its core.

The principles that establish the nomian autonomy of a community must, of course, resonate within the community itself and within its sacred stories. But it is a great advantage to the community to have such principles resonate with the sacred stories of other communities that establish overlapping or conflicting normative worlds. Neither religious churches, however small and dedicated, nor utopian communities, however isolated, nor cadres of judges, however independent, can ever manage a total break from other groups with other understanding of law. . . . The interdependence of legal meanings makes it possible to say that the Amish, the Shakers, and the judges are all engaged in the task of constitutional understanding. But their distinct starting points, identifications, and stories make us realize we cannot pretend to a unitary law.

Sectarian communities differ from most—but not all—other communities in the degree to which they establish a *nomos* of their own. They characteristically construct their own myths, lay down their own precepts, and presume to establish their own hierarchies of norms. Most importantly, they identify their own paradigms for lawful behavior and reduce the state to just one element, albeit an important one, in the normative environment.[101]

As we shall see in Chapter 5, Cover's view is far more sympathetic to the autonomy of sectarian communities than is my pluralist vision. His "non-statist" vision underestimates the element of common citizenship that is the second part of my principle. Recall that this principle values not only independent sources of meaning but also full and equal citizenship. How are both to be maintained? Are they inherently contradictory? How are the centrifugal forces of independent meanings to be contained within the common bonds of community? If religious individuals, communities, and institutions derive their answers to comprehensive questions from separate sources and inspirations, where is the "glue" that holds the polity together? Where is the consensus that assures minimal civility, respect for law, and mutual forbearance?

Part of the answer is found in the fact that groups are not merely *defenses against government*; they are the *agencies of active citizenship*. Political life is not best characterized by the isolation of the voting booth; it is both learned and practiced within the context of associations. Michael Waltzer argues forcefully that democratic citizenship depends on "the strength and vitality of our associations."[102]

The very act of participating in associations should undermine insularity and promote overlapping experiences and commitments. Of course, this is not always the case. But the pluralist vision depends not only on multiple sources of meaning but also on overlapping ones. Its goal is not to foster numerous separate and autonomous communities of meaning but to nurture a complex patchwork of such groups. In this view, no single element of consensus is essential; rather, social cohesion is achieved through the overlap of consensus and conflict—not only within the society as a whole but within individuals as well. The vision of society is not a segmented one but one composed of a web of overlapping roles, identities, and meanings. For these reasons, this principle is far less sympathetic to the separation, insularity, and autonomy of sectarian groups than those of Cover or Berger and Neuhaus would be.

This vision offers a way for both understanding and limiting individual rights. It sees humans as meaning-creating beings and understands freedom as the capability of creating meanings. However, it does not imagine that individuals, sui generis, produce "autonomous" meanings, but it appreciates the social genesis of meanings. Nor does it deny government a role in creating meanings. Hence, while it protects alternative meaning-creating institutions, it does not preclude the educative functions of government as only one—perhaps even a dominant—meaning-creating institution.

The school curriculum cases of the 1980s suggest some applications of this approach. In these cases, Christian fundamentalist parents argued that the exclusion of religious content from public education and the secular humanist values allegedly taught in the schools deprived their children of religious free exercise by denigrating the children's religious beliefs.[103] The pluralist account offers wide protection for private religious schools to create alternative values, but it does not deny government the right to teach values in the public schools. Arguments about whether the public school curriculum taught the "religion" of secular humanism are therefore entirely beside the point. What government may not do is monopolize the teaching of values by burdening or otherwise discouraging other institutions. Hence, while this principle is sympathetic to parents' concerns about government monopoly on the teaching of values, it does not offer much solace to those who want to incorporate religious teachings into the public school curriculum. Religious agendas such as creation science and school prayer seek to use the dominant power of the state to *reinforce* religious values rather than to foster alternative sources of values. In general, this principle argues forcefully against any majoritarian interpretation of the Free Exercise Clause. Moreover, it views the tension between the schools' message and that of parents and churches to be a positive good, even though a painful one. Multiple, conflicting, and overlapping meanings are the source of cohesion and stability in this approach.

The "cult" deprogramming controversies demonstrate another strength of this approach. This view enables us to avoid a fruitless debate about whether beliefs are freely chosen. Just as we avoid questioning whether a Jew is a Jew because she "chose" to be so or simply because she was born of Jewish parents, and whether a Catholic who "chooses" Catholicism after receiving a Catholic education has experienced free exercise of religion, we must not question whether membership in religious "cults" is "freely" chosen—short of physical actions that would be illegal as kidnapping, battery, etc. Traditional Catholic schooling has sometimes looked "coercive" to outsiders, and fraternity initiation rites are often quite coercive. Yet adherents to both practices value immensely the shared meanings they have produced. By the same token, we cannot selectively use a criterion that religious choices must be "autonomous" without being both inconsistent and sociologically naive. Nor is it necessary that all religious beliefs be equally valuable to any observer; what is valued is the plurality of sources of meaning.

This principle offers strong protection for religious practices, understanding them as ways we create, express, and reinforce meanings. Under this principle it would not matter terribly whether the practices were the "commands of conscience" or "merely" the cultural practices of the religious group. This account hearkens to the root of the word religion as a "binding vision," protecting the beliefs, practices, institutions, and identities by which we bind ourselves to each other.

This pluralist principle would be solicitous of the demands for institutional autonomy, but not unqualifiedly so. It reminds us that "freedom of religion" is an abstract term; religions are almost always practiced in social settings. Without denying that individuals can and do have solitary religious experiences, it recognizes that religious meanings perpetuate themselves through collective activities. Hence, protecting religion must include protecting the social institutions that enable it to exist. In Berger's words,

> *all* religious traditions . . . require specific communities for their continuing plausibility. In this sense, the maxim *extra ecclesium nulla salus* has general empirical applicability, provided one understands *salus* in a theoretically rather unpalatable sense—to wit, as continuing plausibility. The reality of the Christian world depends upon the presence of social structures within which this reality is taken for granted and within which successive generations of individuals are socialized in such a way that this

world will be real *to them*. When this plausibility structure loses its intactness or continuity, the Christian world begins to totter, and its reality ceases to impose itself as self-evident.[104]

Appreciating the necessity of religious institutions does not itself imply a constitutional right to institutional autonomy. Rather than positing an abstract right to autonomy, this principle would focus on a concrete question: Does the challenged policy deprive the institution of its ability to perform its role of fostering the religious exercise of its members? The constitutional rights of religious institutions, in this account, are both justified and limited by the underlying principle of religious freedom.

This view would be solicitous of identity claims, such as the claims of "cult" members to maintain insular communities, however bizarre to the majority. This view would not be friendly to governmental demands for uniformity, whether in the education of Amish children or the dress of military officers. Under this reasoning, government should not force choice between religious identity and full participation in society. Not only is that bad for individuals, it is also bad for society. It is in government's interest not to provoke choices that fragment a citizen's identity. Hence, the argument for protecting and accommodating minority practices is not just an individual-rights argument. It also rests on a vision of a society with overlapping rather than segmented commitments.

It is precisely this web of overlapping commitments that holds the society together in the pluralist view. Independent meanings must be maintained within a context of full and equal citizenship. Captain Goldman's problem provides an excellent example of how equal citizenship reinforces the ideal of plural meanings: when the Air Force prohibited Goldman from wearing his yarmulke with his military uniform, it precluded his enjoying full participation as an equal citizen while simultaneously practicing his religion.

There are, however, occasional tensions between the two aspects of the pluralist principle. The demands of common citizenship both help explain the importance of religious freedom and provide some limiting guidelines as well. Very insular groups who stand outside the web of overlapping commitments would not enjoy special rights to insularity. The tension between two elements of this principle—fostering independent sources of meaning and guaranteeing full and equal citizenship—produces the most difficult Free Exercise problems. This problem shall occupy our concern when we attempt to reconcile Free Exercise values in the final chapter.

I shall argue throughout this book that the pluralist interpretation offers the most comprehensive Free Exercise principle. First, it encompasses both individual and communal facets of religion. It understands that religion may be private but may as well be communal. Likewise, it encompasses both deontological and instrumental values. It values the freedom of conscience as an attribute of individual well-being. At the same time, it appreciates the instrumental role of religious liberty in insulating the polity from sectarian conflict and in dispersing political power. Above all, it recognizes religion's own contribution to individual well-being. Understanding the human as a meaning-creating and meaning-needing creature, it protects individual beliefs and their consequent behavior as well as religious identities and institutions because these bonds are among the things that give life meaning.

The path toward constitutional interpretation has taken us, as it always does, on a journey into political and social theory. Identifying what is at stake in Free Exercise claims enables us—indeed, *forces* us—to confront the ways that we define ourselves as a political community and as meaning-seeking creatures.

2

DEFINITIONS OF RELIGION UNDER
THE FREE EXERCISE CLAUSE

THE THRESHOLD PROBLEM

A Jewish parent wants her son excused from public school to attend worship services on Rosh Hashanah. It is the only time of year the family attends the synagogue, but the parent feels that some connection with her son's religious tradition is important, and she does not want the school to penalize him for his absence. Nothing is unusual about this request. Now consider another parent, a passionate music lover for whom music is the center of life's meaning, comfort in distress, and source of hope and inspiration. This parent asks that her son be excused from school for cello lessons during the school day. We would not be surprised if the school grants the first parent's request, reasoning that to deny the Jewish parent's request would violate her First Amendment rights, and denies the second request as one of purely personal preference or convenience. How confident can any decision maker be in saying that one kind of motivation is religious, and hence protected by the Constitution, and the other is not? How can we define—or at least distinguish—a religion, which is, after all, the threshold to First Amendment protection? In this chapter, we consider definitions of religious belief, faith, profession, or motivation that characterize religious conduct, leaving for Chapter 4 the even more difficult problem of recognizing religious *practices*.

The threshold claim encapsulates the underlying dilemma of Free Exercise protection. To provide principled protection for religious exercise, we need to be able to distinguish legitimate Free Exercise claims from spurious ones. But every effort to make such distinctions infuses the Constitution with some particular notion of what a legitimate religion or religious practice is, and that is precisely what the clause should forbid. Words are never neutral; hence, we have no "neutral principles" for ascertaining when a *religious* belief, practice, institution, or identity is genuinely at stake. J. E. Barnhart describes the problem thus:

> A definition of religion which does not exclude any tradition that is already within the general assortment of religious phenomena (Geertz) is a diluted definition pleasing no one. Many who are recognized as strongly religious will protest that a lowest common denominator definition cannot capture the "essence" of religion. . . . Any attempt to expand the definition of religion in order to save it from remaining the diluted lowest common denominator will run into the problem of exclusiveness. . . . The problem here becomes a kind of paradox. If we try to gain depth in our definition of religion, we lose scope and breadth. But if we seek breadth, we lose depth. . . . It seems to be impossible to find a neutral definition that, while enjoying depth, will not offend great numbers of people. We seem to be forced to conclude that no single definition of religion can do the job required by it.[1]

The fact that there are two religion clauses complicates the problem. The Free Exercise Clause has traditionally been considered the protection of the dissenting individual. Free Exercise arguments often occur when a nontraditional adherent attempts to convince a court that her religious beliefs or practices are indeed religious and deserving of constitutional protection. In contrast, the Establishment Clause prevents the politically dominant majority from enacting its own religious agenda into public policy; hence, conventional definitions shared by the community are more appropriate than those of the individual.[2] From time to time, constitutional scholars have suggested that the two clauses require different definitions of religion. Broad definitions seem necessary to protect a wide range of individual religious exercises. However, definitions broad enough to include educational, social service, and patriotic activities would leave many ordinary governmental functions vulnerable to the charge of violating the Establishment Clause. Hence, narrow definitions of religion seem appropriate under the Establishment Clause. Kent Greenawalt, for example, has suggested that the Free Exercise Clause should protect anything that is "arguably religious," while the Establishment Clause should not preclude government from engaging in activities that are "arguably not religious."[3] In a slightly different vein,

Jesse Choper would apply a very restrictive definition of religion when individuals seek religious exemptions from generally applicable laws but would apply broader definitions for other purposes.[4]

Employing different conceptions of religion would have important policy consequences. As Judge Arlin Adams pointed out, such a bifurcated definition inevitably favors new religions and disfavors traditional ones.[5] Overall, most First Amendment scholars prefer to seek a unified definition of religion, pointing out that the very language of the First Amendment suggests a single understanding. As Justice Rutledge wrote two generations ago, " '[r]eligion' appears only once in the Amendment. But the word governs two prohibitions and governs them alike. It does not have two meanings, one narrow to forbid 'an establishment,' and another, much broader, for securing 'the free exercise thereof.' 'Thereof' brings down 'religion' with its entire and exact content, no more and no less, from the first into the second guarantee."[6]

The dual nature of the religion clauses highlights our dual understanding of religious phenomena. Religion involves both an individual, spiritual experience and a social bond. For many Americans, religion is experienced more in terms of a commitment to a people, a congregation, or an institution than as a personal spirituality. Definitions that focus on individual beliefs give a somewhat protestant theological tinge to the characterization of religious experience and hence underemphasize its institutional and communal elements. On the other hand, social and institutional definitions of religion may inadequately protect individual believers or new or noninstitutionalized religious movements. Any adequate understanding of religion must take into account protection for both kinds of religious experiences.

When a group espousing a system of beliefs traditionally understood to be a religion raises a First Amendment claim, the threshold is crossed without controversy. When nontraditional convictions are asserted to be a "religion," courts have the awkward task of deciding what credibility to give to those assertions. Scholars may debate definitions of religions at leisure, but when judges do so, their definitions are authoritative acts of state power. Thomas Hobbes recognized the power of *naming* centuries ago and considered it one of the attributes of sovereignty.[7] The power to name is the power to define the terms of debate. Hence, not only the way religion is defined but also the empowering of those who do so are matters of substantial political significance. We must not forget that judicial definitions of religion are authoritative acts of the state and that almost all definitions advantage some and disadvantage others.

Any serious investigation of the legal definitions of religion entails reflection on the phenomenon of religion itself. Is it to be understood as a particular kind of belief or as a particular kind of motivation within an individual? Or is the defining characteristic of religion the ceremonial and other practices that provide a sense of coherence and identity for a group? Sociologists of religion disagree about whether religion should be characterized by the nature of substantive belief, by a key concept such as sacredness, by function, or by particular kinds of activities. Attempts at legal definitions parallel these approaches with remarkable correspondence. Within the body of First Amendment literature, religion has variously been defined in terms of the content of belief, the nature of its concerns, the function of belief for the believer, and the socio-cultural characteristics of community and practice, as well as combinations of the above.

MAJOR APPROACHES TO THE DEFINITION OF RELIGION

Belief in a Creator, a Supreme Being, a Christian God

For the men who wrote the First Amendment and the judges who interpreted it during most of our history, religion meant a theistic belief based on faith in a deity as understood in Christianity and Judaism. Hence, the core notion of a religion was belief, and the distinguishing feature of the belief was its *content*—belief in a Supreme Being. James Madison's famous 1785 *Memorial and Remonstrance against Religious Assessments* referred to religion as "the duty we owe to our Creator."[8]

Characteristic of this view is the definition offered by the Supreme Court in the Mormon case of *Davis v Beason*: "[T]he term 'religion' has reference to ones own views of his relations with his Creator, and to the obligations they impose of reverence for his being and character and of obedience to His will. One cannot speak of religious liberty, without proper appreciation of its essential and historical significance, without assuming the existence of a belief in supreme allegiance to the will of God."[9]

The narrowest belief-type definitions insisted that religion meant the Christian religion, and mainstream Christianity at that. An extreme example of this kind of reasoning is a statement of the Georgia Supreme Court in 1922. Judge Gilbert, writing for a court with only one dissent, upheld a statute requiring public schools to begin each day with a prayer and a reading from the King James Bible. Assuming that "Christianity is the only religion known to American law," he concluded that the Free Exercise Clause was breached only if the state "gives one Christian sect a preference over others."[10]

While few courts have followed Judge Gilbert's example, most have understood religion within the Western tradition, which places belief in the existence of a Supreme Being at the heart of the religious experience. When Congress provided statutory exemptions for conscientious objection to military service, it specifically provided exemptions only for those whose objections stemmed from "belief in a Supreme Being." The Supreme Court interpreted this requirement in a very traditional way in the 1931 case of *United States v Macintosh*, even in a challenge by a distinguished theologian. Professor Macintosh of the Yale School of Divinity, a Canadian, had applied for United States citizenship but refused to give unqualified promise to defend the country in time of war, reserving to himself the right to decide whether a war was morally justifiable. In refusing his application, the Court ruled that "religion obviously encompasses more than mere belief, faith sentiment or opinion. By its very force, it embraces human conduct expressive of the relation between man and God."[11]

By the middle of the twentieth century, the United States was becoming too religiously plural for such a definition to encompass the extent of religious experience. In 1961 in *Torcaso v Watkins*[12] the Supreme Court recognized nontheistic religions when it struck down a Maryland law requiring that public officials affirm a belief in God. In the Court's words, "[N]either can [government] aid those religions based on a belief in the existence of God as against those religions founded on different beliefs."[13] By the time the conscientious objection statutes were interpreted during the Vietnam War era, the Court recognized that relying on a Supreme Being definition risked violating the Establishment Clause by preferring one kind of religious experience to others.

In spite of the inadequacy of the Supreme Being definition, it is difficult to jettison the notion that religion is a special kind of belief.[14] Shifting the focus from a deity to "the sacred" provides a broad understanding of religion while keeping cognitive content as its central defining characteristic.

Beliefs about the Sacred

Most contemporary scholars of religion place the concept of the *sacred* at the heart of the religious phenomenon. The notion of the sacred entails belief in a reality beyond everyday experience, which gives meaning to everyday reality. These sacred things may be spiritual beings, cosmic laws, natural places, persons, or ideals. Theologian Rudolf Otto describes the sacred as "wholly other," "beyond the sphere of the usual, intelligible, and the familiar." Otto coined the term "numinous" to characterize the compelling, awe-producing and potent experience of a power beyond ordinary experience and explanation—a power that evokes both immense fear (*tremendum*) and profound attraction (*fascinans*).[15] Sociologist Emile Durkheim defines religion as "a unified system of beliefs and practices relative to sacred things."[16] Mircea Eliade, author of some of the seminal studies in comparative religion, sees the distinction between the sacred and the profane as the defining concept of religion. The religions Eliade studied shared not only the sense of the sacred but also the fact that it manifested itself in our world. Eliade called that manifestation a *hierophany*. Sacred spaces or objects could be "windows" through which communication with sacred power became possible. The biblical story of Jacob's dream of the ladder, with ascending and descending angels (Genesis 28:12–22), is a perfect example of this concept.[17] Twentieth-century theologian Paul Tillich spoke of religion in terms of the "transcendent."[18] Peter Berger uses the following description in his classic sociological theory of religion: "The sacred posits a world which legitimates, provides guidance for and helps us make sense of the ordinary."[19] Anthropologist Clifford Geertz understands religion as positing an "inherent structure of reality" in which values are rooted.[20] All of these ideas presume that there exists another "higher" reality, one that impacts upon us in our everyday reality. A textbook for students of religion introduces the study of religion with these words:

> Religions have almost universally made at least some kind of reference to "another dimension." . . . They have been dissatisfied with any suggestion that the immediate environment, or the superficial world of appearances, is the sum total of reality. In one way or another they have pushed beyond whatever "seems" to be the case or whatever "seems" to limit our lives. . . . [T]he great religious teachers do share a premonition that what we ordinarily perceive to be the limits of reality can "somehow" be gotten beyond. And they think it essential to our happiness or enjoyment here and now that we acquire an awareness of an ultimate environment . . . that lies "beyond" our immediate experience.[21]

This approach, like the preceding one, defines religion in terms of beliefs. A defining characteristic of a religion is that it entails a "metaphysical as well as a moral aspect. . . . [A]n understanding of oneself or ones purpose includes an understanding in some measure of some larger reality or whole in which self and others are distinguish and to which ones choice will make a difference. . . . Every religion . . . includes a metaphysical claim about the character of reality."[22] However, belief alone does not capture the experiential dimension of religion understood in this way. The sacred is experienced more than simply believed; when places or objects are seen as windows to the higher reality, people feel the need to behave in extraordinary ways.[23] Hence, the belief is inextricably bound up with religious behavior.

These theological and sociological definitions have found their way into the legal literature. We can see the influence of Eliade's distinction between the sacred and the profane in the legal definition offered by Timothy Hall. He suggests that a cross-cultural understanding of religion is an ontological belief; religion posits a "wholly other" reality, separate from our ordinary world. "Religion consists of beliefs and practices based on a perception of reality as being composed of both sacred ('wholly other') and profane (natural) elements."[24] This approach to definition has the virtue of providing a content-specific notion of religion, without limiting religion to belief in a Supreme Being. Hence, it encompasses many non-Western belief systems and is broadly cross-cultural.

The notion of the sacred carries significant policy implications; it would likely make Free Exercise interpretation more sensitive to certain kinds of claims. The sacred implies something that is set aside, separated from ordinary reality. The complex rituals outlined in *Leviticus* concerning the tabernacle provide a striking prototype, and they are carried through in the sacredness of the ark in contemporary Jewish synagogues. The ark, like the cross in a Christian church, is an object of this world that symbolizes a hierophany. Likewise, the tabernacle in Catholic churches, which contains the host, is a sacred place; rituals that (under normal conditions) cannot be performed anywhere else can only happen in its presence. Objects or places, whether natural or of human creation, may be seen as manifesting a sacred presence. Sacred places suggest an opening between this reality and the transcendent one, where communication with the sacred is made possible. The Ka'ba in Mecca—Islam's most sacred shrine—is such a place, and the giblah in every mosque directs Muslims at prayer to face in the direction of the Ka'ba. To take seriously the concept of the sacred, courts would have to understand that people could believe that some things, places, times, or actions are imbued with transcendent, otherworldly reality.

Eliade also directs our attention to the notion of a sacred *space*: "For [the] religious [person], space is not homogeneous; he experiences interruptions in it; some parts of space are qualitatively different from others."[25] The incorporation of this insight into legal concepts would encourage more sympathetic consideration of Native American claims for protection of sacred lands. Likewise, Sabbatarian claims, which have fared better, would be grounded more firmly in theological understanding: for some people, *time* is sacred. The Sabbath, to believers, is not simply a time for rest and religious reflection, or even for worship; it is a holy time, which, in a sense, belongs to the deity.

Both definitions we have considered thus far—those based on belief in a Supreme Being and those focused on the sacred—share one important characteristic. They understand religion in terms of beliefs about the nature of reality. These definitions are the most common in our tradition, and they pose some particular philosophical and practical problems for adjudication. Because the veracity of beliefs and feelings is indisputable, judges or juries must avoid evaluating it; even judging the sincerity of religious adherents is often problematic. These problems are so significant that they warrant attention in detail; we shall return to them in a separate section at the end of this chapter.

However accurate and appealing belief-type definitions may be as a characterization of religion, they provide an unsatisfying threshold for justifying religious freedom. By focusing purely on the cognitive content of beliefs, without reference to the moral obligations that these beliefs entail, these definitions do not explain why one kind of ontological position should be privileged over others, unless one assumes (as surely our government must not) that certain ontological beliefs are "true." An adequate definition of religion must at least suggest why the actions that stem from beliefs are to be especially protected. Thus, it is not just the nature of the beliefs but the kinds of motivations that the beliefs engender that seems to be at the heart of the phenomenon.

Obligations of Conscience

An adequate definition of religion must at least suggest why the actions that stem from beliefs warrant special protection. One constant answer is that religion is singularly valuable because it is a singularly important source of normative values. An impressive set of definitions reflect the insight that we encountered in the preceding chapter—religion is distinguished, above all, as a system of moral obligations.

An intriguing but unsatisfying attempt to incorporate this insight into what defines religion has been offered by Jesse Choper, who understands the distinguishing characteristic of religion—for some constitutional purposes—to be the belief that actions have "extratemporal consequences."[26] Choper reasons that the underlying purpose of the Free Exercise Clause is to protect people from the agonizing choices between the commands of government and dangers to their immortal souls. Under these conditions—but *only* these conditions—people should be able to claim exemptions from ordinary legal obligations. Of course, as Choper himself recognizes, this characterization excludes religions that do not rest on belief in an afterlife or eternal reward and punishment, as well as those practices that do not take the form of divine commands backed by threats. In his view, the limited scope of this definition is well suited to the limited purpose Choper advocates. When believers demand exemptions from generally applicable government regulations because of religious conflicts, Choper argues that exemptions are constitutionally required only when certain conditions are met — one of those conditions being that "violation of those beliefs entails extratemporal consequences." Precisely because exemptions are fraught with so many practical and legal dangers, Choper intentionally predicates them on a very constricted understanding of religion, even though it commits him to variable definitions for different constitutional problems. While this definition is a beginning toward protecting the sanctity of individual conscience, it does little to protect the institutional and identity interests of religious communities, nor does it offer protection even for individual practices where eternal damnation is not at stake.

Still, Choper has arrived at something critical. It is not just belief in the existence of a transcendent reality that makes religion special, it is the belief that the other reality impinges on the human in a certain way. Religions posit not just that an external reality exists but also that it is normative, prescriptive, and authoritative for human beings. It imposes *duties* on human beings that are "higher" or more authoritative than the duties humans set for each other. This insight suggests that *obligation* is the crucial characteristic of a religion.

This definition shifts our focus from the cognitive content of the belief to the fact that it is both prescriptive and authoritative. In sociologist Milton Yinger's words, "[I]t is not the nature of *belief*, but the nature of *believing* that requires our study."[27] In the same vein, Michael Sandel's powerful critique of Free Exercise thinking, which we encountered in the preceding chapter, suggests a change of emphasis in the definition of religion. The dominant view that the religion clauses protect *voluntary* choice misses the fact that most people do not experience their religious practices as acts of free choice, like consumer choices. Religious commands are powerful precisely because they are felt to be obligatory.[28] Indeed, if religious practices were matters of choice, there would be far fewer powerful reasons for protecting them. It is their obligatory character that makes the protection of these acts seem so compelling.

Several hybrid definitions combine both a cognitive element and a prescriptive one. Recall James Madison's *Memorial and Remonstrance against Religious Assessments*, in which he defines religion as "the duty we owe to our Creator." Madison's definition assumes the existence of a creator while emphasizing obligations. This same conjunction of theistic belief and obligation is captured by Chief Justice Hughes, dissenting in the 1931 case of *United States v Macintosh*: "The essence of religion is belief in relation to God involving duties superior to those arising from any human relation."[29]

Legal scholars have tried to capture this combination of cognitive and prescriptive elements in their attempt to define religion. Ben Clements has suggested a definition that combines both the content and functional elements of the "ultimate concerns" definition. He understands religion as that which addresses fundamental questions of human existence *and* gives rise to obligations of conscience.[30] The second part of the definition encompasses a justification for the religion clauses; they prevent agonizing conflict between obligations to government and obligations to higher authority.

Steven Gey has proposed an intentionally narrow definition of religion that focuses on the conjunction of the sacred and the obligatory: "(1) [R]eligious principles are derived from a source beyond human control; (2) religious principles are immutable and absolutely authoritative; and (3) religious principles are not based on logic or reason, and therefore, may not be proved or disproved."[31] Gey's narrow definition is intended specifically to encompass authoritatively obligatory religious behavior and to exclude others: "Religious principles that are neither immutable nor absolutely authoritative would not lead to a conflict between secular and religious obligations because, by definition, mutable and non-absolute religious obligations can be modified or ignored by the adherent in order to comply with secular duties."[32]

Under this characterization, an act of government that does not require a person to violate her religious conscience would not violate the Free Exercise Clause, no matter how damaging it might be in other ways. We have seen two examples of this kind of reasoning in Supreme Court adjudication. The destruction of Native American sacred lands did not literally require any individual to do something that his religion forbade,[33] nor did paying a sales tax on religious item violate the religious obligation of Bible sellers; hence, the Court found no constitutional violation.[34] The same kind of reasoning would apply to Establishment Clause controversies. Public religious holiday symbols, voluntary school prayers, and public support for religious schools do not require anyone to violate the commands of conscience. Yet, they may infringe the Establishment Clause in other ways. Clearly, defining religion solely in terms of obligations of conscience would greatly constrict our understanding of both religion clauses.

Powerful as the obligation definitions are, therefore, they remain inadequate for much the same reasons that the obligations account of the Free

Exercise Clause is unsatisfactory. To confine religious protection to only those practices believed to be obligatory is inadequate because doing so fails to encompass the nonobligatory religious acts, such as the celebration of holidays. By neglecting the communal and symbolic nonobligatory aspects of religious practice, this approach offers little protection for institutions, identities, and nonconscience-based practices. Moreover, the focus on moral obligations emphasizes the individual and spiritual nature of the religious experience and evokes a rather heroic notion of the individual believer powerfully moved to act by divine inspiration. Hence, while these definitions suggest strong protection for conscientious objection, like other individualist definitions, they give little protection to the social function of religion for communities of believers or to religious practices that bind groups but do not stem from divine commands.

Functional Definitions: Ultimate Concerns and Comprehensive Explanations

Theologian Paul Tillich's characterization of religion as "ultimate concern" has been immensely influential in American legal thinking.[35] Tillich's insight directs attention to the kinds of issues addressed by a putative religion and its role in the life of the believer, not on a specific content. Tillich's works have been extremely helpful in broadening the concept of religion to encompass a greater range of expressions, but at the same time, they have been easily misunderstood.

Simply put, Tillich defines religion as that which concerns "the depth of your life, the source of your being, or your ultimate concern, or what you take most seriously, without reservation." In this view, everyone has a religion. This rather simple interpretation of Tillich's theory gave rise to the "functional approach" in legal definitions, an approach that looks to the depth of a person's motivations as the defining characteristic. This was the approach the Supreme Court used in the Vietnam War era conscientious objector cases.

Congress has long granted conscientious objection exemptions from compulsory military service for persons with religious objections to war. To invoke that exemption, one must be able to show that his objection is a genuinely *religious* one. As we have seen, identifying religious motivations has always posed problems; the faith professed by Macintosh was not sufficient to exempt him from the oath to defend the country required for naturalization in 1931.[36] A religious dissenter fared better in the 1943 conscientious objection case *United States v Kauten*, which foreshadowed those of a generation later. Here, the Second Circuit used functional language in describing religious conscience: "[Conscientious objection] may justly be regarded as a response of the individual to an inward mentor, call it conscience or God, that is for many persons at the present time the equivalent of what has always been thought of as an religious impulse."[37]

This decision provided to the Supreme Court a precedent for expanding the theistic definition of religion when it confronted the Vietnam War era conscientious objector cases. These cases represent the most dramatic departure from traditional content-based definitions and the clearest examples of functional ones. In these cases, the Court expanded religious exemptions from military service to include those whose moral and philosophical beliefs served for them the same *function* as the belief in God did for traditional religious believers.

In the three cases that were combined in *United States v Seeger* the Court was asked to interpret a provision of the Selective Service Act that exempted from combat any person "who, by reason of religious training and belief, is conscientiously opposed to participation in war in any form. Religious training and belief in this connection means an individual's belief in relation to a Supreme Being, involving duties superior to those arising from any human relation, but does not include essentially political, sociological, or philosophical views or a merely personal moral code."[38]

Congress had explicitly used the term "Supreme Being" in defining religious belief, but the courts were aware in the post-*Torcaso* era that this kind of preference for one kind of religion over others risked violating the Establishment Clause. In one of the significant early Vietnam War era cases under this law, the trial judge took the opportunity to provide a very expansive reading of the statutory language. In *United States v Jakobson*[39] Judge Henry Jacob Friendly explicitly relied on Tillich's *Systematic Theology* to find that the applicant met the Supreme Being test even though he referred to a belief in "Godness" rather than God. This case was one of several that were combined in the landmark *Seeger* case. Seeger himself had applied for conscientious objector status, but his answers to questions concerning his religious beliefs were ambiguous. His application left the Court in an awkward position. To deny his application would have limited "religion" to a belief in a Supreme Being—something difficult to do in light of *Torcaso*. Furthermore, to interpret the statute literally would have risked a violation of the Establishment Clause by granting a privilege for one kind of religious belief and denying it to others. Holding the Selective Service Act unconstitutional on these grounds was a result no one wanted. The Court's solution was to "rewrite" the statute, stretching the definition of religion in order to grant Seeger's application. The Court concluded that "Congress, in using the expression 'Supreme Being' rather than the designation 'God' was merely clarifying the meaning of religious training and belief so as to embrace all religions. . . . [T]he test of belief 'in relation to a Supreme Being' is whether a given belief that is sincere and meaningful occupies a place in the life of its possessor parallel to that filled by the orthodox belief in God of one who clearly qualifies for the exemption." Justice Clark's opinion quoted Tillich's *The Shaking of the Foundation*, which defined religion as "the source of your being, of your ultimate concern, of what you take seriously without reservation."[40]

Seven years later, in *Welsh v United States*, the Court continued this expansion, granting conscientious objector status to one who unambiguously rejected labeling his motivations as "religious": "[I]f an individual deeply and sincerely holds beliefs which are purely ethical or moral in source and content but that nevertheless impose upon him a duty of conscience to refrain from participation in any war at any time, those beliefs certainly occupy in the life of that individual a place parallel to that filled [by] God in traditionally religious persons."[41]

While the *Seeger* and *Welch* cases were important expansions of First Amendment protection, a definition of religion that included anyone's ultimate concern or anything that functions parallel to a belief in God bothered many critics. In spite of the expansiveness of this definition, it raises awkward problems for the judicial process. Ought judges probe what is of "ultimate concern" to a complainant? And if they do, then football, family, income, political ideology, or sex might well have to qualify. Moreover, as Kent Greenawalt has observed, most individuals, lacking lexical orders of motivations, do not have "ultimate concerns."[42] Finally, it may even be that "ultimate concerns" are not at the heart of religious experience for many people. Consider Jews who might "religiously" observe the laws of *kashrut* or Christians who might accept communion without ever pondering the profound teachings that these practices dramatize for theologians. It is even possible that reflections on ultimate concerns, like the nature of life and death or the grounding of morality, are discouraged by some religions in favor of observance of church teachings or preserving communal rituals. There may even be a certain intellectual bias in defining religion in terms of ultimate concerns, which may be a disadvantage to religions or religious persons for whom practices or identities, as opposed to reflection, are at the heart of the religious experience.

In truth, these objections are based on an oversimplification of Tillich's point. His own notion of religion is not entirely open-ended; his explanation of "ultimate" is immersed in the notion of transcendence, holiness, and the sacred. Tillich's theory includes both the motivation and cognitive content of belief, as James McBride explains:

> Influenced by Otto's phenomenology of religion, Tillich's "ultimate concern" cannot be reduced to an affective attitude alone. . . . [U]ltimate concern indicates, on the one hand *our* being ultimately concerned—the subjective side—and on the other hand, the *object* of our ultimate concern. Hence, the concept of "ultimate concern" involved by the Court cannot be reduced merely to an affective attitude as legal scholars and justices have implied. If Tillich's notion is to be spared violence, the court must recognize that there exist two poles in "ultimate concern," objective as well as subjective. Does that suggest that this legal notion may be characterized by both affective attitude and cognitive content? But if cognitive content is recognized as an inherent element of "ultimate concern," does that not violate Ballard's prohibition against probing the truth and falsehood of religious claims? [43]

The aspect of Tillich's definition that McBride terms "objective" is a more important characteristic of religion than is sometimes recognized. It reminds us that not every personal obsession is a religion; religion is "ultimate" in the sense of addressing the questions of life for which every human being is presumed to need meanings. Perhaps the term that better captures this sense of ultimate is "comprehensive belief system."

Theologian Franklin Gamwell has developed a theory of religion and of religious freedom that begins with the premise that all human beings, in order to live "authentic" lives, must ask "What is the human purpose?" Religion, for Gamwell, is the attempt to answer this question in an explicit and comprehensive way. Religion, therefore, encompasses both metaphysical questions about the nature of reality and normative questions about how a person should lead her life. Gamwell believes that all humans, indeed all human activities, address these questions implicitly. Religion is the set of cultural concepts and symbols by which we address them explicitly. Specifically, "religion is the primary form of culture in which the comprehensive question is explicitly asked and answered." [44]

Gamwell's insight is echoed in the sociology of religion. Many sociologists recognize the *comprehensiveness of explanations* as one of the cross-cultural characteristics of religion. Milton Yinger, for example, writes that "[r]eligion . . . can be defined as a system of beliefs and practices by means of which a group of people struggles with the ultimate problems of human life." [45] And Clifford Geertz understands religion as a system of symbols that help one interpret the meaning of life itself by "formulating conceptions of a general order of existence."[46]

Judges following this approach look for evidence that a belief system is comprehensive as well as deeply held. Two cases illustrate this judicial approach to religious definition. The first involves the Church of Scientology, and the second stemmed from a prisoner's petition for religious accommodation.

Scientology developed out of a movement called "dyanetics," which was established by the late author Ron Hubbard, and it occupies a disputed border between a profitable enterprise and a church.[47] Scientology, which does not posit a deity, understands the human as having both a physical and spiritual nature. Its practitioners believe that spiritual awareness can be enhanced and irrational behavior reduced by clearing "engrams" from one's mind through intensive counseling sessions called "auditing," for which the subject pays a fee. During auditing, a person's skin responses are measured by an electronic device called an E-Meter, which assists the auditor in determining the subject's spiritual condition. The first of Scientology's numerous legal problems arose when the Food and Drug Administration declared E-meters used by the church and its secular affiliates for "auditing" to be mislabeled—that is, falsely represented as efficacious in treating physical ills. On one hand, if the benefits claimed for E-meters were secular ones, they would be subject to FDA regulation and quite likely to a determination that they did not produce the benefits claimed. On the other hand, if the benefits promoted were *religious* ones, these claims would be beyond the reach of the governmental regulators. To determine whether E-meters promoted secular benefits or religious ones, the court was forced to examine the awkward question of whether Scientology was indeed a religion. In 1969, in *Founding Church of Scientology of Washington, D.C. v United States*, the D.C. Circuit Court decided that Scientology was a religion protected under the Free Exercise Clause, emphasizing the comprehensiveness of the church's doctrines, especially the fact that its "fundamental writings contain a general account of man and his nature comparable in scope, if not in content, to those of some recognized religions."[48] Hence, it concluded that the claims made on behalf of E-meters were of spiritual nature and therefore not subject to prosecution for false or misleading advertising.

The focus on ultimate questions produced an opposite result in the attempt by prisoner Frank Africa to declare his allegiance to the organization MOVE to be religious and to receive dietary accommodations in a Pennsylvania prison. Judge Arlin Adams found his beliefs to be sincere and even ultimate in his life but ruled that they were not a comprehensive system.

In *Africa v Pennsylvania*, the Third Circuit held that however "deep" a sincerely held belief system might be, it did not qualify as a religion if it was not sufficiently "comprehensive."[49]

The criterion of an ultimate and comprehensive belief system raises some serious legal problems. First, a focus on comprehensiveness alone might not distinguish religion from theoretical physics, ontology, or any comprehensive philosophical system; many of these systems also imply prescriptions about how one should live. Any attempt by judges to make this distinction would involve them in the wholly inappropriate role of religious censors, deciding which beliefs are ultimate and which are derivative. Furthermore, to conceive of religion as about ultimate questions makes it almost a totally cognitive phenomenon. Theologically inclined or introspective people might raise questions like: Why are we here? Why is there something rather than nothing? Why is there suffering and evil? Why is one thing more valuable than another? Why must we behave in certain ways?[50] But many "religious" people are unable, or at least disinclined, to ponder these kinds of questions at all; for them, religion is ritual, identity, and some rules to live by. Such a cognitive definition might well deny First Amendment protection to those who cannot articulate profound religious philosophy.

In the end, this promising approach is not adequate for constitutional purposes because it fails to provide workable boundaries. If any ultimately valued and comprehensive belief system is a religion for Free Exercise purposes, it poses serious problems for Establishment Clause adjudication. Conservative Christians during the 1980s, in fact, vigorously campaigned for this broad definition of religion in hopes of having secular humanism declared a religion and thereby banished from public life as an unconstitutional establishment of religion.[51] This strategy was an important element of their challenge to public education. If any ultimate system of values is a religion, and the Establishment Clause prohibits the public schools from teaching religious values, then, arguably, the inclusion of such values in public school curricula entails an unconstitutional establishment of religion. This is precisely the argument Christian fundamentalists made in *Smith v Board of School Commissioners of Mobile County* in objecting to the teaching of secular humanist values in the public schools.[52]

Finally, the functional definition seems to preclude anyone except the most religiously serious person from raising a Free Exercise complaint. But consider the example with which this chapter began: A Jewish parent is irritated that her child's public school examinations are scheduled on Rosh Hashanah, when the family traditionally attends synagogue services. If probed, the parent might readily admit that Jewish holiday celebrations are not among her "ultimate concerns"; she simply believes that respecting religious minorities' traditions are worth making a point about. Would this parent be denied standing to raise a First Amendment issue because holiday worship, or the theology behind it, is not her "ultimate concern?"

In both functional and content definitions, the nature or function of the belief is the defining element; the practices that follow from them are considered derivative. The implicit model here is that religious *actions* flow from religious *beliefs*. But perhaps this reasoning is backward. Emile Durkheim, the "father" of contemporary religious sociology, reminds us that considering only states of mind as intrinsically valuable misunderstands the phenomenon; actions and practices may in fact be crucial in *creating* beliefs. In short, we believe *as a result of* what we do. The focus on belief may be bad social psychology; in addition, it could have dangerous constitutional consequences. If courts focus on beliefs, they may give far too little protection to social practices, institutions, and identities that, Durkheim argues, are the heart of the religious experience.[53]

Communal and Institutional Definitions

Whether we consider religion to be a kind of belief, the commands and motivations it generates, or the function of a belief system, it is understood with reference to the individual adherent. The entire sociological tradition of religious thought directs attention to an entirely different set of phenomena—the shared symbols, practices, and identities that create and sustain a community. Earlier, I quoted a segment of Emile Durkheim's definition of religion; here, the remainder of his definition warrants quoting: "A religion is a unified system of beliefs and practices relative to things sacred, . . . beliefs and practices which unite into a single moral community called a Church all those who adhere to them."[54] For Durkheim, the sense of the sacred is not an individual phenomenon but essentially a communal and institutional one: "In all history, we do not find a single religion without a Church."[55] This focus on group practices, identities, and institutions, and their social functions is typical of most sociological definitions. Milton Yinger, for example, insists that religion is a social phenomenon: it is shared and takes on many of its most significant aspects only in the interaction of the group. Notice again his definition: "Religion, then, can be defined as a system of beliefs and practices by means of which *a group of people* struggles with these ultimate problems of human life."[56]

Stephen Carter's definition emphasizes "group worship" while including the cognitive and conscience elements we observed earlier: "When I refer to religion, I will have in mind a tradition of group worship (as against individual metaphysics) that presupposes the existence of a sentience beyond the human and capable of acting outside the observed principles and limits of natural science, and further, a tradition that makes demands of some kind on its adherents."[57]

These definitions understand religion as not only a source of individual meaning but also encompassing the collective behaviors that create and support that system of meaning. While the earlier definitions focused on individual faith and its function for the believer, social definitions direct our attention to the community created by shared faith and ritual and the ways that social actions sustain faith.

The relatively noncontroversial decision in *Frazee v Illinois Department of Employment Security*[58] is helpful in illustrating both the strengths and weaknesses of this approach. Frazee was a Christian who requested accommodation of a rather traditional Christian practice—keeping the Sabbath; he was unwilling to work on Sundays and therefore unable to find employment. Frazee, however, was denied unemployment compensation because he did not belong to any church. The Illinois courts found his purely personal profession of religious objection to Sunday work insufficient to justify a Free Exercise claim, but the U.S. Supreme Court unanimously reversed the ruling, making it clear that the religious convictions of individuals do merit constitutional protection, even when they are not rooted in the tenets of any particular sect to which the claimant belongs. A Christian, of course, could rely on a long- and well-understood tradition of Sunday Sabbath observance. One wonders what would become of the claim of an individual believer who lacked both institutional affiliation and tradition. The very fact that an "easy" case like *Frazee* raised any controversy at all suggests that any definition that relies totally on religious groups fails to offer adequate protection to religion considered as individual spirituality.

Social and institutional definitions, taken alone, also seem to beg a serious question: What social and institutional criteria enable us to distinguish *religious* communities and institutions from other kinds of associations? Some identifying characteristic is needed to turn the sociological insight to a criterion useful in legal decision making. One of the most promising solutions to this problem directs our attention not to any single characteristic but to a family of indicators that characterize religion.

Indicia and Analogies

A very promising approach to understanding religion avoids any single indicator and attempts to gather together a family of indicia that, cross-culturally, are recognized as pertaining to religious observance. No single element is strictly necessary; a combination of them produce what the ordinary person would recognize as a religion. This is the method of finding "family resemblances," as suggested in Ludwig Wittgenstein's *Philosophical Investigations*.[59] While some religious scholars have looked for the common elements of all religions, others have sought a looser "family" of dimensions that, taken together, capture our understanding of the phenomenon. Ninian Smart identifies social, mythic, ritual, doctrinal, ethical, artistic, and experiential dimensions in all religions.[60] Obviously, none of these dimensions is limited to the religious; we could easily identify many of these qualities in political phenomena, for example. Furthermore, we would not expect to find that every individual religious person partakes of every one of these dimensions. We might find a religious person almost totally ignorant of the doctrine of his faith or unable to appreciate its artistic expression. Still, taken in combination with varying mixes of emphasis and various expressions, these dimensions help us identify a wide range of religious phenomena.

This approach has proven very helpful in First Amendment jurisprudence. When the existence of a religion is in dispute, judges might fruitfully look for combinations of indicators rather than single elements. And because the dimensions, or indicators, are general rather than specific, they would have to recognize likenesses between the beliefs or practice in question and those we easily recognize as "religious." In this spirit, Kent Greenawalt has suggested that judges seek analogies between the putative religion and that which is indisputably religious.

> To use the analogical approach to define the boundaries of religion, one begins with instances of the indisputably religious, instances about which virtually everyone would say, "This certainly is religion." Such instances do not require a consensus about all the concept of religion signifies or about treatment of borderline cases. For example, no one doubts that Roman Catholicism, Greek Orthodoxy, Lutheranism, Methodism, and Orthodox Judaism are religions. Our society identifies what is indubitably religious largely by reference to their beliefs, practices, and organizations. These include: belief in a God, a comprehensive view of the world and human purposes, a belief in some form of afterlife, communication with God through ritual acts of worship and through corporate and individual prayer; a particular perspective on moral obligations derived from moral code or from a conception of God's nature; practices involving repentance and forgiveness of sins; "religious" feelings of awe, guilt, and adoration, the use of sacred texts; and organizations to facilitate the corporate aspects

of religious practice and to promote and perpetuate beliefs and practices. This list could be expanded or organized differently. The main point is that in this society a number of different elements are joined together.

Should any single feature be absent, religion . . . could still exist. . . . Religions need not share any single common feature, because no single feature is indispensable.[61]

Analogies to the external manifestations of religion, such as ceremonies, clergy, or institutional practices of religion would, of course, be a disadvantage to new or noninstitutionalized religions; Greenawalt prefers analogies to the kinds of concerns and motivations traditional religions include.

The use of this method by Judge Arlin Adams in *Malnak v Yogi* is considered a breakthrough in religion clause jurisprudence. *Malnak v Yogi* was an Establishment Clause case in which the public school teaching of the techniques of transcendental meditation was challenged as state inculcation of a religion. Proponents of the program denied that transcendental meditation was a religion; the Third Circuit concluded that it was. Judge Adams's concurring opinion includes a lucid attempt to describe the family of characteristics by which most people understand the word "religion."

There appear to be three useful indicia that are basic to our traditional religions and that are themselves related to the values that undergird the first amendment.

The first and most important of these indicia is the nature of the ideas in question. This means that a court must, at least to a degree, examine the content of the supposed religion, not to determine its truth or falsity, or whether it is schismatic or orthodox, but to determine whether the subject matter it comprehends is consistent with the assertion that it is, or is not, a religion. . . . Expectation that religious ideas should address fundamental questions is in some ways comparable to the reasoning of the Protestant theologian Dr. Paul Tillich, who expressed his view on the essence of religion in the phrase "ultimate concern." . . . As [ultimate concerns] they are to be carefully guarded from governmental interference, and never converted into official government doctrine. The first amendment demonstrates a specific solicitude for religion because religious ideas are in many ways more important than other ideas. New and different ways of meeting those concerns are entitled to the same sort of treatment as the traditional forms.

[T]he element of comprehensiveness [is] the second of the three indicia. A religion is not generally confined to one question or one moral teaching; it has a broader scope. It lays claim to an ultimate and comprehensive "truth."

A third element to consider in ascertaining whether a set of ideas should be classified as a religion is any formal, external, or surface signs that may be analogized to accepted religions. Such signs might include formal services, ceremonial functions, the existence of clergy, structure, and organization, efforts at propagation, observation of holidays and other similar manifestations associated with traditional religions. Of course, a religion may exist without any of these signs, so they are not determinative, at least by their absence, in resolving a question of definition. But they can be helpful in supporting a conclusion of religious status given the important role such ceremonies play in religious life.[62]

Notice that the third indicium concerns group characteristics—sociological or anthropological—that are more appropriate to institutional religious questions than to those of the individual conscience. Several years after developing this test, Judge Adams had the opportunity to use it again. Frank Africa, leader of a religious movement he called MOVE, was imprisoned, and he petitioned for a special diet of raw fruits and vegetables as mandated by his religious beliefs. When his petition came to the Court, the first question was the threshold one. Judge Adams, using his "indicia" approach, ruled that the organization MOVE was not a religion because its beliefs were not comprehensive and because it lacked "formal services, ceremonial functions, the existence of clergy, structure and organization, efforts at propagation, observance of holidays, and other similar manifestations associated with traditional religions."[63] As used, this approach places considerable weight on the social practices of the institution rather than on the conscience of the believers. Presuming that prisoner Africa was a sincere person and that his religious need to consume only raw vegetables was the overpowering command of his deepest convictions, how could he be denied accommodation because the judges found his theology shallow (not involving "ultimate questions") and poorly articulated, and because his "religion" lacked churches, holidays, and clergy? Whereas the earlier definitions seemed to give insufficient weight to the social aspects of religion, this one fails to protect commands of individual conscience in the absence of traditional social manifestations.

Like the previous approaches, this one creates some problems of its own. A judicial approach that would take into consideration all the indicia as necessary to prove the existence of a religion would appear to be overly narrow, excluding from protection religions lacking in formal structures. Conversely, the approach may prove to be overbroad, especially if used (as in its original incarnation) in Establishment cases. A strikingly unsuccessful attempt at a composite definition was attempted by Judge Brevard Hand in the Alabama textbook case, on the basis of which he declared secular humanism to be a religion.[64] His unwieldy composite was unable to distinguish religious questions from philosophical discourse about metaphysics, ontology, and ethics. This case demonstrates a danger in Greenawalt's analogical approach. Almost anyone can concoct analogies, and Judge Hand was able easily to draw analogies between secular humanism and what is "indisputably religious." It is worth noting that in both *Malnak v Yogi* and *Smith* ideas were declared to be religions *against* the arguments of their adherents, who denied that their ideas constituted a religion. In most cases, adherents attempt to claim religious status for their beliefs or practices.

In spite of some difficulties in applying the "indicia" or "analogies" approach to religion, it remains a promising insight. Better than any of the others, it focuses attention on the dual nature of religion as both an individual and a collective phenomenon. Furthermore, the "family of resemblances" idea seems to offer the most promising practical solution to the concrete problems that judges most often confront. The real advantage of this analogical approach is that in avoiding essentialist definitions it removes the necessity of a single constitutional definition of religion at all. Using this method, a judge need ask only whether the specific belief, practice, institution, or identity in question is analogous to the "indisputably religious." Thus, when a person claims that a government act has violated her religious conscience, the nature of her beliefs may be critical. However, when the dispute turns on whether an organization is religious, corporate activities may be more relevant to the inquiry. By limiting the inquiry, this approach enables a judge to focus almost surgically on the aspect of religion that is actually relevant to the dispute at hand.[65]

The use of analogies and indicators is especially compatible with the basic method of our pluralist approach to religious freedom. Pluralist theory rejects essentialism; that is, it does not posit the presence of some fundamental characteristic in the social order. The pluralist theory of social cohesion developed in Chapter 9 uses Wittgenstein's "family resemblances" in arguing that overlapping beliefs, rather than an essential shared core consensus, is sufficient to provide cohesion. The open-endedness of this approach to definition, therefore, is methodologically and philosophically compatible with our general account of religious freedom.

To invoke the constitutional protections of religious freedom, a practice, institution, or motive must be a *religious* one. In most cases, this threshold is crossed without controversy, but occasionally it becomes the heart of the conflict. In these cases, courts may be asked to judge whether the claims are genuinely religious ones or whether the claimant is sincerely religious. Judging either the veracity of religious beliefs or the sincerity of the believer brings government perilously close to making the kinds of judgments the First Amendment seeks to avoid; yet, occasionally, such judgments are unavoidable. When laws provide exemptions from ordinary requirements to protect religious behavior, there is some danger that persons will make "strategic" religious claims; that is, they will seek to shield nonreligious behavior under the umbrella of religious protection in order to gain advantages. Some kinds of exemptions are more likely than others to elicit these kinds of claims. Tax benefits and freedom from administrative regulation provide temptations for insincere religious claims, making investigation into the claimant's sincerity necessary. The most publicized instances of these controversies arise when religious figures are charged with financial fraud.[66] Conflicts over sincerity have also been raised in a variety of contexts, including attempts by prisoners to seek recognition of novel religions in prisons[67] and cases brought by employees seeking religious accommodation in the workplace.[68]

The bitter experiences of the Mormon Church during the nineteenth century illustrate the pitfalls of making distinctions between truth and falsity in religion. At issue was the government's attempts to prohibit polygamy as an affront to public morals and the church's efforts to protect a practice considered a divine command. In the case of *Davis v Beason* the Supreme Court said that Mormon doctrines of polygamy violated "the enlightened sentiment of mankind," notwithstanding "the pretense of religious conviction."[69] Implicit in this and similar decisions was that there were objectively "true" and "false" beliefs and that courts could appropriately determine which beliefs were false and exclude them from First Amendment protection.

While courts have subsequently been more circumspect in making pronouncements about veracity, they have continued to consider sincerity. Nontraditional ministries, especially those that actively seek financial contributions, raise continual problems about the distinction between religious fervor and fraud. The 1917 case of *New v United States* illustrates one approach to making the distinction. Dr. New had claimed all kinds of supernatural powers, including the power to heal, which he professed to have received because of his rare virtue. In prosecuting him for mail fraud, the federal government denied both truth of his claims and his sincerity in making them, thus attacking both veracity and sincerity. The Ninth Circuit made clear that Dr. New was entitled to believe anything he wanted but not to *pretend* to hold beliefs "for false and fraudulent purposes of procuring money." The evidence of Dr. New's "pretense" was hypocrisy: "[H]e was also an habitual indulger in each and every of the sins and practices he pretended to condemn."[70]

The most important and sophisticated attempt by the Supreme Court to wrestle with these problems was the 1944 fraud conviction case of *United States v Ballard*.[71] Guy Ballard experienced a mystical revelation in 1930; subsequently, he, his wife, and son founded a religious movement to propagate the supernatural messages he had received. After he died in 1939, his wife and son were indicted for mail fraud and charged with making false claims (specifically, the power to heal), which "they well knew" were false. The trial judge was sensitive to the difficulty of judging religious beliefs. He therefore separated the question of the truth of the Ballards's religious beliefs from their sincerity and instructed the jury that while the veracity of their beliefs could not be questioned, their sincerity could. The Ballards argued that both questions violated their religious freedom. On appeal, the court noted that they were originally indicted for "false" representations, not insincere ones; hence, the government had to prove their religious representations to be false. The Supreme Court granted certiorari, and a divided Court considered for the first time how to handle the difficult issue of the truth or falsity of religious belief.

The Supreme Court split three ways: Three justices (Harlan Stone, Owen Roberts, and Felix Frankfurter) argued that the Ballards could be punished for making false claims; hence, the veracity of their claims was indeed appropriate for courts. Justice Jackson, dissenting from the conviction, argued that both truth and veracity are beyond the ken of the judiciary because they are inseparable. The majority, in an opinion written by Justice Douglas, took a middle position, finding that the trial court had made the appropriate distinction between veracity and sincerity. The majority upheld the Ballards's mail fraud conviction and affirmed the trial judge's instruction that the jury not consider the veracity of their religious claims, only their sincerity. Justice Douglas's statement remains a classic:

Heresy trials are foreign to our Constitution. Men may believe what they cannot prove. They may not be put to the proof of their religious doctrines or beliefs. Religious experiences which are as real as life to some may be incomprehensible to others. Yet the fact that they may be beyond the ken of mortals does not mean that they can be made suspect before the law. Many take their gospel from the New Testament. But it would hardly be supposed that they could be tried before a jury charged with the duty of determining whether those teachings contained false representations. The miracles of the New Testament, the Divinity of Christ, life after death, the power of prayer are deep in the religious convictions of many. If one could be sent to jail because a jury in a hostile environment found those teachings to be false, little indeed would be left of religious freedom.[72]

The Ballards's conviction for mail fraud was based on the Court's insistence that one can distinguish what one believes from what is believable. In his dissent, Justice Jackson raised a powerful objection to this distinction and argued that both veracity and sincerity should be beyond the ken of the judiciary. His point is a powerful one:

> I do not see how we can separate an issue as to what is believed from considerations as to what is believable. The most convincing proof that one believes his statement is to show that they have been true in his experience. Likewise, that one knowingly falsified is best proved by showing that what he said happened never did happen. How can the Government prove these persons knew something to be false which it cannot prove to be false? If we try religious sincerity severed from religious verity, we isolate the dispute from the very considerations which in common experience provide its most believable answers. . . .
>
> And I do not know what degree of skepticism or disbelief in a religious representation amounts to actionable fraud. . . . Some who profess belief in the Bible read literally what others read as allegory or metaphor, as they read Aesop's fables. Religious symbolism is even used by some with the same mental reservations one has in teaching of Santa Claus or Uncle Sam or Easter bunnies or dispassionate judges. It is hard in matters so mystical to say how literally one is bound to believe the doctrine he teaches and even more difficult to say how far it is reliance upon the teacher's literal belief which induces followers to give him money.

When, in cases like *Ballard*, a person's religious sincerity is in dispute, courts must confront evidence for ascertaining sincerity or its absence. As in the *New* case, disregard for one's own teachings is evidence of insincerity. In addition, commercial or other self-serving motives, evidence of criminal behavior, and frivolity have also been considered as evidence of insincerity. On the other hand, willingness to sacrifice for one's beliefs and long-standing commitment, especially to institutional groups who share one's faith, help establish sincerity.

Conflicts involving the Church of Scientology exemplify the confounding problem of commercial motive, since fees are collected for "auditing" sessions. During auditing, the subject's skin responses are measured by a galvanometer called an E-meter, which assists the auditor in determining the subject's spiritual condition. Because of the church's belief in a "doctrine of exchange," persons receiving auditing are required to pay for this service. We have already encountered the problems that arose when the Food and Drug Administration declared E-meters to be mislabeled, that is, falsely represented as efficacious in treating physical ills. In order to determine whether E-meters were subject to federal regulation, courts were forced to decide whether the benefits claimed for them were physical or spiritual. While claims of physical benefits are regulated and must be subjected to scientific testing, claims of spiritual benefits are beyond the reach of governmental regulators because the issue of religious veracity is not justiciable. In 1969 in *Founding Church of Scientology of Washington, D.C. v United States*[73] the D.C. Circuit decided that Scientology was a religion protected by the Free Exercise Clause; hence claims made on behalf of E-meters were spiritual in nature and not subject to prosecution for false and misleading advertising. On remand, however, the district court judge required the church to cease making medical or scientific claims for its benefits and to situate its claims in a religious context.

Challenges to the religious sincerity of Scientology's organizers did not end. In the late 1970s and early 1980s, several civil suits were brought against the church by former adherents for various fraudulent misrepresentation of the benefits that could be derived from auditing. In *Van Schaick v Church of Scientology*,[74] for example, the plaintiffs argued both that Scientology was not really a religion and that its agents were not sincere in their profession of beliefs but had commercial motives. Part of the conflict concerned the kinds of promises or enticements made by the church recruiters. If the benefits represented were spiritual ones, church recruiters could not be sued by disgruntled former members; if the promises were secular (better physical or mental health), recruiters might be subject to fraud claims for failure to deliver the promised benefits.

In claiming to be defrauded, the plaintiffs alleged that Scientology's founders and present leaders had purely commercial motives in creating the movement. Courts were forced to consider not only the truth of that claim but also the more serious question of whether the religious sincerity and motivations of Scientology's founders was even relevant at all. This argument raises an ancillary issue: How does one prove the sincerity or insincerity of an *institution*? Unlike *Ballard*, which turned on the sincerity of discrete individuals, this case raises far more abstract problems of judging institutional motivations.

Conflicts between religious practices and narcotics laws have been another context for disputes about religious sincerity. In 1964 in *People v Woody*[75] the California Supreme Court ruled that traditional, ritual use of peyote by unquestionably sincere members of the Native American Church was protected by the Free Exercise Clause. But in *State v Bullard*[76] this protection did not extend to drug use without evidence of religious sincerity. And in *Leary v United States*[77] the Fifth Circuit ruled that Dr. Leary's religious faith was simply insufficient to outweigh the state interest in enforcement of its narcotics laws. Perhaps the classic case in this respect is *United States v Kuch*, in which the evidence of insincerity was frivolity.[78] In this case, the district court upheld the conviction for illegal marijuana possession and transportation against a primate of the New American Church who claimed that marijuana and LSD were sacraments of her church and therefore protected by the First Amendment. Examining church documents, the court found no belief in a Supreme Being, no religious discipline, ritual, or tenets to guide daily existence, and, in general, "goofy nonsense."

While "goofy nonsense" may disqualify a claim to religious sincerity, a person making a religious claim need not be theologically sophisticated. While faiths that are grounded in recognized religious groups have an easier time demonstrating their sincerity, neither individually held faiths[79] nor disagreement with other members of one's faith[80] are appropriate grounds for courts to reject the sincerity of one's religious motivations. While obvious hypocrisy and cynicism may call one's sincerity into question, occasional lapses in consistency of religious conduct do not impugn one's sincerity.[81] Courts may also inquire into the origins of beliefs (religious training, for example) to provide evidence of sincerity. Nevertheless, the Supreme Court has affirmed that recently adopted faiths are fully protected.[82]

All of these cases reiterate the essential disagreements that emerged in *Ballard*. The strongest advocates of religious accommodation continue to argue Justice Jackson's point that any judicial examination of religious sincerity inevitably involves scrutiny of the beliefs themselves and hence should be forbidden.[83] Those more sympathetic to secular interests follow Justice Douglas's argument that the truth or falsity of religious doctrine can be distinguished from the sincerity of the believer and that courts may examine the latter when necessary.

Our survey of religious definitions has repeatedly demonstrated how they encompass and promote values. This section attempts to make explicit the connections between the general accounts of religious freedom surveyed in Chapter 1 and the way religion is defined. The first account values freedom of religious choice; open-ended approaches, such as functional definitions, are most consistent with this account. The second account, emphasizing the integrity of religious conscience, is almost perfectly congruent with definitions placing moral obligations at the heart of the religious experience. The third principle is concerned with protecting the state against sectarian conflicts; it would be most compatible with religion as a social phenomenon—shared beliefs, community definitions, and institutional indicators would thus be most appropriate. The fourth account concerns institutions of power; its focus is also on religion as social practice. Hence, indicia—particularly social indicia—would likely be its defining characteristic. The fifth account, the pluralist principle, protects the freedom of religion because religion creates and sustains meanings for individuals and groups. All of the defining elements we have surveyed contribute to that role—suggesting again that the pluralist principle is the most comprehensive view. Clearly, religious beliefs—either about a Supreme Being or about the sacred—are sources of meaning. Functional definitions expand the possible sources of one's ultimate concern, and indicia and analogies draw our attention to other kinds of belief systems or sources of meaning and the social practices that sustain them.

Gamwell's definition of religion as "comprehensive answers to ultimate questions" is particularly interesting in view of the pluralist approach. On one hand, his definition captures better than any of the others the importance of meanings in our individual and communal lives. Intuitively, I find it the most compelling definition. Yet at the same time, it is most problematic for the pluralist approach because the very point of pluralism is to avoid unitary and comprehensive systems of meaning. As we shall see in the last chapter, religions that take "comprehensive answers" most seriously—those that seek either insularity or social transformation in order to inhabit a seamless world of meanings—provide the greatest problems for the pluralist account.

Are we left, then, with Steven Smith's dilemma? Does any attempt to define religion inescapably violate religious freedom by "privileging one religious or secular position over its competitors"?[84] The answer, as I have suggested in the preceding chapter, is yes and no. Yes, any definition of religion inescapably privileges some forms of religious life. No, unlike Smith, I do not believe that this fact vitiates the search for a principled understanding of religious free exercise. It does make us realize the limitations of that search and appreciate, as he does, that much of our judgment is simply prudential. But limited principles and prudential judgments are perfectly consistent with the "mosaic" or "collage" vision of society I have attempted to articulate. While Smith despairs of an effort to find pristine principles, I embrace that failure as itself a kind of success.

Having engaged in this lengthy survey of attempts to define "religion," I finally conclude that what we have sought turns out to be unnecessary. Recall where we began this chapter: the definitional issue is a threshold to specific constitutional claims. In concrete cases, courts do not ask, "What is a religion?" They ask more case-specific questions, such as: "Was a religious belief burdened?" "Was a religious practice penalized?" "Was the autonomy of a religious institution undermined?" "Was a person's religious identity undermined?" Therefore, the questions courts must answer are smaller ones, which do not absolutely require encompassing definitions. Although less intellectually satisfying, an adequate approach would be simply to focus on the nexus between the challenged aspect of religion and the religious exercise being threatened.[85] Thus, if a person claims that government has burdened his beliefs, it is appropriate to ask whether the beliefs he wants protected are *religious* beliefs. Here, the claimant's sincerity as well as the comprehensiveness of his doctrines might well be appropriate considerations. However, if he claims that some aspect of *religious practice* is being threatened, then courts may choose to focus on the relation of the practices to religious doctrine or its function for the community of believers. If institutional concerns are raised, the kinds of issues suggested by Judge Adams's third indicium are appropriate: Does the institution function in ways that most people, cross-culturally, expect of *religious institutions*?

We will confront these questions in depth in Chapter 4, when we consider the nature of religious exercises, and in Chapter 5, when we consider religious institutions. While some of the problems arising under the Free Exercise Clause turn on threats to religious beliefs, most stem from alleged burdens to a religious practice. This issue has its own version of the threshold problem: What is a religious practice? When a worshiper kneels in a pew in a church, we recognize the act as a religious one. But is wearing one's hair in braids, dreadlocks, or sidelocks a religious exercise? Is refusal to wear gym shorts in school a religious practice? When a complex institution, such as a religiously affiliated hospital, social service agency, school, or fund-raising enterprise seeks First Amendment protection, to what extent should those activities or institutions be treated as exercising "religion"? When a minister offers family counseling or a church runs a child care center, or when a religious foundation pays its maintenance employees, or a church lobbies against legislation or does other "secular" acts, courts must often decide whether the institution merits constitutional or statutory protection as a religious one.[86] In short, we cannot set aside the problem of religious definitions as thresholds to the First Amendment; they recur throughout the body of Free Exercise law. This problem in various manifestations shall continue to engage us throughout our deliberations.

3

BURDENS TO RELIGIOUS BELIEFS

THE BELIEF/ACTION DISTINCTION

Reynolds v United States drew a distinction between religious belief and action; beliefs, the Court ruled, were protected absolutely, but actions were subject to government regulation.[1] This distinction has been seriously discredited, and beginning with *Cantwell v Connecticut*, the courts have made clear that the Constitution protects religious actions as well as beliefs.[2] The distinction between belief and action was long considered dead.[3] However, in 1990, the majority in *Employment Division v Smith* revived the distinction and in doing so implied that the Free Exercise Clause is not breached if government does not coerce religious belief.[4] It remains to be seen whether that unlamented distinction will seriously be resurrected.

In a simple, perhaps trivial, sense it is true that beliefs are protected absolutely; governments have neither the technology nor the interest to intrude into the realm of pure thought. It is only some kind of external behavior that raises governmental issues. Even Thomas Hobbes, in the midst of defending absolute sovereignty, noted that the sovereign had power over only the profession of religious belief and utterly lacked the ability to regulate belief itself.[5] Leo Pfeffer quite accurately reminds us that the First Amendment "protects the free *exercise* of religion, a word which surely connotes action."[6]

A great majority of cases turn on some aspect of external behavior—a religious *practice* that is alleged to be burdened. While the distinction between a belief and a practice is unsatisfactory, it may be useful to distinguish the great bulk of cases in which a person is allegedly penalized for *acting* as required by his religious conscience, from those few cases in which the *belief* itself or the profession of belief is allegedly coerced or penalized. Few Free Exercise cases are about religious beliefs in themselves. But interestingly, some are. Our concern for not *limiting* the Free Exercise Clause to religious beliefs should not lead us to neglect those controversies where belief is at the heart of the issue.

Although (or perhaps because) beliefs are intangible and government intrusion into them is speculative, claims about beliefs pose the most abstract Free Exercise problems. On one level, it is tautologically true that "Die Gedanken sind Frei"; on another, almost everything government does shapes or is shaped by beliefs. To help sort through this very abstract problem, we need first to articulate more precisely the ways beliefs are alleged to be harmed. In some Free Exercise cases, persons allege that they have been penalized for holding or professing particular religious beliefs; others allege that they have been coerced to believe or disbelieve or to profess certain religious tenets.

Two inflammatory controversies concerning coercion of religious beliefs sprang to public attention during the 1980s and seem to have peaked by the early 1990s. However, they were more than fleeting political fads; they remind us that religious beliefs remain serious factors in American politics—including judicial policy. Moreover, they remind us that even such an apparently simple guarantee as freedom of religious belief is still very problematic. These controversies force us to confront some very fundamental questions about our understanding of religious freedom.

REQUIRED PROFESSIONS OF BELIEF

In 1961 in *Torcaso v Watkins* the Supreme Court struck down a Maryland law that required public officials to profess belief in a Supreme Being.[7] This law was the archetypal kind of burden on a religious belief; a benefit available to everyone else was denied to those who failed to profess a certain kind of religious belief.

The celebrated flag salute cases raised similar problems. A West Virginia law, like that of several other states in the interwar period, required schoolchildren to salute the American flag and recite the Pledge of Allegiance. Children of the Jehovah's Witness faith refused to salute the flag or to recite the pledge, interpreting both acts of fealty to inanimate objects as idolatry. These children were consequently suspended from public schools. In 1943, the Supreme Court upheld the law,[8] but in 1947 struck down a similar one as a violation of freedom of speech. Justice Jackson, writing for the majority in *West Virginia State Board of Education v Barnette*, noted the absurdity of government-mandated profession of belief:

Here . . . we are dealing with a compulsion of students to declare a belief. . . . [T]he compulsory flag salute and pledge requires affirmation of a
belief and an attitude of mind. It is not clear whether the regulation con-
templates that pupils forego any contrary convictions of their own and
become unwilling converts to the prescribed ceremony or whether it will
be acceptable if they simulate assent by words without belief and by a
gesture barren of meaning. . . . To sustain the compulsory flag salute we
are required to say that a Bill of Rights which guards the individual's right
to speak his own mind, left it open to public authorities to compel him to
utter what is not in his mind.[9]

Clearly, to condition public education upon a profession of faith that conflicts with religious conscience is a penalty upon religious belief. Although
there have been numerous other First Amendment cases concerning professing or forswearing beliefs, most concern political loyalty and hence raise
free speech issues rather than strictly religious ones.

Another issue on the required profession of a belief came before the
Supreme Court in 1977, when a Jehovah's Witness objected on religious
grounds to displaying his state's motto, "Live Free or Die," on his automobile license plate. In *Wooley v Maynard*, the Court ruled that an automobile owner may not be required to display a license plate motto that conflicts
with his religious beliefs.[10]

A small but surprising replay of this issue occurred in 1991, when the
Fifth Circuit in New Orleans ruled two to one that a judge could not force
an atheist juror to swear to or make any other religion-based promise. Robin
Murray O'Hair, editor of *The American Atheist*, had been called to jury duty
in Austin, Texas, and refused to swear to tell the truth or to make any alternative affirmation, stating her belief that even an affirmation was a religious
statement. She was found in contempt of court and jailed, and she filed suit
against the judge. On appeal, the two-judge majority of the Fifth Circuit
ruled that the judge should have allowed her to fashion a generic statement
"of commitment to truth and integrity in the jury box and jury room, and
to do everything that would make for absolute integrity."[11]

Finally, the issue of coerced profession of belief surfaced before the
Supreme Court in 1992 in an Establishment Clause challenge to religious invocations at graduation ceremonies. In *Lee v Weisman* the Court ruled this
customary practice unconstitutional. Justice Kennedy, writing for the majority, expressed concern that such ceremonies coerced students to acquiesce
in the profession of religious beliefs: "[N]o doubt some persons who have no
desire to join a prayer have little objection to standing as a sign of respect

for those who do. But for the dissenter of high school age who has a reasonable perception that she is being forced by the State to pray in a manner her conscience will not allow, the injury is no less real."[12]

COERCED BELIEFS: THE SCHOOL CURRICULUM CASES

The public schools have been one of the main vehicles of socialization in the United States. To appreciate their importance we need only recall the role of the schools in "Americanizing" generations of immigrants, as well as the deep conflict over the role of public schools in perpetuating and overcoming racial discrimination. Hence, it is not surprising that public school curricula are a continuing source of controversy. Ever since public schools became ubiquitous, there have been conflicts between religious groups and public educators concerning the impact of education on children's religious beliefs. In the early years of this century, the Catholic school system was created to provide an alternative to what was considered a pervasive Protestantism of the public system.[13] In the 1960s and 1970s, in the wake of desegregation and of the removal of compulsory prayers and Bible readings, Christian schools became popular among some conservative Protestants as alternatives to public education.[14] More recently, home schooling has been an alternative for some religious parents to keep their children from the kinds of influences they find objectionable in the public schools.[15] All of these alternatives are costly in both financial and social resources. Therefore, many parents have continued to focus attention on the public schools, attempting to bring the public school curriculum into closer conformity with their own values. When their objections are essentially religious ones, their arguments raise both Free Exercise and Establishment Clause issues. Some parents have sought to protect their children's religious beliefs by asking that they be excused from objectionable public school courses; others have sought to have the public school curriculum changed.[16] During the 1980s, politically active conservative Christians were sometimes successful in bringing schools into closer conformity with their values; laws mandating the posting of the Ten Commandments,[17] requirements of teaching creation science on an equal basis with evolution,[18] and laws authorizing moments of prayer or meditation were the result.[19] All of these laws were struck down as violations of the Establishment Clause. Religious groups were more successful in persuading both Congress and the courts to permit the use of school buildings for extracurricular religious activities—or, to be exact, to include religious groups among the kinds of groups permitted to use school facilities.[20] While our focus is not on the Establishment Clause, it is worth noting that these decisions are consistent with the pluralist principle's goal of fostering alternative sources of meanings. When religions seek to use the public schools to *reinforce* religious meanings, this pluralist goal is thwarted; however, including religious along with nonreligious group activities does not raise the same objections.

The textbook controversy occurred against a background of two possibly conflicting sets of precedents. On one hand, the courts had long recognized the affirmative role of the state to educate citizens, including a right to transmit values approved by the majority and necessary for civic functioning in a democracy.[21] At the same time, they have recognized as even more fundamental the right of parents to direct the education of their children.[22] Conflicts between these principles have been a long-standing staple of First Amendment law.

When parents are not successful in mandating changes in the curriculum, they may turn to Free Exercise challenges to request that their children be excused from participating in the offending school practices. These arguments reached national attention during the mid-1980s, but they have a much longer history. For example, in 1921 a California appellate court required a public school to exempt dissenting children from physical education classes that taught dancing, an activity objectionable to the parents' religious beliefs.[23] In 1970, a school district that required ROTC training was ordered to give a diploma to a student who had absented himself from the activity on religious grounds.[24] In 1978, a public school system was ordered to exempt from coeducational physical education classes members of the United Pentecostal Church who objected to interacting with members of the opposite sex wearing immodest attire.[25]

An unsuccessful excusal attempt in the mid-1970s was *Davis v Page*, which pit a school district against members of the Apostolic Lutheran Church, who constituted about 20 percent of the school district. Parents objected to exposing their children to audiovisual projections, drama, music, and dance, the study of evolution, "humanist" philosophy, discussion of personal and family matters, and sexually oriented materials. The court refused to order the school district to excuse the children, finding the Free Exercise rights of the students and their parents subordinate to the state's interest in education.[26]

Coercion of religious belief was at the heart of two cases decided by lower federal courts in 1985 and 1986. A third case, technically an Establishment Clause one, made a similar argument with a slight twist. In all three cases, fundamentalist Christian parents argued that public school reading materials exposed their children to religiously objectionable materials, thereby undermining the tenets of their religious faith. Both Free Exercise cases, *Grove v Mead School District No. 354*[27] and *Mozert et al. v Hawkins County Board of Education*,[28] turned precisely on claims that a religious *belief* was endangered—specifically, that public school children were coerced to disbelieve, or that the legitimacy of their religious beliefs was disparaged, by textbooks. The third case, *Smith v Board of School Commissioners of Mobile County*,[29] alleged that the public schools were inculcating the "religion" of secular humanism in violation of the Establishment Clause. I will consider *Grove* and *Smith* only briefly and devote considerable attention to *Mozert*.

The heart of the Free Exercise challenges was that the state-required textbooks offended religious beliefs and encouraged children to profess beliefs their religious doctrine found objectionable. In these cases, parents claimed that public school textbooks espoused values offensive to their religious values and exposed their children to teachings that undermined the values of their religious faith. By diminishing the importance of traditional religion, parents argued, the textbooks disparaged the children's religious beliefs and implicitly substituted another belief system. At stake was not the religious *practices* of the plaintiffs but rather state policy that exposed their children to ideas in conflict with religious *beliefs*.[30]

The case of *Grove v Mead School District No. 354* was brought by students who objected on religious grounds to reading *The Learning Tree*.[31] The district offered alternative assignments and permitted them to leave the classroom during discussion of the offending book. The children and their parents, however, insisted on its removal from the curriculum, contending that exposure to children who had read the book was itself a danger to their religious values. Both the district and the appeals court denied the request, finding the voluntary accommodation adequate in light of the state's interest in both educational policy and academic freedom.

An unusual Establishment Clause case being reviewed during the same period of time raised very similar issues. Parents in *Smith v Board of School Commissioners of Mobile County* alleged that the public school system was instilling the religion of secular humanism, through both its inculcation of secular values and its failure to give adequate attention to religious values.[32] While this case was not brought as a Free Exercise one, the issues it raises are remarkably similar to those discussed in the two preceding ones. In *Smith* the claimants argued that many "secular" values fit the judicial definition of a religion. Furthermore, even the *absence* of religious material posed a problem. Petitioners argued that the *failure* to mention the role of religion in American history conveyed the clear message that religion was not important. But the school system seemed to be in a bind. Because religion is such a charged topic, any mention of its role was likely to offend some group; hence omitting religion from the curriculum had itself been a decision taken to avoid First Amendment disputes.

The *Smith* case followed a tortured procedural path and illustrated some rather eccentric judicial reasoning. District Judge Brevard Hand issued a 169-page opinion upholding the Establishment Clause challenge to the curriculum. Applying a method rather loosely derived from Judge Adams's reasoning in *Malnak v Yogi*,[33] he ruled that secular humanism is indeed a religion—one whose predominant value was the denial of the supernatural. Further, he held that because the textbooks did not discuss nonsecular issues, they conveyed a preference for secular humanism over theistic faiths. It came as no surprise when the Eleventh Circuit overruled this decision and restored the curriculum.[34]

Mozert et al. v Hawkins County Public Schools resulted from a dramatic challenge to public school curriculum by parents claiming a Free Exercise right to the religious upbringing of their children.[35] In this case, fundamentalist children and their parents raised numerous objections to the Holt Reinhart reading series used in the public schools. The complaints mostly centered on the series' presentation of contemporary pluralism (including readings on different cultures, religions, value systems) as conflicting with their belief in a singular religious truth and system of values. Hence, *Mozert* raises very directly the conflict between parents' religious right to perpetuate beliefs and the state's interest in preparing children for a heterogeneous world in which tolerance of diversity seems necessary for survival.

Parents sought to have their children excused from reading classes using the Holt series and from classroom discussions of the offending material and demanded the right to instruction in an alternative textbook. The U.S. District Court granted summary judgment against the parents on the grounds that the First Amendment does not protect people from exposure to ideas offensive to their religious values. The parents appealed, and the Sixth Circuit reversed and remanded the case for decision on its merits. Upon remand, the district court found that the compulsory use of the Holt series violated the plaintiffs' free exercise of religion and ordered the school to permit students to "opt out" of the reading program. Students would be permitted to leave the room during study of the offending texts and to receive reading instruction at home. Applying the compelling state interest test, the district court found that the children's religious beliefs were burdened and that the state had a compelling state interest in its educational program; hence, the issue came down to the least restrictive means for achieving the state objective. The "opt out" plan was judged the least restrictive means for fulfilling the state's educational goal. The court refused, however, to compel the district to offer alternative instruction, holding that such a program would violate the Establishment Clause.

The school board appealed this decision, and it returned to the Sixth Circuit. On appeal, the circuit court reversed, holding that the compulsory use of the offensive textbooks did not unconstitutionally burden the free exercise of religion. While the decision was unanimous, this case produced three separate opinions, which provide a multiplicity of approaches to alleged burdens on religious belief. Chief Judge Lively ruled that exposure to ideas in conflict with one's religious beliefs does not unconstitutionally burden public school students' Free Exercise rights. Exposure does not constitute compulsion to believe or to act contrary to one's beliefs. Because religious free exercise was not burdened, the compelling state interest test applied by the district court was not necessary. Judge Kennedy's concurring opinion applied the compelling state interest test and found the state's interest in educating children for life in a pluralistic society sufficient to outweigh any Free Exercise burdens. Judge Boggs reasoned that being compelled to read offensive texts did burden the children's free religious exercise but "reluctantly" concluded that such a burden was not unconstitutional according to Supreme Court precedents.

The school curriculum issue provides an opportunity to evaluate some of the accounts of the Free Exercise Clause we surveyed in Chapter 1. The first approach emphasizes individual liberty and the coercion that abridges it. Almost immediately, the notion of coercion becomes problematic. Consider the two interpretations embodied in *Mozert*. Chief Judge Lively's opinion was based on the distinction between exposure and coercion, and he concluded that mere exposure to offensive material does not violate Free Exercise. In his view, the Constitution does not protect people against *offense* to religious values. The children were not required to believe or to engage in (or refrain from engaging in) practices forbidden (or required) by their religion. In contrast, the parents interpreted coercion much more broadly. Given the impressionable nature of children and the compulsory nature of the public school system, *mere exposure* itself did constitute compulsion.

The parents' arguments in *Grove* and *Mozert* would enormously expand the traditional understanding of the Free Exercise Clause. Earlier cases, with the possible exception of *Davis v Page*, concerned school activities that required students to act in ways contrary to their religious convictions—attending coeducational physical education classes in immodest attire or taking military training, for example. These were *actions* in violation of religious conscience and, as we have said, a far narrower Free Exercise claim. The implication of the parents' argument in these cases is that the Free Exercise Clause protects persons from secular, nonreligious cultural influences that challenge or undermine their religious faith.[36] Accepting these claims would have created for public schools an impossible dilemma. To teach anything with normative or religious implications is bound to offend someone's religious convictions; to fail to do so is alleged to teach irreligion or the irrelevance of religion. If this view prevailed, avoiding First Amendment violations would be impossible. If the world is viewed as suffused with religious significance, almost anything has religious impact—and any subject is religiously suspect. Almost nothing in the curriculum could have religiously neutral content, and government would have to exclude anything that might conceivably offend anyone's religious sensibilities.

An additional problem with the emphasis on free religious choice is the one we noted upon introducing it. *Whose* freedom of choice is at stake? Parents assert that their religious liberty includes the freedom to pass along their faith to their children. Can one simply assume that the liberty of parents coincides with that of the children? Recall Justice Douglas's partial dissent in *Yoder*, in which he focused on the liberty of the children separate from that of their parents.[37] The same issue might be raised in these cases, especially when the parents' liberty is exercised in a way that may burden their children later in life.

The second account of Free Exercise emphasizes commands of conscience; such a view would make cases like *Mozert* turn on whether exposure to offending material violated the religious conscience of the plaintiffs. In fact, Judge Lively asked that very question and observed that the parents had no religious obligation to refrain from exposing their children to offending information.[38] Notice that a reliance on this approach would limit Free Exercise protection to instances when specific religious commands are violated. Such a view constricts the First Amendment and the notion of religion itself in ways discussed in the preceding chapters.

The third account emphasizes the danger of political divisiveness. Judge Kennedy noted that an "opt out" program would pose this kind of danger. But this account is a double-edged sword. Both concessions made to conservative Christian groups and the refusals to make concessions produce political dissension. The third approach seems to offer no clear advice in the curriculum cases.

The fourth approach protects religions as ways of constraining the power of government. Those concerned with the immense power involved in the state's educational function might appreciate the role of religious dissenters in checking that power. And yet this approach, like the preceding one, produces a dilemma between the Establishment and Free Exercise Clauses. Whether the secular educators or the religious right capture control of the curriculum, those objecting to it will seek to limit the power of the public school system over the minds of the nation's children.

I believe that *Mozert* and similar cases demonstrate the strength of the fifth account—the fostering of alternative sources of meaning. In this view, the "purpose" of the religion clauses is to enable people to find, develop, and nurture meaning-giving relationships, institutions, sources of information, and identities. Government policies that deprive people of these opportunities would implicate the First Amendment. However, this explanation does not presume that government is excluded from being a source of meaning; it simply is excluded from creating for itself a monopoly.

The parents in these cases were objecting to government's meaning-creating power exercised through the public education system. Their religious beliefs seemed threatened by a public school curriculum that conflicted with the faith they hoped to pass on to their children. The parents' argument brings into question the entire educative function of the state. By the same reasoning, virtually everything government does to influence the beliefs of children would constitute coercion. To reason thus would preclude government from doing anything to inculcate beliefs. The parents' interpretation of coercion would prohibit virtually any educative role for government. This interpretation reflects Robert Cover's concern with the state's dominance, not only in religious meanings but also in meanings in general. His argument makes us appreciate anew the importance of the First Amendment guarantee of alternatives to public education.

The American constitutional treatment of schooling has responded by assuming a twofold form. Certain decisions have acknowledged the dangerous tendency of a state's *paideia* and marked its boundaries through formal specification of the limits of public meanings. *West Virginia v Barnette*[39] and *Epperson v Arkansas*[40] and the School Prayer Cases are the landmarks, though all proceed, in one sense, from *Meyer v Nebraska*. Although these decisions suggest that the state's specification of meaning is most dangerous when religion and politics are concerned, the issues in these cases are presented by every public curriculum. No sharp line between the problems of *Epperson* and those of a typical history curriculum can be drawn. Similarly, the confessional or sacramental character of the utterances in *Barnette* and the school prayer cases distinguishes them only in degree from the confessional character of all claims to truth and meaning.

. . . The public curriculum is an embarrassment, for it stands the state at the heart of the *paideic* enterprise, and creates a statist basis for the meaning as well as for the stipulations of law. The recognition of this dilemma has led to the second dimension of constitutional precedent regarding schooling—a breathtaking acknowledgment of the privilege of insular autonomy for all sorts of groups and associations. . . . The state's extended recognition of associational autonomy in education is the natural result of the understanding of the problematic character of the state's *paiedic* role. There must, in sum, be limits to the state's prerogatives to provide integrative meaning when it exercises its educative function. But the exercise is itself troublesome; thus, the private, insular alternative is specifically protected. Any alternative to these limits would invite a total crushing of the jurisgenerative character. The state might become committed to its own meaning and destroy the personal and educative bond that is the germ of meaning alternative to those of the power wielders.

The school's central place in the *paideic* order connects the liberty of educational association to the jurisgenerative impulse itself.[41]

My own conclusion is more comfortable with the educative role of the state than is Robert Cover's. Cover is concerned that the public curriculum is "an embarrassment" precisely because it "creates a statist basis for meaning." Without denying that insight, my own argument accepts that as one of the functions—even affirmative obligations—of the modern state. In my view, the modern state cannot avoid exercising its meaning-creating power; to avoid violating the First Amendment, it must only be careful to protect alternatives and avoid the temptation toward monopoly. Thus, the pluralist account would reject the parents' arguments. Government is obligated to permit alternate educational arenas, which it does by allowing private schools, home schooling, and, perhaps in limited circumstances, alternative assignments. Government need not abrogate its role in values education for fear of violating the Establishment Clause or of undermining religious beliefs in violation of the Free Exercise Clause. Indeed, once we realize that there is no value-neutral education, the very possibility of abrogating that role is an impossibility if not an absurdity.[42]

Finally the pluralist principle enables us to place this constitutional dispute within the context of a normative vision. In the pluralist view, cultural and philosophical conflicts are not a burden to be avoided; they are to be welcomed. This is not to deny that such conflicts are deeply painful, perhaps especially so to the young. Nor is it to deny the attractiveness of living "seamless" lives within communities of shared meanings. Nevertheless, the pluralist principle recognizes that the United States is neither a seamless society nor an aggregation of autonomous communities of meaning. It consists of communities of overlapping membership in which conflict is moderated by the very fact that individuals are the locus of numerous communities of meaning. Thus, there is no constitutional right for members of the wider society to shield themselves from the very multiple influences upon which our consensus is based.

"COERCIVE PERSUASION" AND THE "CULT" CONTROVERSY

Troubling as the "coerced belief" school cases are, this problem has arisen in even more dramatic contexts. "Coerced belief" is at the heart of the controversies generated by the new religious movements that attained notoriety in the late 1970s through the mid-1980s. During those years, a variety of nontraditional, high intensity, high demand religious groups actively sought recruits among disaffected members of American society—especially young adults. The Unification Church, the International Society of Krishna Consciousness, the Children of God, and The Way International are among many groups that experienced some success in expanding their membership through intense experiences, separation from the wider community, exotic ritual, and comprehensive structures. These movements were popularly referred to as cults, although sociologists agree that the term is pejorative and lacks intersubjective meaning; they prefer the rather awkward term New Religious Movement (NRM).[43]

Sociologist Thomas Robbins has observed several factors that both encouraged the rise of these groups and made them problematic. First, with the decline of other mediating structures, high intensity religious organizations develop to fill the need for identity and meaning. Many of these groups are multifunctional, stretching beyond the activities we have traditionally associated with churches and performing educational, economic, familial, healing, and other functions as well. The broad scope of religious freedom itself has contributed to the phenomenon. Robbins argues that in an increasingly regulated society, the exemptions allowed for "churches" create a "regulatory gap," thus providing incentives for some movements to define themselves as religious. Moreover,

[g]iven the "regulatory gap" . . . any expansion and diversification of the activities and authorities of religious organizations can easily lead to an increase in church-state tension and resentment directed against religious organizations. Groups such as the Unification Church and the Church of

Scientology are situated at the cutting edge of church-state tension because they are highly diversified and multifunctional entities with their fingers in numerous pies. . . .

In short, cults are controversial in part because they are particularly diversified and multifunctional enclaves lying outside the web of regulation which increasingly enmeshes "secular" organizations.[44]

These movements generated intense reactions by the public at large, and especially from family members of new recruits. Opponents characterized "cult" methods as "brainwashing" or "mind control" and argued that recruits were being manipulated for the selfish ends of cult leaders rather than being offered genuine religious experiences. They characterized NRM membership as mental health pathology and thus tended to medicalize the language for analyzing it and to draw from the mental health arena the language and tactics for confronting it.[45] Ultimately, actors on both sides took to the courts as one of the venues of their prolonged battle.

The underlying issue in the "cult wars" is alleged coercion of religious belief—both by the NRMs and by their adversaries. The premise of the anti-cult forces is that since coerced belief is not free, it cannot be the kind of *free* exercise of religion protected by the First Amendment. We will consider first the general argument for a "brainwashing exception" to the First Amendment and then the specific legal contexts in which this argument has arisen.

Coerced Belief: A "Brainwashing" Exception to the First Amendment?

The heart of the argument for a "brainwashing exception" is simple: The First Amendment is intended to protect the *freedom* of religion, not coerced religious conscience. When beliefs are not freely chosen but instilled by coercive means, they are not protected. In other words, "involuntarily" acquired beliefs should be excluded from the First Amendment umbrella. Although the "brainwashing exception" to the First Amendment never reached the Supreme Court, it was extensively explored in several lower courts, with mixed results.

Richard Delgado, the leading advocate of the "brainwashing exception," explains the argument in the context of deprogramming:

Deprogramming is constitutionally suspect only if the first amendment protects *all* religious belief. To suppose that the Constitution protects all religious belief—including coerced beliefs—from state interference is to make the "free" in "free exercise" unnecessary and, indeed, misleading. In order to give the word "free" in the text of the amendment its rightful weight it must be assumed that the clause protects only freely chosen or uncoerced religious belief and action. Thus, deprogramming is not unconstitutional because it endangers only what the first amendment does not protect: unfree religious belief and conduct.[46]

In Delgado's argument, NRMs deprive their recruits of free religious choice by withholding from them the simultaneous knowledge of the nature of the religion and the capacity for free choice. The absence of these two elements means that NRM recruits have not had genuine religious experiences but have been "brainwashed" or coercively persuaded.

> Because of this structuring of the socialization process, *knowledge* of the nature and effects of the religious cult, and *capacity* for free choice — requisites for informed consent — are never present simultaneously. At the outset when capacity is present, knowledge is lacking; sometime after induction, when knowledge is present, capacity is lacking.
> . . . Informational deprivation plays a decreasing role as the new recruit is drawn gradually into the web of cult initiation. Cult leaders disclose details of hierarchy, lifestyle, doctrine, and submission, but only after they perceive that the individual, as a result of an intense and carefully orchestrated process of psychological manipulation has lost the capacity to assess their significance. . . .
> These techniques combine to produce an individual who has neither the opportunity nor capacity to assess critically his or her engagement with the religious group nor to consult outsiders who may introduce an unwanted skepticism. Although the recruit seemingly has committed himself or herself to the cult, the organization's recruiting tactics progressively have undermined the individual's capacity to make a free and open choice. Against this background of questionable influence and pressures, of which the recruit is generally only dimly aware, the recruit's final commitment could seldom be characterized as an expression of free choice or individual autonomy.[47]

In light of this observation, Delgado argues for applying informed consent standards to religious proselytizing, as it is applied to medical or other contexts.[48] Delgado's formulation is based on a rather eccentric notion of informed consent: If the method by which a person becomes a religious convert deprived her both of volitional autonomy and of adequate information about the nature of the group, her conversion lacked informed consent and may be considered not autonomous; hence, deprogramming is justified. His definition of informed consent seems rather disingenuous:

> A special adaptation of informed consent can be used for this purpose. If the cult devotee can appreciate the nature of the forces she has been subjected to, knows that the cult has deceived and manipulated her, but nevertheless prefers to remain with the cult and adhere to its beliefs and practices, it is reasonable to suppose that she has made a free and voluntary rather than a brainwashed commitment. When the cult adherent possesses the information necessary for informed consent, and the original recruiting tactics no longer impair or impede her volitional capacity, a court should give full credence to the cultist's consent. Therefore, deprogramming is justifiable only if the individual adherent lacks either an informed understanding of the process that led to her cult commitment or the volitional capacity to give autonomous consent to it.[49]

Several state legislatures considered enacting such laws at the height of the cult scare, but none was actually adopted. Delgado's critics counter that, in the name of religious freedom, he fails to respect the present religious choices of the religious convert. Furthermore, in the name of consent, Delgado's theory ignores the refusal of converts to consent to deprogramming.[50]

The treatment of religious commitment as though it were a mental health problem has been subject to serious criticism. Two of the closest students of this phenomena, Dick Anthony and Thomas Robbins, describe the logic of his approach as based on

> an affirmation that there exists a specific psychotechnology which can *involuntarily transform beliefs and loyalties* and which can clearly be distinguished from other, less powerful processes and social influences. As such, these formulations imply a sort of loophole in the first amendment. The constitutional prohibition against an inquiry into the validity and authenticity of faith arguably does not apply if the faith in question is not voluntarily held or has been coercively imposed. The rationale for state intervention is even stronger if there has been an enduring *loss of capacity* which, if both coerced and sufficiently devastating, might even legitimate coercive deprogramming.[51]

To evaluate this controversy we must again confront the illusive notion of coercion. Much of the literature on religious coercion is predicated on a parallel between the cult recruitment methods and the kinds of coercion associated with Korean and Chinese treatment of prisoners in the 1950s, as studied by Robert J. Lifton[52] and Edward Schrin.[53] When Lifton was asked to apply his ideas specifically to the cult controversy, he identified several characteristics of "totalism," including milieu control, mystical manipulation, the demand for purity, the cult of confession, the creation of a "sacred science," loaded language, the subordination of human experiences to the claims of doctrine, and the power to dispense existence itself.[54] However, the "coercive persuasion" Lifton and Schrin originally studied was violent, whereas the methods of the NRMs are usually "friendly." Many scholars are highly critical of the parallel made between prisoners of war and religious converts.[55]

At its heart, this argument treats religious conversion as a mental health pathology. The argument was first offered by Eli Shapiro, who was involved in a lengthy battle over the right to "deprogram" his sons.[56] Subsequently, a small group of mental health professionals, most notably Margaret Singer, made a career out of offering expert testimony on the destructive effects of mind control by religious "cults."[57] Hence, the "brainwashing" controversy raises an ancillary problem—that of the expert testimony of psychologists and other mental health experts. The behavioral science community remains divided and is far from convinced that "brainwashing" or "coercive persuasion" is a scientifically defensible concept. Hence, judges in coercive persuasion cases frequently face the evidentiary problem of admissibility of expert witnesses whose theories are not widely held.[58]

To recognize "brainwashing," or to know when a belief is coerced, we must be able to distinguish it from a "freely chosen" one—an exceptionally tenuous distinction. In short, it requires drawing a line between a voluntary and nonvoluntary religious commitment. Anthony and Robbins describe the issue thus:

> Whatever their denotation, which is not always clear, concepts such as brainwashing or mind control connote *involuntariness*. They suggest a distinctive form or influence or psychotechnology which creates involuntary attitudinal and behavioral sequences. A scientific theory which explains such an influences process must, in order to be admissible, enable analysis (and legal authorities) to clearly distinguish brainwashing as a coercive process that creates involuntariness from other less incisively coercive processes, that is, to "draw the line" between groups which thoroughly brainwash from less potent or pernicious groups.[59]

The "brainwashing exception" argument implies that we have a baseline of autonomously acquired noncoerced beliefs against which we can contrast the coercively acquired ones. But since most religious beliefs are acquired as part of childhood acculturation rather than consciously or autonomously, it is difficult to articulate a genuine theory of an autonomous belief against which to contrast a concept of coercion. Moreover, many mainstream religions use some of the methods deemed unacceptable when used by NRMs; the socialization procedures of convents and monasteries are obvious examples. Indeed, the loss of "autonomy" that is observed in NRM recruits may be a kind of self-integration that develops in multifunctional settings. In the wider society, we expect an autonomous self to transcend segmented social roles; but in a multifunctional, communal movement these expectations may be entirely out of place.[60]

Moreover, the notion of "coercive persuasion" is simply inconsistent with the understanding of "coercion" used in other legal contexts. Whereas critics of cult "brainwashing" focus on the mental state of the alleged victim, coercion in other legal contexts focuses on the wrongfulness of the victimizer. Hence, for legal purposes, the term "coercive persuasion" is both conceptually flawed as well as unworkable within the limits of the First Amendment, as Herbert Fingarette concludes:

> [T]he legal wrongfulness of the alleged coercer's conduct is so crucial to coercion or undue influence, [but] . . . there is such great constitutional restraint on the courts in regard to interfering with or making judgments about religion. Methods of persuasion that might be plainly wrong in law when used in, for example, an economic or domestic context, may very well be protected by the claim that they are intrinsic to religious worship. . . . [T]he more likely legal terrain for such claims would be defined by the claim that the purported victim had been rendered or become mentally incompetent in some respect or degree. However, that too, can be a difficult question to settle legally when one person's mental incompetence is another's religious belief or aesthetic practice.[61]

How can one distinguish a religious conversion from brainwashing? Consider the following problem summarized by Anthony and Robbins:

> The confusion . . . is indicated in Delgado's statement that the cult "information is parceled out only as the cult perceives that the person has *"lost the capacity to respond according to his or her ordinary frame of reference"* [Delgado, 1982, p. 551, our emphasis]. So incapacity, therefore, turns out to be an inability to employ one's prior frame of reference, and, presumably, a brainwashed devotee would be distinguished by his or her

not employing his/her old frame of reference. Yet a shift of frame of reference or "universe of discourse" is a frequent meaning of "conversion" itself whether or not it has been "induced." . . . A shift of frame of reference is the empirical indicator of lost capacity, but any "convert" is by definition incapable of seeking things as he or she once saw them. Evidence of conversion is automatically evidence of brainwashing, given a sufficiently pejorative view of the conversion outcome.[62]

Ultimately, then, adjudication of these issues requires courts to inquire into how the beliefs were acquired and to decide whether some kinds of religious influence are illegitimate. These sorts of judicial determination seem precisely the kind of issues the First Amendment was intended to preclude. One of the most serious dangers of the reactions to the cult phenomena is the failure to take seriously religious experience.[63]

Deprogramming: The Legal Issues

The most dramatic response to NRM recruitment was "deprogramming." Some desperate family members hired professional "deprogrammers" to abduct recruits from religious communities and "rescue" their offspring from "mind control." This process often took the form of removing NRM converts by force or deception and holding them against their will while "deprogrammers" used heavy-handed methods to "deconvert" them. Professional deprogrammers flourished briefly from the mid-1970s through the mid-1980s.[64] Typically, a religious recruit was detained, confined, and vigorously "persuaded" to renounce her beliefs and membership. Although the deprogramming controversy raged for less than a decade, it captures some very fundamental, even profound, philosophical problems within Free Exercise Clause interpretation. The highly inflammatory deprogramming controversy occasioned some serious reflection on the nature of religious conversion and of religious belief itself.

Defenders of deprogramming argue that the beliefs were originally acquired by coercive means, possibly including psychological techniques to undermine the convert's resistance, make him dependent upon the religious group, and weaken his critical abilities. They argue that deprogramming is intended to restore autonomy and religious freedom and to counter the concrete harms of cult membership.

When deprogramming is accomplished by physical abduction and holding persons against their will, it opens the abductors to criminal charges of kidnapping. In addition, deprogrammers have been sued for conspiring to violate civil rights under the Ku Klux Klan Act.[65] That law—now 42

USC § 1985(3)—was originally adopted to protect the rights of newly freed slaves; it creates a civil cause of action against persons who conspire to deprive anyone of the equal protection of law, the privileges and immunities of citizenship, or their life, liberty, or property as protected by the Fourteenth Amendment. In its 1980 decision in *Ward v Connor* the Fourth Circuit accepted the argument that minority faiths are protected in the same way as racial minorities and that the federal courts may impose civil remedies for private actions that violate their civil rights.[66]

Judicial rulings on deprogramming are inconclusive. The most frequently cited case is *Peterson v Sorlein*.[67] A young woman joined an organization known as The Way while she was still a minor. Her parents engaged professional deprogrammers, removed her from the cult by deception, and detained her against her will. The "deprogramming" was temporarily successful; she remained with her parents briefly and then rejoined The Way and filed civil suit against her parents for unlawful imprisonment. The Minnesota Supreme Court found that because part of the time she spent with her parents was voluntary (thirteen of the sixteen days), consent rendered the entire course of conduct consensual. Because she had consented after the fourth day of her detainment, that consent was considered by the court to be retroactive. Hence, no false imprisonment occurred.[68]

To avoid charges of kidnapping, parents and deprogrammers developed two defensive strategies. One was the use of the "necessity" or "choice of evil" defense, which permits a jury to acquit defendants if the jury is convinced that the evil avoided through the abduction outweighs the evil of the abduction.[69] More significantly, parents have attempted to legitimize deprogramming by obtaining court-ordered conservatorship under state statutes. The process begins with a writ of habeas corpus ordering the cult to produce the recruit for a court hearing on mental incompetence. Parents typically present evidence of personality change, and if they are successful, the judge may grant a temporary (usually a fifteen- to thirty-day) conservatorship for the purpose of deprogramming.[70] The cases generated by this tactic involved courts in the task of assessing mental capacity, responsibility, and autonomy as it relates to religious commitments. The most significant case on this strategy is *Katz v Superior Court*, in which a California court denied a plea for temporary guardianship for the purpose of deprogramming.[71] The court relied on the majority reasoning in *United States v Ballard*,[72] refusing to question the validity of a religious faith.

Overall, most constitutional scholars have been very critical of deprogramming. Because deprogramming routinely involves forcible restraint and other coercive methods in order to "persuade" people to renounce their present religious beliefs, it seems to belie the professed goal of the anticult movement to promote religious freedom by eliminating coerced religious conversions. One author captures the spirit of these criticisms by terming deprogramming "the new exorcism."[73]

Civil Suits against NRMs

While anticult activists experienced some early judicial successes in legitimating deprogramming activities, the weight of First Amendment doctrine was against them. *Katz* was a substantial defeat. As a result, they developed an additional strategy aimed at imposing financial losses on these organizations. Former NRM members or their families brought tort actions against religious groups for fraud, false imprisonment, intentional infliction of emotional distress, and other harms, or sued them under the old Ku Klux Klan Act for conspiring to violate their civil rights. When these suits demanded punitive as well as compensatory damages, the financial stakes often ran into the millions of dollars. Notice that these are the *same* statutes and legal strategies used by NRM members *against* deprogrammers.

A complex case brought against the Holy Spirit Association in California illustrates the complicated connection between First Amendment issues and civil law remedies. In the case of *Molko and Leal v Holy Spirit Association*[74] a former member of the Unification Church brought a civil suit against the church for fraud and intentional infliction of emotional distress. Two lower California courts summarily dismissed the suits, following the reasoning in *Katz* that the First Amendment provided a barrier against interferences with religious practices. The California Supreme Court reversed, and the majority opinion, written by Judge Stanley Mosk, seemed to create a First Amendment exception. In the majority's view, coercive persuasion alone does not constitute a cause of action, but coercive persuasion in combination with deliberate and blatant deception of the identity of the church is actionable. Judge Mosk thus adopted Delgado's reasoning, which we considered in the preceding section. Hence, the California Supreme Court established a narrow exception to First Amendment protection—deliberate concealment of the identity of the organization along with coercive persuasion deprive a religious movement of First Amendment protection.

Two subsequent cases suggest continued ambivalence over such claims. *George v ISKCON*[75] was an action brought by a former member and her mother, alleging infliction of emotional harm as well as wrongful death of her father, whose death was attributed to his distress over his daughter's involvement in the Hare Krishna movement. The jury heard testimony from Dr. Singer that the plaintiff's "will was overcome," and it subsequently awarded the claimant $30 million in damages. An appeals court reversed part of the judgment but left standing an award of $2.9 million on her claim of wrongful death and emotional harm. In contrast, in *Murphy v ISKCON*[76] the Massachusetts Supreme Court dramatically reduced an award against the Hare Krishna movement on Free Exercise grounds, noting the impossibility of separating the group's actions from its religious beliefs.

The "Cult Wars" and Principles of Religious Freedom

While the practice of forcibly attempting to change the religious beliefs of those thought to be under the influence of "cults" has faded from public attention, it reminds us that beliefs themselves remain very controversial and that the courts have occasionally been used to legitimize private efforts to change people's religious beliefs.

One of the striking things about the legal and sociological literature on the "cult wars" is its relative isolation from the rest of Free Exercise literature. It is as though there are two bodies of professional thought that have not come into contact with each other—the mainstream literature on religious freedom and the literature on the topics we have been considering. Except for Delgado's argument, most discussions are not well situated within a general approach to the Free Exercise Clause. Delgado's argument is clearly embedded within our first Free Exercise principle; its entire focus is on the freedom of religious *choice*. He approvingly quotes Thomas Jefferson's preamble to the Virginia statute on religious freedom, "God made man's mind free, and deliberately chose that religion should be propagated by reason and not coercion," as well as Locke's referring to a church as a "voluntary society of men, joining themselves together of their own accord."[77] For Delgado and his supporters, religious freedom is at the heart of the First Amendment; religion without freedom is not included within that protection. NRMs and their legal defenders counter with their own emphasis on freedom of choice; they remind us that government-sanctioned deprogramming and similar methods emphasize the government's refusal to respect the religious choices of church members.

A parallel problem is raised if we follow the second account and focus on liberty of conscience. Just what do we mean by conscience? Opponents of NRMs deny that the conscience claims of "cult" members can be genuine; worse, they find some of the actions commanded by conscience under "cult" control to be downright "unconscionable." NRM members demand that the commands of their conscience be taken as seriously as those of the mainstream. Unless courts are willing to address this conundrum, the second approach is not likely to provide useful guidance.

The third and fourth accounts of religious freedom focus attention on the public consequences of these conflicts. The third account emphasizes civil peace and seeks to depoliticize religious conflict, while the fourth one emphasizes private institutions as alternatives to governmental power. But when an issue becomes as politically volatile as the "cult wars" of the 1980s, it is not clear that any judicial strategy avoids religious conflict, especially if legislatures have joined the fray. Nor is the avoidance of governmental power—the goal of the fourth account—likely when partisans of both sides invoke the civil law as their weapons.

The cult cases pose some serious problems for the pluralist account, because they push the principle to its limit and demand a justification for its values. NRMs in this view are "tolerated" because they provide sources of meaning for people who seem particularly to need them. But is any source of meaning—at least any source of *religious* meaning—to be protected? So far our arguments have assumed that meaning itself is crucial for both individual well-being and social binding. Moreover, NRMs, like other multifunctional groups, illustrate an ambiguity in the concept of pluralism. These movements would be reasonably consistent with pluralism that is understood to be a confederation of relatively autonomous subgroups. However, the view of pluralism emerging here emphasizes overlap rather than autonomy. Insular and multifunctional organizations preclude this overlap by keeping members' associations and loyalties within the singular organization as much as possible. To this extent, they pose a problem for the pluralist vision I have advocated. When we return to the pluralist vision in the concluding chapter, we will revisit the special problems that insular groups pose for pluralism in both theory and practice. These cases, therefore, ultimately demand that partisans and judges probe the value and limits of our commitment to pluralism.

4

THE NATURE OF RELIGIOUS EXERCISES

THE PROBLEM

The scope of religiously motivated behaviors is virtually incalculable. Religious codes dictate a variety of means by which people worship: kneeling, standing, eating, fasting, ingesting alcoholic beverages or hallucinogenic drugs, making symbolic sacrifices or sacrificing live animals, covering or uncovering their heads or feet in houses of worship, singing, meditating, chanting, preaching, and speaking in tongues, to name only a few. Religious laws frequently mandate certain kinds of personal care and hygiene, including bathing, dressing, health care, diet, and hairstyle. Religious mandates cover comportment in the world at large in such areas as social responsibility, education, child rearing and relations between the sexes, medical practices, appropriate employment, financial decisions, and countless other aspects of life.

Religious practices range from liturgical or ceremonial activities done inside religious institutions, to secular practices motivated by religious faith. They range from those that are obligatory (confession for Catholics), to those that are optional (singing in the church choir). They range from those authoritatively sanctioned by recognized churches, to those based upon the private conscience of an individual believer.

Similarly extensive is the regulatory range of modern government. Federal, state, and local governments regulate virtually every aspect of contemporary life, from the production and processing of foods and drugs, to education, employment, transportation, housing, finances, building, and zoning. Given the scope of both religious practices and government regulation, it is no surprise that they clash from time to time. People may perceive that government burdens their religious exercise when it either requires (or encourages) behavior that the religion forbids (or discourages) or forbids (or discourages) behavior that the religion requires (or encourages). The range of both religious practices and governmental actions that potentially burden them are virtually boundless. When a government regulation negatively impacts on a person's ability to act in accordance with religious conscience, she may seek redress through the judicial system by claiming violation of her constitutional right to the free exercise of religion. Before we are in a position to consider the resolutions of these conflicts, we need to think more precisely about what it means for an individual to engage in a religious exercise. Subsequently, we will have to analyze what it means to "prohibit" a religious exercise and then consider the special Free Exercise problems of religious institutions. Only then will we be in any position to shed light on possible solutions.

CENTRALITY: A FALSE START

Because the range and diversity of religious practices is virtually boundless, courts need a common language for evaluating them. From time to time judges have experimented with the concept of "centrality"; the more central the practice to the religion, the more constitutional protection it merited. There is a persuasive plausibility to this approach. Surely a core religious act —the sacrifice of the Eucharist—deserves more protection than an optional one that some members feel religiously encouraged to perform. Courts have sometimes asked for evidence about the centrality of the practice to the religious life of the person or group making a Free Exercise claim. But judging the centrality of a practice to religion was always bothersomely close to evaluating religious doctrine. In Justice Scalia's words, "What principle of law or logic can be brought to bear to contradict a believer's assertion that a particular act is 'central' to his personal faith? Judging the centrality of different religious practices is akin to the unacceptable business of evaluating the relative merits of differing religious claims. . . . It is not within our judicial ken to question the centrality of particular beliefs or practices to a faith."[1]

Since few religions provide lexical lists of required or prohibited practices, it is not at all clear how crucial a challenged practice may be. For example, how "central" is it for Jewish men to keep their heads covered? Was the practice of polygamy central to Mormon belief, or was it dispensable? Was the objection to secular education for teenagers central to Amish belief or merely a strategy for protecting the religious subculture? In the absence of authoritative statements of doctrine—a characteristic of most non-Catholic religious groups in the United States—courts lack a place to turn for authoritative answers to these questions. Hence, satisfaction of these criteria is not a simple matter in any religious system; but it may be especially difficult in those that lack either formal definitions of orthodoxy or formally sanctioned promulgators and interpreters of the faith.[2]

Another problem with centrality is that it entails some of the same problems we encountered in Chapters 1 and 2 in approaching religion as a system of obligation. The practices considered central to a religion are likely to be those required by its doctrines. But, as we have seen, approaching religion as consisting essentially of required practices reduces religion to a body of rules and hence fails to appreciate the social and communal aspects of religious life. To paraphrase a previous example, singing in a church choir may not be central to any religious belief system, but it may be precisely the activity that links an individual believer to a religious community.

Because of these difficulties, the courts have abandoned attempts to judge centrality in recent years. Justice O'Connor defended this desertion at some length in *Lyng v Northwest Indian Cemetery Protective Association* against the dissenters' arguments to retain the practice.

> [T]he dissent proposes a legal test under which it would decide which public lands are "central" or "dispensable" to which religions . . . and would then decide which government programs are "compelling" enough to justify infringement of those practices. . . . We would accordingly be required to weigh the value of every religious belief and practice that it said would be threatened by any government program. Unless a "showing of centrality" . . . is nothing but an assertion of centrality, . . . the dissent thus offers us the prospect of this court holding that some sincerely held religious beliefs and practices are not "central" to certain religions, despite protestations to the contrary from the religious objectors who brought the lawsuit. In other words, the dissent's approach would require us to rule that some religious adherents misunderstood their own religious beliefs. We think such an approach cannot be squared with the Constitution.[3]

While the centrality issue is a troublesome one, abandoning judgment based on centrality has recently permitted the Court to uphold laws that had devastating effects on practices that were indispensably central to a religion. Indeed, in *Lyng* the devastating effect of the governmental road-building project was stipulated and beyond dispute. And in *Smith* the majority upheld a prohibition on a core religious ritual, without considering its centrality. Abandoning the search for centrality has left courts in need of a way of recognizing when actions may constitute religious exercises. Since virtually any action may be imbued with religious meanings, I propose that judges consider the contexts in which these actions occur.

A TYPOLOGY OF RELIGIOUS PRACTICES

Religions create and sustain meanings in a multiplicity of settings. For purposes of simplicity, we might consider three general categories: worship practices (ritual, liturgy, etc.), religious mandates concerning personal care, and religiously motivated practices diffused through the general culture.

Worship practices are those by which people attempt to get in touch with the transcendent or the sacred; sometimes these are individual acts of spirituality, but more often, they occur in a communal setting in a specific location designated for that purpose. These are the kinds of religious practices of most immediate concern to the Constitution's founding generation. Moreover, and more importantly, these acts are the core creators of meaning that the religion clauses seek to protect; they are the "plausibility structures" that enable people to maintain religious meanings and identities.[4] Let me emphasize that this category does not restate the issue of centrality. I emphatically do not imply that ritual and liturgy are more central to religion than social service ministries; as a matter of personal conviction, I believe the contrary. However, worship activities are mostly confined in both location and impact to willing participants. Their impact on the wider community is more often circumscribed, and the occasions of conflict with state interests ought to be few. It should take a very great compelling state interest to justify interference with these activities.

Emanating from worship practices are the religious mandates concerning personal care—dietary and cleanliness practices, religiously mandated health care, clothing, hairstyles and other appearance requirements or prohibitions. Many of these activities implicate constitutional privacy protections in addition to those of the Free Exercise Clause. These kinds of activities seem to be particularly crucial to the protection of religious identities; braids for Native Americans, head coverings and dietary restrictions for Jews and Muslims, and health practices of Christian Scientists have become the identifying symbols of religious identity. They also merit strong protection, including accommodation, wherever possible. However, unlike worship practices, which are usually confined to specific settings, these activities are carried on in a variety of settings. As we carry around our bodies and come into contact with others, state demands are more likely to be compelling, i.e., demands for vaccinations to combat communicable diseases. However, less than compelling state benefits, such as the extra modicum of safety that might be obtained by requiring that basketball players remain bareheaded, or the added discipline produced by requiring that military officers wear only uniform head coverings, are not sufficient to outweigh these very personal attributes of religious identity. In short, while the state may occasionally have compelling reasons for restricting religious behavior concerning personal care, such occasions should be few.

Beyond this circle are diffuse religious activities, which are conducted in society at large and often in the idiom of the wider society. These practices combine religious and other kinds of meanings and thus raise the most complicated problems. When religious individuals and institutions operate within the idiom of the broader culture, the opportunities for conflict grow, and the interests of the state become more numerous. Here, the religious adherent is operating in multiple roles, including both citizen and religious observer. Religious accommodation in the workplace or school seems legitimate under these circumstances as long as they promote pluralism in the public sphere. Because these kinds of activities raise the most complex problems, they ask for some very delicate judgments that return our attention to the informing principle of the religion clauses themselves.

I want to reiterate that I have arranged these categories of religious practice on a nominal, not an ordinal, scale; the arrangement does not suggest a declining order of significance or restate the issue of centrality. Indeed, many religious people insist that the interpersonal, ethical behavior mandated by their religious beliefs is more important than their rituals or personal care. I do not offer the distinction between the second and third categories as one between "self regarding" and "other regarding" behavior, since I doubt that the very distinction is a tenable one. Surely practices as personal as one's own hygiene may deeply affect others. What I suggest here is that there are concentric circles of activities in which, as one moves outward, separating religiously imbued meanings from other meanings attached to the same activity becomes increasingly difficult. Ritual and personal care activities may not be more important, but they should be easier to protect because they are more physically circumscribed. Hence, there ought to be fewer good reasons for government to interfere with them.

The typology I suggest here is superficially similar to the "concentric circles" of religious activities that Bruce Bagni has advocated for evaluating the activities of religious institutions.[5] Bagni proposes that the Free Exercise Clause protects "purely spiritual" matters at the epicenter of a church's functions, but as church activities emanate from this core, they merit less constitutional protection. His proposal is intended to guide courts in evaluating the autonomy claims of religious institutions, while mine is aimed at understanding individual religious activity. More importantly, while my proposal is concentric in a certain sense, it rejects the ordinal scale of constitutional protection that is at the heart of Bagni's argument.

RITUAL PRACTICES

Ceremonial, liturgical, or sacerdotal practices—which I shall collectively call rituals—are typically done in a religious community or institution, or in formal worship services, symbolizing foundational myths or directly relating participants to the divine. These are the kinds of "practices" that would have been best understood by the people who wrote and ratified the First Amendment. At first blush, these practices seem to be an epiphenomena to the beliefs they represent, but some observers of religion find them to be the heart of religion itself.[6] Any serious approach to Free Exercise protection must appreciate the crucial functions performed by religious ritual: "[R]itual is often central to the ability of religious systems to transmit values and apply those values to control the conduct of adherents. If the Constitution protects religious communities not as anachronistic curiosities, but as important components in creating standards of belief and behavior in modern societies, the Court must take more seriously the importance of religious ritual practices."[7]

Steven Gey has argued that rituals are the *only* kinds of religious practices that should be protected by the First Amendment. His argument is thought provoking: "To extend First Amendment protection beyond worship practices plays havoc with the regulatory state by providing unlimited exceptions to uniform policy. Furthermore, any broader definition of religious practices raises unsolvable Establishment Clause problems because most of the ordinary activities of government could be seen as establishing a religion."[8] While most First Amendment scholars have not been sympathetic to Gey's limited interpretation of Free Exercise, his emphasis on rituals does shed an interesting light on the surprising number of instances in which they have been the focus of conflict. The following discussions illustrate some of the legal conflicts occasioned by controversial worship practices.

Snake Handling

Occasionally, government finds religious ceremonies so objectionable that it makes performing them a crime; the practice of snake handling by some Holiness churches is one dramatic example. These churches, mostly in the Southeast, take literally the verse from Mark 16:115–18: "These signs will attend those who believe: in my name they shall cast out devils, they shall speak in new tongues; if they carry snakes or if they drink a lethal drink, it shall not harm them; they shall lay hands upon the sick and they shall be well." As acts of faith, at certain services ministers and other church members handle snakes and drink strychnine. More than once, state legislatures have enacted statutes specifically banning this religious ritual. Kentucky legislators, for example, explicitly outlawed snake handling "in connection with any religious service or gathering."[9] The issue emerged again in the 1970s, when the Supreme Court of Tennessee upheld an injunction against both practices, on the ground that the snakes posed a danger in a crowded place and that the state's interest in preserving life to have a healthy citizenry was a sufficient interest to justify the prohibition against poison. Notice that the laws in question in these cases, like the 1993 animal sacrifice one discussed below, specifically target a religious practice.[10]

The snake handling cases might seem a constitutional oddity were it not for the two dramatic Supreme Court cases of 1990 and 1993, both stemming from laws prohibiting religious rituals. In the much criticized *Smith* case, a divided Court upheld a prohibition against ingesting peyote, even in a religious ritual. Three years later, a unanimous Court struck down a municipal ordinance banning ritual animal slaughter.

Ritual Peyote Use

Both Supreme Court watchers and religious activists were shocked in 1990, when a six to three majority upheld an Oregon law prohibiting the use of peyote, a drug that has long been used as a crucial part of the religious ceremonial practices of the Native American Church, as applied to its ritual use by members of the church and upheld the denial of unemployment compensation benefits for two church members fired from their jobs for ritual peyote use.[11]

As long as hallucinogens have been prohibited by state and federal narcotics laws, exemptions for ritual peyote use have been controversial. Since 1964, when in the case of *People v Woody*[12] the California Supreme Court ruled that ritual peyote use in Native American Church services was protected by the Free Exercise Clause, the issue had seemed settled. Subsequently, both federal law and the laws of twenty-three states provided statutory exemptions. Oregon, however, had not done so. When Alfred Smith and Galen Black were fired from their jobs for participating in a peyote ceremony, the once-settled question was opened again and prompted the most controversial religious freedom case of the decade. Smith and Black's request for unemployment compensation was denied because their termination was deemed to be for a work-related cause. The Oregon courts reversed that denial, refusing to hold a religious ritual a work-related cause for termination. Citing a long string of U.S. Supreme Court cases, the Oregon Supreme Court ruled that such acts are protected by the First Amendment. On remand after the first Supreme Court hearing, the Oregon Supreme Court reemphasized its position: Although ritual use of peyote was not exempted from the state's narcotics laws, the law's enforcement in those circumstances would violate the First Amendment. Thus, when the Supreme Court reversed and held that ritual use need not be exempted from "laws of general applicability," it was upholding a criminal law that the state had declined to enforce; hence, it was ruling on an issue that had not been raised.

Among the peculiarities of Justice Scalia's majority opinion is his failure to confront the fact that the exercise being prohibited was a religious *ritual*—the kind of act most uncontroversially "religious." In contrast, the dissenters took very seriously the religious context of peyote use. While agreeing with the majority that courts ought not delve into the "centrality" of religious acts, they noted that, for members of the Native American Church, peyote rituals are "an integral part of the life process." "Respondents believe, and their sincerity has *never* been in doubt, that the peyote plant embodies their deity, and eating it is an act of worship and communion. Without peyote, they could not enact the essential ritual of their religion."[13] The dissenters noted the "devastating impact" of prosecuting them for an act of worship—an impact all the more troubling in view of Congress's policy of protecting the religious freedom of Native Americans symbolized in the American Indian Religious Freedom Act.

Animal Sacrifice: Church of Lukumi Babalu Aye, Inc., and Ernesto Pichado v City of Hialeah [14]

Santeria, an Afro-Caribbean religion combining elements of Yoruba practices with Roman Catholicism, evolved among the descendants of slaves in Cuba and elsewhere in the Caribbean. It was brought to the United States with the migration of Cubans in the middle of this century. "The Santeria faith teaches that every individual has a destiny from God, a destiny fulfilled with the aid and energy of the *orishas* (spirits). The basis of the Santeria religion is the nurture of a personal relation with the *orishas*, and one of the principle forms of devotion is an animal sacrifice. . . . Sacrifices are performed at birth, marriage and death rites, for the cure of the sick, for the initiation of new members and priests, and during an annual celebration."[15] In both Cuba and the United States, Santeria is usually practiced in secret, but in 1987 a group leased land in the city of Hialeah, Florida, and announced its intentions to establish a church. These announced plans were met with "concern and distress" by many members of the Hialeah community, and in response, the city council called an emergency meeting. The council adopted a resolution declaring the city's commitment to prohibiting acts by religious groups "inconsistent with public morals, peace and safety." The city sought counsel from the state attorney general, who advised that banning ritual sacrifice would not be inconsistent with the state's laws prohibiting "unnecessary" killing of animals. The council then adopted a number of resolutions prohibiting animal sacrifice and the possession of animals intended for ritual slaughter but specifically exempting virtually any other kind of animal killing. Both the district and appeals courts upheld the prohibition; the Supreme Court granted certiorari.

These facts presented the Supreme Court with a straightforward issue. The city council had passed ordinances specifically aimed at a religious ritual the majority of the community found abhorrent.[16] The Court did not give any particular significance to the fact that the prohibited religious act was a *ritual* one, but rather, they focused on the fact that an unpopular religious practice was targeted by a "religious gerrymander" that managed to prohibit animal sacrifice while protecting most analogous forms of animal killing.

Ritual Acts in Prisons

The Bill of Rights' emphasis on protection of persons accused of crimes makes it clear that prisoners do not lose constitutional protections. However, the very nature of a penal institution implies that these rights are greatly reduced and constricted. Federal Bureau of Prisons regulations contain rather extensive protections for religious freedom "within the constraints of budgetary limitations and the security and orderly running of the institution."[17] These protections include access to religiously mandated diets, services, ceremonies, and meetings, defense against religious coercion, and accommodation of work schedules to the requirements of religious faiths. The enforcement of these guarantees is left to judgment of the warden concerning budget, security, good order, and fairness. In addition to relying on the Free Exercise Clause and the Bureau of Prisons Guidelines, prisoners may also bring complaints of denial of civil rights under the 1871 Civil Rights Act and federal and state habeas corpus claims. The Equal Protection Clause may also be invoked when prisoners complain of religious discrimination or unequal treatment. However, except during the heyday of the Warren Court, the judiciary has been extremely deferential to the decisions of prison administrators.

During the period from the mid-1960s to mid-1970s, incarcerated Black

Muslims brought to the federal courts a number of cases demanding religious rights, and they were soon followed by members of other minority religions. In *Cruz v Beto*[18] in 1972 the court ruled that a Buddhist prisoner could not be denied the same religious opportunities afforded to prisoners of other faiths.

Beyond rather basic acknowledgments, however, the Supreme Court has not been vigorous in supervising prisoners' religious rights. The most significant contemporary precedent is *O'Lone v Estate of Shabbaz*,[19] decided in 1987 by a divided Court. This Free Exercise complaint was brought by Muslim prisoners whose work schedule prevented their attending weekly religious services. Because of prison overcrowding and supervisory costs, prisoners scheduled to work outside the prison main building were not permitted to return to the building in time for the Friday afternoon service of Jumu'ah, the only weekly congregational service of the Muslim faith. Justice Rehnquist, writing for the five-member majority, acknowledged that this service was indeed a central part of their faith, but he nevertheless upheld the prison authorities' decision. The majority emphasized its deference to the judgment of prison administrators and ruled that prison regulations burdening religious freedom are constitutional if they are reasonably related to valid penological interests. Prison officials need not show that there are no less burdensome alternatives for meeting those interests, as the court of appeals would have required. The majority were impressed by the fact that Muslim prisoners "retain the ability to participate in other Muslim religious ceremonies." They are not "deprived of all forms of religious exercise." The majority also found it significant that their religious interests were being accommodated in other ways, including their dietary ones.

The four dissenters, in an opinion authored by Justice Brennan, were less impressed than the majority by other forms of accommodation: "Jumu'ah . . . cannot be regarded as one of several essentially fungible religious practices. The ability to engage in other religious activities cannot obscure the fact that the denial at issue in this case is absolute: respondents are completely foreclosed from participating in the core ceremony that reflects their membership in a particular religious community."[20] The dissenters would have held prison officials to a stricter standard, requiring that they demonstrate that both the restriction was genuinely necessary and less burdensome alternatives were not available to meet prison interests.

While the Supreme Court has heard relatively few religious rights cases from prisoners, the lower courts have heard many. In *Hadi v Horn*[21] the Seventh Circuit found no constitutional violation in the occasional cancellation of Muslim services when the chaplain was not available and when the chapel was used for recreation purposes. In *Brown v Johnson*[22] the Sixth Circuit upheld a prison ban on group worship by a gay church.

A number of controversies regarding religious rituals in prisons have been initiated by Native Americans, whose faiths require access to ritual objects, such as sweat lodges, medicine bags, eagle feathers, and various plants, and often the presence of a medicine man.[23] In asserting their rights to religious rituals in prisons, Native Americans can rely not only on constitutional guarantees but also on statutory protection offered by the American Indian Religious Freedom Act.[24] However, their petitions have been met with mixed results. Many prisons, for example, do provide sweat lodges, but some administrators consider them safety hazards.[25] In *Allen v Toombs*[26] the Ninth Circuit rejected a petition of two prisoners in disciplinary segregation at Oregon State Penitentiary who had been denied access to sweat lodges and pipe bearers because of security concerns. Choice of clergy to perform ceremonies may also be a source of controversy. In *Saoa Bahin v Gunther*,[27] for example, prisoners complained that the medicine man the state had provided to prisoners was one whose practices were contrary to the beliefs of many of those he served. The Eighth Circuit ruled that the Constitution does not require prisoners to have chaplains of their own choosing, but it also ruled that the prison may not provide only a single religious perspective and required the state to rotate a variety of medicine men in the prison program.

The issue of prisoners' religious rights took on a new significance during the debate over the 1993 Religious Freedom Restoration Act. Probably the most serious controversy generated during its consideration was the very significant opposition that came from prison administrators. They feared that the act, which would require accommodation of all prisoners' religious needs unless prison officials could show a compelling interest in refusing to do so, would play havoc with prison order and discipline. An amendment to exempt prisoners from the act was debated but in the end not adopted.

Ritual Acts and Free Exercise Principles

As we might expect, the first two accounts of free religious exercise are most helpful in thinking about ritual religious acts. Interestingly, protection of free religious choice would protect these acts better than the protection of religious obligation. Holiness members are not *obligated* to handle snakes; they do so as voluntary expressions of faith. Likewise, peyote is not an *obligation* for members of the Native American Church; it is a method of achieving higher spiritual awareness. Taken together, the individualist principles do an adequate job of explaining and justifying religious freedom in these areas.

Yet, something seems to be missing. As we have seen, both freedom of choice and freedom of conscience are individualized principles. Yet, the core significance of rituals seems to be that they are not individual behaviors but collective ones, which have meaning only because they are done with a certain community of worshipers and in a particular setting. (Carrying around snakes in one's living room and ingesting peyote on the back porch would not be considered religious practices; indeed, they would probably be considered blasphemous.) However, neither the third account, which views religious freedom in terms of preventing civil conflicts, nor the fourth, which is concerned with limiting the power of government, seems particularly helpful in resolving to these controversies.

Again, the pluralist account seems to provide the missing piece. These practices are valuable for individual worshipers because they sustain shared meanings and identities. A society that values a complex mosaic of meanings and identities rather than unified ones cannot fail to appreciate the contributions of these ritual acts to that mosaic.

RELIGIOUS PRACTICES CONCERNING PERSONAL CARE

The second kind of religious practice includes religiously mandated acts concerning a person's own body—what she eats, how she dresses, and the way she takes care of her health, for example. Jews and Muslims wearing head coverings and keeping religiously mandated dietary restrictions, Native Americans wearing braids, Orthodox Jews and Sikhs wearing beards, Rastafarians wearing dreadlocks, and Sikhs wearing turbans, as well as the bathing rituals of Orthodox Jews provide other examples. When Captain Goldman complained about the Air Force's refusal to let him wear his yarmulke while in uniform, he was attempting to exercise a religious practice of this type. When Jehovah's Witnesses refuse blood transfusions or Christian Scientists refuse medical care for themselves on religious grounds, they are also making this kind of claim. For many religious traditions, personal care practices are grounded in divine commands, transcendental beliefs, or ultimate concerns. As Judge Arlin Adams recognized in creating his composite definition, many religions are sufficiently comprehensive to include rules or views on very ordinary matters such as diet, periods of rest, and dress. These are not themselves "ultimate concerns," but they are intimately connected to a religion that does address such concerns. Once a belief system has been credited as a "religion" through an examination of its "ultimate" nature, its teaching on other matters also must be accepted as religious.[28]

The following sections summarize some of the representative legal conflicts concerning personal care.

Religious Refusal of Blood Transfusions

Jehovah's Witnesses interpret the Bible as prohibiting the receipt of blood in any form, including lifesaving transfusions. When a member of this faith suffers medical emergencies requiring blood transfusions as a lifesaving procedure, transfusions are sometimes given by court order over the objection of the patient. Courts have long recognized a general right to bodily integrity grounded in common law as well as on constitutional privacy and religious freedom doctrines. The privacy interest in refusing medical treatment is still tentative, but the First Amendment right is more secure. Either right may be outweighed by a compelling state interest. The state interest in protecting the patient's minor children has usually been considered sufficient to override the religious preferences of the patient.[29] When there are no minor children involved, courts have tended to be more solicitous of the patient's own decision. Some courts balance patients' religious rights against the interests of medical staff in practicing medicine according to the commands of their consciences.[30]

In a way, the failure to protect religious refusal of medical care suggests a shortcoming we observed in *Lyng*. In both instances, authorities seem unable to imagine and take seriously belief systems out of the mainstream—in this instance, a belief system that places less emphasis on life than on purity and obedience. Protecting alternate sources of meaning requires a willingness to take seriously the fact that other people could hold entirely different worldviews.

These cases are related to the ones that follow—those in which parents with religious objections to medical care are prosecuted for failure to seek treatment for their children. Many of the religious, medical, ethical, and emotional issues are the same. Yet, while the preceding cases concern the personal care of one's own body, the following ones concern the responsibilities and rights of parents concerning the physical and spiritual care of their children.

Prosecutions for Religiously Motivated Refusal of Medical Care for Children

Interpretations of religious liberty seldom involve life or death decisions, but in the conflict between religious healing and mainstream medicine, they sometimes do. When parents choose religious healing methods for their children in lieu of mainstream medicine, and the child dies, the parent may be charged with child neglect or abuse. A number of such cases have pitted Christian Scientists against state and local officials, and the resulting judicial decisions have created a patchwork pattern.[31] Before we discuss this problem and related cases, a preliminary word must be said about classifying this issue as *personal* care. Clearly, the care of one's children's bodies is not quite the same as the care of one's own; hence "personal care" is not quite an accurate characterization of this practice. However, because of the deep affinity between parents and children and the fact that the personal care of children is the parents' responsibility, this classification seems appropriate. Clearly, however, it occupies an ambiguous position in the classification system.

Prosecution of Christian Scientists for the failure to obtain medical care for their children illustrates a curious conflict between legislative accommodation of religion and judicial refusal to accommodate. In almost every state (forty-five at my last count) child welfare statutes contain provisions protecting parents against prosecution for resorting to spiritual rather than medical healing practices. The Massachusetts statute, for example, states: "A child shall not be deemed to be neglected or to lack proper physical care for the sole reason that he has been provided remedial treatment by spiritual means alone in accordance with the tenets and practices of a recognized church." Until the last decade, the federal child abuse regulations issued by the Department of Health Education and Welfare contained a similar accommodation for religious healing. However, in 1983, revised regulations specifically defined failure to provide medical care as child neglect and included a provision for overriding parental judgment. And a series of state decisions in the late 1980s suggests that state exemption statutes cannot be relied upon to protect parents from prosecution when spiritual healing fails and the child dies. These cases raise the question of whether statutory exemptions provide parents with a statutory defense to charges of manslaughter or felony child abuse. A typical case is *Walker v Supreme Court of Sacramento County*.[32] Here, a father was found guilty of involuntary manslaughter and child endangerment after his four-year-old daughter died of meningitis while receiving care from a Christian Science practitioner and nurse. Walker's defense relied on the fact that treatment by prayer is defined as "care" under California statute. The court, however, ruled that the accommodation in the health code did not supersede the relevant criminal statutes, nor did the prosecution violate his religious free exercise.

Personal Care in Prisons

Individual decisions regarding personal care are greatly constricted within prisons, which exercise control over many personal aspects of the individual's life, including diet, dress, hairstyle, and personal hygiene. These rules occasionally conflict with religious mandates. State and federal prisoners whose religiously based personal care practices conflict with prison regulations have initiated a number of Free Exercise challenges.[33] Demands for accommodation for religious mandates concerning hair and beards have generally not been met with favorable results. A Jewish prisoner's petition to be allowed to retain his beard was denied in *Friedman v Arizona Department of Corrections*.[34] Similarly, Native American requests for exemptions to prison rules on hair length have often been denied based on prison officials' concerns about proper identification and their fear of granting preferences.[35]

Requests for religiously mandated diets have had more mixed results. As we have seen previously, in *Africa v Pennsylvania*[36] a prisoner who claimed a religious obligation to consume only raw fruits and vegetables was unsuccessful because the court was not persuaded that his beliefs constituted a religion. However, both Muslim and Jewish prisoners have successfully raised First Amendment demands to receive diets free from pork products.[37]

The disciplinary routine of a prison quite overtly tries to sever the inmate from previous communities, attachments, and identities. Uniform clothing, hairstyles, living quarters, food, and routines detach a person from individualized identities. Prison officials must consider whether the fostering of religious sources of meaning and identity are beneficial or harmful to the overall purpose of the institution. Because religion so often functions as a creator of values, prison officials might do well to appreciate the role personal care practices play in expressing and maintaining them.

Religious Attire

Goldman v Weinberger,[38] one of the most widely discussed contemporary Free Exercise cases, illustrates problems posed by religious attire for people in institutional settings. Captain Goldman, an Orthodox Jew, had been wearing his yarmulke with his Air Force uniform for some years without incident. After receiving a complaint, his commanding officer enforced the uniform code and forbade him to wear his yarmulke while he was in uniform. Captain Goldman appealed this ruling, and the Supreme Court upheld it, deferring to the Air Force's expressed need for uniformity in order to maintain discipline and to avoid discriminating among religions. Yarmulkes are reasonably unobtrusive, but the majority worried about a military forced to permit turbans, dreadlocks, robes, braids, and other religious symbols. In 1989, Congress reversed that decision by enacting a law permitting the wearing of conservative religious apparel by members of the armed forces while they are in uniform.

Public schools have occasionally been the venue of similar problems. In *Menorah v Illinois High School Athletic Association*[39] the Seventh Circuit considered a regulation prohibiting high school basketball players from wearing any headgear against the Free Exercise complaint of an Orthodox Jew whose religion required head covering. Also in this category are public school cases discussed in Chapter 3, in which students refused to participate in mandatory physical education classes because of religious prohibitions of immodest attire.[40]

For teachers, too, religious attire has raised Free Exercise problems. Pennsylvania had a statute forbidding teachers to wear distinctive religious garb in public classrooms. In 1984, a Muslim woman was fired for wearing a scarf and long dress, as mandated by her religious beliefs. She filed a religious discrimination complaint with the Equal Employment Opportunity Commission. A federal trial judge ruled in her favor in 1989, but in 1990, a unanimous Third Circuit denied her petition, ruling that the statute served a compelling state interest in preserving an atmosphere of religious neutrality in the public schools and did not discriminate against any particular religion.[41]

Refusal of Autopsies

Several faiths profess religious objections to the desecration of bodies after death—beliefs that sometimes conflict with state laws requiring autopsies. Since the *Smith* decision ruled that religious exemptions were not constitutionally required, lower court judges have upheld the performance of autopsies against the religious traditions of the deceased and the strong objections of their families.[42]

Personal Care and Religious Freedom Principles

Religious personal care freedoms are accounted for by both of our individualist principles, freedom of choice and freedom of conscience, although again, neither account is adequate alone. Some of these personal care activities are chosen; others may be religiously required. In addition, many of them serve the important function of announcing to the world a person's religious affiliations. We have already seen how little help the notion of religious choice is in understanding these practices. If choice were the only issue, there would be no problem in demanding that Captain Goldman choose between his military career and his favorite hat. Yet, obligation is not entirely sufficient either. No judge is in a position to inquire whether these practices are done because of obligation or because they sustain a religious identity. As we have noted previously, the notion of choice is a very poor explanation for either Goldman's insistence on keeping his head covered or Jehovah's Witnesses' willingness to die for their faith. Obligation is clearly a better explanation for behaviors that entail such massive sacrifices as those undertaken by the Christian Science parents. Still, it seems not adequate to capture the fundamental importance of these perhaps bizarre practices.

The pluralist principle seems best able to protect religious personal care practices because it appreciates the significance of identity- and meaning-sustaining practices. The sacrifices people make, whether in maintaining restrictive diets or refraining from medical care, are certain kinds of discipline that define their lives. The choice of garments or diet or hairstyle is often a way of locating oneself within a community; hence, it is crucial to a person's identity. In general, a society that values pluralism would seem compelled to place exceptionally high value on religious diversity with respect to personal care.

DIFFUSE RELIGIOUS ACTIVITIES

The most common but perhaps least noticed kinds of religious activities are the broad range of activities occurring in the general society but mandated by religious beliefs. These kinds of "practices" cause the most problems, precisely because they are diffuse. *Sherbert v Verner*[43] was a landmark case in many ways, one of which is that it is seldom noted. The Court had no problem in recognizing that Ms. Sherbert's refusal to work on her Sabbath was a religious *practice*. The gravamen of Ms. Sherbert's claim was not that she was prevented from going to church but that *she could not go to work.* "Not going to work" is not a "practice" in the delimited way that kneeling is. Yet, it is a behavior mandated by a religious conviction. One's willingness to abide by requirements for driver's licenses or license plates, or food stamps, or one's marriage or child-rearing practices may all be manifestations of a religious faith. One's behavior as an employer or landlord may be mandated by the tenets of her faith; these are no less religious acts because they are conducted in the "secular" environment rather than in a house of worship. Yet, they are impossible to separate from nonreligious elements of the same acts; the act of an employer is no less that of an employer because it is engaged in for religious reasons. Because people do not make clear distinctions between "religious life" and "secular life," religious perspectives often affect work activities, relations with government, voluntary associations, leisure, and family life. All of these contexts provide opportunities for conflicts between religiously motivated behavior and the regulatory state. Frequently, the administrative requirements associated with governmental services conflict with religiously inspired behavior. Hence, these kinds of activities pose the most difficult problems for judges trying to reconcile conflicting values.

The following sections illustrate some of the common sources of conflict between receipt of a government benefit and the free exercise of religion.

Religious Practices in the Workplace

Employment laws offer some of the most frequent opportunities for religious conflict because their requirements rest at the convergence of so many individual, organizational, and governmental relationships. The following sections survey some of the most common contexts in which religious liberty issues arise in the workplace.

UNEMPLOYMENT COMPENSATION CASES

The landmark case establishing a right to religious accommodation emerged from a problem as apparently mundane and "secular" as unemployment compensation. Adelle Sherbert, a Seventh-Day Adventist, was unable to continue her employment when Saturday work became required. She was terminated for refusal to work on Saturday and denied unemployment compensation because her termination was viewed as voluntary. Typical regulations deny such benefits to persons who have quit their jobs voluntarily, have been terminated from their jobs for cause, or have refused to make themselves available for employment. When a person's religious practices are the source of her quitting, termination, or unavailability, the denial of unemployment benefits would involve the state in the obstruction of religious free exercise. The decision in *Sherbert v Verner* [44] in 1963 established not only that religious practices are protected but also that the denial of state benefits to a person who refused to accept a job that required her to work on her Sabbath would constitute a breach of the Free Exercise Clause. In *Hobbie v Unemployment Appeals Commission of Florida* [45] the Court affirmed that these guarantees apply to newly acquired religions as well as to long-held ones. Similarly, in *Thomas v Review Board of the Indiana Employment Security Division* [46] the Court ruled that the state could not deny compensation to a person whose religious conviction prohibited his working on armaments, even when his understanding of his obligations differed from those of his co-religionists. And in *Frazee v Illinois Department of Employment Security* [47] a unanimous Court reaffirmed the same reasoning, granting benefits to a Christian who refused to work on his Sabbath, even though his belief was not based on the teachings of an identifiable sect or church to which he belonged. The religious practices involved in the unemployment compensation cases are varied. *Sherbert, Hobbie,* and *Frazee* involved a refusal to work on a Sabbath. In *Thomas,* however, the religious practice at issue was a conscientious refusal to work in the production of armaments. This case, too, stretches our traditional understanding of what constitutes a religious act. These cases appear to provide obvious precedents for the 1990 *Smith* case.[48] The *Smith* majority, however, made a peculiar use of this sequence of cases. Justice Scalia argued that unemployment compensation cases are the *only* ones in which the courts have used the compelling state interest test, and then he proceeded to treat *Smith* as though it were a criminal conviction instead of the unemployment compensation case that it actually was.

TITLE VII PROTECTION FROM RELIGIOUS DISCRIMINATION

Title VII of the 1964 Civil Rights Act forbids employers to discriminate on the basis of religion as well as on race, sex, or national origin. While these are statutory protections, they raise issues parallel to some constitutional ones. The parallel is derived from a recognition that threats to religious freedom come not only from government but from other sources of power as well, such as employers. Employers exercise power outside the authoritative system of government, but religious discrimination in the workplace may as effectively "penalize" religious exercise when it comes from a private power source as does a criminal prohibition emanating from government. By adopting the Civil Rights statutes, Congress has undertaken an affirmative obligation to protect individual employees from employment decisions that burden their religious exercises. However, the law requires that employers accommodate the religious needs of employees only when they can do so without "undue hardship." A 1972 amendment to the law made this limitation quite specific: "The term 'religion' includes all aspects of religious observance and practice, as well as belief, unless an employer demonstrates that he is unable to reasonably accommodate an employee's or prospective employee's religious observance or practice without undue hardship on the conduct of the employer's business."[49]

Not surprisingly, many disputes turn on the question of what constitutes an undue hardship. In *Trans World Airlines v Hardison* the Supreme Court took a rather narrow view of the employer's duty to accommodate, ruling that the employee's religious need to refrain from working on the Sabbath did not require the employer to violate its seniority system and collective bargaining agreement.[50] Similarly, in *Ansonia Board of Education v Philbrook* the majority upheld a school board decision denying a teacher the right to use his personal leave for religious observance or personally to pay for a substitute during his absence.[51] In general, neither the Burger nor the Rehnquist Courts have been particularly sympathetic to the petitions of religious employees.

While religious discrimination is generally prohibited, occasionally religion may be a bona fide occupational qualification. Thus, in 1984, the Fifth Circuit upheld the requirement that a helicopter pilot flying over the city of Mecca be of the Muslim faith, since Saudi Arabian law forbids non-Muslims from flying over the holy city on pain of death.[52] However, a similar argument by Baylor College of Medicine was rejected when it had refused to assign Jewish physicians to rotations in Saudia Arabia out of concern for their safety.[53]

Special accommodation for the religious needs of employees may raise Establishment Clause problems by offering to those invoking religious excuses privileges not accorded to others and by requiring others to conform their behavior to the religious needs of their coworkers. For that reason, in *Estate of Thornton v Caldor*[54] the Court overturned a Connecticut statute that provided all employees with a right to refrain from work on their Sabbath. The majority reasoned that privileging Sabbath observance but not other employee interests violated the Establishment Clause.

Employers, as well as their employees, may find their religious interests compromised in the workplace, but unless they are religious institutions,[55] they cannot rely on either constitutional or statutory protections. In general, private employers who wish to carry their religious commitments into the workplace have not fared very well when their practices have run afoul of the Title VII religious rights of their employees. For example, in *Townley Engineering and Manufacturing Company v EEOC*, the Ninth Circuit ruled that an employer could not force its employees to attend religious service.[56] The Townleys, devout Christians and owners of a company that manufactured mining equipment, had argued that their religious commitments and their intention to run a Christian business rendered their establishment a religious corporation with statutory exemptions from Title VII coverage. The majority concluded that "the beliefs of owners and operators of a corporation are simply not enough in themselves to make the corporation 'religious' within the meaning of [that law]."

The *Townley* decision provoked a theologically sophisticated dissent from Judge John Noonan. Judge Noonan criticized the majority for forcing the Townleys to fragment their lives between religious and secular activities, a theological position that was adverse to their faith. For the Townleys, their faith demanded an integration of their religious and business lives. Thus, in Noonan's argument, the decision had forced upon them an objectionable theology, in clear violation of their Free Exercise rights.

Cases like *Townley* pose serious dilemmas for Free Exercise interpretation. To protect the religious rights of employees the state must insist that employers forego their own religious mandates. Employers occupy a dual role.

Not only are they religiously motivated individuals, they are also holders of social power. Hence, just as government may not use its power to establish a religion or deny free exercise, the employer may not use her power advantage to similar ends.

OTHER EMPLOYMENT PRACTICES

One of the earliest Free Exercise cases was *Prince v Massachusetts*,[57] in which a religious practice was alleged to conflict with state efforts to eradicate child labor. In that case the Supreme Court upheld a child labor prosecution brought against a Jehovah's Witness parent who allowed her daughter to accompany her on the religiously mandated act of proselytizing by selling religious tracts. A 1989 case provided a contemporary replay of that conflict. Members of the Shiloh True Light Church, a separatist religious group, believed in home education and vocational apprenticeships for their children. Through a church arrangement, church members apprenticed their children to work in the enterprises of like-minded co-religionists. In the course of their employment, the children not only worked in violation of minimum wage and child labor laws, but some also worked with heavy machinery and in dangerous occupations in violation of Fair Labor Standards Act laws. When the Department of Labor sought to enforce applicable statutes, the religious employers raised Free Exercise objections. However, the Fourth Circuit ruled that religious motivations could not immunize commercial enterprises from their Fair Labor Standards obligations.[58]

Miscellaneous Free Exercise Conflicts

Even ordinary administrative record keeping may also require what religious conviction forbids. In Nebraska, a person whose literal interpretation of the biblical prohibition against graven images prevented her from having her photograph taken for her state driver's license won an exemption from that requirement.[59] And a divided Court upheld the claim of a Native American family who objected on religious grounds to providing a social security number for their infant daughter as a condition of receiving government benefits, but the Court permitted the government to use the number it had assigned for its own internal purposes.[60]

Other conflicts are slightly more exotic. In the early 1990s, several disputes arose when religiously motivated landlords, in apparent violation of state or local ordinances against marital status discrimination, refused to rent housing to cohabiting couples of opposite sexes. No trend has yet developed in these disputes. In Alaska, the state supreme court upheld the statute against the Free Exercise claims of the landlord,[61] but in Minnesota, the court held that the state-protected religious rights of the landlord out-weighed the state interest in protecting unmarried couples.[62]

Diffuse Religious Activities and Free Exercise Principles

Most religions seek ultimately to sacralize the "secular"—that is, to pro-vide transcendental meanings for the ordinary occurrences of life and to prescribe norms for living in accordance with transcendent values. Some of these norms are perceived as choices, some as obligations, but all help fulfill the human need to make the world comprehensible. The absence of these meanings is the misery of anomie; the unity of meanings is the totalitarian ideal. Between these extremes lies the pluralist vision, a society encompass-ing a multiplicity of meanings. However, when the different approaches to meanings are diffused throughout ordinary life, they challenge us to decide how much plurality a society can sustain. Is accommodation of religiously motivated labor practices too complicated to administer equitably? Is accom-modation of the government bureaucracy to individual spiritual needs too costly and too divisive? The principle of fostering diverse sources of mean-ing does not require rejecting the need for common ones. Ultimately, the pluralist account provides direction but not concrete solutions. The concrete controversies we have seen make us recall that even the best abstract prin-ciples serve only as guides, not as algorithms.

CONCLUSIONS

Our survey of controversial religious practices confirms the common under-standing that the Free Exercise Clause is essentially a protection for religious minorities. None of the cases discussed here was brought by a dominant religious group—groups presumably able to protect themselves within the majoritarian political process. Claimants here were Fundamentalist Protes-tants, Jews, Muslims, Native Americans, and some very marginal groups.

This survey also conveys a striking absence of any unifying approach to religious exercise. The courts' inability to provide a coherent perspective re-flects the genuine difficulty of protecting religious practices in a religiously plural society where the very definition of a religious activity lacks consen-sus. The range of personal religious convictions and the practices they man-date seem almost infinite, raising an endless potentiality of Free Exercise claims. The advantage of the pluralist account is that it enables us to rec-ognize religious practices in a multitude of settings and to appreciate their significance for both the individual practitioner and society as a whole.

My simple typology directs attention to the context of a religiously mandated act. Some practices are worship rituals, which are sometimes private but more often communal. Some stem from religious mandates concerning personal care. The most problematic religious exercises are religiously mandated activities diffused throughout the ordinary activities of life. None of these acts is intrinsically any more or less important than any other. The first advantage of this formulation is that it avoids the mistake of distinguishing religious from secular acts—a distinction that seems to fly in the face of most religious teachings. A second advantage is that the focus on contexts helps illuminate both the religious significance of the act and the countervailing social interest. While it does not provide a solution to balancing these interests, it does suggest that the more localized the act, the less reason there should be for interfering with it.

There is a danger in my formulating the issue in this way. By arguing that government will have less reason to burden ritual and personal religious practices, I have perhaps inadvertently minimized their significance—or in Mark Tushnet's language, marginalized them: "The rhetorical strategy of proponents of free exercise exemptions is to minimize the impact of the exemptions on the government's interests. They do so by emphasizing that religious practice has minor social consequences. . . . Careful definition of the incremental impact will always show that the religious practice plays a marginal role in the accomplishment of social goals. . . .[T]he law can take religion into account only because, and to the extent that, it is not socially significant.[63]

Tushnet's point is valid, but the problem he raises seems to be an unavoidable one. To determine the limits of pluralism in concrete instances requires weighing the impact of a challenged practice on the rest of society and protecting those that seem least costly. "Marginalized" practices with trivial social costs will inevitably fare better than costly ones. Fortunately, the compelling state interest standard[64] attempts to rectify this problem by putting the law's thumbs on the scale in favor of the religious practice when the balance is made, and by requiring that the religious practice be protected unless it endangers a public interest of the first importance.

Before we are ready to consider the balancing of religious practices against other interests, we need to consider yet another whole aspect of religious exercise—the practices of religious groups and institutions. For reasons that will become apparent in the Chapter 5, group and institutional religious practices raise even more complex Free Exercise problems than do those of individuals.

5

THE AUTONOMY OF RELIGIOUS INSTITUTIONS

A THEORY OF INSTITUTIONAL RELIGIOUS RIGHTS

We frequently refer to the constitutional guarantees of the first eight amendments as "individual rights"; this usage is consistent with the liberal philosophy that understands individuals, and only individuals, to be rights bearers. Characteristically, our courts declared corporations to be persons in order to clothe them with constitutional rights.[1] It is no accident that our Constitution is remarkably successful in protecting individuals but both hesitant and awkward in extending those guarantees to collectivities.[2]

In the same philosophical vein, we typically understand religion to be a matter of private choice or conscience. Religious institutions (churches or their cognates) are conceived as voluntary associations, created or joined by individuals to facilitate their shared goals. The church (not the building) is an abstraction—a collective term for an aggregation of persons. As such, a church can have no conscience; only its members do.[3] Traditionally, for a church to raise a Free Exercise claim, it must speak on behalf of its individual members, asserting their rights. It may be successful in asserting "representational standing," speaking vicariously on behalf of the Free Exercise rights of individual members.[4]

Oddly enough, the popular phrase for the First Amendment religion clauses, "separation of *church* and state," belies this understanding. In general, I find this a poor formulation, but it does suggest one important insight: it associates religion with the institution in which it is practiced. The catchphrase captures our recognition that a religion depends upon the communities and institutions that sustain and propagate it. It reminds us that religion may not be as much about individual choice or conscience as about a "binding vision." For members of some religions, probably Jews and Muslims, the sense of "peoplehood" is an overarching object of religious commitment. For Catholics, the church as an institution is itself sacred. The church is not an organization that people create or join because of shared values; it is the creator and sustainer of those shared values.

One of the most dramatic affirmations of this view is from the Amish brief in *Wisconsin v Yoder*, quoted by Robert Cover in his "Nomos and Narrative": "There exists no Amish religion apart from the concept of the Amish community. A person cannot take up the Amish religion and practice it individually. The community subsists spiritually upon the bounds of a common, lived faith, sustained by common traditions and ideals which have been revered by the whole community from generation to generation."[5]

Contemporary communitarian thinkers are reconsidering the individualist notion of religion and are rediscovering the role of religious communities. In their view, groups or institutions are prior to individuals.[6] The stories and rituals of the group are often constitutive of the identity of the individual; they create what Robert Bellah has called our "communities of memory."[7] This observation reminds us that religion is almost always practiced in social settings—and for good reason. Without denying that individuals can and do have solitary spiritual experiences, it recognizes that religious meanings perpetuate themselves through collective activities. This theory hearkens back to the foundational insight of religious sociologist Emile Durkheim, who wrote that "[i]n all history, we do not find a single religion without a church."[8] We are reminded again of the words of Peter Berger on the necessity of religious institutions to the existence of religion itself:

> [A]ll religious traditions . . . require specific communities for their continuant plausibility. In this sense, the maxim *extra ecclesium nulla salus* has general empirical applicability, provided one understands *salus* in a theoretically rather unpalatable sense—to wit, as continuing plausibility. The reality of the Christian world depends upon the presence of social structures within which this reality is taken for granted and within which successive generations of individuals are socialized in such a way that this world will be real *to them*. When this plausibility structure loses its intactness or continuity, the Christian world begins to totter, and its reality ceases to impose itself as self evident.[9]

The communitarian understanding of persons has stimulated a Free Exercise jurisprudence that goes beyond protecting individual believers and posits that religious institutions may have First Amendment rights not reducible to the rights of individual members. More than a generation ago, the nation's most eminent scholar of religion and law extolled what he saw as the Court's acknowledgment of "a corporate liberty for churches" in its decision in *Kedroff v St. Nicholas Cathedral of the Russion Orthodox Church*.[10] His conclusion may have been premature; it was not until the 1980s that scholars and courts began seriously to debate whether religious *institutions* could claim First Amendment rights. The terms of this argument were initiated in 1981 in an article by Douglas Laycock in which he proposed "a right to church autonomy": "Quite apart from whether a regulation requires a church or an individual believer to violate religious doctrine or felt moral duty, churches have a constitutionally protected interest in managing their own institutions free from government interference."[11]

An additional source of inspiration for thinking about church-state relations occurred in 1982, when Robert Cover published a groundbreaking article providing a philosophical context for appreciating the special rights of those communities that sustain values: "The religion clauses of the Constitution seem to me unique in the clarity with which they presuppose a collective, norm generating community whose status as a community and whose relationship with the individuals subject to its norms are entitled to constitutional protection."[12]

The concern for church autonomy generated a broadly ecumenical conference of religious activists in 1982 and again in 1986.[13] The Dawson Institute of Church and State sponsored a conference on the same topic in 1992.[14] Recently, it has become one of the major themes in scholarly interpretations of the Free Exercise Clause. Many thinkers now argue that institutions, in their own right, merit constitutional protection even when individual conscience claims are not involved, and perhaps even when doing so compromises the rights of individual members.[15] The focus on groups and institutions implicates the broader questions of pluralism and the role of autonomous associations in the American polity.

The argument for institutional autonomy is immensely complicated by the proliferation of religious activities. As the notion of a religious practice expands to include educational, healing, broadcasting, and social service ministries, in addition to the financial arrangements for supporting them, the institutions whereby these practices are accomplished can themselves claim immunity from state regulation. According to an expansive interpretation of the Free Exercise Clause, the protection of religious practices includes not only ceremonial or liturgical ones but also church ministries in the broadest sense, the financing of these ministries, and the administrative decisions regarding the ordinary housekeeping details of institutional existence. Further, as religious groups diversify their economic activities, courts are ultimately asked to decide which parts of expansive economic enterprises are protected from taxation and other regulation by virtue of being "religious activities."[16]

Angela Carmella has recently offered a theological underpinning for the First Amendment protection of institutional rights.[17] The argument is grounded in the concept of what Catholic theologians call "inculturation"—clothing the core faith in the cultural expressions of its particular adherents. Religions differ on the appropriate balance between acculturization (adopting the surrounding culture) and remaining outside it in order to maintain a critical perspective.[18] Acculturated religious responses engage the prevailing secular world and are compatible with it. Acculturated religious activities may include the way churches act upon the world through education or through providing health, counseling, or social services. Carmella summarizes the idea in this way:

> In broad terms, acculturated conduct refers to churches and their role in moral discourse, their provision of human services and philanthropy, their creation and operation of institutions, and their efforts at maintenance and reform of civic life. Churches use the media, own property, raise funds, espouse moral-political positions, operate all types of programs that address social and spiritual needs, and establish and operate institutions such as hospitals and universities. Churches do not function only to reject and insulate themselves from the wider culture, to live according to distinctive practices, or to engage in civil disobedience and challenge existing mores. Churches are in constant dialogue with the wider culture. They routinely tolerate, support, appropriate, adapt, and transform—and are transformed by—the values, institutions, and practices of the culture.[19]

Acculturated activities are no less "religious" than those that are "pervasively sectarian"; they are equally legitimate ways in which religions encounter the world. Precisely because they are such familiar "secular" activities, Carmella argues, judges and juries fail to recognize them as religious and to accord them First Amendment protection. For that reason, we may be better at recognizing "countercultural" religious activities than "acculturated" ones. Yet, to fail to encompass these activities and the institutions that provide them within the First Amendment umbrella would be to miss a very important element of religious exercise in contemporary life.

Given the complex structures and multiple functions of both modern religious institutions and the modern state, it is not surprising that the two intersect on numerous fronts. Carmella argues that conflicts arising in these instances should be resolved according to

> a broad presumptive autonomy for religious conduct under the religion clauses. This presumption would capture the entire process of acculturation and protect the ecclesiological judgments of churches. . . . This broad presumptive autonomy for all types of religious conduct respects the institutional separation created by the founders' disestablishment decision, and permits religious exercise to flourish independently, preserving in particular the fluidity and dynamism of the continuous conversation between church and culture. . . .
>
> This author proposes that the state exempt religious conduct (or fashion comparable accommodation) from regulation unless the state can demonstrate that the exemption will (1) frustrate a compelling governmental interest; (2) threaten to breach the institutional separation between church and state; or (3) coerce, compromise, or influence the religious beliefs of those who do not benefit from the exemption.[20]

One way we have traditionally attempted to shield religious institutional activity is for government to avoid unnecessary "entanglement" with it. The term "entanglement" originated in Establishment Clause adjudication. Since enunciated in *Waltz v Tax Commission*[21] and formalized in *Lemon v Kurtzman*,[22] excessive entanglement between church and state has been one of the three strands of the dominant Establishment Clause test. While the term has its roots in Establishment Clause adjudication, numerous Free Exercise claims are predicated upon the resistance of religious institutions to state scrutiny, certification, record keeping, and the like, and the state's hesitation to become involved in such entanglement. Not surprisingly, arguments for religious institutional autonomy frequently entail overlap between the two religion clauses. Typically, those arguing for autonomy invoke both clauses.

Not every constitutional scholar is impressed with the case for constitutional rights of religious organizations. Ira Lupu, for example, reminds us that "our constitutional tradition tends to be more respectful and cognizant of individuals, who are more vulnerable to state power when standing alone." He can find no Free Exercise principle autonomy that would extend beyond individuals to organizations:

> All these attributes of free exercise claims—religious commitment, the urge to relieve religious suffering, free and private choice of convic-

tion, and sincere embrace of such conviction—can only be understood as reflecting qualities of autonomous human beings. But if free exercise exemption rights are thus rights of autonomy, organizations may not possess them. Organizations qua organizations are incapable of emotion and self-consciousness. Organizations cannot experience the indignity or shame associated with a loss of autonomy. More importantly, organizations cannot hold convictions or make spiritual commitments, and they cannot demonstrate the sincerity with which organizational positions are held. Recognizing organizational claims to free exercise exemptions from secular law thus tends to undermine the entire structure and legitimacy of free exercise law.[23]

To the extent that religious institutions enjoy constitutional protection, Lupu argues, the right grows out of the freedom individual members have to form associations. Institutions do not have group rights beyond that which individuals would have. Thus, individuals may have associational rights to form "members only" groups that may imply a right to hire church members only. But since individuals have no right to discriminate on the basis of race or sex, neither do religious institutions, religious doctrine notwithstanding.[24] Lupu concludes that the Free Exercise Clause does not require exemptions for religious organization and that, moreover, the Establishment Clause forbids them. To grant such exemptions would enable dominant groups to gain rights unavailable to others, thus threatening the principle of *equal* religious liberty.[25]

As we have seen, the very notion of religious group rights remains highly controversial; in addition, it implies countless subsidiary controversies. To implicate the Free Exercise Clause is not to conclude that its guarantees are absolute; autonomy claims must still be weighed against competing ones. And not surprisingly, religious institutions raise their own threshold problems. In an environment of multifunctional organizations, how can one identify a *religious* institution?

THE THRESHOLD QUESTION

The argument for religious institutional rights has a threshold condition: The institution seeking First Amendment protection must be a *religious* one. But as churches and their cognates become multifunctional, it is virtually impossible to disentangle the religious parts of institutions from nonreligious ones.[26] The existence of a religious institution is not a simple black and white phenomenon. Multifunctional religious institutions may include financial, social service, and even political entities, subdivisions, or activities.

Carmella argues that the balance between state and church is always tilted toward the state because the state is in the position authoritatively to *define* for itself the distinction between the two entities. For that reason, she would tilt the definition to provide the widest possible latitude for religious self-definition:

> Herein lies the paradox: the state is incompetent to act in matters of religion, but the state defines what conduct is religious and therefore outside its jurisdiction, and what conduct is secular and therefore within its jurisdiction. The fact that the state has ultimate definitional authority requires tremendous vigilance on the part of each of the branches of government, and the judiciary in particular, to ensure that the boundaries between church and state are functioning as intended; that is, enabling religion to flourish without frustrating the state's basic ordering role.[27]

Hence, we shall encounter threshold questions in virtually every context in which religious institutional rights are raised. The expanding notion of a religious ministry makes it very difficult to distinguish religious from non-religious functions of religious institutions. Providing education, feeding the hungry, sheltering the homeless, and healing the sick, in addition to participating in the activities by which these ministries are supported, are just a few of the functions of religious ministries. Often, courts must determine which specific *activities* of religious institutions are religious.[28] Two contrasting approaches to similar cases illustrate this problem. In *Needham Pastoral Counseling Center v Board of Appeals* a pastoral counseling center associated with a Protestant seminary applied for a building permit to expand a local church for its counseling activities. Although buildings for religious functions were permitted under the zoning laws, the zoning board, trial court, and appellate court all ruled that counseling was not a religious use, and the application was denied.[29] In contrast, in *Lutheran Social Services v United States* the Eighth Circuit recognized the danger of distinguishing between activities that were part of a religious ministry, and thus qualified for tax exemption, and those that were secular. To avoid having to make this distinction, the Court extended the law's exemption for churches to include their auxiliaries to a separately incorporated agency that provided child care, adoption services, counseling, residential treatment, camps, and chaplaincy services.[30]

Individuals do not easily distinguish between religious and secular components of their reasoning. Similarly for institutions, there is no clear separation between "religious acts," "political acts," or "social service acts." How are courts to make distinctions that do not exist in our own life experience? One answer, proposed by Bruce Bagni, is to make a distinction between the "purely spiritual or integral facets of the actual practice of the religion"—the epicenter of a religion—and three concentric "emanations" from the core. The first emanation would contain church-sponsored community activities (such as its social service ministries), the second would encompass its "purely secular business activities," including its employment relationships with employees who perform "nonspiritual" functions, and the third would include the totally secular world. In Bagni's view, "the spiritual epicenter of a church must be outside the scope of civil regulation. . . . Only the most compelling government interest . . . might justify regulation of some practices within the epicenter." Once outside the epicenter, however, "the church subjects itself to secular regulation proportionate to the degree of secularity of its activities and relationships."[31] While this approach has a surface plausibility, it has not gained much support because rather than avoid the threshold problem, it puts squarely in courts' hands the determination of what is a "spiritual epicenter" and what is an "emanation"—a determination that itself would seem to violate the Free Exercise Clause.

Another answer—that offered by the most expansive interpretation of the Free Exercise Clause—is that the making of this distinction is itself fraught with Free Exercise perils, and it may not be made by government at all.[32] The very act of distinguishing religious from nonreligious activities entangles government with religion in ways likely to violate both religion clauses. To avoid this problem, Douglas Laycock argues for the virtual total autonomy of churches from all government regulations: "[A]ny activity engaged in by a church as a body is an exercise of religion." Any activities of a religious institution are, ipso facto, religious; thus an institution need not demonstrate that the activity it seeks to shield from government is itself a religious activity.

This latter view was endorsed by the Supreme Court in 1987, when it was forced to deal with the threshold problem in *Corporation of the Presiding Bishop of the Church of Jesus Christ of Latter-Day Saints v Amos*.[33] The original complainant had been terminated as a custodian in a church-owned gymnasium when he failed to remain a member in good standing of the church. He raised a religious discrimination complaint, and his former employer responded that a 1972 amendment exempts religious institutions from provisions of the law covering religious discrimination. He challenged the exemption as a violation of the Establishment Clause because it provided special treatment for religious employers. Several threshold questions emerged. Is a nonprofit gymnasium owned by a church a religious institution? Is a custodian performing a religious function? The church answered affirmatively to both questions. In its decision, the Court suggested that fine distinctions between religious and nonreligious activities were inappropriate for government to make and ought to be made only by the religious institution in question. The Court held that the threshold question—whether an activity of a church is a religious activity—was itself a distinction reserved for the institution alone. Thus, it left the determination of what was a religious function up to the church, reasoning that a deference to the religion's own judgment is necessary to keep courts from second guessing religious doctrine concerning its ministry. Justice Brennan's concurring opinion expresses this point well:

> What makes the application of a religious-secular distinction difficult is that the character of an activity is not self-evident. As a result, determining whether an activity is religious or secular requires a searching case-by-case analysis. This results in considerable ongoing government entanglement in religious affairs. Furthermore, this prospect of government intrusion raises concern that a religious organization may be chilled in its free exercise activity. . . . As a result, the community's process of self-definition would be shaped in part by the prospects of litigation. A case-by-case analysis for all activities therefore would produce excessive government entanglement with religion and create the danger of chilling religious activity. . . .
>
> This substantial potential for chilling activity makes inappropriate case-by-case determination of the character of a nonprofit organization, and justifies a categorical exemption for nonprofit activity. Such an exemption demarcates a sphere of deference with respect to those activities most likely to be religious.

Clearly, *Amos* does not answer once and for all the complex threshold questions about religious institutions. Nor does it specify what rights an institution can expect once it is past the threshold. We turn our attention now to the specific contexts in which these controversies arise. They include school certification, the labor relations of religious institutions as employers, taxation, church political activities, internal church disputes, and church discipline—plus brief mention of religious broadcasting and church zoning. We will then reflect on the justifications and limits of institutional autonomy through the perspectives of our five proposed accounts of religious freedom.

School Certification

During the past generation, evangelical Christian schools became the most rapidly increasing sector of private education in the United States.[34] Whereas the older Catholic and Lutheran schools had long since adapted to state educational requirements, these newer schools became sources of numerous legislative, administrative, and judicial conflicts concerning the proper role of government, church, and families over education. Among the issues that raised constitutional questions, the most common were objections to state certification requirements, on the grounds that they were an intrusion of government on a religious ministry. Teaching, like preaching, is a way of inculcating the beliefs and values of the faith; for many churches, educational functions are a part of their religious missions. Hence, religious schools have objected to governmental supervision of their schools for the same reason they would object to governmental censorship of Sunday morning sermons.[35] For example, in *State ex rel. Douglas v Faith Baptist Church* a church-related school based its refusal to meet teacher certification requirements on its insistence that education was part of church ministry and not subject to state approval.

> It is their position that the operation of the school is simply an extension of the ministry of the church, over which the State of Nebraska has no authority to approve or accredit. . . . Defendants further maintain that, because their philosophy is Christian, and that of the State Department of Education is not, the latter is not capable of judging the philosophy of education of the defendants' school. Finally, because the state school laws require inspection of the school by the county superintendent, the defendants cannot submit to school control because the State has no right to inspect God's property.[36]

Significantly, the school did not articulate any concrete harm of teacher certification; rather, it simply insisted that state certification of a religious ministry was *itself* prohibited by the Free Exercise Clause. Similarly, in *Kentucky State Board for Elementary and Secondary Education v Rudasill*[37] the state supreme court held that the state could not impose on church-related schools the educational standards for curriculum, textbooks, and teacher certification used for public schools. Ministries must not be state licensed, certified, inspected, or otherwise regulated under the Free Exercise Clause.

In response to a similar challenge,[38] North Carolina passed a law excluding nonpublic schools from all education laws except those dealing with fire safety, sanitation, and immunization. School certification cases continue to pose some of the most sensitive church autonomy dilemmas because of the importance of education in the propagation of faiths and because the very point of church-sponsored education is to suffuse all learning with religious perspectives.[39]

Labor Relations: The Autonomy of Religious Institutions as Employers

When churches function as employers they are subject to most of the normal state and federal regulations that characterize employment law. Occasionally, religious institutions resist compliance with these laws on the grounds that compliance would compromise their religious mission and excessively involve government in their internal affairs. Such challenges have arisen concerning applications of the Equal Employment Opportunity Act (and cognate state acts), the Fair Labor Standards Act, and the National Labor Relations Act. (Both the EEOC cases and the NLRB cases are based on statutory construction and therefore are not, strictly speaking, matters of constitutional law.) These cases illustrate some truly agonizing conflicts among values and demonstrate how inadequate is any understanding of constitutional rights that poses the problem as a simple conflict between individuals and government. Moreover, they often raise conflicts between the two religion clauses. Compliance with these employment laws may violate the Free Exercise rights of religious employers. But exemptions for religious employers raise the specter of preferences prohibited by the Establishment Clause; furthermore, they may even suggest violation of the Equal Protection Clause by denying to employees of religious institutions benefits that the government provides for other persons. The following sections survey some of the most frequent contexts in which these controversies have arisen.

COLLECTIVE BARGAINING AND THE NATIONAL LABOR RELATIONS ACT

One of the most significant precedents in the development of religious institutional autonomy was the 1973 decision in *National Labor Relations Board v Catholic Bishop of Chicago*.[40] The National Labor Relations Board had recognized a collective bargaining decision made by teachers of the Chicago Catholic school system and thus required the diocese to bargain with them in good faith. The diocese refused, arguing that submitting itself to NLRB jurisdiction would interfere with ecclesiastical control of a religious institution and thus violate its First Amendment rights. The Supreme Court, expressing a concern for the dangers of entanglement, reached a decision on statutory rather than constitutional grounds. In the absence of specific congressional intent to include religious schools, it read the National Labor Relations Act as exempting religious schools from NLRB coverage. Behind that decision was its acceptance of the church's argument that governmental collective bargaining authority might impinge on church governance and matters of curriculum and religious doctrines. While the Supreme Court decision in this case has been the most significant statement of deference to institutional autonomy within the collective bargaining context, lower courts have not been eager to extend its guidance beyond educational settings.[41] Numerous lower court decisions have held religious institutions bound by the collective bargaining provisions of the National Labor Relations Act when no doctrinal issues or ministerial functions appeared to be compromised.

WAGES, WORKING CONDITIONS, AND THE FAIR LABOR STANDARDS ACT

Some religious institutions acting as employers have paid wages below statutory minimum wage requirements or have created working conditions that violate other provisions of the Fair Labor Standards Act. When prosecuted, they have argued that these special conditions are part of a religious ministry and are thus protected as religious exercises. Generally, courts have refused to exempt religious employers from this act. The Supreme Court affirmed this approach in *The Tony and Susan Alamo Foundation v Secretary of Labor*.[42] This controversial foundation trained and employed hard-core unemployed persons (mostly rehabilitated drug addicts and former criminals) in its commercial establishments and provided them with food, clothing, and shelter, but not wages. The foundation was cited for violations of the Fair Labor Standards Act for failure to pay minimum wage. The foundation claimed that payment for work was an anathema to the religious beliefs central to their mission and that FLSA compliance would substantially burden their religious exercise. Noting the competitive advantages this arrangement provided for the foundation's enterprises, the Court rejected its Free Exercise claim, reasoning that workers who did not wish to be so compensated could simply return the money to the foundation.[43]

A similar result was reached in the case of *Dole v Shenandoah Baptist Church*,[44] in which the church-related school paid its staff less than a minimum wage but provided a head-of-household supplement for married men (and divorced women with children). This policy violated both the FLSA and EEO standards. The church claimed a Free Exercise exemption, arguing that its employees were all ministers and thus exempt, that the practice was based on its sincere religious belief that men should be primary breadwinners, and in general, that the school was a church, not an enterprise within the definition of the law. The Fourth Circuit had no trouble rejecting the arguments for statutory exemptions and further ruled that compliance with the law would not excessively burden the church, since its religion did not require either low salaries or sex-based pay differences.

EMPLOYMENT DISCRIMINATION

The 1964 Civil Rights Act and its revisions, plus the various cognate state acts, prohibit employers from discriminating in the terms and conditions of employment on the basis of race, sex, national origin, religion, pregnancy, disability, and age.[45] The law thus creates an individual right to be free from discrimination and expresses a powerful public policy against tolerating such discrimination. But it is also a double-edged sword. While the law enhances the liberty of individual employees, it occasionally constricts the liberties of religious institutions as employers to make employment decisions in accordance with their religious scruples. While few religions make it a duty to discriminate, many do believe in certain divisions of labor between the sexes, in the segregation of the races, or in maintaining a religiously homogeneous institution. Hence, compliance with civil rights laws sometimes requires acts the religion finds unacceptable. When antidiscrimination law conflicts with the religious compunctions of a religious institutional employer, however, the controversies raise major conflicts between the individual rights of citizens and the institution's own religious vision.

Congress recognized the special needs of religious institutions to take religion into account in making employment decisions. Hence, Section 702 of the Civil Rights Act provides that these prohibitions shall not apply "to a religious corporation, association, or society with respect to the employment of individuals of a particular religion to perform work connected with the carrying on of such corporation, association, or society of its activities."[46] The autonomy necessary for religious institutions to make hiring decisions based on religious classifications is thus much greater and more clearly grounded in statute than that required for such institutions to take race, sex, pregnancy, national origin, age, or disability into account. Yet, all of these issues force courts to weigh the relative value of individual rights granted under the law against the pluralist value of autonomy for groups to live by their own values. To side with the individual is to impose on voluntary associations a uniformity of values inconsistent with their own collective choices.[47] To side with the institution leaves individuals harmed, often mistreated, and less protected than other members of society. In the sections that follow we consider separately the problems raised by religious discrimination and those posed by the other categories protected under Title VII.

Religious Discrimination In spite of the broad language of the Civil Rights Act, it is obviously not illegal for a Catholic church to consider only Catholics for the position of priest, or for a fundamentalist school to require doctrinal conformity in the selection of its teachers. There has never been any question that religious institutions may take an applicant's religion into account when they are hiring ministers and other religious personnel; Congress made that intention quite clear by exempting "a religious corporation, association, educational institution, or society with respect to the employment of individual of a particular religion to perform work connected with the carrying on . . . of its religious activities." In a 1972 amendment, Congress broadened the exemptions by deleting the word "religious" before "activities."

In practical terms, the religious exemption means that religious employers may take into account factors that other kinds of employers may not.[48] Thus, it privileges religious institutions to do things that would otherwise be illegal. This exemption suggests a certain tension between the two religion clauses as well as between the religious rights of individual employees and religious institutions. Does this special privilege to discriminate violate the Establishment Clause of the First Amendment? Would the failure to exempt religious institutional employers violate their Free Exercise rights?

In 1987, the Supreme Court faced head-on the conflicts of values in *Corporation of the Presiding Bishop of the Church of Jesus Christ of Latter-Day Saints v Amos*.[49] We have already encountered this case in the context of the boundary between religious and secular employment. Now we consider the substance of the discrimination complaint. In the case, a long-term employee was terminated from his job as custodian for a nonprofit gymnasium owned by the Mormon Church when he failed to receive a temple recommend, a document verifying that he was a church member in good standing. His termination would ordinarily have constituted a clear case of religious discrimination, but because his employer was a religious institution, it was exempt from the religious discrimination provisions of Title VII. He challenged this exemption as a preference in violation of the Establishment Clause. The Supreme Court upheld the law's exemption against that challenge, ruling that an exemption necessary to protect the free exercise of religion cannot violate the Establishment Clause.

Behind the issue of whether a custodian in a church-owned gymnasium may keep his job, Frederick Mark Gedicks sees a principle of religious preservation:

> Forcing the Mormon church to retain an unfaithful employee and to pay his salary with tithing funds would have undermined the sacrifice narrative that is so prominent both in Mormon history and in contemporary Mormon life. If the church community sought to interpret this narrative to accommodate the use of tithing to benefit the unfaithful, it would be forced to dilute and perhaps even to abandon the powerful concept that tithing is the sacred means by which Mormons build the Kingdom of God. The church's vision of itself as a people of sacrifice would fade into one of a people of prudence.
>
> . . . That the Mormon church might itself choose prudence over sacrifice is not constitutionally significant. That it should be forced to do so by the government is theological violence.[50]

But there is another way to look at this decision. For example, Steven Gey observes that it upholds the religious rights of an institution at the expense of the statutory religious rights of an individual. He views it as an ominous transformation of the principle of religious accommodation—changing what began as a protection for dissenting individuals into "a way of enforcing the norms of the religious community." This and similar decisions "represent the elevation of religious doctrine and organization over individual conscience and nonconformity."[51] His criticism is a pointed one: "The regulation being lifted to avoid burdening the free exercise of religion is a regulation protecting the free exercise of religion. The Court is able to interpret a regulation fostering free exercise as a burden on free exercise only by specifically favoring one form of free exercise over another. Specifically, the Court favors free exercise in the form of the theological integrity of religious organizations over free exercise in the form of personal freedom of conscience and belief."[52]

Race and Sex Discrimination The Civil Rights Act does not exempt religious institutions from the race, sex, and national origin discrimination prohibitions. Yet, courts have treaded delicately when applying these provisions to churches and church-related institutions. Powerful interests on both sides are at stake in these conflicts. On one hand, the state has a strong policy interest in eliminating the evils of discrimination, as well as a concrete interest in guaranteeing remedies for wronged individuals. On the other hand, religious institutions sometimes assert claims of conscience in conflict with the law, and sometimes of a more generalized interest in autonomy.[53]

When faced with this conflict in practice, courts have read into the civil rights law something almost parallel to the religious exemption. When asked to apply antidiscrimination provisions to religious entities, courts tend to examine the impact of compliance on the *religious functions* of the institution, thus in effect exempting institutions whose religious mission would be compromised by compliance—a process very deferent to the institution's view of its religious mission.

The first case of this nature established this pattern of deference. *McClure v Salvation Army* was a sex discrimination suit brought by a female officer in the Salvation Army, alleging that she received lower pay and benefits than her male counterparts. The Fifth Circuit dismissed her suit, fearing that allowing "secular interests" to interfere with church-minister relationship would intrude upon matters of church administration and ecclesiastical concern.[54]

The second major case was *EEOC v Mississippi College*, alleging sex discrimination in faculty hiring by a Baptist college.[55] Unlike the Salvation Army in the *McClure* case, the Baptist-affiliated college was not a church, nor were its professors ministers. The Fifth Circuit rejected both Establishment Clause and Free Exercise objections to EEOC jurisdiction. Application of the civil rights law did not produce sufficient entanglement to violate the Establishment Clause, and neither did equal employment opportunity violate the religious beliefs of the Baptist college; hence, the Free Exercise Clause was not breached.

Building on the wide latitude given to church-minister relations in the earlier case, the seminaries of the Southern Baptist Convention, an organization with strong commitment to the separation of church and state, attempted to insulate their seminaries wholesale from Title VII jurisdiction. In the mid-1970s the presidents of the six seminaries of the convention agreed to join in refusing to submit EEO forms on race, sex, national origin, tenure, and compensation data as required of all institutions of higher learning. They further agreed that Southwestern Baptist Seminary, the largest among them, would serve as defendant in the expected litigation.[56] The seminary argued that as a pervasively sectarian institution it was immune from EEO regulation and the governmental entanglement it would produce. In *Equal Employment Opportunity Commission v Southwestern Baptist Theological Seminary*,[57] the district court agreed and denied EEOC jurisdiction over the seminary. The court reasoned that in the pervasively religious seminary's environment, employment decisions were virtually inseparable from religious ones, and any attempt to separate them would excessively entangle government with religion. On appeal, however, the Fifth Circuit partially reversed and attempted to fine-tune the distinction between covered and exempt employees. The decision exempted from EEO jurisdiction only ministers (defined as those directly involved in teaching or the supervision of teaching) and granted EEO jurisdiction over other administration and staff.

The most troublesome case is *Ohio Civil Rights Commission v Dayton Christian Schools, Inc.*[58] This private, fundamentalist school hired teachers based on explicitly religious criteria. It refused to renew the contract of a married teacher when it found out she was pregnant, basing its decision on the religious conviction that mothers with young children should not work outside the home. Under ordinary circumstances, this termination would have clearly violated the state law against sex discrimination. The teacher, receiving no redress at the school, consulted an attorney and filed a claim with the Ohio Civil Rights Commission, which found probable cause to conclude that the school had violated the state Civil Rights Act. But the Dayton Christian school offered a powerful defense; its beliefs about the role of mothers were *religious* beliefs, and as a religious institution it was obligated to practice its own teachings.

The already difficult issue was complicated by an additional twist. When the school administrators learned that the teacher had engaged an attorney and brought the issue before civil authorities, all possibility of reconciliation was lost and they terminated her employment. This kind of retaliation is clearly illegal under the civil rights law. But the school again had a religious defense. The school argued that in going outside the school authorities, the teacher had violated religiously required respect for authority as well as a biblical injunction against one Christian suing another. Hence, they argued that the firing was religiously justified and protected as an act of religious freedom. The school sought a declaratory judgment that the Ohio Civil Rights Act could not be constitutionally applied to its action in this instance.

This case—and many like it—place the courts in a terrible dilemma. Frederick Gedicks, making the case for the priority of the group right, has summed up the dilemma succinctly:

On the one hand, the teacher suffered a loss of employment because of action that the legislature had declared unlawful through the Act. Exempting the school from the Act, and thereby upholding the school's refusal to reinstate the teacher, would have significantly injured the teacher. On the other hand, those who make up the community of Dayton Christian

Schools — the people who work there, who send their children there, who attend school there, who teach there, who set the policy of the school and manage its assets — had created a unique form of education. . . . Requiring the reinstatement of the teacher would force the school to accommodate a course of conduct that it believed was wrong and would prevent the school from effectively teaching one aspect of its distinctive religious philosophy. This disposition would implicate the constitutional free exercise and associational rights of those connected with the school. It would also dilute religious pluralism, by forcing upon the school conformity to majoritarian values and practices relating to gender discrimination.[59]

By the time the case reached the Supreme Court, the religious issues had been superseded by jurisdictional problems of federalism, so the Supreme Court was able to avoid the Free Exercise issues by deferring to the authority of the state. It let stand a decision enabling the local Human Rights Board to hear the case.

Gedicks argues that enforcing the norms of nondiscrimination on the Dayton Christian School would have created a religious threat far beyond the issue of employment policy. The religious school would have been confronted with the choice of facing legal penalties or of changing its beliefs and practices to conform with majoritarian norms.

> Thus, there are two dimensions to the threat to group existence that inheres in government regulation of group membership. Whether the group will remain physically intact, and if so, what kind of group it will be. The group that refuses to change a core concern to comply with valid regulation may be liquidated and cease physically and legally to exist. The group that chooses to abandon a core concern in order to comply with regulation loses its definitional boundaries, thereby transforming itself into a different group. In either event, the group has ceased to be, having been extinguished by the government's regulatory intervention.[60]

Religious opposition to homosexuality has created several conflicts between religious doctrine and governmental antidiscrimination policies. In *Madsen v Erwin* a former employee of the *Christian Science Monitor* brought suit under the Massachusetts Civil Rights Law, alleging that her termination had been based on her sexual preferences.[61] The court ruled, however, that her employer was an "arm" of the Christian Science Church, engaged in a religious activity, and that the church asserted a religious objection to homosexuality. In this case, her termination was an "ecclesiastical decision," and her discrimination claim was dismissed.

A somewhat parallel issue emerged at Georgetown University, although, technically, this issue involved the university's obligations under a local antidiscrimination ordinance rather than employment discrimination. In *Gay Rights Coalition of Georgetown University v Georgetown University*,[62] the D.C. Court of Appeals ruled that the District of Columbia's antidiscrimination statute banning sexual preference discrimination in access to services and facilities appropriately applied to Georgetown, a Catholic university. The university had refused to recognize two gay student groups, arguing that recognition would imply endorsement of the clubs' activities and purposes, which its religious doctrines prohibited. The court ruled that the university recognition need not imply endorsement and that it was not permitted to withhold facilities and services from the two gay student groups. While the court admitted that extending recognition would burden the university's religious free exercise, the majority was persuaded that the compelling interest in eradicating sexual discrimination outweighed the burden to Georgetown's religious beliefs.

Taxation and Regulation of Religious Financial Activity

Recognizing the desirability of fostering nonprofit institutions, Congress has included religious institutions among those exempted from federal income taxation. To receive this exemptions, an institution must meet the statutory guidelines defining a church or religious institution. Section 501(c)(3) of the Internal Revenue Code exempts from income taxation a religious organization that meets the following three requirements:

1. It must be organized and operated exclusively for religious purposes;
2. No part of its net earnings may inure to the benefit of any private shareholder or individual; and
3. It must not engage in substantial lobbying activities or intervene in any political campaigns.[63]

In addition, Section 170 of the Internal Revenue Code permits taxpayers to deduct contributions to these organizations — a major incentive for private support.

The exemption is crucial to the financial health of religious institutions but raises problems at both margins. On one hand, the exemption is an invitation for unscrupulous profiteers to gain fraudulent tax advantages for commercial activities. On the other hand, it is an invitation for overzealous or religiously biased prosecutors to selectively investigate and prosecute unpopular religious movements. Both of these problems raise threshold problems of distinguishing churches and their cognate institutions from non–tax exempt commercial institutions.

Federal tax exemptions for churches have not been judicially tested, but a precedent regarding state property taxes has traditionally been taken as authoritative. In *Waltz v Tax Commissioner*[64] the Supreme Court upheld the constitutionality of New York's property tax exemption for churches against a challenge that it violated the Establishment Clause by providing public financial support of religion and coercing nonmembers to contribute to that support. Tax exemptions for churches have been only moderately controversial in our history, but as both mainline and marginal religions develop immense capitalist empires, and as distinctions between religious and other activities blur, all three provisions of the 501(c)(3) exemption will provide arenas of conflict between governmental interests in fair allocation of the tax burden and the interests of churches in preserving their internal autonomy.

"EXCLUSIVELY RELIGIOUS ACTIVITIES"

In order to qualify for the 501(c)(3) exemption, a religious organization must be organized and operated exclusively for a religious purpose; however, as we have repeatedly seen, the threshold definition of a "religious" purpose is extremely imprecise.[65] The definitional problems that we have observed in other contexts become extremely prominent when significant financial issues are at stake. The dilemma becomes even more convoluted because of a regulation intended to simplify administration of this provision. Whereas most tax-exempt organizations are required to file a statement of activities as well as an informational tax return justifying their exempt status, "churches, their integrated activities, and conventions or associations of churches, and organizations claiming to be churches" are excused from these requirements. Hence, another definitional problem is raised: What is a church?[66] The Treasury Department has promulgated a singularly unhelpful definition:

> The term "church" includes a religious order or a religious organization if such order or organization (a) is an internal part of a church, and (b) is engaged in carrying out the functions of a church. . . . A religious order or organization shall be considered to be engaged in carrying out the functions of a church if its duties include the ministration of sacerdotal functions and the conduct of religious worship. What constitutes the conduct of religious worship or the ministration of sacerdotal functions depends

on the tenets and practices of a particular religious body constituting a church.[67]

The looseness of this definition and the IRS's hesitation to investigate church claims have helped preserve the autonomy of religious institutions. At the same time, critics argue that the reporting exemption deprives government of the information necessary to prosecute fraud and abuses perpetrated under cover of religion. Fraudulent schemes to avoid payment of income taxes by bogus churches have been a perpetual problem under this provision, as have the "churches" that have protested taxes such as the mail-order Universal Life Church.[68] Attempts to enhance law enforcement against potentially illegal exemption claims raise fears among legitimate churches that their own financial autonomy and privacy may be violated—or that they may have to bear overwhelming record keeping costs. Hence, the IRS has chosen to tread very softly on this treacherous ground.

"BENEFITS TO INDIVIDUALS"

Distinguishing between a church and its officers constitutes a problem in administering the 501(c)(3) exemption. The complex commercial activities of the Unification Church and its leader provided the most dramatic example of this issue during the 1980s.[69] In particular, the prosecution of the much-reviled Reverend Sun Myung Moon at the height of the "cult scare" raised for religious freedom advocates the specter of selective prosecution. Reverend Moon was charged and convicted of filing fraudulent tax returns by failing to report income that he received, controlled, and used from accounts held in his own name but that he claimed were held in trust for the church and used for religious purposes. The case of *United States v Sun Myung Moon*, therefore, raised the threshold problem of distinguishing "religious" from "business" from "personal" activities.[70] The government argued that the disputed funds were for personal and business, not religious, purposes. In his brief on behalf of Reverend Moon, Lawrence Tribe argued that the distinction between the religious and the economic or personal is "itself a constitutionally protected religious distinction" and that juries must accept the appellant's own definition of what is religious.[71] The courts were not impressed with this argument and responded thus: "The First Amendment does not insulate a church or its members from judicial inquiry when a charge is made that their activities violate a penal code. Consequently, in this criminal proceeding, the jury was not bound to accept the Unification Church's definition of what constitutes a religious use or purpose."[72]

A similar if less dramatic problem concerns the income earned by members of religious orders employed outside their communities. Salaries earned by Catholic regular clergy who have taken vows of poverty are not taxable when earned as agents for their orders, but the question of agency is ambiguous when they are employed outside the order. When the payment is made to the individual and turned over to the order and when the payment is made directly to the order, the courts have ruled that these earnings are taxable individual income.[73]

CHURCH PARTICIPATION IN ELECTORAL
CAMPAIGNS AND POLITICAL ADVOCACY

Section 501(c)(3), which provides tax exemptions to exclusively religious organizations, strictly precludes such organizations from "participat[ing] in or interven[ing] in . . . any political campaign on behalf of any candidate for public office" and specifies that "no substantial" part of its activities be devoted to influencing the making of public policy. However, the statute is not clear on the meaning of the words "campaign," "candidate," and "public office." Even more imprecise is the distinction between religious activity and public-policy advocacy. The exemptions and their restrictions have been subject to criticism from several directions.[74] Some critics believe that the exemptions themselves violate the Establishment Clause; others believe that these exemptions pose a Free Exercise danger; in exchange for the tax benefits, the advocacy role of churches in moral issues is chilled. In order for churches to qualify for tax exemptions they must limit political and lobbying activities that are clearly within their moral interests. Indeed, there is serious concern that the political advocacy limitation poses an unconstitutional condition on the receipt of a public benefit by requiring that religious and other nonprofit organizations forego their First Amendment rights as a condition of receiving the exemption. However, the Supreme Court rejected this argument in the case of *Regan v Taxation with Representation* and upheld the limitation.[75]

In practice, this exemption entails the constant threat of nonuniform enforcement by the Internal Revenue Service. Stanley Weithorn and Douglas Allen provide the following examples:

> Jesse Jackson's 1988 run for the presidential nomination was frequently endorsed by black churches, but that action was never followed by any significant Internal Revenue Service enforcement activity.
>
> Jimmy Swaggert Ministries, which endorsed Pat Buchanan's presidential bid, was the subject of a recent "press release" which indicated that enforcement action not only had fallen short of revocation but was no

more than a slap on the wrist and the extraction of a promise, in effect, "not to do it again."

John Cardinal O'Connor's threat to excommunicate prochoice Catholic politicians running for reelection evoked no Internal Revenue Service Sanctions.[76]

Uneven enforcement of the political limitations was precisely the issue in the case of *Abortion Rights Mobilization, Inc. v Regan,*[77] which began with an even more convoluted issue: Who may have standing to challenge the tax-exempt status of a religious organization? In this case, a coalition of abortion rights groups challenged the 501(c)(3) status of the Catholic Church because of the church's political activities in opposition to abortion rights. The suit alleged that in failing to enforce the political limitations, the government had exhibited a favoritism that violated the Establishment Clause. The district court found that several of the plaintiffs had shown sufficient personal injury to gain standing to challenge the exemption, but after several years of convoluted litigation, the Second Circuit ruled that none had standing.[78] It appears unlikely that any plaintiff in the near future will be granted standing to challenge the exemptions of another taxpayer.

While religious autonomy advocates are deeply troubled by the chilling effect and intrusiveness of the political advocacy limitations, to date only one church has lost its exemption for participating in political activity.[79]

THE PUBLIC POLICY EXCEPTION: *BOB JONES*
AND LIMITS OF INSTITUTIONAL AUTONOMY

Perhaps the most significant conflict between governmental policy and religious autonomy was the case of *Bob Jones University v United States.*[80] The case came to the Supreme Court after a complicated administrative and political history. The simple issue was whether the Internal Revenue Service had the statutory and constitutional power to deny tax exemptions to a religious university that practiced religiously motivated race discrimination.[81] At the time the university's tax troubles came to a head, it forbade interracial dating and marriage, advocacy of these practices, or belonging to groups that advocated them.[82] Two preliminary questions preceded the constitutional one. The first was a matter of statutory construction and administrative law: Had Congress authorized the IRS to withhold the tax deduction? The second dealt with an interpretation of the Internal Revenue Code: Does the long-standing requirement that charities must serve a public purpose in order to receive tax-deductible status also apply to tax exemptions in 501(c)(3)? The Court answered both questions in the affirmative. The third issue was the constitutional one relevant here: Is the denial of a government benefit such as tax-exempt status for an action motivated by sincere religious belief a violation of the Free Exercise Clause? In an eight to one decision, the Court ruled that it was not. A practice of a religious institution, even if sincerely religiously motivated, may deprive the institution of its tax exemption if the policy is contrary to public interest. Even though the loss of this financial benefit would be a costly one, the university could still practice its religious tenets. Applying the compelling state interest test, the majority found the "overriding governmental interest" in eliminating racial discrimination sufficiently compelling to justify whatever burdens the university suffered. But Justice Burger's majority opinion was not clear about the magnitude of the public policy sufficient to invoke this penalty. Would a church's conflict with any congressional policy be sufficient to justify revoking tax exemptions, or would only the violation of a constitutionally protected interest be sufficient grounds?

The university's advocates had not specifically argued its case in terms of institutional autonomy but rather relied on the more traditional (and perhaps more powerful) argument for the sanctity of religious conscience. Nevertheless, the conflict between institutional autonomy and the public interest seethed just below the surface. This case forces us to consider the limits of pluralism; in fact, it shall be one of the focal points for our more detailed explorations of the pluralist account in the concluding chapter.

Perhaps the most profound commentary on the *Bob Jones* case was that offered by Robert Cover.[83] Cover, as we have seen, is extremely sympathetic to insular religious communities, but ultimately even he recognized that a truly compelling public commitment may sometimes override that of a religious association. Cover would have accepted the university's defeat more readily had the majority opinion been phrased in terms of the government's profound commitment to racial equality. But Chief Justice Burger's opinion spoke merely of deference to congressional public policy—a goal insufficient, in Cover's view, to justify the sacrifice of the university's autonomy. Cover argues that the normative autonomy of Bob Jones University deserved more protection, unless the Court was willing to assert a much stronger commitment to racial equality—not merely a "public policy." The Court's decision took away too much from Bob Jones while giving too little to racial equality:

> It is a case that gives too much to the statist determination of the normative world by contributing too little to the statist understanding of the Constitution. . . . In the impoverished commitment of Chief Justice Burger's opinion, the constitutional question was not necessary, but the

Court avoided it by simply throwing the claim of protected insularity to the mercy of public policy. The insular communities deserved better— they deserved a constitutional hedge against mere administration. And the minority community deserved more—it deserved a constitutional commitment to avoiding public subsidization of racism.[84]

SECTION 170 DEDUCTIONS

Among the constitutional problems raised by religious tax deductions, none is more interesting than that raised by the Church of Scientology; the conflict between the IRS and the Church of Scientology forced a consideration of the very definition of a religious activity. The core activity of Scientology is "auditing," for which a "fixed donation" is required, according to church doctrine.[85] When members attempted to take Section 170 deductions for these donations, the Internal Revenue Service disallowed them because they were "fees for service." The church argued that because the doctrine of exchange was a religious belief, the fixed donations were not like ordinary commercial activity but were protected religious acts. The Internal Revenue Service denied charitable contribution exemptions for payments to the Scientology church for auditing because they were regarded as quid pro quo exchange for services. This denial was challenged by a church member in *Hernandez v Tax Commissioner*.[86] The Supreme Court upheld the findings of the Internal Revenue Service. Writing for the majority, Justice Thurgood Marshall ruled that the denial violated neither religion clause; it did not discriminate against a religion or excessively entangle church and state. In fact, to have permitted deductions for religious services would have required the IRS to distinguish between secular and religious services, thus entangling church and state. Furthermore, the incidental burden on religious free exercise was more than justified by the government's interest in maintaining a sound tax system free from "a myriad of exceptions flowing from a wide variety of religious beliefs."

Section 170 provides tax deductions for contributions "to or for the use of" qualified organizations. But even the meaning of those words is ambiguous. Consider the issue of Mormon missionaries. Traditionally, when young men are called to service as Mormon missionaries, they are supported by their parents, who provide for their needs as determined by their religious supervisors. When parents attempted to deduct the funds used in supporting their offsprings' missionary activities as contributions "for the use of" the church under Section 170, the Internal Revenue Service disallowed the deduction. In *Davis v United States*, the Supreme Court affirmed the ruling of the Internal Revenue Service and the lower courts that these expenditures were not deductible contributions because they were not literally "for the use of" the church.[87] In a similar vein, religious school tuition paid in the form of contributions to the parish have been held to be fees for service rather than contributions.[88]

SALES TAXES

While exemption from income and property taxes has been a long-standing legislative policy, other kinds of taxation have also raised constitutional problems. During the past decade, sales tax exemptions have been controversial under both religion clauses. For example, in 1989 a Texas law granting sales tax exemption to religious sellers of religious articles was held to be an unconstitutional establishment of religion.[89] The next year, the Supreme Court majority rejected a claim by Jimmy Swaggart Ministries for exemptions from California sales taxes as a constitutional right.[90] In the latter case, the majority found significant the fact that Swaggart's religion did not have conscience-based objections to paying sales taxes.

Churches as Sources of Public Policy Advocacy: Other Contexts and Problems

American history is interwoven with the activities of churches in support of or in opposition to public policies. Indeed, some of the most heroic chapters in our history have been the stories of church leadership in the abolition of slavery and in the civil rights movement. Religious institutions have been important sources of moral opposition and policy initiatives in virtually every aspect of public policy. In our own times, one only has to think of the role of churches as opponents of the Vietnam War, abortion rights, and capital punishment and as supporters of universal health care and racial equality. At its best, this is the tradition Robert Cover describes as "redemptive constitutionalism": "People associate not only to transform themselves, but also to change the social world in which they live."[91]

Does the involvement in political advocacy render a church a political action committee, subject to campaign disclosure laws? Consider the Bemis Pentecostal Church of Tennessee, which because of its moral objection to alcohol became involved in a local referendum concerning the sale of alcoholic beverages by running radio advertisements opposed to the measure. The courts ruled that these campaign activities were subject to the Campaign Finances Disclosure Act because they were political and not religious.[92]

We have seen how a church's political and social activities run afoul of IRS restrictions; however, potentially even more serious consequences befall churches whose special agendas are outside the mainstream. The Sanctuary

Movement of the 1980s illustrates how these activities often place religious institutions on a collision course with public authorities.

During the early 1980s a number of religious groups organized what was called a "Sanctuary Movement" to protest U.S. policy of tolerating human rights violations in Central America and its immigration policy, which denied refugee status to Central Americans fleeing persecution. The Sanctuary Movement was active within segments of the Catholic Church, the United Methodist Church, the Presbyterian Church, and the Unitarian Universalist Association, among others. Many of its activities were legal, including providing legal advocacy on behalf of persons seeking asylum. In addition, some members publicly announced that they would engage in acts of civil disobedience and violate immigration law by offering shelter to refugees residing illegally in the United States.[93]

In 1982 the government initiated an undercover investigation to obtain evidence of violation of immigration laws. Its agents became active participants in the movement, and their testimony became a major part of the record in the prosecution of Sanctuary activists. In 1989 fifteen Sanctuary activists were charged with violating the United States Immigration and Nationality Act by smuggling, transporting, and harboring refugees from El Salvador via Mexico into the United States. Eleven defendants were ultimately convicted. Their trial raised numerous issues of immigration and criminal law. Among the First Amendment issues raised was the use of government infiltration of religious institutions and use of testimony obtained through informers. Government infiltrators participated not only in the illegal activities but also in the religious life of member churches; they surreptitiously taped religious worship services and recorded license plate numbers of cars in church parking lots. The defendants in *United States v Aguilar*[94] argued that these methods violated both the First and Fourth Amendments and, hence, the evidence the agents gathered was inadmissible. The court thus had to consider not only the constitutional issues concerning "invited informers" in general but also the particular problems of such informers in religious settings. The Ninth Circuit summarized the defendants' argument and its response thus:

> The critical aspect of appellants' argument is their suggestion that the first amendment and the fourth amendment are necessarily intertwined in the context of an informer's infiltration of a church. Based upon first amendment principles, appellants contend that society is prepared to recognize

as reasonable churchgoers' expectations that "they could meet and worship in church free from the security of federal agents and tape recorders." A churchgoer need not "assume the risk that apparent fellow worshipers are present in church not to offer homage to God but rather to gain thirty pieces of silver." . . . Appellants' position is premised on the theory that the first amendment provides them with an additional expectation of privacy making the invited informer rationale inapplicable. The first amendment requires this heightened expectation of privacy because a "community of trust" is the essence of a religious congregation and the ability of a person to express faith with his fellow believers "withers and dies when monitored by the state." Appellants argue that government "spying" on religious activities necessarily chills a person's ability to exercise freely his religious faith. . . . While privacy, trustworthiness, and confidentiality are undoubtedly at the very heart of many instances of free association and religious expression and communication, the Court has recognized that legitimate law enforcement interests require persons to take the risk that those with whom they associate may be government agents.

Subsequent to the prosecutions in this case, several churches brought civil action against the government for violation of their religious freedom stemming from government infiltration of churches. Thus, *Presbyterian Church USA v United States* [95] is a companion case to *Aguilar*. While the trial court in this case entered summary judgment against the churches, the Ninth Circuit partially vindicated their constitutional claim. The court had no difficulty finding a compelling state interest in enforcing immigration policy, but it gave serious attention to the second prong of the compelling state interest test: were government activities that were burdening religious exercise the least restrictive means available to achieve the government's interest. The court in this case entered a declaratory judgment limiting "invited informers" in religious institutions to the specific invitations extended to them, restricting them to investigations only with a "good faith purpose," and precluding them from "unbridled and inappropriate covert activity" aimed at abridging First Amendment freedoms.

Civil Conflicts and Internal Church Disputes
One of the dangers to the autonomy of religious institutions occurs when a church becomes embroiled in a civil dispute and the parties themselves seek recourse in the civil courts. These disputes arise most frequently from some sort of schism: a local congregation divides over some irreconcilable difference, or a local church decides to split off from the denominational group.

In these cases, quarrels over who gets the church's property, like other property conflicts, are often taken to state courts. Judicial involvement in church civil disputes poses the threat of the kind of entanglement that would violate the Establishment Clause; it also implicates the Free Exercise interest in maintaining the autonomy of religious institutions.

For the first century of our history courts resolved these disputes according to the Pearson Rule, otherwise known as the "implied trust" or the "departure from doctrine" standard. Considering the church to be a trust, courts examined the creeds of disputants and awarded church property to the faction whose doctrines appeared closer to that of the institution at its founding. In other words, the losing faction would be the one who was perceived to have departed from the founding doctrine. Needless to say, this approach required courts to interpret often esoteric theology, an area upon which judges claim no special expertise and that appears, from contemporary perspective, to involve extreme entanglement as well as evaluation of religious doctrine. Clearly, the Pearson Rule stacked the cards in favor of orthodoxy and against doctrinal evolution.

A clear break with this method appeared in the Civil War era case of *Watson v Jones*.[96] The case resulted from a struggle between two factions of a local Presbyterian church for control over the church building when the church split over the question of slavery. One faction argued that the parent denomination had departed from its original doctrine while the local congregation remained theologically true to the original faith and, hence, was the rightful owner of its property. The Kentucky Supreme Court ruled that by departing from its original doctrine the parent church had dissolved the implied trust in which the property was held, and it therefore awarded the property to the local congregation. The U.S. Supreme Court reversed, refusing to engage in examination of theological doctrines: "The law knows no heresy, and is committed to the support of no dogmas." Instead, the Court announced the broad principle of deference to internal decision-making procedure of religious institutions in internal disputes. That is, when the church itself provides an authority or a mechanism to resolve property disputes, a court must defer to that body—hence insulating the autonomy of the church from judicial inquiry. The task of the courts is to ascertain what is the appropriate decision-making structure of the church and then to withdraw itself from further consideration.

Two other significant cases illustrate this standard. In *Kedroff v St. Nicholas Cathedral of the Russian Orthodox Church* the Supreme Court struck down a New York statute that had transferred control of the Russian Orthodox churches from the governing hierarchy in Moscow to the North American diocese following the Russian Revolution.[97] In spite of the political interest in freeing the American church from control by Moscow (in this cold war era), the Court recognized a stronger interest in preserving religious authority free of legislative interference. The Court characterized its precedents as protecting "a spirit of freedom for religious organizations, an independence from secular control or manipulation—in short, power to decide for themselves, free from state interference, in matters of church government, as well as those of faith and doctrine." *Serbian Eastern Orthodox Diocese v Milivojevich* arose when a priest who had been defrocked by the mother church in Belgrade challenged the action in the Illinois state courts.[98] The Illinois Supreme Court found gross irregularities in the procedure and set aside the hierarchy's decision. The Supreme Court reversed, ruling that the First Amendment forbade courts to oversee the internal procedures of a hierarchical church.

In 1969 the Supreme Court incorporated into the Fourteenth Amendment its prohibition of the "departure from doctrine" approach. The Free Exercise Clause, incorporated into the Fourteenth Amendment, forbids state courts to resolve a church issue through their own interpretation of church doctrine. The problem arose from a claim by two local Presbyterian churches that their parent organization had violated its constitution and departed from accepted doctrine and practice by ordaining women, making pronouncements on social and political matters, and changing church teachings. A state court had ruled on the substance of the complaint, and the Supreme Court overruled because the First Amendment does not permit the "departure from doctrine" standard to be applied by the state. The Court insisted that there are "neutral principles of law" available for resolving church property disputes without necessitating consideration of religious doctrines and practices.[99]

A third approach to adjudicating church property disputes is to treat the disputes like any other civil disputes and apply appropriate legal principles, such as contract. *Jones v Wolf*[100] involved a religious schism in which two factions claimed to represent the "true church" and hence claimed ownership of church property. Applying "neutral principles" of contract law, the Court examined deeds, corporate charters, state statutes, and the constitution of the parent church in resolving the dispute. In congregational churches and in the absence of documents granting authority elsewhere, courts may rely on the principle of majority rule as rebuttable presumption in determining which faction was entitled to speak for the church. Advocates of church autonomy find the "neutral principles" approach far too intrusive an approach to church conflicts.

The church dispute issue that most appalled church autonomy advocates was the brief but dramatic incident in which the attorney general of California placed the Worldwide Church of God in receivership because of alleged financial mismanagement. The dispute began when followers of an ousted church leader made allegations of financial mismanagement by the new leadership. The state attempted to investigate by examining church records. When it appeared that the records were being destroyed, the attorney general sought and received a court order appointing a receiver to control and audit church finances, but not to interfere with "ecclesiastical affairs." This condition lasted for over two months before the proceedings were dropped. The attorney general argued that the church was a public trust and hence subject to supervision and state financial oversight on behalf of the public.[101]

Internal Church Discipline

Civil cases involving internal church discipline require us to consider the scope and limits of associations' rights to define the terms of their own membership.[102] These cases arise from painful disputes between churches and their own members. On one hand are individuals who believe that they have been abused by their churches in ways that constitute civilly actionable torts; hence, they call on the power of the state for redress against the injury. On the other hand are religious institutions defending their rights to define their own rules of membership and to require members to live according to the dictates of the institution. For many Christian churches, the discipline of members is a scripturally based requirement for a community of the faithful. To vindicate the individual complainant, courts find themselves second-guessing the internal decisions of religious bodies. Such cases, therefore, sharply illustrate the discord between individual and institutional rights in this area. To argue a priority of either is to overlook the painful but very real tension inherent in the notion of a group right.

The shunning ("withdrawal of fellowship") cases illustrate these competing Free Exercise claims. Here the right of a group to practice a religion is posed against the right of a former member not to practice. One example is *Paul v Watchtower Bible and Tract Society of New York*, in which the plaintiff was prohibited from recovering damages for shunning by Jehovah's Witnesses because of possible violation of Free Exercise.[103]

The most well publicized of the church discipline incidents was the case of *Guinn v Church of Christ*.[104] Guinn had been a member of the Church of Christ; when she became involved in a romantic relationship of which her church disapproved, the ministers ordered her to break off the relationship. When she did not do so, the church not only imposed a shunning but also publicly denounced her as an adulterer. Guinn attempted to withdraw from the church but was not successful. She sued, and the trial court awarded her damages. A divided Oklahoma Supreme Court reversed and remanded, ruling that only those actions taken after her withdrawal from the church were actionable. This case provides an important insight into the notion of religious choice. If one accepts the notion that religious groups have constitutionally protected choices, then the disciplinary approaches of these churches have some constitutional standing. However, this is true only so long as the church is a voluntary association, where members have a right to leave. Gedicks finds in this simple conclusion one of the significant limits of a religious institutional autonomy right:

> Two concepts, voluntarism and value creation, are useful in articulating the boundaries within which a right to religious group self-definition should operate absolutely. The importance of religious groups to individual and social life, which gives the groups their strong claim to constitutional protection, is intertwined with the assumption that the creation or maintenance of an individual's membership in such groups is voluntary. The protection against governmental tyranny that is offered by a religious group to its members is of little personal value to one who is being coerced to join or to stay within the group. People in such situations need governmental intervention and protection. Similarly, it makes little sense to speak of the contribution of religious groups to personality development when the group is forcing its norm of individual identity on a member who does not wish to stay within the group. Accordingly, deference to a religious group's membership decisions is not appropriate in any situation in which group members are not free to leave the group.[105]

Other Issues, Briefly
ZONING, HISTORIC PRESERVATION, AND CHURCH BUILDINGS

Another source of church-state conflict concerns actual church buildings. Zoning and landmark designation have placed government in a position of exercising "design control" over the physical attributes of church structures, occasionally in opposition to the congregations that worship there. Since the adoption of the Historic Preservation Act of 1966 and the subsequent passage of cognate state acts, numerous important structures, including churches, have been designated as historic landmarks. Once so designated, these buildings must be maintained in accordance with guidelines established by the relevant preservation authority, frequently at substantial economic cost.[106] In the case of churches, this designation cedes to that authority control over some of the physical attributes of a house of worship and hence raises Free Exercise problems. If a church is simply a building like any other, the religious harm may be insignificant. But if, as Angela Carmella argues, religious architecture conveys religious meanings, then government has denied to the religious community a very significant part of its religious life. Carmella provides an impressive introduction to the realm of ecclesiastical architecture and argues thus:

> Ecclesiastical architecture has always been inextricably linked with basic religious choices made by worshipping communities. In both functional and visual aspects, the house of worship reflects and influences all dimensions of a religious community's life—its primary theological principles, its liturgical practices, its faith renewal movements, its doctrinal development, its missional goals, and its identity. The purpose of the structure is a religious one; religious choices are embodied in it; those choices in turn shape the individual and communal religious experience and either foster or constrain the spiritual development of the adherents. Because of the symbiosis between the building and the worshipping community, the design manifests religious expression. The semiotic nature of the house of worship renders its "religious" and "aesthetic" aspects indistinguishable. Therefore, when the government controls ecclesiastical design or dictates design orthodoxy to any religious community, it invades the sphere of religious decision making, compels some form of religious expression while suppressing others, and distorts the development of doctrine and the religious formation of adherents. Such state action severely compromises the religious community's freedom to adapt its worship structure to its liturgical, theological, doctrinal, and missional goals, and consequently, its ability to protect its own expression and vitality.[107]

The several most significant cases involving this issue suggest different directions in judicial thinking when churches have challenged landmark designation. *Saint Bartholamew's v City of New York*,[108] for example, focused on the economic impact of landmark designation. This case was brought by a landmark Park Avenue Episcopal Church in New York that wanted to demolish its community house adjacent to the church in order to construct an office tower to raise funds for its church programs. The Second Circuit, following *Smith*, treated the designation as a neutral law with only incidental religious burden and upheld the landmark authority's refusal to permit the destruction.

When the challenge has been phrased in religious terms, courts have been more receptive to church claims. For example, in *First Covenant Church v*

City of Seattle[109] a religious community challenged its designation as a landmark. The relevant law contained a "liturgical exemption" that purported to protect the ability of churches to make changes in accordance with liturgical developments but nevertheless provided for consultation with a secular authority on design changes. The Supreme Court of Washington held that the designation violated both federal and state religious guarantees, finding particularly offensive the law's requirement "to seek secular approval of matters potentially affecting the church's practice of religion."

Another case, *Society of Jesus v Boston Landmarks Commission*,[110] concerned a dispute about the *interior* of a church, including its altars. In this dispute Immaculate Conception Church was subject to a law that required preservation of its interior space and that did not include a liturgical exemption. When the Jesuits sought to move the front and side altars of the church to a more central location in accordance with changes mandated by Vatican II, the commission denied them permission to remove two of the original side altars. The Massachusetts State Judicial Court found adequate state constitutional protection of religion to overcome the state interest in historical preservation. It is worth noting that in both of these cases, state courts chose to rely on state constitutional religious freedom guarantees to avoid the debilitated interpretation of the federal Free Exercise Clause in the wake of *Smith*.

The unlikely issue of church architecture proved to be divisive enough to provide the first challenge to the 1993 Religious Freedom Restoration Act to reach the Supreme Court. The dispute began when Saint Peter Catholic Church, in Boerne, Texas, applied for a building permit to expand the church building. Because the church occupied an area that had recently been designated a historic district, the permit was denied. The bishop then challenged the denial as a violation of the Religious Freedom Restoration Act, which forbids government from burdening religious exercise unless the burden is the least restrictive means of furthering a compelling government interest. The district court struck down the act, but the circuit court reversed. In June 1997 the Supreme Court struck down the law as exceeding the constitutional powers of Congress.[111]

FINANCIAL SOLICITATION

The 1980s were replete with religious financial scandals; some of the most prominent involved fraudulent fund-raising by popular televangelists; others were based on distrust of the financial motives of "cults." But controversies over money and politics are much, much older, perhaps coeval of religion itself. These kinds of problems enmesh government in a conflict between two kinds of duties—its constitutional duty to protect religious freedom and its duty to protect citizens against fraud. While these disputes have raged in local law enforcement agencies and in the press, it is interesting that those reaching the Supreme Court have all involved marginal and unpopular faiths.

Financial solicitation rights were among the early Free Exercise disputes litigated by the Jehovah's Witnesses in the 1940s. Part of the Witnesses ministry involves distributing and selling religious literature house to house. Recall that the conviction for child labor upheld in *Prince v Massachusetts*[112] was against an aunt taking her niece on such a mission. Additionally, the Supreme Court twice considered whether this practice was taxable under local ordinances requiring peddlers to purchase licenses. To the Witnesses, this requirement amounted to the taxing and licensing of a religious ministry. In 1942 in *Jones v Opelika*[113] the Supreme Court upheld the tax on the grounds that the selling of religious literature was simply commercial activity. But only two years later, in *Murdock v Pennsylvania*,[114] a five to four majority vacated that decision and ruled that the sale of religious literature was a religious act that could not be licensed or taxed.

As the 1980s dawned, the issue reemerged, once more pitting local authorities against marginal religious groups. The first involved ISKCON, or the International Society for Krishna Consciousness—the very visible Hare Krishna movement. Members of this faith engage in a practice known as Sankritan, which includes public chanting, selling religious articles, and soliciting donations for support of the faith. Members of ISKCON challenged a rule of the Minnesota State Fair that required all commercial, charitable, and religious organizations to sell or distribute literature and solicit donations from only assigned locations on the fairgrounds. These assigned booths were rented by the state authority on a first-come, first-served basis. Although there was no evidence that the rental process was discriminatory, ISKCON argued that the ruling limited its ability to engage in the religious practice of Sankritan. In *Heffron v International Society for Krishna Consciousness*[115] a divided Supreme Court upheld the rule as an appropriate time, place, and manner restriction, which was constitutional in light of the state's compelling interest in crowd control.

The next year the Supreme Court considered another case involving financial solicitation, this one posing Minnesota against the Unification Church. The state had long imposed certain registration and reporting requirements on charitable organizations but had exempted religious organizations. However, a 1978 amendment required registration by religious organizations that solicit more than 50 percent of their funds from nonmembers. The Unification Church challenged that regulation as blatant religious discrimination.

In *Larson v Valente*[116] a bare majority struck down the rule on both Free Exercise and Establishment grounds because it constituted a preference of some denominations over others.

These financial solicitation cases are only one aspect of the broader issues of financial regulation, many of which we have already encountered in other contexts. These brief notes only give the barest suggestion of the kinds of constitutional problems raised when government interests cross paths with church fund-raising efforts.

RELIGIOUS INSTITUTIONAL AUTONOMY AND GENERAL THEORIES OF THE FREE EXERCISE CLAUSE

Having surveyed the concrete contexts in which religious institutions raise Free Exercise claims, we are now in a position to evaluate them. To do so requires some general sense of the "purpose" of the religion clauses; hence, we return to the five accounts that have been the source of guiding principles.

Promoting Individual Choice

The most common explanation of the First Amendment religion clauses is that they protect free religious choice. Most of the standard arguments for free religious choice focus on *individual* choices; hence, this explanation is far more effective in protecting individual religious practices than in encompassing the autonomy of religious *institutions*. In fact, the focus on individual autonomy provides one of the strongest arguments *against* the case for institutional rights, as Ira Lupu explains: "Free exercise principles protect autonomous, individual choices, not choices dependent upon group membership. Persons claiming Free Exercise clause exemptions must individually bear whatever burdens and sacrifices those exemptions entail. Group based exemptions, by contrast, may confer benefits on individuals who are only nominally committed to the group faith."[117]

Autonomy, as we have seen, is a difficult concept, whether for the individual or the group. Recall the potential conflict raised by Justice Douglas's concurring opinion in *Yoder* between the autonomy of the Amish community and the potential autonomy of any individual Amish child who might wish for wider choices.[118]

Frederick Gedicks has avoided the individualist bias of this approach and applied the choice argument to religious *groups*. He proposes a "right of self-definition," including a broadly understood right of religious groups to choose their own members. His points of departure are two employment discrimination cases, *Ohio Civil Rights Commission v Dayton Christian*

Schools[119] and *Corporation of the Presiding Bishop of the Church of Jesus Christ of Latter-Day Saints v Amos*,[120] both of which involved religious group membership decisions. These cases pose sharp conflicts between the associational freedom of those prevented from affiliating with the religious group and the associational freedom of members favoring exclusion. While recognizing the values at stake on both sides, Gedicks comes down squarely on behalf of the associational rights of groups.

> There are . . . always at least two distinct individual interests at stake in individual-government-religious group conflicts: the interests of a nonmember or nonconforming member in being free from religious discrimination by the group, and the interest of group members in maintaining the integrity of their existing relationships with and within the group. Nonmembers or nonconforming members of a religious group who insist on the right to belong to the group without conforming to beliefs and practices considered important by the group, insist upon the right to belong to the group on their own terms, rather than those of the group itself.
>
> It is unclear why the autonomy of the nonmember or the nonconforming member should prevail over that of the conforming member in such situations; at most, they cancel each other out. In fact, individual interests may well weigh more heavily on the side of religious group self-definition than on that of government intervention in any definitional balance. When the government intervenes in religious membership decisions on behalf of nonmembers or nonconforming members, it "kills" the group, causing it to change a fundamental aspect of its character or even physically to disband. Religious pluralism, and the choices of those individuals whose personal identity and life are tied to the group, are reduced because the group that stands behind the personal identity of conforming members no longer exists. On the other hand, when the government refrains from intervening in membership decisions, religious pluralism and individual choice are maximized. The religious group remains intact and undistorted for all those members who reference their personal growth and identity to it, while nonconforming members and nonmembers are still free to join other groups whose core concerns more closely match the self-concepts and aspirations of such persons. Thus, in considering the interests of conforming members versus those of nonmembers and nonconforming members, any weight to be added to the definitional balance of individual, government, and religious group interests should fall on the side of protecting religious group self-definition.[121]

Gedicks's argument is both powerful and troubling. His notion of associational freedom is a broad one indeed, including not only the freedom of individuals to associate but also that of groups to evolve free of external influences from government or unwelcome members. His persuasive references to self-identity, core concerns, and group narratives mask the fact that the group membership being referred to is often merely an employment relationship. To understand employment as an associational right may be to inflate it with unrealistic constitutional baggage. We must recall that the "association" at stake in *Amos* was the job of a custodian in a gymnasium. The association at stake in *Dayton Christian School* was a woman's job as a teacher. Does the elegant concept of "group membership" genuinely convey what is at stake in these cases? Gedicks's broad definition of membership may dignify simple employment discrimination. Indeed, the arguments for associational freedom seem to be almost a more elegant restatement of those made in opposition to 1960s era civil rights laws.[122] In short, while neglecting associational freedoms of religious groups appears to be a mistake, overemphasizing and romanticizing them seems to be equally perilous.

There is an additional fundamental problem with articulating religious freedom in terms of choice, one we have seen in this and the preceding chapters. To understand religious practices as choices badly mistakes the nature of religion; for believers, its commands are not choices, but obligations. To treat claims to religious free exercise as matters of choice is to trivialize religion and to ignore the tragedy that befalls people forced to choose between the commands of the state and those of their consciences. Perhaps for this reason, the court has often looked to religious doctrine in determining the burdens of compliance with governmental requirements.

Protecting Freedom of Conscience

Many of the cases raising institutional-rights questions are argued in terms of religious conscience. In some instances compliance with law conflicts with the religious tenets of the faith. This was the case for the churches involved in the Sanctuary Movement and in some of the race and gender discrimination cases, for example. These instances produce strong cases for religious institutional exemptions. However, the burdens to conscience raised in these instances were not really on churches as institutions but on their individual members. "By their nature," Lupu argues, "institutions cannot have a conscience or a faith."[123] Conscience, as we have seen, is essentially an individualized concept; to apply it to an institution may be to reify the collectivity in an inappropriate way.

Still, courts have frequently accepted the conscience arguments of religious institutions, as in some of the gender discrimination cases we have observed. We have also observed that conscience claims cut both ways. When a church cannot raise a conscientious objection to a compliance with a state regulation, the absence of religious tenets contrary to law becomes a reason for enforcing compliance. For example, in *Jimmy Swaggart Ministries v Board of Equalization*, the ministry was unable to show that paying a sales tax violated a religious belief.[124] The same was true in several of the employment discrimination cases.

To be able to base an argument on the religious conscience of an institution, one must be able to assert with some confidence what the institution's conscience requires. Thus, arguments about the conscience of a religious institution fall back almost immediately on the practical question of how to ascertain what it is. Who speaks for the institution, and how is its "conscience" to be ascertained? It is difficult enough to discover the beliefs of a person. How are decision makers to ascertain the conscience of an institution? Clearly hierarchical religious institutions may have an answer to this problem, but in others, there may be no single spokesperson authorized to articulate the conscience requirements for the institution.

The 1977 Fifth Circuit decision in *Brown v Dade Christian Schools* illustrates this problem.[125] A religious school under court order to cease its racially exclusive admissions policy argued that the order violated its religious freedom. The members of the Fifth Circuit Court, sitting en banc, disagreed over the method of ascertaining an institution's professed religious commitments. Judge Hill's plurality opinion concluded that the school could not raise a Free Exercise claim because it had failed to show that racial discrimination was based on a religious conviction. Judge Hill took note of the absence of references to segregation in the school's written literature as well as to the statements of its pastor and school president. The concurring opinion by Judge Goldberg criticized the "constrictive" approach to ascertaining religious beliefs taken by the plurality, fearing that it inadequately recognized religious convictions not based on official documents. He was persuaded that the school did have a Free Exercise claim but concluded that segregation was not central to their faith, but a "minor tenet" of their religion, which would neither jeopardize the continued existence of the church nor threaten its members' chances of achieving salvation. Hence, the government's interest in promoting racial equality easily outweighed the school's religious claims. The dissenters, in contrast, were persuaded that racial segregation was indeed a religious belief of the church, based not only on its members' biblical interpretations but also a congregational vote and the unwritten beliefs of its members. Judge Roney's dissenting opinion expands the notion of a religious institutional belief beyond the official written doctrine of an institution.

In my view, the problems illustrated in *Dade Christian Schools* are virtually insurmountable; religious convictions always end up being the convictions of *someone*. Hence, while the appeal to institutional conscience is a promising approach, it remains an essentially individualist one. If this is true, the conscience argument makes the institutional rights argument superfluous. If an association claims that its activity is done because of religious conscience, its members' claims are individual ones, and the fact that the members are acting as an institution adds nothing to the argument.

For this and other reasons, the conscience argument seems to be an insufficient ground for a right to institutional autonomy. Even in initiating the debate, Douglas Laycock insisted that institutional rights should extend beyond the bounds of activities strictly required by religious conscience. Laycock's original case for a right to religious institutional autonomy quite explicitly encompassed not only the activities required by religious conscience but also a much broader range of institutional activities.

> Many activities that obviously are exercises of religion are not required by conscience or doctrine. Singing in the church choir and saying the Roman Catholic rosary are two common examples. Any activity engaged in by a church as a body is an exercise of religion. This is not to say that all such activities are immune from regulation; there may be a sufficiently strong governmental interest to justify the intrusion. But neither are these activities wholly without constitutional protection. It is not dispositive that an activity is not compelled by the official doctrine of a church or the religious conscience of an individual believer. Indeed, many would say that an emphasis on rules and obligations misconceives the essential nature of some religions.[126]

Strong advocates of church autonomy, like Laycock, Carmella, and Gedicks, are concerned with protecting the fluidity of religious doctrines. Churches are complex institutions that may encompass a diversity of views and ever-evolving customs, practices, and obligations. Carmella argues that even the relations between church and state are matters of theology and ecclesiology, both of which should be left to the determination of the church itself. For government to intervene in these matters not only risks invading religious doctrine as it is but also compromises the future development of religious doctrine.[127] In the same vein, Gedicks recalls the Mormon Church's coerced renunciation of polygamy and insists that state intervention will almost inevitably shape the direction of religious doctrines.[128]

There is much to be said for this argument, but it may beg the wider question. Religious doctrine is perhaps inevitably shaped by its confrontation with the culture at large—everything from consumer fashions to technology. If such influences are constant and inevitable, why should government be singularly excluded from exerting its authority? More to the point, as pervasive and subtle as governmental influences are, is it even imaginable that government could be so precluded?

Protecting the State from Sectarian Conflicts

As we have seen, for Madison and Jefferson, the religious liberty guarantees were, above all, "articles of peace." In a society already becoming religiously heterogeneous, the separation of religion from political conflict was a natural solution to a potential danger. By separating church and state, both structurally and functionally, sectarian conflicts would be less likely to spill over and cause civic ones. This rationale has most often been articulated in Establishment Clause issues, most notably those in which religious institutions are the recipients of public resources. Increasingly these kinds of arguments spill over into Free Exercise issues. In *Larson v Valente*, for example, the Court spoke of the risk of "politicizing religion."[129]

During the past decade, religious interest groups have become some of the most powerful actors in American politics at all levels; the combining of religious and political conflict is a fact of contemporary public life. What guidance would this approach to Free Exercise (church-state separation) offer in the present context? It appears to me that it would offer only situational guidance rather than a consistent principle. In some instances, it would counsel leaving a wide clearing around powerful religious institutions and deferring to their own institutional needs, as the Court did in both *Corporation of the Presiding Bishop of the Church of Jesus Christ of Latter-Day Saints v Amos*[130] and *NLRB v Catholic Bishop of Chicago*.[131] In both cases, the Supreme Court refused to enforce labor laws to powerful religious institutions, fearing that doing so would impact ultimately on the religious decision-making authority of the institutions. Hence, this perspective might argue for broad accommodation of religious institutional interests. But similar reasoning suggests an opposite conclusion; a blanket refusal to grant exemptions to religious institutions might be less divisive than granting them selectively.

The accommodating of religious groups raises again the question of whether any accommodation should be the role of the courts or the more politically sensitive legislatures. This, of course, is the point of Justice Scalia's controversial argument against judicial accommodation in the *Smith* case.[132] But to argue that such decisions ought properly to be decided by legislatures, as Justice Scalia does, is to turn the religious guarantees from a right to an element of the pluralist bargaining process.

Fostering Independent Sources of Power and Alternative Public Policies

Pluralist theory suggests that the great genius of the American political system is the dispersal of power among the branches of government, between central and local institutions, between public and private economic sectors, to the free press, and among voluntary associations. Religious institutions serve as additional means of checking the power of government. They are the "mediating institutions" that buffer individuals from bureaucracies and perform community functions parallel to those performed by government. Moreover, they provide additional points of entry into the political system and offer policy alternatives that expand the political agenda.

The church-based civil rights, social justice, prolife, and pacifist movements, the Sanctuary Movement, and the Catholic Bishops' Letter on the Economy illustrate some ways independent religious institutions foster alternative conceptions of public policy and influence government toward those ends. When churches perform these functions, however, they raise the threshold problems we encountered earlier. Religiously motivated political activities risk violating campaign contribution disclosure laws. The Sanctuary Movement protesting immigration policies ran afoul of criminal statutes and prompted a campaign of government infiltration. These problems seem to stem from unrealistic line drawing. These activities are indeed "political," but they are no less "religious." Indeed, for "redemptive" groups, the religious vision commands an alteration of the entire society. It may be that the "redemptive" activities of religious communities are among the most important functions they perform for the polity as a whole.

Overall, this approach to religious freedom should be more favorable to the claims of religious groups who privately pursue alternatives to government than to those who seek to change governmental policy. However, the *Bob Jones* case[133] underscores the ambiguous limits of this argument. A pluralist should have been very sympathetic to a private school pursuing its own moral vision. However, when that vision conflicts with highly charged and important policy commitments, the argument begins to fray. The alternative public policy vision—important as it is—does not provide us with guidelines to its own limits.

Fostering Independent Sources of Meaning

This approach to religious free exercise takes as its point of departure one of the distinctive features of the human condition—the need for meaning. Among the many sources of meaning, religion has always been particularly important because it situates the person within the cosmos, addresses ultimate questions, and helps make sense of those situations in which our everyday understandings are most sharply called into question. Autonomous religious associations help prevent individuals from anomie and, at the same time, counteract the totalizing unity of imposed meanings.

Among the ways that groups create meanings are through common narratives, as Frederick Gedicks eloquently explains:

> Narrative is particularly important for religious groups. A group's narrative is its vision of itself, of what its members aspire to be both individually and communally. Shared by all of a religious group's members to some extent, the narrative constitutes the interpretive structure against which those members assess the meaning of their lives. Because core concerns are the definitive referent for determining who is and who is not a member of the group, the group's narrative exerts considerable force on those who value group membership. Again, this is especially true of religious groups, for a religious narrative is a source of moral authority in the lives of those who wish to become or to remain members of the religious group to which narrative pertains. It is, therefore, an arbiter of disputes among members of the group, as well as an authoritative normative guide for personal decisions.[134]

Gedicks builds upon this insight an argument for the right of religious groups to "self-definition." Like Laycock, he shifts the focus away from what a group professes at a certain time and argues that the First Amendment should protect the rights of the religious institution to develop its own doctrines and narratives and to practice, profess, and propagate its evolving vision.

State intervention into the affairs of a religious community frequently destroys the daily development of a group's historical and theological narratives. Accordingly, government regulation may seriously disrupt and distort the spiritual life of the community even when the state's demands would not violate clearly identifiable doctrines, beliefs, or practices. Such intervention breaks the link between evolution of group meanings and group authority, and thus reinterprets and recasts such meaning. Historical and theological narratives often exist as unconscious or subconscious phenomena in the lives of individual members. Thus, focusing attention on an aspect of religious group life that otherwise would be perceived by the group as unremarkable may interfere with the normal development of the community's spiritual life and may channel that development in new directions which would not have been taken. . . .

Only the religious group itself is capable of accurately assessing the significance of government burdens on its religiosity, because only the group can accurately identify and interpret the relevant historical and theological narratives.[135]

Robert Cover makes perhaps the broadest argument for the independence of "jurisgenerative communities" to define for themselves not only their own shared meanings but also their own understandings of law itself.

Groups assume different constitutional positions in order to create boundaries between the outside world and the community in which real law grows—in order to maintain the jurisgenerative capacity of the community's distinct law. We ought not lightly to assume a statist perspective here, for the *nomos* of officialdom is also "particular"—as particular as that of the Amish. And it, too, reaches out for validation and seeks to extend its legitimacy by gaining acceptance from the normative world that lies outside its core.

The principles that establish the nomian autonomy of a community must, of course, resonate within the community itself and within its sacred stories. But it is a great advantage to the community to have such principles resonate with the sacred stories of other communities that establish overlapping or conflicting normative worlds. Neither religious churches, however small and dedicated, nor utopian communities, however isolated, nor cadres of judges, however independent, can ever manage a total break from other groups with other understanding of law. . . . The interdependence of legal meanings makes it possible to say that the Amish, the Shakers, and the judges are all engaged in the task of constitutional understanding. But their distinct starting points, identifications, and stories make us realize we cannot pretend to a unitary law.

Sectarian communities differ from most—but not all—other communities in the degree to which they establish a *nomos* of their own. They characteristically construct their own myths, lay down their own precepts, and presume to establish their own hierarchies of norms. Most importantly, they identify their own paradigms for lawful behavior and reduce the state to just one element, albeit an important one, in the normative environment. Even an accommodationist sectarian position—one that goes to great lengths to avoid confrontation or the imposition upon adherents of demands that will in practice conflict with those imposed by the state— establishes its own meaning for the norms to which it and its members conform.[136]

Although Cover draws most of his examples from religious communities, his argument applies equally to any "jurisgenerative community." It thus raises the question, "Why are religious communities special—why are they worthy of special protection?" Gedicks proposes an answer to this question. Religious groups are special in that they *create* values:

[Many other organizations] do not form the foundation of an individual's self concept or provide a significant check on state power. Indeed, such organizations are usually parasitic with respect to their group values. They do not originate or create values, but only reflect values that have their origin in more foundational groups. Thus, they are carriers rather than creators of meaning.

The moral values that inhere in the communal life of religious groups are the result of the fact that such groups normally create rather than merely reflect values. Religious groups are among those institutions in American society that teach people to find and nurture personal meanings and values in their individual lives. Indeed, given the continuing and pervasive influences of religious traditions in the lives of many Americans religious groups must be considered to be among the most significant sources of American values.[137]

We must not be too hasty to accept this argument, for to do so is perhaps to both reify and romanticize groups. The narratives of groups are subject to change through all sorts of external reasons beyond the groups' control. Is government precluded from being among them? Furthermore, one might well challenge an account of religious freedom so inclusive as to encompass something as amorphous as a community's right to self-development of its theology. William Marshall and Douglas Blomgrin challenge the argument:

[T]heological development is not itself theology, or even if it is theology, ephemeral development of doctrine cannot properly be held to be within the ambit of first amendment protection. An equally persuasive argument is that the genesis and development of theological principles is a process no different from the development of political, artistic, or literary ideas in the secular world. The mere fact that secular affiliations or organizations may develop ideas through the interactive process does not imbue these groups with constitutional interests. . . . The proposition then, that the process of theological development should be singled out for special treatment appears to be without justification.

Religion, then, although it can and should be free from government coercion, cannot be insulated from government action that might affect religious values. This, of course, does not leave religion at the state's mercy. In the absence of coercion, the religious institution itself ultimately determines whether to be theologically influenced by governmental or societal action. This is the fallacy of the direct effect argument. It seeks not to protect church from government, but rather to protect religious institutions from matters within their own volition.[138]

Does the Laycock/Gedicks/Cover argument underestimate the role of the state as a legitimate creator of values? Do they make too broad a case? What happens when religious meanings are outside the toleration limits of the general consensus? Have these authors misrepresented value-creating communities? And why are *religious* meanings especially privileged?

The argument for jurisgenerative communities is immensely appealing. It evokes a world of insular, "authentic" communities sustained by shared narratives and normative commitments. Yet, our survey of cases reminds us that very few of the actual disputes involved such communities. Most institutional autonomy claims are not raised by either insular or redemptive communities; they are raised by institutions that are a part of the wider society and who share, in various degrees, the patchwork of overlapping norms. The idea behind American pluralism is that these groups are not insular but overlapping. These groups create, foster, and reinforce meanings within the context of a multiplicity of other meaning sources.

The search for the scope and limits of religious institutional rights takes us beyond the scope of constitutional law and into political philosophy. It suggests the continual tensions between centrifugal and centripetal forces within a polity. These tensions are especially sharp in a democracy; autonomous institutions seem to be necessary for democratic ones to survive, but at the same time, they are sources of threat. Ultimately, I reach a conclusion as mixed and inelegant as pluralism itself. I conclude that religious institutions do have First Amendment rights but that there is no constitutional right to institutional autonomy per se. I would recognize a rather wide latitude for religious institutions to characterize their activities as religious exercises. These clearly include "acculturated religious practices." However, recognizing activities as religious practices does not preclude their being other kinds of practices at the same time. Religious counseling is no less counseling, religious education is still education, and a religious hospital is still a hospital.

The search for line drawing between secular and religious, between church and state, has led us astray. It is an attempt to separate phenomena that are not separate. The image of a mosaic collage is helpful. Individuals and groups may be part of more than one picture simultaneously. Indeed, the overlap itself provides coherence for the polity as a whole.

Autonomous institutions, or in Cover's terms, "jurisgenerative communities," create and sustain shared meanings for their members. In addition, they contribute to the constellation of understandings that shape the polity as a whole. Some aspire to be "redemptive communities," but most perform both functions while immersed in countless other overlapping "communities." For such institutions to claim a right to "autonomy" belies their multifunctional nature. The challenge is not to protect them *from* entanglement with surrounding pressures but to protect them *within* the entangled institutional complexity of our existence.[139]

6

THREATS TO RELIGIOUS IDENTITY

UNDERSTANDING RELIGIOUS IDENTITY

"Since the memory of man runneth not to the contrary," religious identity has been one of the most pervasive and persistent ways in which humans define themselves and each other. Religious identities are among the fundamental ways that people locate themselves in their social environments and understand the meanings of large events and everyday occurrences. Because of the continuing importance of religious identity, to both the society as a whole and individual well-being, some aspects of religious identity may warrant protection as part of the Free Exercise Clause of the First Amendment.

Before we focus on the constitutional contexts of religious identity, we should consider the connections between religious identity and the phenomenon of religion itself. As usual, Emile Durkheim's ideas are the point of departure. Durkheim stated the relationship between religion and social group with characteristic drama and power: Religion is coterminous with the creation of a people.

> If religion has given birth to all that is essential in society, it is because the idea of society is the soul of religion. . . . The collective idea which religion expresses is far from being due to a vague innate power of the individual, but it is rather at the school of collective life that the individual has learned to idealize. Thus both with the individual and in the group, the faculty of idealizing has nothing mysterious about it. . . . He could not be a social being, that is to say, he could not be a man, if he had not acquired it.[1]

Durkheim's insight led sociologists to explore the subtle connections between religion and personal identity. In the 1970s Hans Mol elaborated a complex theory of religious identity, beginning with a definition of religion as "the sacralization of identity."[2] Mol posits an enormous human need for identity, order, and a sense of place.[3] Just as the lower primates are attached to and defend territory, humans express this sense of place through attachment to symbols. This need for integration exists in precarious tension with the forces of differentiation, adaptation, and change. Mol understands the human condition in terms of a dialectic between differentiation and integration. Religion is a strong force for integration and identity. "The precariousness of human identity has led man to repeatedly wrap it in 'don't touch' sentiments."[4] This is precisely the function of sacralization, the process by which symbol systems become taken for granted, stable, and seemingly eternal. Moreover, religion always appears to modify or stabilize the differentiations it has been unable to prevent. Sacralization protects conceptions of reality and personal identity and when necessary enables them to accommodate and legitimate necessary changes. "Religious practices give special underpinning to particular conceptions of order within a culture, thus making the security of the individual less precarious."

To understand religion is to understand the mechanisms through which sacralizations occur. Mol calls one such mechanism *objectification*, "the tendency to sum up the variegated elements of mundane existence in a transcendental point of reference where they can appear more orderly, more consistent, and more timeless." Another is *commitment*, the emotional attachment to identity that "anchors a system of meanings in the emotions and, given time, develops into awe which wraps the system in 'don't touch' sentiments." In addition, *ritual* "maximizes order, reinforces the place of the individual in his society, and strengthens the bonds of a society vis à vis the individual"; it also "restores identity when disruption has occurred." Mol recognizes that highly differentiated societies like ours no longer can be integrated by universal religions: "[S]ectarian groups in these highly differentiated societies seem to derive at least some of their success from being buffers between the heterogeneity of the social whole and the threat of personal alienation."

It is not just that religion sustains identity for the individual; the converse is equally true. Religious identity provides what Peter Berger calls the "plausibility structures" that make religion possible. Without participating in a social group that makes plausible the religious claims of the believer, without its rituals, myths, and other legitimating practices, the individual finds it exceedingly difficult to sustain the religion.[5] Thus, religious identity is not just an outgrowth of religion, it is essential for the very existence of religion.

Anthropologist Clifford Geertz focuses on the way meanings and motivations are sustained through socially created symbols.[6] His work stresses the functions religion performs for the individual in confronting bafflement, death, and suffering, and in his need to make moral decisions. Geertz reminds us that the "solutions" to these problems are not matters of private, individual conscience but of socially created systems of symbols. To be religious is to partake in the system of symbols and, hence, to have an identity with people who share the system of symbols.

Fr. Andrew Greeley's observations of contemporary American Catholics have added empirical details to these theories. Greeley has identified what he calls a striking "loyalty factor" that seems to account for a great deal of the stability of church membership. He concludes that "religion is an essential component of your identity and social location (so, too, for many people in many places, are your politics and ethnicity). You have to be something and Catholicism is your heritage; it is a component of your selfhood. No one, not even the Pope, much less Cardinal Ratzinger or some bishop, is going to take it away from you!"[7]

All of these insights suggest that legal thinkers need to give much more serious attention to religious identity interests in our understanding of the Free Exercise Clause. They lead me to conclude that the protection of religion—belief or practice—is simply not comprehensible without the protection of religious identity. Identity, in this view, is prior to both belief and practice; it creates both, even while it is created by both.

Even this extremely brief survey of religious sociology confirms the fact that religious identity is as much a part of the phenomenon as is individual spirituality or theology. Such a focus should make us far more sensitive to threats to identity values than we would have been by taking a purely individualistic approach. These reflections on the nature of religion impact our thinking about the Free Exercise Clause and suggest that identity claims are not poor relations to the belief and practices claims; rather, they are absolutely central to the very existence of religion. But at the same time, they raise powerful problems: How can religious identity be distinguished from other aspects of one's personal identity? How is religious identity to be reconciled with the other aspects of identity that make claims upon us and compete with our allegiance?

Recent contributions to social theory have enhanced our understanding of the relation between the individual self and the identities, associations, and commitments that constitute it. As communitarian thinkers have come to challenge the once-prevailing liberal individualism, identity seems to have been rediscovered. Liberalism, with its emphasis on autonomy and choice, necessarily separates the self from its choices, commitments, and identities; these can be picked up and discarded at will, leaving the self intact. Man[8] enters society as a consumer, selecting those commitments and joining voluntary associations that suit his purposes. People's identities are adopted and changed as they make their own lives.

Contemporary communitarians reject this view of the self and insist that identities (ethnic, geographic, gender, religious, tribal, or familial, etc.) are *constitutive* of the self. Michael Sandel calls this the "situated self," and his description of this view has become classic:

> Communitarian critics of rights-based liberalism say we cannot conceive ourselves as . . . bearers of selves wholly detached from our aims and attachments. They say that certain of our roles are partly constitutive of the persons we are—as citizens of a country, or members of a movement, or partisans of a cause. But if we are partly defined by the communities we inhabit, then we must also be implicated in the purposes and ends characteristic of those communities. . . . Open-ended though it be, the story of my life is always embedded in the story of those communities from which I derive my identity—whether family or city, tribe or nation, party or cause. On the communitarian view, these stories make a moral difference, not only a psychological one. They situate us in the world, and give our lives their moral particularity.[9]

Many First Amendment thinkers have been tempted to jettison the notion of individual choice altogether, but, paradoxically, doing so would ignore our own cultural and constitutional heritage, as well as much of the empirical evidence about religious choices. At the same time, the notion that identities may indeed be chosen is experiencing its own renaissance. Ethnic identities, once almost totally ascriptive, are increasingly a matter of choice, since intermarriage among groups has given individuals a multiplicity of ethnic heritages from which to choose.[10] Furthermore, recent sociologists are impressed by the "economic" behavior of individuals in "choosing" religious identities—and the remarkable success of high-demand religions in competing for those choices.[11]

It appears, therefore, that any thorough approach to the Free Exercise Clause must incorporate both individual and communitarian insights in understanding religious freedom. A provocative anonymous "Note" written a decade ago in the *Harvard Law Review* suggests such a direction.[12] The note's author notices that the two religion clauses of the First Amendment seem irreconcilable from the perspective of classical liberalism and its individualistic conception of the self. But when the self is understood as the nexus between separateness and collective identity, the two religion clauses merge into a single protection for the freedom to acquire and maintain identities. The author posits the human self as the fulcrum of two aspects in dynamic equilibrium—the separate and unique identity and the collective. Like background and foreground in a painting, they are mutually defining. Protection of religious liberty is crucial for maintaining both aspects of the self.

The religion clauses protect each of the two processes that create the dual self. The first process through which identity emerges is the process of choice. Choices that determine the individual's separate identity and define his connection to other human beings are protected by the Free Exercise clause. In order for choice to be effective, however, background social institutions must allow for the formation of both aspects of the self. Each community must be free to create a collective identity, but no community should be so overpowering that it threatens the individual's ability to define himself in opposition to it. The establishment clause protects this second process, through which an individual's identity is formed by the influence of communities. The clause ensures the right of both religious and political communities to influence identity independently, but it protects the individual from the potentially overwhelming power of their alliance. The two religion clauses thus protect the processes by which socialization and individual choice together shape the contours of human identity.

Individuals are influenced by a wide range of constitutionally protected communities, of which religious groups are only one. But the special constitutional protection for religion is more than just a historical accident. Defined functionally, a religion is a system of belief that is essential to the self-definition of the believer. Thus, a society that failed to protect religion would foreclose the individual's choice of the most fundamental part of his identity.[13]

Furthermore, several elements of First Amendment doctrine combine to create a unified protection for identity. The Free Exercise Clause enables a person to participate in her or his own religious community while remaining a full participant in the political community. The same "Note" continues: "The individual choice of identity can be protected only if the political community offers him full membership regardless of his association with a religious community."[14] In the author's view, the Establishment Clause contains two essential elements: state neutrality among religions and separation of church and state. Both are necessary for maintaining the plurality of identities. The former protects what he calls "horizontal plurality."

> [N]eutrality fosters horizontal plurality—that is, it fosters a society in which a multiplicity of communities that exert a particular kind of influence (for example, religious influence) can coexist. . . . [N]eutrality does ensure that the comparative vitality of the competing communities to which people are exposed will depend on the popular appeal of the ideas they offer and not on the government's preference. . . . Plurality provides a contrast among communities that allow members not only to acquire distinctive group characteristics, but also to recognize that those characteristics are theirs by virtue of membership in the group. The contrast among communities also apprises the individual to the possibility of separating himself from any given group. Thus, horizontal plurality aids in the formation of both the collective and separate aspects of identity.[15]

The separation of church and state protects what the author calls "vertical plurality," "the simultaneous influence of several communities upon an individual whom they all claim as a member."

> Modern society is full of overlapping communities; an individual may belong to a family, a neighborhood, an ethnic group, a church, and a nation. Two of these intersecting communities—a church and a state—are kept distinct by the doctrine of separation. . . . The competition of secular and sacred communities ensures a balance between the separate and collective aspects of the self. Plurality prevents the overwhelming influence of a monolithic community from destroying separateness. . . . [V]ertical plurality also provides a basis for collective identity; the contrast among groups makes us aware of the extent of our membership in each as well as the extent of our separateness. . . .
> Vertical plurality preserves individual autonomy by maintaining a bal-

ance between two powerful institutions — a balance reminiscent of those maintained both by federalism and by the separation of powers within the federal government. Entanglement threatens this balance by bringing church and state into such close cooperation that they can no longer act as checks upon each other. When entanglement becomes an impediment to vertical plurality, it violates the establishment clause.[16]

This approach to religion clause jurisprudence is remarkably similar to the theory of pluralism I have articulated. When we evaluate identity claims in light of the four accounts of religious freedom at the end of this chapter, we will have occasion to return to these insights.

THE CONSTITUTIONAL CONTEXT OF
RELIGIOUS IDENTITY CLAIMS

The following sections introduce and illustrate three kinds of Free Exercise problems that seem to rest on perceived threats to religious identity. A religious identity may be threatened when by some official action a person is made to feel like an "outsider" because of her religious identity, or when official action subjects members of some religions to public disapprobation because of their religious identities. Additionally, the state may deprive a person or group of a symbol of religious identity. Finally, the state may deprive a group of the ability to create or sustain a religious identity. As always, not all claims are valid. Indeed, I shall conclude that some forms of the argument are more plausible than others; and some are quite problematic. Nevertheless, all are worthy of our attention. In the section that follows, I shall examine the general argument more critically, considering whether religious identity claims are worthy of constitutional protection, and if so, what might be their scope and limits.

Denigrating a Religious Identity or Marginalizing
a Person Because of Religious Identity

One of the emerging themes in Establishment Clause jurisprudence is a conception of the harm that is done to nonparticipants when majoritarian religious symbols or practices are incorporated into public life.[17] On several occasions, Justice O'Connor has attempted to formulate an approach to Establishment focusing on state endorsement of a religion or its symbols and the feelings of exclusion felt by religious minorities. The best statement of this point is her concurring opinion in *Lynch v Donnelly*, upholding public display of a crèche in Pawtucket, Rhode Island:

[A]ny endorsement of religion is invalid because it "sends a message to nonadherents that they are outsiders, not full members of the political community, and an accompanying message to adherents that they are insiders, favored members of the political community. Disapproval sends the opposite message. . . . What is crucial is that a government practice not have the effect of communicating a message of government endorsement or disapproval of religion. It is only practices having the effect, whether intentionally or unintentionally, that make religion relevant, in reality or public perception, to status in the political community." [18]

Government-sponsored religious exercises present identity problems to persons who do not wish to participate. To abstain from participation requires one to publicly separate herself from the community of participants. [19] The harm here is foisting on one the sense of being an outsider in one's country. We are familiar with harms to religious identity through the Establishment Clause, but certain kinds of deprivations might also implicate the Free Exercise Clause as well.

Denigration of one's religious identity by a public official would constitute this kind of harm. Either an individual or a religious institution should be able to claim Free Exercise protection against public denigration of religious identity without showing any further harm. But some claims of this sort may be problematic. Consider the occasional objections of Jewish parents to the reading of Shakespeare's *The Merchant of Venice* in public schools because of its characterization of Jews. Their argument is that the use of this material in public school curricula subjects Jewish children to disapprobation by association with the play's villain. The Alabama textbook cases, oddly enough, raise another version of this claim. In these cases, fundamentalist parents argued that their religion was being denigrated by *omission*; the failure to mention the role of religion in American life disparaged religion and parents' ability to sustain the Christian identity of their children. They argued that their children's religion had been demeaned and delegitimized by the textbooks' failure to recognize their role in society and their beliefs. [20] While I do not find either of these latter arguments compelling, I do find them illustrative of the genre of arguments that are worthy of First Amendment consideration.

The "Conceptions of Self" note described above captures the heart of this aspect of Free Exercise protection, although its author places more emphasis on the *choice* of identities than I think is warranted:

The boundary of permissible state action must therefore be determined by the effect such action has on the individual's choice of identity. . . .

When state action deprives the individual of full membership in the political community because of his choice of a particular religious affiliation, the state interferes with free exercise. The individual's choice of identity can be protected only if the political community offers him full membership regardless of his association with a religious community. Actions that merely make it less convenient to choose a particular religious identity do not violate the Free Exercise clause; they do not bring the membership requirements of the two communities into conflict. But government actions that condition a legal right, privilege, or duty of citizenship upon a certain choice of religious identity do prohibit free exercise, because legal rights and duties define full membership in the political community.[21]

By extension of this argument, many burdens to religious exercise are kinds of religious denigration. If we consider the group context of religious experience, we appreciate that laws aimed at unpopular religious practices are in fact methods of communicating to people that they are marginal. Laws like Hialeah's ordinance against animal sacrifice,[22] in the words of Kenneth Karst, are exercises in "status domination":

> Status domination is a zero-sum game, and one group's achievement of dominance is matched by the "status harm" to another group. The harm can be described as a stigma, or as the hurt of exclusion. The harm is experienced by a group of people, and it centers on their group membership. Some justices have been astute to recognize the importance of this injury to equal citizenship in deciding cases under the Establishment Clause, but the problem of status domination also implicates the Free Exercise clause. To understand why, we must pay serious attention not only to the liberty of individuals but also to the relations among groups.[23]

Attention to the group context of religious controversies may bring to light acts of discrimination in what otherwise appear to be "individual acts of unfairness." "Given the group-based focus of religious politics, an environment of group discrimination is likely to lead either to overt discrimination, as in the Hialeah case, or to indifference to religious minorities."[24] Recognition of the group context of religious discrimination does not itself create any new group rights to religious identity; it does make Free Exercise jurisprudence more attentive to the identity harms created by either discrimination or selective indifference.

Deprivation of Symbols of Religious Identity

Identity can easily become a sentimentalized abstraction. It is made concrete by actions that symbolize identity for the actor and other members of her community. Hence, denial of a symbol of religious identity may be the kind of deprivation that feels most oppressive to members of religious groups. In both *Goldman v Weinberger*[25] and Indian prisoner cases[26] individuals argued that they were denied an important external symbol of religious identity. It appears to me that religious identity makes much better sense of both of these cases than do claims based on religious conscience. Recall that in discussing religious conscience, we encountered a serious problem. If a judge demanded to know whether Captain Goldman felt religiously compelled to cover his head, the state would be delving into far more theological inquiry than should be permissible under the First Amendment. However, if we simply recognize that a yarmulke is an important Jewish religious symbol, these kinds of questions are entirely avoided. Similarly, in a Native American prisoner case, judges raised awkward questions about the centrality of braids in Cree religious belief. That form of inquiry also proved to be fraught with difficulties. Again, a simpler starting point would be the recognition that braids are a symbol of religious identity; inquiry could proceed from that point.

An illustrative parallel, fortunately outside the American experience, is *forced* religious identity, such as the Nazi requirements that Jews wear the detested yellow stars. This tragedy provides painful examples of the destructive use of forced symbols of identity.

Deprivation of a symbol of religious identity might not stand alone as a constitutional claim, but the concept is useful in helping comprehend the nature of some kinds of religious practices. Some of the problems we observed in Chapter 5 in recognizing religious practices might be clarified by considering religious identity symbols as part of religious practices.

Depriving a Group of the Opportunity to Create or Sustain a Religious Identity

Wisconsin v Yoder could be seen as a religious identity case if one apprehends that what was at stake was the right of a religious community to protect its collective identity by limiting external influences on its youth. There is some statutory precedent for approaching religious rights in this way. Under the American Indian Religious Freedom Act, Native Americans may make First Amendment claims for the protection of sacred sites or objects by arguing that the places or objects or practices are necessary to maintaining the *identity* of the religious group.[27] Thus, the statute creates for Native

Americans a kind of right to religious identity. Under this interpretation, the petitions of Native Americans to protect religious sites might also be viewed as religious identity claims. This approach makes more sense of the sacred land cases than do interpretations based on religious conscience.

To pursue this line of reasoning would require judges to consider the ways in which identities are created and maintained. We have already observed how important rituals are in sustaining the sense of belonging. Likewise, personal care requirements that set the person apart from nonbelievers are identity creators. Observant Jews define themselves, in part, as persons who faithfully keep the dietary restrictions of Orthodox Judaism; Christian Scientists define themselves (and are defined by others) as those who abjure mainstream medicine. Again, these examples do not necessarily create a freestanding constitutional right to a religious identity. However, they do deepen our understanding of the importance of these practices to religious freedom.

In spite of its initial attractiveness, an alleged right of a group to develop or sustain a religious identity raises immense threshold problems. What kinds of groups could claim such rights? Does a group without an identity have a collective right to develop one? What would make an identity a *religious* one? Is this a collective right, and if so, of whom? In light of the continually fragmenting nature of many American religious groups, the religious identity argument would seem to raise almost impossible boundary problems. At the very least, it would take extremely careful articulation to construct this kind of claim. However, I maintain that Free Exercise jurisprudence would be enriched by being open to well-constructed claims regarding identity rights.

EVALUATING RELIGIOUS IDENTITY CLAIMS

Considering identity claims requires us to confront the nature of both religion and the American polity. Our points of departure are, as always, the five proposed accounts of the religion clauses. How would each of our proposed accounts approach religious identity claims?

The first two seem relatively simple and relatively unsympathetic to identity claims. In fact, the first account, which understands the First Amendment as protecting freedom of religious *choice*, is virtually antithetical to the notion of religious identity expounded by sociologists. Religion—to put it crudely—is a way of *foreclosing* choices. Religion sacralizes certain identities. In Mol's words, it puts "don't touch" signs around a commitment and enables the identity bearer to treat it is something "given" rather than something to be continually reevaluated. There is a virtual antipathy between the free choice notion of the First Amendment and a demand for special deference to religious identities.

The second account is perhaps less hostile but almost as unsympathetic. It views religious freedom in terms of the protection of individual conscience. There is, of course, a considerable overlap between religious conscience and religious identity. For example, in Hans Mol's analysis, morality provides concrete rules by which members of an identity group recognize themselves and each other.[28] But to focus on religious identity is to see morality as in service to identity, whereas to focus on conscience would be to understand that relationship reversed. Hence, while protecting actions commanded by religious conscience might well guard the rules that sustain identity, identity claims would have no independent weight.

The remaining principles take better account of religion as a communal phenomenon, although not always sympathetically. The third account attempts to protect the state from religious controversy. While this approach understands that religion is a group phenomenon, it emphasizes the disruptive and divisive functions of religion in a heterogeneous society. Strongly held—and certainly exclusive—religious identities would be viewed from this perspective as potential sources of conflict and divided loyalties. (The long-held distrust of Catholics and Jews in Protestant America was often phrased in terms of their extranational loyalties.) In short, one should not look to this view for strong support of religious identity claims.

The fourth account, which views religion as a source of countervailing power, is far more sympathetic. One can hardly overemphasize the importance of religious identities as sources of political power. In this approach, fostering a plurality of religious identities would help counter the totalizing and monopolizing tendencies of the state. Still, this is a defensive argument. This view does not appreciate the value of identities as attributes of well-being but rather sees them as instrumental defenses against excessive governmental power. Such an instrumental concept of religion offers poor protection for religion when public well-being is perceived to be at stake.

The fifth account is undoubtedly the most sympathetic to religious identity claims, while it still offers guidance for limiting them. In this view, the underlying "purpose" of the religion clauses is to protect alternate sources of meaning within the context of full and equal citizenship. Since religious identities are among the most important sources of meaning, they are crucial to both individual well-being and a healthy polity. This approach is unabashedly pluralistic; it celebrates modernism and the fragmentation of identities that many religious conservatives bemoan.[29]

Segmented identities seem to be a key characteristic of pluralism (perhaps of modernity itself). This point is nicely described by Samuel Heilman in his discussion of the alleged dangers to Jewish solidarity posed by sectarian disagreements over "who is a Jew." Heilman persuasively argues that in contemporary society such disagreements do not pose the schismatic danger they once did because we are accustomed to fluid identities:

> The modern society reflects the compartmentalization of individual life by creating divisions in all sorts of domains and at the same time frequently effacing those divisions. . . .
>
> What does all this mean for Jewish unity? It means, first that we can no longer consider modern Jews only in terms of their corporate identity. . . . They are not only Jews; they are Jews and lots of other things. And sometimes they may choose to make their Jewishness primary, active, and salient; while at other times, it remains secondary, dormant, or irrelevant to their lives. For many, it is only one aspect of their identity. . . . [I]n the modern world, partial affiliations and divided loyalties are perfectly normal and acceptable. In such a world, the idea that one either is a Jew or one is not is replaced by the notion that in some circumstances and ways one may be Jewish while in others one may not be. Compartmentalization is a fact of modern existence.[30]

An essential feature of pluralism is the discouragement of exclusive identities. The pluralist vision welcomes segmented, fluid ones. The religion clauses are successful when they enable people to maintain religious and national identities, unsuccessful when government forces a choice between them. A pluralistic vision would therefore likely be exceptionally sympathetic to Captain Goldman's petition to wear his yarmulke *with* his Air Force uniform. The very point of Goldman's petition was to wear the symbol of *both* identities, in effect, to be an Orthodox Jew while being a U.S. military officer. Similarly, this vision would likely be sympathetic to Little Bird of the Snow, who wishes to retain her Native American religious identity while still partaking in the benefits of the welfare state.[31] Likewise, it would support the arguments of members of religious subcultures who seek to preserve the conditions necessary for the maintenance of identity against governmental intrusion. For the same reasons, this approach would easily protect persons against at least the most egregious official denigration of their religious identities.

The pluralistic approach also offers guidance on Establishment cases. While it favors separate and partial identities protected by the Free Exercise Clause, it would clearly reject efforts to imbue the public sphere with religious meanings. This approach looks with disfavor on any unified identity system. We recall the words of the author of the note on "Conceptions of the Self": "The religion clauses, by mandating a social commitment to plurality and choice, protect the formation of the separate and collective aspects of identity. Government must share its influence over the individual's identity both with various other communities and with the individual himself. The political community must be willing to accept — to the limits of its legitimacy — the individual's commitment to other identities."[32]

Of course, some religions reject pluralism and aspire to monistic identity; the demand that America be declared a Christian nation expresses such a vision. The Establishment Clause is an important protection against this kind of affront to pluralism. As we shall see in Chapter 9, persons and groups that find multiple identities painful pose the most serious challenge to this pluralist vision. Some do so by retreating to insular communities that strive for a "seamless" existence. Others take a "redemptionist" stance and seek to reform the wider society. Together, they illustrate some of the most admirable and frightening elements of American society. Yet, the pluralist theory, with its preference for fragmented identities, is ultimately unsympathetic to both. We shall have to consider whether this facet of the pluralist vision proves to be its strength or its fatal flaw.

Should religious identity claims be constitutionalized as part of our understanding of the Free Exercise Clause? At this point, a right to religious identity is probably not strong enough to stand alone, but its recognition would be extremely helpful in understanding what is at stake in several other kinds of Free Exercise controversies. For example, a greater appreciation of religious identity would help courts understand the functions that controversial religious practices perform for their members. This understanding, in turn, should be especially important when the protection of religious communities or institutions is at stake. Even if we stop short of recognizing identity interests as independent constitutional claims, appreciating the importance of religious identity would surely enrich our understanding of the beliefs, practices, and institutions by which religion is sustained.[33]

7

BURDENS ON RELIGIOUS EXERCISE

TO PROHIBIT AND TO BURDEN

The opening words of the First Amendment are a clear admonition against searching for legal understanding in the literal meaning of the individual words. The religion clauses read: "Congress shall make no law respecting an establishment of religion or prohibiting the free exercise thereof." To "prohibit" a religious exercise is indeed a very serious infringement on religious liberty, but it is only one of the ways in which liberty may be trammeled. At least since *Sherbert v Verner*,[1] the Court has considered First Amendment issues invoked when religious exercise is *burdened*. But what constitutes a burden, and how serious must it be to present a constitutionally cognizable problem? How confident can we be in distinguishing a major impediment to religious worship from a *de minimis* annoyance?

The notion of a *burden* serves as another threshold to the Free Exercise Clause—or in Ira Lupu's words, a "gatekeeper." Lupu argues that recent court decisions have raised the threshold, allowing judges to avoid constitutional issues by determining that harms to religion are insufficiently serious to trigger constitutional protection.[2] Any full account of religious freedom must include an account of what harms religion, and that involves thinking about the ways religion is vulnerable. In keeping with our nonessentialist approach to religion in general, in this chapter I will argue that burdens to religious freedom cannot be reduced to any single element.

Harms to religious freedom are experienced in a variety of ways. This chapter begins by surveying and analyzing the ways that government acts may adversely affect religious exercise. The remainder of the chapter is devoted to attempts to bring coherence to this variety by searching for an inclusive understanding of what is at stake when religion is burdened. Every interpretation of burdens on religion implies its own view of what religion is and why it is important.[3] Those who hold an individualist view of religion, based on either choice or conscience, tend to focus on coercion as the paradigmatic harm. Those who view religion as a group phenomenon tend to see some form of inequality as the essential violation. The least controversial case in recent Free Exercise history, the 1992 animal sacrifice case, illustrates both kinds of harm and will serve as our introduction to both approaches. Hialeah's ordinances against animal sacrifice exemplified *both* paradigmatic burdens to religious exercise—the coercion of religion through a criminal penalty of its worship ritual and a poorly disguised animus directed at a religious minority. While both approaches capture important characterizations of religious harms, neither alone provides a sufficient common denominator. The pluralist account encompasses the strengths of both, and ultimately, this is the approach that enables us to understand what is at stake when religious freedom is burdened. Nevertheless, we must be very cautious in our conclusions. Even if we were able to identify religious harms with certainty, we would not be able to conclude that the First Amendment has been violated; some burdens are justified by countervailing social interests. In Chapter 8 we will continue the inquiry by focusing on the ways religious freedom and other interests are balanced.

A SURVEY OF BURDENS TO RELIGIOUS FREEDOM

Burdens on religious freedom are experienced in a number of ways. Some laws literally prohibit a religious exercise; some condition government benefits on behavior inconsistent with religion; others make a religious practice impossible; and some do not seem to fit any of these categories. In order to make sense out of this unruly list of burdens we must return to our general theories to determine what is at stake when religious freedom is denied.

Penalties on Religious Acts

The most obvious burdens on religious freedom are those, like the ordinances in the Santeria case, that literally prohibit a religious exercise. Criminal penalties on religious practices—especially worship practices such as snake handling, peyote ingestion, and animal sacrifice—seem particularly egregious because they violate the most literal reading of the First Amendment. Personal care and acculturated religious practices, ranging from polygamy to the use of prayer rather than traditional medicine to cure the sick, have been also subject to criminal penalties. And finally, *religious institutions* have been subject to criminal penalties, such as those imposed for violation of the Fair Labor Standards Act.

Criminal sanctions are not the only kind of legal penalties on religious acts. Laws authorizing civil damages have the same effect. Equal Employment Opportunity statutes allow persons harmed by discrimination a cause of action to seek civil damages. When employers are assessed civil damages for religiously motivated but discriminatory employment practices, they too may argue that their religious practices have been penalized. Civil penalties against "cults" for their recruiting practices likewise illustrate this kind of burden.

These prohibitions infringe on the freedom of religious choice and, in many cases, of conscience as well. Still, all of us can imagine religiously inspired acts that would uncontroversially violate the criminal law. Acts of terrorism by religiously motivated groups obviously fall into this category.

The 1990 *Smith* case illustrates some of the complexities of laws penalizing religious practices.[4] Because criminal penalties so overly "prohibit" a religious exercise, one might think such laws would be the most suspect. Oddly, however, Justice Scalia's majority opinion in *Smith* treats criminal laws as *least* likely to require accommodation. Even odder, the *Smith* majority treated what appeared to be an ordinary unemployment compensation dispute as a criminal case in order to reach that conclusion. The very ambiguity of the legal issues provided the justices opportunities to reflect on the particular problems of criminal penalties against religious practices.

Recall briefly the situation: Smith and Black had been terminated from their jobs for using peyote during a ceremony of the Native American Church; their request for unemployment compensation was denied because they were fired for "job-related" wrongdoing. They appealed the denial, and both the appellate and Oregon Supreme Court ruled that religious exercises could not be considered misconduct for purposes of denying state benefits. The criminal law was irrelevant at this point.

Oregon petitioned for certiorari to the U.S. Supreme Court, which vacated the state decisions and remanded the case to the Oregon courts to determine whether state law prohibited sacramental peyote use. The Supreme Court reasoned that if a state could punish an act by criminal law, it could justify the lesser penalty of denying benefits. It is important to recall that *Smith* itself is not a criminal case. Neither Smith nor Black—nor anyone else for that matter—had been prosecuted in Oregon for peyote use in a religious ritual.

On remand, the Oregon Supreme Court concluded that (unlike twenty-three other states and the federal government) Oregon law "makes no exception for the sacramental use," but it also noted that if the state should ever attempt to enforce the law against religious practice, that prosecution would violate the Free Exercise Clause of the U.S. Constitution. Hence, in the state court's view, the existence of the criminal law was irrelevant to the unemployment compensation issue.

The U.S. Supreme Court again granted certiorari. In April 1990 it overturned Oregon's judgment that the application of the criminal statute to religious practices would be unconstitutional. The specific question before the Court in *Smith* was the denial of unemployment compensation for engaging in a religious ritual. The precedents requiring unemployment compensation when religious acts have led to job termination were too consistent to explain away. The only distinguishing factor in this case was the existence of a criminal law prohibiting peyote use. For the majority, the existence of the criminal statute distinguished *Smith* from the preceding cases. Consequently, the majority treated this as a criminal penalty case—although Oregon's highest court had twice ruled that the criminal penalty was irrelevant to Smith and Black's right to unemployment compensation, since a state criminal penalty on a religious observance would violate the Free Exercise Clause.

Both Justice Blackmun's dissent and many of the Court's critics have pointed out that the majority was thus ruling on a purely hypothetical issue —and resting a major constitutional ruling on an issue that had never arisen and that the highest state court had ruled to be irrelevant. Justice Blackmun's dissent points to the extraordinary judicial activism that was involved in formulating this as a criminal penalty case: "I have grave doubts . . . as to the wisdom or propriety of deciding the constitutionality of a criminal prohibition which the State has not sought to enforce, which the State did not rely on in defending its denial of unemployment benefits before the state courts, and which the Oregon courts could, on remand, either invalidate on state constitutional grounds, or conclude that it remains irrelevant to Oregon's interest in administering its unemployment benefits program."

The criticism Justice Scalia's opinion elicited has been well deserved. Nevertheless, his point bears serious consideration. To insist that people have a constitutional *right* to exemptions from the criminal law for religiously motivated behavior would render ineffectual the criminal law and produce a kind of anarchy. If nothing else, the public interest in a rule of law informs Scalia's position. The argument's relative merits and its adversaries will be considered at length in Chapter 8, when we consider various approaches to reconciling Free Exercise conflicts.

Denial of Benefits

Far more common than outright prohibitions are the denials of government benefits because of some aspect of religious practice. Typically in these instances, a government benefit is conditioned on the recipient foregoing some aspect of her religious practice. The landmark case on unconstitutional conditions of governmental benefits involved a problem of this kind. Adelle Sherbert, a Seventh-Day Adventist, was unable to continue her employment at a South Carolina textile mill when Saturday work became required.[5] She was terminated for refusal to work on Saturday and denied unemployment compensation because her termination was viewed as voluntary. Typical regulations deny such benefits to persons who have quit their jobs voluntarily, who have been terminated from their jobs for cause, or who have refused to make themselves available for employment. However, when a person's religious practices are the source of her quitting, termination, or unavailability, the denial of unemployment benefits would involve the state in the obstruction of religious freedom. Kathleen Sullivan has observed a small and seldom noticed peculiarity in this reasoning: "Ms Sherbert could not have obtained unemployment compensation by violating her conscience; if she worked on Saturday, she would not have needed unemployment compensation."[6]

The decision in *Sherbert v Verner* in 1963 established that state denial of benefits to a person who refused to accept a job that required her to work on her Sabbath would constitute a denial of Free Exercise. In its decision the Court made it quite clear that the First Amendment forbids the denial of benefits to an individual for his religious practices as well as their outright prohibition. "It is too late in the day to doubt that the liberties of religion and expression may be infringed by the denial or placing conditions upon a benefit or a privilege. . . . [T]o condition the availability of benefits upon this appellant's willingness to violate a cardinal principle of her religious faith effectively penalizes the free exercise of her constitutional liberties."[7]

Subsequent unemployment compensation cases have affirmed that this benefit cannot be denied to persons who have lost their jobs for engaging in religious practices. In *Hobbie v Unemployment Commission* the Court reaffirmed that principle, applying it to a person who had adopted a new religion after accepting employment.[8] In *Thomas v Review Board* the Court ruled that the state could not deny compensation to a person who resigned his job because his religious conviction prohibited his working on armaments, even if other members of his faith felt no such moral restrictions. Chief Justice Burger made the reasoning regarding denial of benefits in this case quite clear: "Where the state conditions receipt of an important benefit upon conduct proscribed by a religious faith, or where it denies such benefits because of conduct mandated by religious belief, thereby putting substantial pressure on an adherent to violate his beliefs, a burden upon religion exists. While the compulsion may be indirect, the infringement upon free exercise is nonetheless substantial."[9]

In *Frazee v Illinois Department of Employment Security* a unanimous Court reaffirmed the same reasoning, granting benefits for a Christian who refused to work on his Sabbath, even though his belief was not based on the teachings of an identifiable sect or church to which he belonged.[10]

The activist regulatory and welfare state multiplies the contacts between government and religious observers. Regulations and requirements that to the majority seem religiously neutral occasionally do conflict with religious commitments. When these requirements are conditions for the receipt of government benefits, Free Exercise conflicts arise. As we have seen, these conditions may arise even from ordinary administrative record keeping requirements, such as the social security number in *Bowen v Roy*,[11] or the requirement of a photo driver's license in *Quaring v Peterson*.[12]

Religious institutions, as well as individuals, may consider that their governmental benefits are purchased at the price of foregoing constitutional rights. The Internal Revenue Code 501(c)(3) provides tax exemptions for nonprofit institutions on the condition that they refrain from participating in political campaign and that no substantial portion of their activity is devoted to political advocacy. These restrictions have been challenged as imposing unconstitutional conditions for receipt of a governmental benefit, but they were upheld by the Supreme Court in *Regan v Taxation with Representation*.[13]

These cases force us to consider whether, when, and why religious freedom is burdened by conditioning a governmental benefit upon foregoing some religious practice. After all, there is a certain plausibility to thinking of these cases as simple bargains arrived at by mutual agreement. If government is free to grant or withhold benefits at will, why may it not impose whatever restrictions it chooses on them? And why is it wrong for government to impose conditions upon benefits that individuals are free to accept or refuse at their own volition?

Recently, in a seminal article on unconstitutional conditions, Kathleen Sullivan produced a systematic attempt to address that very question. Her analysis sheds considerable light on our understanding of religious free exercise. "The doctrine of unconstitutional conditions holds that government may not grant a benefit on the condition that the beneficiary surrender a constitutional right, even if the government may withhold that benefit altogether. It reflects the triumph of the view that government may not do indirectly what it may not do directly."[14]

After surveying a range of explanations for why unconstitutional conditions are wrong, she proposes an impressive argument about the harm of such conditions. She begins her argument by noting that constitutional guarantees "do not just protect individual rightholders piecemeal," but they affect the "distribution of power between government and rightholders generally, and among classes of rightholders." Her argument is worth quoting at length:

> Unconstitutional conditions, no less than "direct" infringements, can skew this distribution in three ways. First, they can alter the balance of power between government and rightholders. Preferred constitutional liberties generally declare desirable some realm of autonomy that should remain free from government encroachment. Government freedom to redistribute power over presumptively autonomous decisions from the citizenry to itself through the leverage of permissible spending or regulation would jeopardize that realm. Second, an unconstitutional condition can skew the distribution of constitutional rights *among* rightholders because it necessarily discriminates facially between those who do and those who do not comply with the condition. If government has an obligation of evenhandedness of neutrality with regard to a right, this sort of redistribution is inappropriate. Third, to the extent that a condition discriminates de facto between those who do and do not depend on a government benefit, it can create an undesirable caste hierarchy in the enjoyment of constitutional rights.[15]

Each one of the concerns expressed in this theory is relevant to our understanding of burdens to free religious exercise, and each corresponds loosely with the kinds of concerns encompassed in our five approaches to religious freedom. First, unconstitutional conditions infringe upon spheres of autonomy, which are not only necessary to preserve self-determination but also to check the power of the state. Second, benefits can be so targeted as to endanger government equality, neutrality, and evenhandedness among its citizens. Finally, conditioned benefits affect the distribution of rights among individual citizens; conditions have vastly different impacts depending on where the affected person is situated in the social hierarchy. Those who need the governmental benefit are much less free to exercise their constitutional rights than those who do not. "[B]ackground inequalities of wealth and resources necessarily determine ones bargaining position in relation to government, and ... the poor may have nothing to trade but their liberties."[16] In

Ms. Sherbert's case, for example, she was far less able to continue her Saturday worship than was another member of her faith who did not need either a job or unemployment compensation. To Sullivan, these dangers would not automatically invalidate all conditions to government benefits but would certainly require strict scrutiny.

Making Religious Acts Impossible

Some of the greatest burdens on religious practice are virtually invisible because the very possibility of these acts has been precluded. Some government acts simply make it impossible for a person to engage in a religious practice. For example, local courts may appoint a guardian ad litem to consent to blood transfusions on behalf of members of the Jehovah's Witness faith whose religion forbids it. People who are given court-ordered blood transfusions are simply not able to practice their religion; their choice—even the choice to act and suffer a penalty—is effectively removed. They are often physically, as well as legally, in no position to object to the transfusion; they can only passively receive it.[17] I suggest that this burden is even more powerful than is typically recognized. Unlike laws penalizing religious actions, which a person may choose to violate, these laws simply remove the opportunity to engage in the act.

Governmental destruction of Native American sacred lands, the religious sites necessary for ceremonies, is another dramatic example of this kind of "burden." The analogy—although perhaps an exaggerated one—would be the "burden" on ancient Judaism by the destruction of the Temple; in that case, mandated rituals were simply no longer possible. The government's act was not a penalty on a religious practice; it simply prohibited the practice altogether. The case of *Lyng v Northwest Cemetery Protective Association*[18] illustrates these kinds of threats to religious freedom and the perils in the refusal to recognize them.

As part of the tragic history of U.S. acquisition of the North American continent from Native American peoples, many of their sacred sites came to be owned by the U.S. government. As long as the lands were in remote places and "undeveloped," Native Americans continued to maintain the sacred sites and use the land for traditional worship practices. As pressure for development and other uses of these lands grew, government often had to choose between traditional Native American practices and other uses. Because the sites were considered sacred, once they were devoted to other uses, long-standing religious rituals, integral to the spiritual life of a people, were no longer possible.

In spite of legal challenges, in recent decades these sites have been taken over for water developments, tourist facilities, and other projects.[19] The 1988 *Lyng* case involved a conflict between the continued ceremonial use of National Forest Service lands in Northern California and the building of a road to make local logging more efficient. A study by the National Forest Service had concluded that the road "would cause serious and irreparable damage to the sacred areas which are an integral and necessary part of the belief systems and lifeway of the Northwest California Indian peoples" and recommended abandoning the project. Nevertheless, the service decided to proceed with the plan, prompting a Free Exercise challenge. Both the district court and Court of Appeals enjoined the building of the road on Free Exercise grounds.[20]

Reversing the lower courts, the Supreme Court approved the road building project, and in the process, signaled some important shifts in Free Exercise law. First, the Court rejected the centrality test, refusing to consider whether the ceremony in question was central to the religious life of the people in question. Second, the majority viewed the road project simply as internal governmental business indistinguishable from the government's use of social security numbers approved in *Bowen v Roy*.[21] Justice O'Connor argued that no religious group could expect government to conduct *its own business* in conformity with that group's religious needs. Finally, and directly to the point here, the majority substantially diminished the notion of harm to religious free exercise.

In discussing the concept of sacredness in Chapter 2, I argue that *Lyng* and similar decisions rest upon the majority's narrow conception of a religion—and the failure to take seriously the notion of the sacred, a crucial characteristic of religion. There is perhaps an implicit, but misplaced, parallel between the lands and a church. A church, after all, can be moved. The church may be consecrated, but consecration is a human act, and human acts can also deconsecrate it. The lands were sacred in a different way. The place itself was associated with the divine, and certain religious experiences could happen only there.

Furthermore, the majority's decision seems to rest on a peculiarly limited definition of the word "prohibit" in the First Amendment; the government did not actually "prohibit" any religious practice by penalizing it or depriving its adherents of privileges enjoyed by others. Quoting *Sherbert v Verner*, the majority said: "The crucial word in the constitutional text is 'prohibit'; 'For the Free Exercise clause is written in terms of what the government cannot do to the individual, not in terms of what the individual can extract from the government.' According to this reasoning, the 'incidental effects of the governmental program make it more difficult to practice certain religions, but . . . have no tendency to coerce individuals into acting contrary to their religious beliefs.' "[22]

Making a religious practice more difficult, the Court ruled, is not the kind of act that must be justified by compelling state interest. Hence, because of the way the religious practice was burdened (removing the resource that had made it possible), the government was not required to show compelling state interest sufficient to override the religious freedom. By minimizing the notion of harm, the majority avoided the compelling state interest test and relied instead on its finding that the challenged policy was religiously neutral and uniform in application.

The *Lyng* majority seemed to imply that rendering a religious practice impossible is somehow less burdensome on religious exercise than a penalty or the denial of a benefit. In fact, because it does not *compel* behavior but only precludes it, it is no burden at all. Justice Brennan's dissent is devastating on this point:

> None of the religious adherents in *Hobbie*, *Thomas*, and *Sherbert*, for example, claimed or could have claimed that the denial of unemployment benefits rendered the practice of their religions impossible; at most, the challenged laws made those practices more expensive. Here, in sharp contrast, respondents have claimed—and proved—that the desecration of the high country will prevent religious leaders from attaining the religious power or medicine indispensable to the success of virtually all their rituals and ceremonies. . . . Here the threat posed by the desecration of sacred lands that are indisputably essential to respondents' religious practices is both more direct and more substantial than that raised by a compulsory school law that simply exposed Amish children to an alien value system. And of course, respondents here do not even have the option, however unattractive it might be, of migrating to more hospitable locales; the site-specific nature of their belief system renders it nontransportable. . . . [R]eligious freedom is threatened no less by governmental action that makes the practice of ones chosen faith impossible than by governmental programs that pressure one to engage in conduct inconsistent with religious beliefs.[23]

What insights would our various understandings of the Free Exercise Clause offer on *Lyng* and similar cases? Clearly, if the clause is understood to protect either the freedom of religious choice (our first account) or the protection of religious conscience (our second account), no great harm has been done. No act is compelled, nor is any conscience violated. Nor is interreligious hostility exacerbated, as in the third account, nor is the power of a countervailing institution adversely affected, as in the forth account. Hence, any of these explanations of the Free Exercise Clause would find no constitutional obstacle to the destruction of sacred lands. However, the fifth account seems to argue differently. If the First Amendment protects alternate sources of meaning and the ritual performed on the sacred land is a source of spiritual power to members of the community, they are denied the acquisition of that spiritual growth when its source is removed. That the majority cannot quite conceive of an irreplaceable sacred place complicates the problem for the Native American believers, but it should not diminish the seriousness of their loss. Indeed, only the fifth account enables us fully to appreciate the significance of *Lyng*. The overall failure of the *Lyng* decision is that the Court majority could not take seriously or protect alternate systems of meaning.

Additional Burdens

Not every burden on religious freedom fits into the categories described above. Consider the law overturned in *McDaniel v Paty*,[24] which had prohibited members of the clergy from holding public office. The prohibition neither makes a religious practice impossible nor penalizes it, and although it does deny a benefit, that does not seem to capture the heart of the harm. The harm in this case is a public demonstration of distrust of the civic commitments of members of the clergy—the fear that clergy will be advocates for their own sects rather than pursuers of the public interest. Distrust is also the main message in *Larson v Valente*;[25] Minnesota's law conveyed a clear public statement that religions that seek significant support from nonmembers cannot be trusted to solicit or use their funds honestly.

The *Mozert*[26] case raises a different problem. The school curriculum entailed no obvious penalty, nor even denial of benefit, nor was religious practice made impossible. Rather, parents were alleging that their children's beliefs were diminished, delegitimated, and marginalized by the subject matter in public school materials that conflicted with their own religious principles. These cases are only illustrative of the wide variety of ways people perceive their religious freedom to be burdened. Lacking any essential elements for identifying burdens, we must return to our basic principles to discover what liberties are at stake.

RELIGIOUS FREEDOM AND ITS BURDENS

Neither what defines religious practices nor the actions that burden them seem to be reducible to a common core. However, our survey does illuminate several distinct approaches to the way harm is formulated. When religion is conceived as a matter of choice or conscience, coercion of the individual is the harm. The approaches that emphasize the group basis of religion emphasize unequal treatment as the essential harm. The 1993 Santeria case illustrates both kinds of harms and, hence, both approaches.

Church of the Lukumi Babalu Aye, Inc., and Ernesto Pichado v City of Hialeah [27]

Laws passed specifically to target a particular religion for unfavorable treatment have been fortunately rare in our history. Thus it was somewhat surprising when one reached the Supreme Court during the 1993 term. Even more surprising was the fact that the law in question had been upheld by the district courts and Appeals Courts; seldom has a law seemed so uncontroversially invalid. The Afro-Caribbean religion known as Santeria involves the worship of deities and celebration of life-cycle events by offering sacrifices of chickens, goats, and other animals. In both the United States and the Caribbean, it is usually practiced clandestinely. When a congregation in Hialeah, Florida, announced plans to lease property for a church and practice openly, the city council adopted a resolution that declared the city's commitment to prohibiting acts by religious groups "inconsistent with public morals, peace and safety" and then adopted a number of resolutions prohibiting animal sacrifice and the possession of animals intended for ritual slaughter. At face value these ordinances constituted a law "prohibiting the free exercise of religion." Moreover, they specifically exempted virtually any other kind of animal killing.

The district court upheld the laws on the grounds that "specifically regulating religious conduct does not violate the First Amendment when [the activity] is deemed inconsistent with public health and welfare."[28] On appeal, the Eleventh Circuit affirmed in a one-paragraph per curium opinion.[29] When the case reached the Supreme Court, the justices unanimously struck down the ordinances. Since there was no question that the ordinances prohibited a form of worship, at issue was whether the prohibition could be justified. Hialeah argued that the laws were valid secular public health measures; the church characterized them as religious discrimination—the kind of laws that the *Smith* majority three years previously had declared to be the prototype for Free Exercise violations. Although the decision in favor of the church was unanimous, the Court divided into two factions: Justice Kennedy, writing for himself and Justices Scalia, Rehnquist, White, and Thomas, accepted the *Smith* distinction between targeted and inadvertent burdens; Justices Souter, Blackmun, and O'Connor rejected the *Smith* reasoning.

Justice Kennedy's majority opinion began from the premise that laws specifically targeting religions must meet compelling state interest scrutiny. The question for the majority was how to identify such laws. The offending statute's use of words with religious significance, such as "ritual" and "sacrifice," undoubtedly suggests a focus on religion, but that use was not dispositive since those words can also have secular meanings. Much more significant was the law's "religious gerrymandering." Through a complex set of definitions, exclusions, and exemptions, the law managed to prohibit the killing of animals in religious rituals but permit virtually every other kind of animal killing commonly practiced.

> Ordinance 87-40 incorporates the Florida animal cruelty statute . . . punishing "whoever . . . unnecessarily kills any animal." . . . Killings for religious reasons are deemed unnecessary, whereas most other killings fall outside the prohibition. The city . . . deems hunting, slaughter of animals for food, eradication of insects and pests, and euthanasia as necessary. There is no indication in the record that respondent has concluded that hunting or fishing for sport is unnecessary. Indeed one of the few reported Florida cases decided under s.828.12 concludes that the use of live rabbits to train greyhounds is not unnecessary. . . . Respondent's application of the ordinance's test of necessity devalues religious reasons for killing by judging them to be of lesser import than nonreligious reasons. Thus, religious practice is being singled out for discriminatory treatment.[30]

The law was not "generally applicable" either.[31] The city council defended the law as necessary to protect public health and to avoid unnecessary cruelty to animals. However, gerrymandering had rendered the law both over- and underinclusive on both points.

> Respondent claims that [the] Ordinances advance two interests: protecting the public health and preventing cruelty to animals. The ordinances are underinclusive for those ends. They fail to prohibit non-religious conduct that endangers these interests in a similar or greater degree than Santeria sacrifice does. The underinclusion is substantial, not inconsequential. Despite the city's proffered interest in preventing cruelty to animals, the ordinances are drafted with care to forbid few killings but those occasioned by religious sacrifice. Many types of animals' deaths or kills for nonreligious reason are either not prohibited or approved by express provision. For example, fishing . . . is legal. Extermination of mice and rats within a home is also permitted. Florida law . . . sanctions euthanasia for

"stray, neglected, abandoned or unwanted animals . . . ," destruction of animals judicially removed from their owners "for humanitarian reasons," or when the animal "is of no commercial value," the infliction of pain or suffering "in the interest of medical science," the placing of poison in one's yard or enclosure, and the use of a live animal "to pursue or take wildlife or to participate in any hunting" and "to hunt wild hogs."

The city concedes that "neither the State of Florida nor the city has enacted a generally applicable ban on the killing of animals." It asserts, however, that animal sacrifice is "different" from the animal killings that are permitted by law. According to the city, it is "self evident" that killing animals for food is "important"; the eradication of insects and pests is "obviously justified," and the euthanasia of excess animals "makes sense." These *ipse dixits* do not explain why religion alone must bear the burden of the ordinances, when many of the secular killings fall within the city's interest in preventing the cruel treatment of animals.

The ordinances are also underinclusive with regard to the city's interest in public health, which is threatened by the disposal of animal carcasses in open public places and the consumption of uninspected meat. Neither interest is pursued by respondent with regard to conduct that is not motivated by religious conviction. The health risks posed by improper disposal of animal carcasses are the same whether Santeria sacrifice or some non-religious killing preceded it. The city does not, however, prohibit hunters from bringing their kill to their houses, nor does it regulate disposal after their activity. . . . [R]estaurants are outside the scope of the ordinance.

The ordinances are underinclusive as well with regard to the health risk posed by the consumption of uninspected meat. Under the city's ordinances, hunters may eat their kill and fishermen may eat their catch without undergoing government inspection. . . .

We conclude, in sum, that each of Hialeah's ordinances pursues the city's interests only against conduct motivated by religious activity. The ordinances have every appearance of a prohibition that society is prepared to impose upon [Santeria worshipers] but not upon itself. . . . This precise evil is what the requirement of general applicability is designed to prevent.

The inescapable conclusion of this gerrymandering was the fact that the law specifically was aimed at prohibiting Santeria religious practices. Another factor in Justice Kennedy's opinion was the legislative record, which was replete with specific statements of intent to outlaw Santeria practices. The use of this kind of evidence prompted a separate opinion by Justice Scalia, who (joined by the Chief Justice) rejected reliance on legislative intent.

The First Amendment does not refer to the purposes for which legislatures enact laws, but to the effects of the laws enacted. . . . This does not put us in the business of invalidating laws by reason of the evil motives of their authors. Had the Hialeah City Council set out resolutely to suppress the practices of Santeria, but ineptly adopted ordinances that failed to do so, I do not see how these laws could be said to "prohibit the free exercise" of religion. Nor, in my view, does it matter that a legislature consists entirely of the pure hearted, if the law it enacts in fact singles out a religious practice for special burdens. Had the ordinance here been passed with no motive on the part of any council man except the ardent desire to prevent cruelty to animals . . . , they would nevertheless be invalid.

On the surface, the disagreement between Justices Kennedy and Scalia here is a minor one—the significance of evidence of intentional animus. In fact, this question is a familiar one in equal opportunity law; is discrimination to be observed by evidence of intent or by evidence of disproportional effect?[32] In the case of religious rather than racial discrimination, Justice Scalia is satisfied with evidence of effect rather than intent. How should courts treat laws that target religion and are not of general applicability? For the majority in this case, such laws invoke the strictest scrutiny. "A law that targets religious conduct for distinctive treatment or advances legitimate governmental interests only against conduct with a religious motivation will survive strict scrutiny only in rare cases."[33] But Justice Blackmun, concurring for himself and Justice O'Connor, would be far more rigorous: A law specifically targeting religion simply could not meet the strict-scrutiny test and would therefore automatically be unconstitutional. "Unlike the majority, I do not believe that [a] law burdening religious practice that is not neutral or not of general application must undergo the most rigorous of scrutiny. In my view, regulation that targets religion in this way, *ipso facto*, fails strict scrutiny."[34]

Because the Santeria case involved such unambiguous burdens to religious freedom, it did not require the Court to develop a comprehensive approach to the problem of burdens. Hialeah's law was both coercive and discriminatory, two kinds of burdens that are often quite distinct. We now turn our attention to each burden separately.

Individualist Approaches: Coercion as the Essential Burden

One comprehensive approach to both religion clauses emphasizes the protection of *religious freedom* and religious coercion as the essential danger to it. We examined this theme in some depth in Chapter 2. This idea has played an important role in Establishment Clause adjudication during the past decade; some commentators see coercion as the common denominator of Establishment Clause violations. In this view, governmental accommodation is constitutional unless it coerces belief or participation.[35] Justice Kennedy, in particular, has looked for evidence of coercion as the deciding factor in determining whether government-sanctioned religious expression constitutes a prohibited establishment. For example, in *Allegheny County v ACLU*, the perplexing decision involving a crèche, Christmas tree, and a gigantic menorah, Justice Kennedy's partial dissent reasoned that government is free to accommodate religion as long as it neither coerces anyone to support or participate in it, nor gives "direct benefits to religion to such a degree that it in fact establishes one."[36] And *Lee v Weisman* seemed to turn on whether dissenting graduates were coerced by the inclusion of a religious invocation at their graduation ceremony.[37]

To those who understand the Free Exercise Clause as a protection either for personal autonomy or private conscience, the threat to be avoided is coercion. One of the clearest (and most telling) statements of this position was Justice O'Connor's opinion in *Lyng v Northwest Indian Cemetery Protective Association*,[38] in which she is quite explicit in framing the nature of harm to religious freedom in terms of coercion to believe or to act contrary to the tenets of one's religion: "[T]he challenged government action would interfere significantly with private persons' ability to pursue spiritual fulfillment according to their own religious beliefs. In neither case, however, would the affected individuals be coerced by the Government's action into violating their religious beliefs; nor would either governmental action penalize religious activity by denying an equal share of the rights, benefits, and privileges enjoyed by other citizens."

The *Lyng* decision illustrates one of the most serious shortcomings of this approach. As we have already discovered, being coerced to act contrary to one's faith is only one of many ways in which religion may be impeded. The theory of coercion seems to conceive of religion as either a choice or an individual moral commandment; it seems unable to encompass the ways in which collective and institutional religious activity may be impeded.

Finally, as we repeatedly have seen, the concept of coercion itself is an extremely difficult one to apply in concrete instances. As Kathleen Sullivan points out, any view of coercion rests upon normative views of what is proper or uncoerced behavior—a concept for which neither legal literature nor philosophy has developed an adequate understanding. In surveying the legal contexts in which coercion plays a role, Sullivan discovers that "in each of the settings, . . . 'coercion' constituted more than a lack of choice (reasonable alternatives) on the part of the offeree. In each, a finding of coercion depended on some moral condemnation of the offer itself. In other words, the concept of coercion is inescapably normative."[39]

This means that every definition of coercion depends on how the theorist believes one should exist in the absence of coercion. But philosophers disagree on what should be the norm. Robert Nozick focuses on rationality. According to him, coercive offers (threats) involve a departure from "the normal or expected course of events" that makes the recipient worse off—that is, puts him in a position the rational person would consider undesirable.[40] Other thinkers emphasize coercion as a departure from equality[41] (but what is equality?) or from desert.[42] Some libertarians even think that no offer is coercive.

We have observed the practical implications of these problems in judicial efforts to identify "coercive persuasion" by religious "cults." No workable standards ever emerged for distinguishing coerced from noncoerced beliefs.[43] Similar problems have arisen in attempting to recognize coercion in Establishment Clause cases. Recall the dispute between Justice Kennedy and his associates over whether children asked to stand for a religious invocation at a graduation ceremony were coerced to participate in a religious ceremony. Would a "rational student" consider herself worse off? Is a teenager, perhaps a sensitive member of a religious minority, "rational?" Should the subjective preferences of this teenager be the determiner of constitutionality?[44]

There is a certain commonsensical inclination here to agree with the spirit of Justice Stewart's famous aphorism: We may not be able to define coercion, but we know it when we see it. I suspect that there are good occasions for an intuitive use of the concept of coercion, but the philosophical and psychological difficulties the concept presents should make us exceptionally wary of relying too heavily on it.

Finally, we repeatedly have encountered situations in which religious freedom has been violated but there is no evidence of coercion. Since most of these situations involve some kind of religious inequality, we turn our attention to arguments about that notion.

Group Approaches: Animus, Discrimination, and Inequality as Burdens

Those who approach religion as a group phenomenon are likely to focus on the relative treatment of religious groups as the measure of religious freedom. For the most part, religion is not a matter of private faith but of collective practice, and the relations among religious groups are the sources of many conflicts. Interreligious hostility may cause some groups to use political power to disadvantage others. Simple ignorance, indifference, or insensitivity may have the same effect. Both religion clauses can be seen as attempts to preserve religious equality within a more or less majoritarian political system. Some of the broadest—and some of the narrowest—approaches to religious freedoms are based on this view. In narrow views, only laws with obvious discriminatory intent or effect violate the Free Exercise Clause. In the broader approaches, even religiously "neutral," secular laws that incidentally disadvantage a religious group may violate its right to free exercise. Roughly, this dispute parallels the Fourteenth Amendment debate about whether equal protection is violated not only by intentional discrimination but also by systemic inequality that produces disparate impact.

Although the United States has an enviable record of religious liberty overall, de jure religious discrimination and outright animus have not been absent from our experience. We have already encountered this kind of animus in the Santeria case. The law against polygamy challenged in *Reynolds*[45] was the result of a similar animus, and so was the prohibition against clergy holding public office that the Court struck down in *McDaniel v Paty*.[46] The regulation on religious fund-raising overturned in *Larson v Valente*[47] was undeniably aimed at nonmainline religions, and state prohibitions on snake handling may also reflect this kind of hostility.

In the narrow approach to religious equality, these kinds of overt discrimination are clearly unconstitutional, but beyond that, the religion clauses should pose only minimal restraints on the ability of religious groups to jockey for advantage within the political process. The Establishment Clause does not prevent symbolic or even financial support of religion as long as the benefits are not discriminatory, nor does it prevent the representative branches of government from choosing to accommodate religious interests. Valid, secular laws that have only an inadvertent negative impact on a religious exercise pose no constitutional violation and do not require exemptions. This kind of reasoning seemed to motivate Justice Stevens's concurring opinion in *Goldman v Weinberger*,[48] in which an Orthodox Jew was denied an exemption from military uniform requirements so that he could wear a religiously mandated head covering with his uniform. Justice Stevens readily admitted that a small yarmulke seemed innocuous enough to permit without any disruption but feared if this exemption were required, the military would be equally required to permit saffron robes, dreadlocks, turbans, and all manner of other religious garb that would detract from discipline and uniformity.

With the majority opinion in *Employment Division v Smith*,[49] this kind of reasoning became a full-blown theory. Justice Scalia articulated an interpretation of religious discrimination as the only kind of pure Free Exercise violation. Justice Scalia's controversial majority opinion narrowed the guarantee to encompass only laws that specifically target religious practice for unfavorable treatment. Generally applicable laws, neutral in intent, that inadvertently disadvantage a religion or its practices, do not raise First Amendment problems; they need not be justified by compelling state interests and do not require accommodation. In Justice Scalia's reasoning, any other conclusion would play havoc with general laws and make every man a law unto himself.

Justice Scalia's argument rests on a distinction between neutral laws that inadvertently burden religion and laws that specifically target a religion. He concludes that neutral laws that inadvertently burden religion warrant neither exemptions nor justification by the strict-scrutiny standard. Those who take a broader approach to religious equality deny that Free Exercise protection is *limited* to laws that target specific religious practices. Most commentators agree with Justice O'Connor's analysis: "The First Amendment . . . does not distinguish between laws that are generally applicable and laws that target particular religious practices. . . . There is nothing talismanic about neutral laws of general applicability or general criminal prohibitions, for laws neutral toward religion can coerce a person to violate his religious conscience or intrude upon his religious duties just as effectively as laws aimed at religion."[50]

Moreover, many observers doubt that the distinction between targeted and neutral laws is, even in principle, sustainable. Attempts to differentiate between the two reduces religious equality to a mere formal neutrality, requiring only that a law be religion blind and that it not, at face value, discriminate against religion. The effort to reduce religious liberty to equality suffers from two serious flaws. The first is that the notion of religious neutrality contains the same ambiguities (perhaps even impossibilities) that critics find in the notion of formal neutrality under the Equal Protection Clause. The second is that the very parallel between religious freedom and equal protection is seriously flawed because religious liberty requires considerably more than mere equal treatment by government, as we shall see below.

An enormous body of litigation under the Equal Protection Clause has emerged from attempts to identify discrimination. Are only de jure differences prohibited? What about laws that appear neutral but mask discriminatory intent? What about laws that lack that intent but have substantial disproportionate impact? These same problems emerge when granting religious liberty is viewed as a matter of avoiding discrimination. And while it is difficult enough to identify the characteristics of a racially neutral law, it is even more difficult (if not impossible in principle) to identify a religiously neutral law. The very distinction between neutral and discriminatory laws is deeply flawed. It relies on an oversimplified understanding of both legislative intentions and pluralism. The needs of religious majorities are taken into account in the legislative process almost without thinking about them—i.e., schools and government offices are closed on Sundays and Christmas and Easter holidays. These "accommodations" to the Christian calendar are so ordinary that they appear neutral to us. But laws that appear quite neutral to a majority may seriously burden a religious minority—even though that was never their intent. And the unfamiliarity of minority religious practices may make legislators and administrators selectively indifferent or insensitive to the needs of persons out of the mainstream. Michael McConnell summarizes this problem succinctly:

> It should be apparent why a mere absence of attention to religious consequences on the part of the legislature cannot prove the legislation is neutral. In a world in which some beliefs are more prominent than others, the political branches will inevitably be selectively sensitive toward religious injuries. Laws that impinge upon the religious practices of larger or more prominent faiths will be noticed and remedied. When the laws impinge upon the practices of smaller groups, legislators will not even notice, and may not care even if they do notice. If believers of all creeds are to be protected in the "full and equal rights of conscience," then selective sensitivity is not enough. The courts offer a forum in which the particular infringements of small religions can be brought to the attention of authorities and (assuming the judges perform their duties impartially) be given the same sort of hearing that more prominent religions already receive in the political process.[51]

Moreover, even if formal, genuinely equal treatment were possible, that is not what the Free Exercise Clause requires. As Douglas Laycock has noted, this reasoning understands the Free Exercise Clause as merely an adjunct to the Equal Protection Guarantee, requiring only that religion may not be treated more disfavorably than any other activity.[52] Reducing Free Exercise to mere equality would eliminate the substantive impact of the guarantee, as Laycock forcefully explains: "[T]he Free Exercise clause creates a substantive right, and the Court has reduced it to a mere equality right. The Free Exercise clause does not say that Congress shall make no law discriminating against religion, or that no state shall deny to any religion within its jurisdiction the equal protection of the laws. Rather, it says that Congress shall make no laws prohibiting the free exercise of religion. . . . On its face, this is a substantive entitlement, not merely a pledge of non-discrimination."[53]

Finally, the general goals of the Equal Protection and Free Exercise Clauses are normatively different. The goals of equality concern ignoring irrelevant differences, while the goals of the religion clauses foster differences in the interests of heterogeneity and pluralism.

> [T]he ideal of racial nondiscrimination is that individuals are fundamentally equal and must be treated as such; differences based on race are irrelevant and must be overcome. The ideal of free exercise of religion, by contrast, is that people of different religious convictions are different, and that those differences are precious and must not be disturbed. The ideal of racial justice is assimilationist and integrationist. The ideal of free exercise is counter-assimilationist; it serves to allow individuals of different religious faiths to maintain their differences in the face of powerful pressures to conform.[54]

The preserving of differences is at the heart of the pluralist approach to religious free exercise. We turn now to that approach to see what light it might shed on our understanding of how religious freedom is harmed.

The Pluralist Approach

It will be no surprise that the pluralist account provides the most thorough explanation for the variety of harms religious freedom may suffer. In this view, religion is valued as a source of meaning, both individual and collective, both freely chosen and ascriptive, rooted in both belief and a multiplicity of practices. To prevent, penalize, or otherwise endanger the actions and structures that maintain those meanings endangers what is most valuable about religion. This formulation encompasses the dangers posed by coercion but is not limited to it. But pluralism is not only a theory about group independence and separation; it is also a theory of common citizenship. The pluralist account also demands that members of all religions be treated with equal respect as full citizens of the commonwealth. As we have seen, intentional discrimination, selective indifference, or ordinary insensitivity can deprive citizens of this kind of equality.[55] Thus, the concept of religious harm requires a sensitivity to the group and institutional context in which religion is practiced. Equality must be more than purely formal and must preserve diversity in practice. Doing so implicates the very controversial issues of exemptions and other forms of religious accommodation and involves the balancing of religious freedom with other interests.

The pluralist approach conceives of religious freedom as a mosaic of protections for a variety of actions from a variety of burdens. There is no "essential" feature of such burdens; hence, the form a particular burden takes may not be constitutionally significant. But once again, identifying that religious free exercise has been burdened does not end our inquiry. What remains are judgments about when these burdens are outweighed by other social considerations. In the next chapter, we move beyond the threshold of burden and consider if, when, and under what conditions the First Amendment requires accommodation of religion. In short, how does the Constitution guide us in balancing religious freedom against other valued aspects of our public lives?

8

ACCOMMODATING, EXEMPTING, AND BALANCING: RELIGIOUS FREEDOM AND THE POLITICAL PROCESS

We refer to the first ten amendments as constitutional *rights*. To identify something as a right is to recognize, at first view at least, a valid claim to its protection, even in the face of strong conflicting values. Sometimes the costs to these other values are substantial indeed, and sometimes they are even sufficient to outweigh rights claims. When a right is constitutionalized, it is protected from change through the ordinary political process. One of the major tasks of constitutional jurisprudence is to offer principles for reconciling conflicts between rights and the countervailing values that emanate from the political process. In spite of the immense intellectual talent invested by both scholars and advocates in attempting to reconcile competing values, no proposed solution seems to offer consistently successful guiding principles.

These conflicts are typically articulated in two overlapping arguments—one about the accommodation of religious interests, and the other about the importance of countervailing interests. Both arguments are embedded in a broader debate about the nature of American politics. The debate over accommodation raises the inference of special privilege and invokes competing conceptions of neutrality and equality. The debate over compelling state interests inevitably raises questions about the relative value of legislative or judicial decision making and brings about competing concepts of democracy.

It will be helpful to recall how Free Exercise cases originate. They arise when someone perceives that government has created a conflict between civic and religious commitments. The simple cases result when someone challenges a law that targets a specific religious practice for disfavorable treatment. These instances are rather rare. However, the city ordinance banning religious animal sacrifices, struck down in 1993 in *Church of the Lukumi*

Babalu Aye, Inc., and Ernesto Pichado v City of Hialeah,[1] demonstrates that legislatures are still capable of passing law with animus to specific religions.

More typical and complex problems occur when religiously "neutral" laws inadvertently impinge on religious practices. In these instances, affected persons may either work to have the law changed or seek legislative and administrative exemptions to accommodate religious practice. Many, perhaps most, potential conflicts are solved this way. Failing this option, they may go to federal court and demand an exemption as a constitutional right required by the Free Exercise Clause of the First Amendment. At this point the problem becomes a judicial one, and a court must weigh the competing claims of state and religious values. Both legislative and judicial solutions raise serious constitutional questions: Does the Free Exercise Clause demand that religious adherents receive exemptions from ordinary legislation in order to accommodate their religious needs? If so, what standards should courts use in weighing the state's interests against the religious burdens? May legislators voluntarily accommodate religions in ways not strictly required by the Free Exercise Clause, or does such legislative accommodation violate the Establishment Clause by granting preferences to religions?

A simple way to characterize these issues is in terms of majority rule in conflict with religious minority rights. In this interpretation, the acts of the elected branches of government or the agencies under their control represent democratic decision making and are said to reflect majority will. In contrast, intervention by courts is inherently antimajoritarian. When religious minorities whose interests are not protected in the political process demand accommodation as a constitutional right, they are demanding intervention by an unelected judiciary. Also, when legislative accommodation is challenged in court as a violation of the Establishment Clause, that intervention, too, is seen as countermajoritarian. Those with strong commitments to representative decision making naturally advocate judicial restraint under these circumstances.

Pluralists tend to reject the foregoing description and, along with it, the very distinction between political majorities and minorities. In this view, most government enactments are the result of a temporary coalition of interests representing not a majority but those groups whose interests are at stake. Public decision making is almost always a minority phenomena; what makes the situation democratic is that the coalition of minorities is fluid.[2] Of course, some groups are more politically favored as coalition partners and hence more successful than others; at worst, some groups are so disfavored they are never wanted as coalition partners, or perhaps they are excluded entirely from effective participation, and their interests are never represented.

The distribution of power within government helps provide access to many different groups; those who may be disadvantaged in dealing with one institution may find more favorable access in another. Congress may be attentive to certain kinds of interests, and courts to others; federal agencies have particular constituencies, but state agencies, city councils, and other institutions are receptive to others. In this view, there is no sharp distinction between elective and nonelective branches of government. Every branch is designed to provide access to some different combination of interests, and the judiciary is simply another policy-making branch of government, with its own constituencies and procedures. In this view, judicial intervention is not condemned as undemocratic; democracy results from the multiplicity of access points that exist for different interest groups.

These competing images of American politics provide the political context for arguments about how to balance religious rights and competing values. "Compelling state interests," "accommodation," and "exemptions" are the common parlance of contemporary Free Exercise controversy. The controversial 1990 *Smith* case[3] focused public attention on these issues, mobilized religious interest groups, and ultimately drew a response from not only the State of Oregon but also the U.S. Congress.[4] Without trying to reproduce the immense literature already available on these issues, I shall summarize the major themes they raise and the problems all of them entail. Doing so will provide the opportunity to situate the discussion of religious freedom within its political context.

ACCOMMODATION OF RELIGION

Free Exercise jurisprudence most often arises at the margins of law. Seldom do claimants challenge the constitutionality of law; instead, they seek exemption in order to "accommodate" the religious practice. It is important to remember that judicially ordered accommodations are not the beginning but usually the end of the political process. Religious interest groups with sufficient political power may be successful in having accommodation written into legislation or administrative regulations. Part of the confusion in constitutional doctrine stems from the fact that the term "accommodation" is used to describe both judicially ordered exemptions, which are deemed to be constitutional *rights*, and legislatively granted exemptions or other benefits, which are not constitutionally required. Judicial and scholarly opinion is massively fragmented concerning the appropriateness of both policies.[5] Some constitutional scholars favor both;[6] some favor neither.[7] Some favor legislative but not constitutionally required accommodations,[8] and some favor required but not legislative ones.[9]

It is tempting simply to adopt different words for the two kinds of policies, but doing so would do violence to the terms in which the argument has developed. I shall try to maintain the distinction by using the terms *legislative accommodations* to refer to the (arguably) permissible but not required ones, and *Free Exercise accommodations* to refer to those that are (arguably) required as a matter of constitutional right.

Accommodation of both forms raises constitutional problems; however, the arguments under the two clauses are quite different, and in some views, potentially contradictory. Legislative accommodation of religion raises Establishment Clause problems when a religious majority or dominant group seeks to use public resources for religious purposes or to carry on religious acts in "the public square." Permitting this kind of accommodation usually involves lowering the metaphorical "wall of separation" between religion and the state. In contrast, accommodation to enhance free exercise often means heightening the wall of separation, preventing the state from intruding on religious life. Separationists—those who understand the religion clauses to require a strict separation between church and state—therefore tend to favor Free Exercise accommodation but not Establishment Clause accommodation. In contrast, accommodationists understand the essence of the clauses as promoting the widest possible range of religious expression; they tend to support accommodation under both clauses, even when it seems to lead to contradictory approaches to the two clauses.[10]

Having made a clean distinction between legislative and judicially ordered accommodation, the next step is to qualify to almost to the point of obliteration. First, "legislative" itself is a misleading term because many accommodations are administrative. Many, if not most, are matters of simple selective enforcement by law enforcement agencies. It is almost inconceivable, for example, that a local prosecutor would choose to bring charges of serving alcohol to a minor to a Jewish family celebrating a Passover seder. These kinds of "accommodations" are so pervasive they are unseen.

Administrative accommodation is significant for other reasons. When an administrative agency has discretionary authority, granting religious exemptions is simple, and failing to accommodate raises the inference of discrimination against religion. However, when discretion is lacking, special exemptions infer special favors to religion. Justice Scalia made much of this distinction in *Smith*. When agencies have an individualized process for ruling on the motives of applicants, the failure to consider religious ones might be a violation of religious freedom. But other rules, such as the criminal law, are not supposed to be enforced with the same kind of discretionary authority. This fact does not, I think, require us to agree with Scalia's constricted notion of exemptions, but it does suggest that the institutional structure of decision making makes a difference in where we locate the authority for granting exemptions.

Consider the institutional difference between *Sherbert* and *Goldman*. South Carolina's unemployment compensation agency was specifically empowered to make individualized judgments about whether a person's unavailability for work was legitimate or not. "A state that puts in place a discretionary process to assess reasons for quitting work, and then turns a deaf ear to adherence to religious commandments as good cause, opens itself to the conclusion that it is not giving equal regard to the deep religious commitments of non-mainstream believers."[11] The circumstances in *Goldman v Weinberger* illustrate both flexibility and inflexibility. The situation preceding the dispute illustrates simple administrative accommodation. Although the military rule regarding headgear was absolute and authorized no exceptions, Capt. Goldman had in fact been accommodated throughout most of his military career without incident. And the military practice had unofficially permitted officers to wear yarmulkes while they were in uniform on a case-by-case basis. Still, when confronted with an official request for accommodation, the military fell back on its inflexible rule. In defending its refusal to accommodate Goldman's request, the Air Force expressed a fear that accommodating a relatively innocuous yarmulke would require accommodating dreadlocks, saffron robes, and turbans, or else force the military to discriminate among religious.[12] When the Supreme Court refused to rule that Goldman's exemption was required by the Free Exercise Clause, Congress enacted a law that created the exemption legislatively.[13]

There is a third ambiguity to the distinction between legislative and Free Exercise accommodations. How should one classify the 1993 Religious Freedom Restoration Act? Undeniably, it is a legislative enactment. However, it puts congressional authority behind an interpretation of the Free Exercise Clause, in effect ordering courts (and presumably other government bodies as well) to accommodate religious practices unless doing so would violate a compelling state interest.[14] With these ambiguities in mind, we shall only briefly consider legislative accommodation, and at greater length Free Exercise accommodation.

Legislative or Permissible Accommodation and the Conflict between the Religion Clauses

When religious groups desire public support for religious activities or to engage in religious activities "in the public square," or to create legislative exemptions from general obligations, they may be successful in achieving these "accommodations" through the political process. Such accommodations are not strictly required by the Free Exercise Clause and may or may not be permitted by the Establishment Clause. They occupy the "disputed border" between the two religion clauses. Many thinkers who deny there is a Free Exercise *right* to religious exemptions nevertheless favor legislatively granted ones.

Some kinds of legislative accommodation provide overt financial or symbolic support for religion. The provision for allowing chaplains in the military, prisons, and legislatures is one example. Financial assistance to religious schools is another, and religious activities in the public schools remain perpetually controversial. The first judicial reference to this kind of accommodation was Justice Douglas's description of the released-time program the court upheld in *Zorach v Clauson*: "When the state encourages religious instruction or cooperates with religious authorities by adjusting the schedule of public events to sectarian needs, it follows the best of our traditions. For it then respects the religious nature of our people and accommodates the public service to their spiritual needs."[15]

The difference between symbolic or financial support and a mere adjustment of schedule is a subtle one. Was the school system merely adjusting its schedule, or was it using the mechanisms of compulsory education to pressure children to attend religious training? Like *Zorach*, most accommodations can be seen either way.

Symbolic and financial assistance to religious groups raises many important Establishment Clause questions that are beyond the scope of our study. We cannot avoid them entirely, but we will focus on legislatively granted exemptions to general laws aimed at accommodating religious interests. Typical state exemptions include the Texas law that exempted religious publications from sales taxes, policies accommodating the schedules of religious minorities into school calendars, and state exemptions for sacramental peyote use. Congress has engaged in legislative accommodation by providing for religious conscientious objection to military service, exempting persons with religious objections to receiving social security benefits from paying social security self-employment taxes, exempting those with religious objections to labor unions from paying union dues, and exempting religious institutions from some of the requirements of Title VII of the Civil Rights Act. All of these policies raise Establishment Clause questions. To grant exemptions from valid, neutral laws for persons whose motivations are religious and to deny the same consideration to persons with equally pressing nonreligious motivations appears to be the kind of special privilege for religion that the Establishment Clause forbids.[16]

A classic example of this problem was raised in the case of *Estate of Thornton v Caldor*.[17] The State of Connecticut repealed its Sunday closing laws but created a statutory right for any employee not to work on his or her Sabbath. In 1981 the Supreme Court ruled that the law impermissibly advanced a particular religious practice by requiring employers and fellow employees to adjust their behavior to the requirements of Sabbath observers. This decision illustrates the very thin line between required and prohibited accommodation of religion and forces us to confront the disputed border between the two clauses.

The Court took the opposite approach to the "disputed border" problem in *Corporation of the Presiding Bishop of the Church of Jesus Christ of Latter-Day Saints v Amos*.[18] In this case the majority not only upheld a legislative exemption for religious institutions from Title VII prohibitions on religious discrimination but also interpreted the exemption very broadly.

Advocates of accommodation argue that this "disputed border" problem arises only if one mistakenly imagines that the Establishment Clause is meant to ensure separation. In their view, the correct understanding of the two clauses taken together is that they protect religious liberty. Hence, actions taken to promote religious free exercise, specifically to remove governmental impediments to religious free exercise, cannot be seen as violations of the Establishment Clause. For accommodationists, such as Michael McConnell,[19] the Establishment Clause is a weak adjunct to the Free Exercise Clause and poses little or no impediment to government efforts to facilitate religious practices. In the words of Richard John Neuhaus, "The no-establishment part of the relation clause is entirely and without remainder in the service of free exercise."[20]

Various members of the current Supreme Court support wide legislative latitude in granting permissive accommodation. Justice O'Connor supports such accommodations so long as they do not "endorse" religion. Chief Justice Rehnquist does so on originalist grounds. Justice Kennedy argues that accommodation is permissible so long as it does not coerce unwilling participation. Justice Scalia does so on majoritarian grounds, as suggested in his dissents in *Edwards v Aguillard*[21] and in *Texas Monthly v Bullock*[22] and his majority opinion in *Smith*. In *Aguillard* he rejected the majority's decision that Arkansas's moment of silence law violated the Establishment Clause and argued that it simply removed a state-imposed obstacle to religious exercise. In *Texas Monthly v Bullock* the majority struck down a provision of a Texas law that exempted religious publications from sales taxes. Scalia dissented, believing that the exemption was an entirely appropriate permissive accommodation. And in *Smith*, while he rejected a constitutional right to accommodation, he advocated legislative solutions. While Scalia denied any Free Exercise *right* to religious exemptions, he insisted that legislatures are free to grant them as part of the normal political process. Scalia recognizes that the majority approach leaves religious liberty within the political process. "Values that are protected against government interferences through enshrinement in the Bill of Rights are not thereby banished from the political process." He readily admits that "leaving accommodation to the political process will place at a relative disadvantage those religious practices that are not widely engaged in; but that unavoidable consequences of democratic government must be preferred to a system in which each conscience is a law unto itself."[23]

Legislative accommodations have also attracted some serious critics. Ira Lupu challenges the premises that religious liberty is the single core value of the two religion clauses. He believes their goal is *equal liberty*. To diminish the Establishment Clause is to risk sacrificing religious *equality*, thereby enabling religiously dominant groups to use the political process to gain unequal advantages.[24] Lupu advocates a strong right to Free Exercise accommodation but finds legislative ones objectionable on numerous doctrinal, normative, and institutional grounds. He reads the Establishment Clause as prohibiting legislative accommodations because by their nature they are divisive and favor politically successful religious groups rather than marginal ones. Furthermore, resting the accommodation power in courts rather than legislatures creates a more principled approach to religious freedom. Lupu would even prohibit legislatures from anticipating constitutional challenges and granting exemptions likely to be required by the Free Exercise Clause; exemptions must only be granted by court order.

His point about legislative decision making is hard to deny; legislative accommodations are often inconsistent, unprincipled, and sometimes divisive. Nevertheless, they are so much a part of our ordinary legislative practice that it is difficult to imagine their absence. We take for granted such simple accommodation as religious excuses for school absences, or exempting religious sacraments from laws forbidding serving alcohol to minors. Imagine how contentious life would be if every one of these simple accommodations required a court case. Moreover, our constitutional tradition holds all government authorities to constitutional standards; it seems almost perverse to deny legislators the opportunity to exercise their own constitutional judgment about religious freedom.

My own approach would accept *both* legislative accommodations *and* a vigorous enforcement of Establishment Clause limits. The Free Exercise Clause mandates religious accommodation for those persons and practices not protected in the political process, and the Establishment Clause prevents public policy from being captured by a dominant religious interest. Moreover, legislative and administrative accommodations are often the simplest and most humane ways of protecting religious freedom. We must bear in mind that the judicial process is an adversarial one—a crucial last resort, but surely not to be preferred to consensual or negotiated ones. From a pluralist perspective, the patchwork of administrative, legislative, and judicial solutions protects the strength and resiliency of the system. Congressional actions reversing *Goldman* and *Smith* illustrate the strength of the Madisonian system of divided and overlapping power. The more institutions involved in a decision, the more persons and interests have access to the entire process. The results are seldom elegantly principled, but the porousness of the processes is itself advantageous.

The 1994 *Kiryas Joel*[25] case illustrates the frustrating but ultimately beneficial interplay of legislative and judicial approaches to religious interests. The citizens of Kiryas Joel, predominately members of the Satmar Hasidic sect of Judaism, educated most of their children in private religious schools but were unwilling or unable to provide the full range of rehabilitative services in private schools for their disabled children. Before 1985, disabled children had been receiving state services on the grounds of private religious schools—a legislative accommodation. In 1985, the Court held that this kind of accommodation violated the Establishment Clause.[26] Subsequently, the New York legislature accommodated the village by creating its own public school district—again, a legislative accommodation aimed at meeting the needs of a disabled children within a minority religion. I do not think we should fault the village for exercising its political power to persuade the legislature to grant this unusual accommodation; nor should we fault the legislature for granting it. Constitutional doctrine is not the highest priority of either interest groups or legislative bodies. Hence, it was perfectly appropriate for the Supreme Court to remind both that the Establishment Clause forbids religious gerrymandering. The Court was right to forbid this kind of political accommodation. Interestingly, Justice Souter's majority opinion itself suggested some administrative solutions to the problems his ruling created. In the long run, the conflicting solutions of legislature and judiciary reflect the strength of pluralist institutions of government.[27]

These few paragraphs provide only the smallest hint of the debate raging over religious accommodation in Establishment Clause jurisprudence. However, since our focus is religious free exercise, the remainder of our discussion shall be on Free Exercise accommodation.

Free Exercise Accommodation and the Values of Neutrality and Equality

When religious interest groups fail to receive accommodation through the legislative or administrative process, they may go to the courts and demand accommodation as a matter of constitutional right. Typically, they seek a judicial order exempting them from the religiously burdensome aspects of the law. These demands compel courts to consider whether the Free Exercise Clause requires religious accommodation in the form of exemptions to generally applicable laws, and if so, under what conditions, and what are the scope and limits of such accommodation?

Arguments about constitutionally required accommodation invoke passionate discussion and ultimately demand that we explore the meaning and value of governmental neutrality, the nature of discrimination, and the position of religious groups in American life. Beginning with *Sherbert v Verner*,[28] the Supreme Court has considered at least some degree of accommodation to be required by the Free Exercise Clause. In that case, the Court ruled that Ms. Sherbert, a Seventh-Day Adventist, could not be denied unemployment compensation when she lost her job and was unavailable to work on Saturdays, her Sabbath.

Critics of this decision, and of the jurisprudence it engendered, object to the inference that the Free Exercise Clause privileges religious motivations over nonreligious ones. Ms. Sherbert's religiously motivated unavailability to work is entitled to a kind of preference that she would not receive for nonreligious but equally strong reasons for not working. If she were unavailable to work because of sick children at home, or an ethical objection to working in a segregated work force, or a compelling commitment to participate in political meetings or musical recitals instead of working, she would not be constitutionally entitled to unemployment compensation. In other words, the Court read the Free Exercise Clause as privileging religion over other interests.

After *Sherbert*, three more unemployment compensation cases were decided based on this line of reasoning. In *Thomas v Review Board of the Indiana Employment Security Division*[29] the Court ordered unemployment compensation for a worker whose religious convictions prevented him from working in the production of armaments (even when other members of his faith had no such scruples); in *Hobbie v Unemployment Appeals Commission of Florida*[30] the Court ruled that recently acquired religious convictions were as protected as long-standing ones; and in *Frazee v Illinois Department of Employment Security*[31] a Christian who refused to be available for work on Sunday was entitled to unemployment compensation even though he was not a member of any specific church. Outside of the unemployment context, the most significant exemption ruling is *Yoder v Wisconsin*, in which the Supreme Court granted an exemption from the state's compulsory education law for an Amish community with religious objections to public schooling for its teenagers beyond the age of fourteen.[32] *Yoder* stands out as the most significant and unambiguous commitment to Free Exercise exemptions.

Beyond this series of cases, the picture gets hazy. Exemptions have been granted in several other religious rights cases, but always with some ambiguity. *West Virginia Board of Education v Barnette*,[33] the landmark decision that Jehovah's Witness children may not be required to salute the flag in violation of their religious principles, was in fact decided on grounds of freedom of speech. *Wooley v Maynard*[34] upheld the right of a Jehovah's Witness to refuse to display a religiously objectionable state motto on his license plate; however, the majority relied on a general First Amendment right not to be required to profess an objectionable idea. *Jensen v Quaring*,[35] which granted an exemption to Nebraska's law requiring a photograph on a driver's license, was decided by an equally divided court without an opinion; hence, the exemption granted by the lower court was allowed to stand. Most constitutional scholars took issue with Justice Scalia when in *Smith* he said that exemptions had never been ordered outside the unemployment compensation context or in "hybrid cases," but it is true that the Court has turned down more demands for Free Exercise exemptions than it has granted. Demands for Free Exercise exemptions were rejected in the following instances. In *Tony and Susan Alamo Foundation v Secretary of Labor*[36] the Court rejected demands for exemptions from the Fair Labor Standards Act; in *Goldman v Weinberger*[37] it rejected a demand for exemptions from military uniform requirements; in *U.S. v Lee*[38] it turned down a demand that an Amish employer be exempted from paying social security taxes for his Amish employees who did not accept social security benefits; and in *Bob Jones University v United States*[39] the Court refused to grant an exemption to a religious university to accommodate its religious belief in separation of the races. In *O'Lone v Estate of Shabbaz*[40] the Court denied a claim by Muslim prisoners for adjustments in prison work schedules to accommodate religious services, and in *Jimmy Swaggart Ministries v Board of Equalization*[41] the Court refused to exempt sales of religious items from a state sales tax.

A substantial tradition of constitutional scholarship considers the preference for religion as mistaken jurisprudence. The key value for the critics is neutrality. A generation ago Philip Kurland argued that neutrality was the heart of the religion clauses: religion should not be used to confer either a benefit or a disability. In his view, the exemptions granted to persons with religious motivations are like subsidies that are not available to persons with other kinds of motivations and should be constitutionally prohibited.[42] Numerous Supreme Court opinions invoke the value of government neutrality, equal treatment, and nonpreference between citizens regardless of religious belief.[43] For critics of exemptions the privileging of religious over nonreligious motivations raises serious Establishment Clause problems. Moreover, by inevitably preferring some religions over others, they raise Free Exercise problems as well. In a society as religiously heterogeneous as ours, it is impossible for every religious motivation to be accommodated; it would result in precisely the kind of "anarchy" that Justice Scalia spoke of in *Smith*. Hence, accommodation implicitly violates equality.

Kurland has some powerful followers among today's constitutional scholars. Ellis West has argued persuasively against constitutionalizing religious exemptions. (He finds legislatively granted ones less objectionable.) West presents six arguments against such exemptions: First, they violate the primary First Amendment value of neutrality toward religion and inevitably lead to invidious discrimination among religions; second, granting them is politically divisive; third, they encourage false and self-serving religious claims; fourth, there are no principled ways to balance the demands for exemptions against the interests of the state; fifth, granting them fosters entanglement between religion and government; and sixth, granting them inevitably leads to conflicts between the Free Exercise Clause and the Establishment Clause.[44] His most persuasive theme is the mischief of tampering with neutrality:

> [W]hen the government gives exemptions to some religious persons that it does not give to all, that constitutes special or favored treatment for their religion or for them because of their religion. The discrimination can be threefold in nature. First, the exempted persons or groups are not required to do or refrain from doing something that others are required to do or not to do. Second, exemptions . . . may give those religions or churches an unfair advantage over other religions, secular ideologies, churches, nonprofit organizations, or businesses with which they compete for members and money. The discrimination is tripled if the persons and groups not favored with exemptions have a duty or burden, such as taxes,

shifted to them because of the exemptions given to the religious individual or groups.[45]

In the same spirit, William Marshall has been a consistent critic of religion-based exemptions. His view situates the religion clauses within the First Amendment protection of *communication*. At the heart of the First Amendment is the protection of the equality of ideas; hence, Marshall understands the boundaries of free exercise as congruent with those of free speech in general. In his view, to go beyond that and to grant religious exemptions would be to offend the equality of religious and nonreligious ideas.[46]

Perhaps the most profound philosophical objection to accommodation is that made by Steven Gey.[47] Gey finds the philosophical underpinnings of religion inconsistent with those of democracy. Religion's guiding principles are derived from a source beyond human control, are immutable and absolutely authoritative, and are incapable of proof or disproof. In contrast, democracy considers all governmental actions reflections of temporal human authority whose legitimacy rests on the acquiescence of its subjects, and it must treat all questions as open. Accommodation of religion, therefore, is inconsistent with the underlying logic of democratic government.

> [R]eligious doctrine is distinctive in part because it is derived from an extra-human, transcendental force or reality. Accommodation problems arise in the free exercise context when a religious adherent seeks to avoid general social obligations imposed by secular authorities on the ground that such behavior violates a duty imposed by the higher, transcendental authority. In the accommodation cases, the Court has interpreted the Free Exercise clause to mean that the state usually may, and sometimes must, respect such transcendental obligations. In all such cases, one of the following scenarios occurs: the state subordinates its legitimate secular objectives to the religious principles relied upon by the adherent, the state subsidizes the religiously motivated behavior, or the state shifts some social burden from the adherent to a nonadherent. Each of these consequences conflicts with the interpretation of the establishment clause.[48]

In view of these rather persuasive academic criticisms of exemptions, Justice Scalia and the *Smith* majority were not entirely alone in rejecting them. As I noted earlier, Scalia read the precedents as limiting exemptions to the context of unemployment compensation and to cases in which religious rights were combined with other constitutional claims—the so-called hybrid cases. Except in those circumstances, the Free Exercise Clause is breached only when laws specifically target religious practice for unfavorable treatment; generally applicable laws that are neutral in intent do not raise the same First Amendment problems. Hence, the First Amendment requires only that a law be religion blind and not on its face discriminate against religion; it does not require religion-based exemptions.[49]

In Justice Scalia's view, exemptions are particularly inappropriate when the law in question is a *criminal* one. The state has an overwhelming interest in uniform applicability of the criminal law. According to Justice Scalia, "We have never held that an individual's religious beliefs excuse him from compliance with an otherwise valid law prohibiting conduct that the State is free to regulate."[50] In contrast, unemployment compensation cases already involve a procedure for making individualized determination; hence, it is not unreasonable to include religious excuses among other good reasons for the inability to work.

Scalia's point about uniform applicability of laws returns us to Kurland's original argument for neutrality. In spite of the many deficiencies in Justice Scalia's *Smith* opinion, he joins an important tradition in First Amendment thinking, and that whole tradition poses a serious challenge to advocates of exemptions. Hence, any justification for Free Exercise accommodation must come to terms with the value of neutrality.

Several powerful arguments take on that challenge. Most reject the premise of neutrality itself. The simplest arguments note that if neutrality ever made sense, it is a concept appropriate to a much simpler form of government. Neutrality might have been appropriate in an era of limited government, when most governmental regulations took the form of prohibitions—such as criminal penalties. But the regulatory state has so multiplied the interactions among governmental institutions, religious institutions, and individuals that simply avoiding penalties no longer assures freedom of religious practice. The multiplicity of regulations almost guarantees that one of them will conflict with someone's religious convictions. For example, the requirement of having a photograph on a driver's license will have an impact on those who believe that such photographs are "graven images" prohibited in the Bible. Regulations about the equipment worn by high school athletes will have an impact on either those who believe that the clothing is immodest or those who are religiously required to cover their heads at all times. Hence, without accommodation, persons will inadvertently and constantly be deprived of the ability to practice their religion while they participate as full members of the larger society. To refuse accommodation will deprive them of the benefits of full citizenship, causing harm to not only the individuals but also the society by fragmenting identities and making people choose between civic and religious commitments.

A deeper probe challenges the notion that exemptions are truly privileges. Many ordinary regulations already accommodate widely practiced religions; they are simply so much a part of our lives that we fail to see them. School closings for Christmas and Easter and Sunday office closings reflect the needs of the Christian majority. However, when Jews ask for excused absences from schools for the Jewish High Holidays, we notice the accommodation request. Religious majorities protect themselves legislatively; the very point of making religious freedom a constitutional *right* is to protect those whose interests will not be reflected in majority decisions.[51] The *Sherbert* case reaffirms this point. South Carolina law had already accommodated Sunday Sabbath observers by providing that no employee be required to work on that day in violation of religious conscience.

Pursuing this point leads us to question whether the very notion of neutrality even makes sense. The policy favored by Kurland, West, Marshall, and others appears now as a purely formal neutrality, which may mask significant substantive mistreatment. We are familiar with this idea in the jurisprudence of equal protection, and we have long recognized that formal equality often reinforces substantive inequalities when background conditions are unequal. Some of the lessons learned in combating race and gender discrimination are relevant to the religion clauses. Religious minorities are not really in an equal position with members of mainstream groups with respect to the burdensome laws. "The person whose religious life is invaded by a legal provision is not similarly situated to the person for whom the provision has no such effect. The impact of the legal provision on those differently situated persons is not equal."[52]

The most cursory knowledge of religious group conflict in American history reminds us that religious minorities have long suffered both overt and purposeful discrimination as well as "selective indifference" to the burdens of laws that seem to be religiously neutral. Discrimination and "selective indifference" are all the more prevalent when the religious beliefs and practices in question are so incomprehensible to the majority that it cannot really appreciate their religious impact. In these instances, exemptions are necessary to create a substantive equality that mere formal equality overlooks. For Christopher Eisgruber and Lawrence Sager,[53] the "selective insensitivity" to religious minorities suggests the key to understanding the Free Exercise Clause. They argue that the distinguishing characteristic of religion in the United States is not its singular value, but its singular vulnerability. Religious accommodation is not to be justified because religion merits special privileges but because doing so is necessary to achieve *equal respect*. Discrimination against religious groups, often in the form of insensitivity, is the real threat the Free Exercise Clause confronts; hence, the model of equal protection provides appropriate analogies and guidance. According to Eisgruber and Sager, there are several reasons for religious discrimination and it takes several forms.

> Religious commandments are not necessarily founded on or limited by reasons accessible to nonbelievers; often they are understood to depend on fiat or covenant and to implicate forces or beings beyond human challenge or comprehension. Religion is often the hub of tightly knit communities, whose habits, rituals, and values are deeply alien to outsiders. At best, this is likely to produce a chronic interfaith "tone deafness," in which the persons of one faith do not easily empathize with the concerns or persons of other faiths. At worst, it may produce hostility, even murderous hatred, among different religious groups. . . . From the perspective of some faiths, it is desirable to convert nonbelievers rather than to injure them. . . . [T]hey may even have the welfare of the unbelievers fully in mind as they seek to shape the legal regime to discourage or prevent the nonbelievers from pursuing their own faiths. Even when conversion is not their aim, dominant faiths (or clusters of faiths) that recognize the value and concerns of others may nevertheless use political power to favor themselves. . . .
>
> These nonantagonistic variations may be "kinder, gentler" forms of discrimination, but they remain stark failures of equal regard.[54]

This interpretation sheds a different light on *Sherbert*. South Carolina had provided a discretionary process to assess reasons for quitting work; the state's fault was turning a deaf ear to Ms. Sherbert's religious commitments, suggesting that it was not "giving equal regard to the religious commitments of non-mainstream religious believers."[55]

While most of the debate over religious exemptions occurred in the court, the most decisive recent step was congressional adoption of the Religious Rights Restoration Act. This act would seem to require accommodation of religion except when a compelling governmental interest would be threatened by the exemption. Although the law has been challenged, it does seem to create a strong presumption of a right to accommodation.[56]

Ultimately, the argument about religious exemptions has led us to consider the concept of equal citizenship. If we are persuaded that more than formal neutrality is necessary to achieve equal citizenship, then subtler problems must be addressed. The issue then becomes not *whether* religious practices must *ever* be accommodated but rather under what conditions and with what limitations? When should courts require such accommodations as a matter of constitutional right? How deferent should courts be to legislative judgments when religious exercises are burdened?

If we accept the argument for Free Exercise exemptions in general, we are still confronted with determining their limits. Michael McConnell, the preeminent advocate of accommodation, proposes two governing limitations. First, exemptions are constitutional when they relieve religious persons of burdens *created* by government; they are only constitutional when they do not create inducements for nonbelievers to adopt the religion in question or to feign religious motivations. McConnell's argument rests on a basic distinction between "government 'benefits' or 'inducements' to religion on the one hand, and the lifting of government 'restraints' or 'inhibitions' on religion, on the other."[57] In illustrating this distinction, he suggests that public school prayers and tax exemptions for ministers provide unconstitutional inducements for people to engage in religious practices. However, permitting Jewish military officers to wear yarmulkes, allowing Amish buggy drivers to refrain from displaying bright orange signs on their buggies, and providing pork-free diets for Jewish and Muslim prisoners are not likely to induce anyone to adopt these religions. This point has arisen before. Recall that in considering religious sincerity in Chapter 2 we found it to be controversial mainly in instances in which religious persons would have been exempt from some otherwise burdensome regulation or cost. And in Chapter 3, we encountered the suggestion that part of the dramatic rise in new religious movements might be the incentive for "nonreligious" movements to call themselves religious in order to be exempt from governmental regulation.[58] In light of these examples, McConnell's suggestion seems to be a promising one, although it leaves considerable room for controversy at the margins.

McConnell's second limitation—an accommodation must not pose an undue burden on nonbeneficiaries—would be more difficult to regulate. In his words, "An accommodation that imposes costs on others disproportionate to the alleviation of a burden on religious practice could be a form of favoritism for religion."[59] This stipulation raises all kinds of questions about how to weigh disproportional burdens. Would the tax burden shifted to nonreligious publications by tax exemptions for religious ones pose an undue hardship? Was accommodation of Sabbath observers' employment schedules an undue burden on fellow employees? Is the traffic risk of encountering unmarked slow buggies on public roads too great a burden on non-Amish drivers? What about the administrative burden to the State of Nebraska in providing alternatives to driver's licenses with a photograph, or the administrative costs of administering food stamp programs without social security numbers for identification? In surveying these "costs" or "burdens," we quickly notice that they are not easily compared. Some impose economic costs on nonbeneficiaries and, among these, some costs are widely dispersed and others are more localized. Some costs are primarily inconvenience or irritation. Should the annoyance of nonbeneficiaries be considered a burden, and if so, what degree of burden should be assigned to it? And finally, when the religious practice in question is outside the social consensus, how should burdens to social consensus be weighed?

Of course, these problems are not specific to McConnell's proposal; they arise every time courts must balance religious interests against other values —as we shall see in the section that follows.

Guidelines for Free Exercise exemptions are neither unambiguous, self-enforcing, or free of social or economic costs. Almost always, the benefits to religious claimants conflict with other values, and when the conflicts reach the courts, judges must measure the relative weights of the religious rights against countervailing interests. How these interests should be weighed and by whom are the subject of major controversy in themselves.

COMPELLING STATE INTERESTS: THE DEBATE IN *SMITH*

In First Amendment cases, as in other individual-rights cases, judges are asked to weigh the relative importance of an individual-rights claim against the state's interest in its limitation. In ordinary balancing, the state must show only that the challenged law is reasonably related to legitimate interests, not necessarily that it is the best way to achieve them. This kind of balancing essentially replicates the legislative process; hence, dominant interests generally prevail. In fact, the very notion of balancing reduces *rights* to *interests* and weighs them along with all other social interests.[60] Hence, balancing of interests often places the individual claimant at a disadvantage because more widely shared interests can easily outweigh the interests of dissenting individuals or groups. Furthermore, this procedure allows for considerable judicial sleight of hand over exactly *what* is to be balanced. Whether the state weighs in with the entire policy or simply its interest in not granting exemptions makes an enormous difference.[61]

The compelling state interest approach is aimed at redressing this imbalance by adding extra weight to the individual's claims. This method reflects the view that the whole point of having a Bill of Rights is to remove certain liberties from the ordinary balancing of the political process. Ordinarily, the person challenging the constitutionality of a law bears the burden of proof. Failing to overcome this burden leaves the law intact. In some situations—mostly those suggested in Justice Stone's famous Footnote Four of the opinion in the *Carolene Products* case,[62] the Courts have reversed this burden of proof and assumed a law to be unconstitutional, leaving its defenders with the burden of establishing its constitutionality. Such laws are subjected to "strict scrutiny," requiring their defenders to show that (1) the challenged law served not just an important public purpose but a genuinely *compelling* one; (2) the law was well tailored to achieve that purpose; and (3) the purpose could not be achieved by some less burdensome legislative method. Particularly during the Warren Court years, this standard was used when laws were challenged as burdening "fundamental freedoms" or "discrete and insular minorities." In theory, the compelling state interest test places a heavy obligation on government to establish that burdens on fundamental rights are justified by extremely important state interests that could not be achieved in any less objectionable way.

The application of the compelling state interest standard to Free Exercise cases was made explicit in *Sherbert v Verner*: "When religious practices are burdened by acts of government, the government must demonstrate that the burden is necessary to achieve a compelling state interest which can be achieved in no less burdensome way."[63] Perhaps the single clearest statement of this doctrine is in *Wisconsin v Yoder*: "[O]nly those interests of the highest order and those not otherwise served can overbalance legitimate claims to the free exercise of religion."[64] *Yoder* offers a good example of how this method operates. In that case, the Court agreed with Wisconsin that the state had a compelling interest in fostering education and agreed that the compulsory education laws in general were well tailored to achieve that purpose. However, it found that the state's educational goals would not be harmed by exempting Amish students fourteen to sixteen years old from these laws since the Amish community's educational practices were capable of achieving many of the goals the state sought to enforce.

After *Yoder*, the compelling state interest test was widely understood to be the prevailing method of constitutional analysis in Free Exercise cases. While the standard gives special significance to religious freedom claims, that extra weight has not often been sufficient to outbalance state claims. In spite of the standard, government claims have prevailed against Free Exercise challenges before the Supreme Court only in *Yoder* and the four unemployment compensation cases. Hence, when *Smith* reopened the question in 1990, the jurisprudence of compelling state interest was at odds with itself. No case in this generation has fueled battles over religious freedom like the majority's cavalier treatment of religious liberty in *Smith*. Because the majority, concurring, and dissenting opinions in *Smith* so pointedly capture the controversy surrounding the compelling state interest test, we shall use those opinions as the focal point for discussing this doctrine.

When the *Smith* case was argued, litigants on both sides assumed the compelling state interest standard to be the appropriate standard of review. Neither party had challenged the use of that standard in its briefs. Thus, when the majority rejected this standard, they made a significant reversal in constitutional policy on an issue that was neither raised nor argued by the litigants.

As we have seen, the *Smith* majority held that the Free Exercise Clause is directly breached only by laws that specifically target religious practice for unfavorable treatment, not by generally applicable, religiously neutral laws. Consequently, laws inadvertently burdening religious exercise need not be justified by a compelling state interest. Because the majority did not believe that the employment of generally applicable laws on religious practices required special justification, it did not question either the state's interest in a drug policy, which included sacramental peyote use, or the extent of the relation between this law as enforced and the state's interests.

Recall that strict scrutiny begins by assuming that any law burdening religion is unconstitutional, leaving the state with the burden of showing a state interest in retaining it. Justice Scalia invokes an image of anarchy that this doctrine would create. Especially in a religiously plural society, virtually every ordinary policy, from labor to health, foreign to education, could potentially burden the religious interests of some faith. In Scalia's words, to hold such laws presumptively invalid—at least as applied to religiously motivated persons—would be "to make an obligation to obey . . . a law contingent upon the law's coincidence with religious beliefs, except where the State's interest is compelling," and to permit an individual "to become a law unto himself."[65] This risk is all the more troubling, he argues, because "we are a cosmopolitan nation made up of people of almost every conceivable religious preference." Hence, "we cannot afford the luxury of deeming *presumptively invalid*, as applied to the religious objector, every regulation of conduct that does not protect an interest of the highest order." Scalia then recounts what critics term a "parade of horribles" to illustrate the disarray of governmental policy that would result from such a doctrine.

In Justice Scalia's view, this argument is especially strong in the case of the criminal law. He finds it particularly pernicious to hold *criminal* laws presumptively invalid as applied to persons with religious motivations. Thus, he took great pains to suggest that the compelling state interest doctrine was itself an aberration, applicable only in unemployment compensation cases, not in other circumstances, and most certainly not in cases involving the criminal law.

The compelling state interest standard is vulnerable on another count as well. It is inconsistent with judicial restraint. The presumption of unconstitutionality is a presumption against the judgment of representative institutions. Scalia forcefully identifies the countermajoritarian implications of the compelling state interest approach and the fact that it enables a dissenting minority's interest to outweigh determinations made in the political process, thus disrupting the normal course of public policy. Furthermore, to remove the balancing from the legislative process and place it in the hands of unelected judges, is to enhance the power of courts to substitute their judgment for those of elected officials. Justice Scalia's majoritarianism, therefore, moves him to reject judicially mandated exemptions but to take a very permissive attitude toward legislative ones.

Justice Scalia's vigorous rejection of the compelling state interest test did not win majority support. Justice O'Connor's concurring opinion in *Smith*, as well as the vigorous dissent authored by Justice Blackmun, provide a strong defense of compelling state interest. To O'Connor, the test is not an anomaly but rather "a fundamental part of our First Amendment doctrine." Without serious judicial scrutiny, the fate of minority religions would indeed be left up to the political process, which is precisely what the Bill of Rights is intended to prevent.

> The very purpose of a Bill of Rights was to withdraw certain subjects from the vicissitudes of political controversy, to place them beyond the reach of majorities and officials and to establish them as legal principles to be applied by the courts. . . . The compelling interest test effectuates the First Amendment's command that religious liberty is an independent liberty, that it occupies a preferred position, and that the Court will not permit encroachments upon this liberty, whether direct or indirect, unless required by clear and compelling governmental interests "of the highest order." "Only an especially important government interest pursued by narrowly tailored means can justify exacting a sacrifice of First Amendment freedoms as the price for an equal share of the rights, benefits, and privileges enjoyed by other citizens."[66]

Like the dissenters, she would retain the compelling state interest test; unlike them, she believed that Oregon had shown a compelling state interest in maintaining the consistency of its antidrug policy.

Recognizing both the burdens that the law places on the ability of people to exercise their religion and the state's interest in combating illicit drugs, she understands the critical question as "whether exempting respondents from the state's general criminal prohibition will unduly interfere with fulfillment of the governmental interest." She concludes that "uniform application of Oregon's criminal prohibition is essential." Hence, she reasons that Oregon has shown sufficiently overriding interest to justify applying the law to religious uses of peyote.

Justices Harry Blackmun, William Brennan, and Thurgood Marshall joined Justice O'Connor in the first two sections of her concurring opinion — those in which she challenged the majority's Free Exercise doctrine. They departed from her opinion that the state had shown a compelling interest in refusing to exempt sacramental peyote use. Their disagreement focuses on what is to be balanced, and how the balancing is to be done. Citing Roscoe Pound, one of the originators of the balancing of interests approach to jurisprudence, Blackmun reminds the majority that individual interests are not to be balanced against the general purpose of the law; clearly, general public purposes would always prevail over individual interests. "It is not the State's broad interest in fighting the critical 'war on drugs' that must be weighed against respondents' claim, but the State's narrow interest in refusing to make an exception for the religious, ceremonial use of peyote." From this perspective, the dissenters conclude that virtually nothing is lost by granting the exemption. Rejecting Justice O'Connor's emphasis on uniform applicability of drug laws, the dissenters point out that both the federal government and twenty-three states exempt sacramental use of peyote from criminal prosecutions, without reported problems. Moreover, Blackmun asserts, Oregon itself provided no evidence of the alleged dangers of peyote use; hence, he notes, the majority argument "rests on no evidentiary foundation at all." With no evidence of any harm to drug enforcement that has come from exempting sacramental peyote use, the dissenters would have required the exemption.

The compelling state interest argument was replayed, albeit inconclusively, three years later in *Church of Lukumi Babalu Aye v Hialeah*. While the Court unanimously overturned the city's ban on religious animal sacrifices, its members were split in their reasoning. The minority used the occasion to attack the *Smith* precedent and argue for a return to a compelling state interest standard.

While these disagreements left the Court's position inconclusive, Congress took the initiative in 1993 to adopt the Religious Freedom Restoration Act, which legislatively restored that standard for constitutional review in cases where federally supported programs were involved.[67] The statute could not be more clear about Congress's attitude toward the *Smith* precedent. Among the findings are that "[I]n *Employment Division v Smith*, the Supreme Court virtually eliminated the requirement that government justify burdens on religious exercise imposed by laws neutral toward religion; and the compelling interest test as set forth in prior Federal court rulings is a workable test for striking sensible balances between religious liberty and competing prior government interests." The first stated purpose is "to restore the compelling interest test as set forth in *Sherbert v Verner* and *Wisconsin v Yoder*, and to guarantee its application in all cases where free exercise of religion is substantially burdened."

As we noted previously, Congress's entrance into the debate complicates any simple distinction between majoritarian decision making and the protection of rights. Hence, the compelling state interest debate unfolds into a larger one about the nature of American constitutionalism. Before Congress passed the Religious Freedom Restoration Act, the positions on either side of the issue were a bit more clear. Those who understand our institutions as essentially majoritarian tended to find Justice Scalia's argument persuasive. Those who emphasize constitutional limitations as hedges against majoritarianism understand that the very point of having a constitution is to remove certain protections from the ordinary political process, to give them, if not absolute status, at least the kind of special weight that the compelling interest standard offers. The adoption of the statute placed the popularly elected branch of government squarely on the side previously identified with antimajoritarian arguments. By invalidating the law, the Court further complicates any simple distinctions, reinforcing my distrust of the majority/minority distinction.[68] Indeed, the interaction of multiple institutions is at the heart of the pluralist interpretation articulated below.

A STRUCTURAL AND PLURALIST INTERPRETATION OF THE DEBATE

Clearly, no single principle seems to provide adequate balance for reconciling the value conflicts raised under the Free Exercise Clause. However, this absence seems not so much a failure of principle as further evidence of the nonessentialist, pluralist nature of this constitutional problem. Still, there is something to be learned from these arguments and counterarguments. If we consider the issues from the perspectives of institutional structure, we may find a certain wisdom in this apparent muddle. They illustrate the (perhaps inadvertent) wisdom of our fragmented and even illogical system of overlapping governmental powers. The compelling state interest standard, as we have seen, is countermajoritarian[69] in that it empowers courts to consider balances in different ways than do legislative or administrative bodies. Most initial policy decisions are made by legislative or administrative entities that can be presumed to be responsible to mainstream interests or to politically favored minorities. When these policies are challenged in court, an alternative institution is invoked, and when courts use the compelling state interest standard, they measure the balance with different weights. The different institutions and different measuring devices contribute a crucial redundancy to the system of constitutional protections. They do not literally guarantee anything, but they increase the opportunities for religious interests to be given a serious hearing.

The same argument applies to accommodation. Legislative (or administrative) accommodation provides a first-instance opportunity for religious interests to be taken into account in the decision-making structure. Often accommodation is simple and relatively noncontroversial. Sometimes, of course, it produces the very problems its detractors point out; it may be unfair, biased toward favored religions, contentious, and unprincipled. For that very reason, the Establishment Clause provides a constitutionally protected method for removing the issue to a different venue, where the accommodation may be challenged. In these cases, the courts provide a place for conflicting interests to be heard and to be weighed on a different scale than that used in the original instance. None of this guarantees that the judicial decision will be different from the legislative one, but the redundancy both improves the opportunities for a good decision and helps legitimate any decision rendered. Free Exercise accommodation provides "a second opinion" for religious interests not accommodated in the first instance. Perhaps the real genius of our constitutional guarantees within a structure of fragmented government is that the process provides more access points for these protected interests to influence government. While this procedure is far from a "guarantee" in the literal sense, it is an important protection nevertheless.

The focus on the institutional implications of constitutional doctrine is consistent with our general approach to Free Exercise itself. These multiple venues of decision making are part of the larger vision of pluralism, in which religion plays so crucial a role.

9

THE PLURALIST THEORY OF FREE EXERCISE

The very forces that create a people and draw them into the bonds of community are those that separate them from others. Cultural traditions, ideology, class, geography, language, and ethnicity are powerful sources of both unity and division. Among these, religion is singularly potent because religious meanings tend to be comprehensive. Religious beliefs, rituals, practices, associations, institutions, and identities both create a sense of belonging and define the "other" who does not belong. Ancient societies did not distinguish between religious and political institutions; hence, religion was not a category separate from politics, economics, or culture. But Scripture reminds us of the difficulties Rome experienced in trying to govern an empire characterized by deep religious differences. For contemporary societies, containing a heterogeneous population in a single and harmonious political community remains elusive. Indeed, Franklin Gamwell calls the existence of multiple religions in one political community the distinguishing feature of modernity and the separation of religion and government as the distinguishing characteristic of modern politics.[1]

These features exemplify one of the perennial problems of political life—the tension between centrifugal and centripetal forces in a society. Throughout most of human history, the protection and promotion of common cultural values were understood to be two of government's most basic functions. The vision of true unity is a powerful one, nowhere explained more powerfully than in Plato's *Republic*. Religion, art, literature, and all of learning are in the service of the polis.[2] In systems based on Plato's vision, religion is either dominated by the state or simply does not exist as an independent phenomenon.

An alternative vision of unity subordinates the state into the religious authority system. The Catholic Church prior to the Second Vatican Council clung to this vision, even after the Protestant Reformation and nationalism had rendered it unattainable. In our own day, this vision seems increasingly attractive to advocates of Islamic republics in the Muslim world. Even in the United States, where religious and political separation made its earliest official appearance, many have always believed that some common spiritual and moral premises are necessary for civil peace and that the shared Judeo-Christian tradition is the background condition for our constitutional system.[3] Not surprisingly, those who hold this view also believe that the constitution permits (if not requires) governmental support of this common tradition.

The contemporary variant of this argument, increasingly prominent in the United States since the mid-1980s, is communitarianism, whose influence on religion clause jurisprudence we have seen throughout this book. Political theorists such as Michael Sandel,[4] Alasdair MacIntyre,[5] and Charles Taylor[6] have been its leading advocates. While they differ on particular points, all share the sense that atomistic individualism has created a malaise by depriving us of opportunities to sustain meaningful lives within a community of shared purposes. The communitarians reserve some of their harshest criticism for our society's excessive emphasis on rights. Rights by their very design are defensive; while they may be very effective in protecting us against invasion, they serve us poorly in developing the communal attachments, purposes, and values that seem to be essential for human happiness. The goal of this school of thought is to restore a community of shared purposes in which human beings can flourish as social beings.

The communitarian vision coexists in the United States with the more dominant theory of liberal individualism, which demands from the state a pristine neutrality, not only about religious commitments but also about other cultural, economic, and "lifestyle" choices as well.[7] Some liberals reach this conclusion because they believe that individual autonomy is a natural right, while others are simply convinced that depoliticizing these issues promotes civil peace, efficiency, and, ultimately, truth. Individualist liberalism has dominated our political thought and approach to religious liberty for much of our history, but its domination has never been complete.

While communitarians have attacked liberals for misunderstanding the nature of human attachments, liberals have attacked communitarians for refusing to recognize the potential for oppression implicit in their theory. In Avagail Eisenberg's words, "communitarians require us to suspend our disbelief about the nasty side of political power which is exercised by communities."[8] Moreover, by lavishing attention on nonvoluntary attachments, communitarians tend to underestimate the importance of voluntary ones.[9] The failings of both positions suggest the need for a richer way of understanding individual and collective life.

Somewhere between these poles lies a vision that appreciates the multiple sources of meaning and provides space for individuals to make or find their own meanings, while still recognizing the need for social cohesion. I have used the term *pluralism* to refer to this vision. Pluralism emphasizes the role of "mediating institutions," such as families, voluntary associations, and religious, educational, and economic institutions, as sources of values, meanings, and identity. To protect this diversity, pluralists oppose the accumulation of power in any institution and thus advocate both the fragmentation of governmental power and the existence of countervailing sources of power.

In many ways, the term "pluralism" is unhelpful because it is claimed by thinkers all over the political spectrum. Beyond its advocacy of diversity and limited government, the term itself dissolves into a plurality. In particular, pluralists disagree on the degree of autonomy that associations should enjoy in a good society. This disagreement, as we have seen, has serious consequences for religious freedom because so much of religious life is practiced in groups and institutions. European pluralism, with its English,[10] Catholic,[11] and Dutch Calvinist[12] variations, adheres to an almost metaphysical understanding of groups as having personalities and something akin to sovereignties. American conservative pluralism, represented here by Peter Berger and Richard John Neuhaus, emphasizes the role of intermediate institutions as transmitters of values and as buffers between individuals and the large, impersonal institutions of modern society, such as corporations and government.[13] Conservative pluralists tend to advocate a vigorous autonomy for these institutions, particularly religious ones.[14] In contrast, American liberalism is less concerned with replacing government with private associations than with making government accountable and accessible to diverse citizen influences. These views have been much discussed among social philosophers, and the public debate on multicultural education has popularized many of their key arguments.

My intent here is to neither give a full theory of pluralism nor survey the vast literature on the subject. Frankly, in a country rent by racial, ethnic, and economic divisions, and one lacking a strong activist tradition of citizenship, the issue of religious freedom alone cannot carry the weight of a whole theory of pluralism. Instead, I want to focus on those elements and interpretations that are relevant to religious freedom. It is important to emphasize that this vision does not purport to be an empirical description of the American political system; it is a regulative ideal. Cumulative inequalities continue to thwart its ideals of representation; profound divisions are as characteristic as crosscutting allegiances. The pluralist ideal is indeed an *ideal*—a constitutional aspiration.

Any commitment to pluralism raises an overwhelming question for not only constitutional theory but the polity itself: Can our institutions accommodate attachments to what Edmund Burke called "the small platoons" in a manner consistent with the need for an overall consensus and common identity? Is an individual's identification with an economic, religious, or ethnic group wholly consistent with her or his identity as an American? If our constitutional law fosters a sense of belonging to particular cultural groups, will it undermine the unity of the nation? What does it mean to belong to America? Who belongs?[15]

A pluralist approach to the free exercise of religion must give an account of the centrifugal force of religious freedom, which nurtures and protects diversity, autonomy, mediation, and all of Burke's "small platoons." And, it must protect sufficient centripetal forces to foster social coherence and sustain the bonds of common citizenship. I must reiterate that I do not offer here a full theory of pluralism. Rather, I have tried to take from the pluralist traditions those insights that are necessary to ground an approach to religious free exercise. We have encountered these elements piecemeal throughout the foregoing chapters; I wish now to bring them briefly together and then to demonstrate the light they shed on Free Exercise problems.

The pluralist interpretation of the Free Exercise Clause is embedded in Madisonian political thought. Given that the causes of faction "are sown into the nature of man," how can factional warfare and majority tyranny be avoided in a democracy? Madison's answer is perhaps the outstanding American contribution to political philosophy; he argues that the dangers of faction are minimized by the multiplicity of factions. "Either the existence of the same passion or interest in a majority at the same time must be prevented, or the majority, having such co-existent passion or interest, must be rendered, by their number and local situation, unable to concert and carry into effect schemes of oppression."[16]

The fragmentation of groups is reinforced by the fragmentation of government powers. Madison's "Federalist 51" describes a government structure that enables ambition to counter ambition.

[T]he greatest security against a gradual concentration of the several powers in the same department, consists in giving those who administer each department, the necessary constitutional means, and personal motives, to resist encroachments of the others. . . . Ambition must be made to counter ambition. The interest of the man must be connected with the constitutional rights of the place. It may be a reflection on human nature, that such devices should be necessary to controul the abuses of government. But what is government itself, but the greatest of all reflections on human nature? If men were angels, no government would be necessary. If angels were to govern men, neither external nor internal controuls on government would be necessary. In framing a government which is to be administered by men over men, the great difficulty lies in this: You must first enable the government to controul the governed; and in the next phase, oblige it to controul itself. . . .

In the compound republic of America, the power surrendered by the people is first divided between two distinct governments, and then the portion allotted to each, subdivided among distinct and separate departments. Hence, a double security arises to the rights of the people. The different governments will controul each other, at the same time that each will be controuled by itself. Second, it is of great importance in a republic, not only to guard the society against the oppression of its rulers, but to guard one part of the society against the injustice of the other part. Different interests necessarily exist in different classes of citizens. If a majority be united by a common interest, the rights of the minority will be insecure. There are but two methods of providing against this evil. The one by creating a will in the community independent of the majority, that is, of the society itself [a heredity authority, which Madison rejects]; the other by comprehending in the society so many separate descriptions of citizens, as will render an unjust combination of a majority of the whole, very improbable if not impractical. . . . Whilst all authority in it will be derived from and dependent on the society, the society itself will be broken into so any parts, interests and classes of citizens that the rights of individuals or of the minority, will be in little danger from interested combinations of the majority.[17]

Of course, divided power alone does not adequately describe constitutional democracy. It is, in effect, a limiting addendum to a representative democracy.[18] Madison realized that the guarantees of representative government and (more or less) majority rule do not provide adequate protection against majority tyranny. His genius was to attain that protection by structuring government to prevent the accumulation of power. A Bill of Rights might not be just a "parchment guarantee," but it is at best a supplemental protection. Thus the constitution created not only an extended and federal republic, with its numerous separate and independent governments, but also the separation and "blending" of powers among the three branches of the national government, so that no single one could act without the consent of the others. The fragmentation of political power and redundancy of functions within government multiplies the points of access for groups attempting to influence public policy, thus enhancing citizen impact on government.

Twentieth-century political scientists developed Madison's insights into full-blown theories. Early thinkers such as Arthur Bentley[19] and David Truman[20] constructed "interest group" explanations of American politics, and by 1960 Robert Dahl was creating a well-developed pluralist interpretation of American politics.[21] Dahl's work remained in the tradition of liberal individualism by showing how individuals join groups and engage in political action in order to pursue their individual interests. The multiplicity of groups provides overlapping patterns of consensus and conflict that build bridges across the chasms of intergroup conflict. Groups defeated on one policy issue are potentially part of a winning coalition on another issue. Because political and social allegiances are overlapping and coalitions are constantly shifting, groups moderate their demands and take into account those whose support they need in some later controversy. The constantly shifting coalition of groups should minimize the likelihood that any one group is a permanent loser. Over time, ideally at least, public policy comes to represent an inclusive concern for all participants.

Of course, this characterization is an ideal, not an empirical description of American politics, and political practice continues to fall short of this ideal. In practice, the impact of political and economic inequalities in skewing the pubic agenda raises serious challenges to the optimistic assumptions of this faith.[22] Religious minorities are far from the only groups who remain effectively disenfranchised by exclusion from coalition partnerships. The distortion of equal representation provides one the best justifications for the role of the courts in protecting minorities who are systematically excluded from the political process.[23] This understanding of judicial power abandons the "majority rule/minority rights" dichotomy inherent in much of the literature of constitutional jurisprudence and instead views legislators, administrators, judges, and all other officials as legitimate actors in this system of fragmented power and multiple access points. As we saw in the previous chapter, this "jurisdictional redundancy" has significant consequences for religious freedom in practice.

The works of Robert Dahl and other political scientists have made very important contributions to the understanding of American politics. However, these works, by intent, limit their focus to interest-group competition on the distribution of powers in a democracy. They do not address the impact of associations on individual identity or social equality, or the other implications of pluralism.[24] A new generation of pluralist social thinkers developed the theory in other directions. For example, Michael Walzer's influential book *Spheres of Justice* has greatly enriched our appreciation of the connection between a plurality of values and social inequality.[25]

Differences are seldom "just differences"; they usually convey evaluative connotations as well. Waltzer recognizes the role of groups in providing social meanings and the importance of social boundaries surrounding the separate spheres. He also recognizes that separate spheres have distinct criteria for allocating values. His theory of complex equality accepts the legitimacy of inequalities in different spheres of life, so long as they are not cumulative—that is, so long as a person's advantages in one sphere do not imply advantages in another. Distributive justice must accept these inequalities but avoid "dominance," the condition in which the distribution of goods within one sphere overflows to affect the distribution in another.

So far, what seems to be missing in all of this talk about groups is an appreciation for the variety of groups and the significance of their differences. These distinctions are crucial to the communitarian/liberal debate, as Avigail Eisenberg has shown: "Communitarians claim that liberals ignore those aspects of the self that cannot be shed as easily as are affiliations with political parties and social clubs. . . . Communitarians are mostly interested in associations and obligations that are constitutive of the individual in the sense that no self exists apart from the constitutive elements."[26] Eisenberg thus makes a very important refinement to pluralist thinking by distinguishing three kinds of associative ties: the involuntary, nonvoluntary, and voluntary. Voluntary associations are assumed and changed at will. Nonvoluntary associations are affiliations acquired either at birth or in circumstances in which an individual cannot exercise volition; thus they cannot be easily shed. "[C]onverting from Catholicism to Judaism often does not entail discarding all elements of Catholicism or adopting all elements of Judaism. Rather, it usually means becoming a 'Jewish convert' or an 'ex-Catholic,' even in one's own eyes."[27] Finally, involuntary associations are those a person rejects but cannot avoid "because the association is linked to a characteristic that she possesses involuntarily, such as being a woman or black, and this characteristic influences how she is treated by others."[28]

Clearly, these distinctions—particularly that between voluntary and nonvoluntary associations—shed much light on the debate we encountered in Chapter 1 about whether religion is to be understood as a choice. We encountered another variation of it in the context of religious institutions.

Thus, a theory of religious pluralism would be well served to take seriously the "nonvoluntary" nature of many kinds of religious associations.

Pluralism in all its varieties confronts the following problem: How can people, profoundly divided on the most foundational questions, nevertheless live together in relative peace and justice? In the liberal tradition, John Rawls finds the answer in an overlapping consensus derived from the shared fund of principles suffused through the political culture.[29]

In my view coherence is maintained not so much by an essential core of common beliefs as by a family of concerns (in the Wittgensteinian sense). This family of concerns, in turn, is fostered by the crosscutting patterns of cleavage, identity, conflict, and commitment among citizens. My insistence on cohesion as well as plurality underlines the importance of common citizenship in my approach. It is crucial that religious minorities enjoy full freedom to engage in divergent practices *while* participating in the system at large. The goal is inclusive citizenship in which people never have to choose between loyalties.

How well does this ideal reflect real possibilities in American society? Perhaps Americans are too polarized for any overlapping consensus to exist. James Davison Hunter's book entitled *Culture Wars* envisions an increasing polarization of American society into two opposing and mutually exclusive camps.[30] The split, which he defines as "not theological or ecclesiological," is a result of profound differences over "how to order our lives" and, ultimately, over what is moral authority. On one side is orthodoxy, with its commitment to externally definable and transcendent authority, and on the other side is progressivism, where rationality and subjectivism are the authority. Increasingly this cleavage cuts across traditional denominational lines—dividing conservative and progressive elements of the same denomination and uniting religious groups that historically have had little overlap. If Hunter is right, this polarization is profoundly "religious" in the sense that religion is about comprehensive meanings. Hence, my faith in a pluralist overlap of values is sadly unfounded. Adding to the seriousness of this possible polarization is the loss of bridges between the two traditions. Mainline liberal Protestantism and its educational institutions long served as a bridge between orthodox Christianity and "secular humanism." The dramatic decline of mainline Protestantism may be an indication that the bridge is disappearing, leaving the society as a whole culturally polarized.

Of course, this pessimistic thesis of polarization considers only the religious/cultural dimension of social life. A full pluralism depends on overlapping interests and commitments based on economic and professional interests, geographic and ethnic identities, friendships, voluntary associations, and countless other factors to blunt the sharp lines of religious divisions. Nevertheless, empirical evidence of religious polarization that reduces multiple characteristics of religion to a single dividing line seriously decreases the likelihood of a pluralist solution to religious conflict.

The pluralist vision of American society will appeal to many but by no means all readers. I have argued that the "purpose" of the religion clauses is to foster alternate sources of meaning. Important as religions are, they are not the only sources of meanings. The state is not barred from being an important source of meaning—it is simply precluded from holding a monopoly on that function. This vision accepts, celebrates, and fosters a vision of overlapping and crosscutting attachments that many have identified as a characteristic of modernism. The goal is to enable a person comfortably to be a Muslim, an American, a Texan, a homemaker, a voluntary association member, and many others at the same time.

The notion of overlapping and crosscutting group affiliations (rather than exclusive ones) is crucial to this pluralist view. Avigail Eisenberg explains the role of multiple affiliations:

> In order for the individual to have the power to shape her own identity, she must enjoy many affiliations and, crucially, no single group or community may dominate and direct her development. Each group provides for the individual a different vantage from which she can critically assess her attachments to other groups. Reassessing one's attachments requires that a multiplicity of contexts be accessible to the individual. The individual need not be conceptualized as unencumbered by all attachments at once in order to understand how she is the author of her life and identity.[31]

This vision promises individuals "an opportunity to participate in our public life as equals while maintaining such ties to the minority cultures as they may choose."[32] At the same time, it promises equal opportunity to choose integration within the common identity. Ultimately, intellectual honesty is required of a pluralist to confront a difficult question: Does this vision make promises that no polity can deliver? As we survey the implications of this idea for Free Exercise interpretation, we must bear in mind the immense task it imposes upon our political system.

THE SCOPE AND LIMITS OF PLURALIST FREE EXERCISE

Where does all this take us in the jurisprudence of the religion clauses? Its guiding ideal is to foster independent religious beliefs, meanings, and identities, and the institutions that sustain them within the context of common citizenship. This principle is similar to one offered by Michael McConnell. In his view, "[t]he great evil against which the Religion Clauses are directed is government induced homogeneity—the tendency of government action to discourage or suppress the expression of differences in matters of religion." Thus, religion clause cases lead courts to one basic question: "Is the purpose or probably effect to increase religious uniformity, either by inhibiting religious practice (a Free Exercise clause violation) or by forcing or inducing a contrary religious practice (an Establishment Clause violation) without sufficient justification?"[33]

While I can find no fault with McConnell's words, my interpretation of them would be somewhat more limited than his—especially his approach to the Establishment Clause. In Free Exercise controversies, my approach is more demanding on the obligations of common citizenship than is his. The pluralist principle does not simply protect alternate sources of meaning; it does so "within the bonds of equal common citizenship." Again, McConnell's words are appropriate: "[T]he American polity should be such that every citizen can be a full and equal participant in civil society without being forced to sacrifice his religious identity."[34] A fundamental aim of the First Amendment religion clauses is to assure to persons of all religions the benefits of equal and common citizenship. The paradigm Free Exercise failure in this respect is the case of *United States v Macintosh*,[35] in which a religious pacifist was denied American citizenship because of his refusal to swear to defend the country.

"Equal common citizenship" involves the subtle relationship between identity and differences. Sometimes equality means ignoring irrelevant differences, sometimes it means taking relevant ones into account. The problem, of course, is knowing which is which. Differences are relevant, not in the abstract, but within social context. Background conditions, such as economic status or political power, may affect religious ones. In the United States, the difference between Catholics and Protestants may be simply a difference; in Ireland, the difference is one that conveys a power inequality. Once we are aware of the background conditions surrounding religious exercise, we recognize problems of status domination, selective indifference, and downright animus as part of the context that must be taken into account in order to preserve religious equality. These observations help us appreciate what is often at stake when religious freedom is threatened. Religious minorities are vulnerable to both intentional exclusion and "selective indifference." The insistence upon a genuine equality for a variety of religious expressions demands much more than a mere formal neutrality in government policy.[36]

This element of the Free Exercise issue captures the spirit of Justice O'Connor's Establishment Clause approach. Beginning with her concurring opinion in *Lynch v Donnelly*, O'Connor has argued that the Establishment Clause is breached if religious symbolism conveys a message of exclusion to others. "Endorsement sends a message to non-adherents that they are outsiders, not full members of the political community, and an accompanying message to adherents that they are insiders, favored members of the political community."[37]

The principle of common citizenship aims at inclusion, and inclusion is a double-edged sword. While religious minorities are guaranteed the right of common citizenship, they do not enjoy Free Exercise rights to exclude themselves from the public mosaic of meanings. The "bonds of common citizenship" idea expresses both an expansive and limiting principle. It is expansive in that it implies accommodation that enables those who wish to do so to participate in the benefits of the wider society. But it is limiting in that it does not imply a guarantee of strong autonomy rights to insular groups who reject common citizenship, nor does it offer much comfort to the "redemptive communities" whose religious exercise involves capturing of governmental power to impose unitary meanings. For their doing so would both curtail alternate sources of meaning for others and deny to them the symbols of equal citizenship.

The pluralist approach counsels a broad, but not infinitely expandable, definition of religion. Above all, it resonates with the nonessentialist "family of indicators" approach associated with Judge Adams's opinion in *Malnak v Yogi*.[38] Judge Adams's three indicia, in spite of all their problems, capture best what is of value in religious sources of meaning. The first element, that religion is valuable because it is a source of both answers to ultimate questions and ultimate values, reflects the pluralist insistence that while the state may be an important source of values, it ought not be the ultimate one. The second element in Judge Adams's definition—"comprehensiveness"—captures the important insight that a function of religious beliefs is to organize other kinds of beliefs—to "bind" them into a unifying whole. The final element—institutional and social indicators—invokes the concrete ways that meanings are created and sustained and reminds us that the First Amendment protects not just alternate meanings but also their sources and their manifestations.

Undoubtedly, the comprehensiveness of religious beliefs is the source of immense civil/religious conflict, as the textbook and curriculum cases illustrated.[39] In these cases, parents attempted to remove from the public school curriculum reading materials that conflicted with their religious beliefs.

Overall, the courts found no First Amendment requirement that the public schools refrain from confronting students' religious beliefs. In the pluralist account, religious beliefs are protected but are not immune from confrontation by the state or other cultural influences. The painful confrontation of beliefs is a *positive good* in this vision. In general, the pluralist view is expansive in protecting and fostering religious meanings at odds with commonly held ones. However, it has only limited sympathy for exclusive meanings of any sort.

We have repeatedly observed that meanings are not disembodied, purely cognitive phenomena but are inseparable from the practices that create and sustain them. This observation implies a very broad, but not infinite, protection for religious practices. The role of a challenged practice in fostering a system of meanings might become a point of contention. Of course, petitioners can be expected to argue that every practice is essential to the preservation of meaning. However, the state is likely to be skeptical. Judges will still have to make difficult judgments in this area. In spite of the fact that centrality has not proven to be a useful jurisprudential tool, there is something to the notion that some practices are more crucial than others. For example, payment of social security taxes did not seem to deprive Lee of his Amishness, but depriving him of the opportunity to educate his children in his faith would certainly have done so. This distinction makes sense of the different results in *Wisconsin v Yoder*[40] and *United States v Lee*.[41] The Amish approach to education was protected in *Yoder*, but in *Lee* the Court rejected a claim of an Amish businessman for exemption from the social security tax for his Amish employees who for religious reasons do not accept social security benefits. Here, it is difficult to find any forced choice between religious conviction or identity and the obligations of citizenship. It is true that Lee was required to pay a tax for which he received no personal benefit, but the very nature of taxation, like the pooled risk in an insurance program, makes that inevitable. Even as a member of an insular community, Lee shares common citizenship with his fellow Americans; paying the tax does not deny him religious meanings, identities, or practices.

Can we square the *Lee* decision with the unemployment compensation cases in which individuals were unavailable for their ordinary employment because of their religious convictions?[42] The Supreme Court held in all these cases that denial of benefits violated their constitutional right to free exercise of religion. That is, the state was constitutionally obligated to recognize religion as legitimate grounds for being unavailable to work. These decisions enabled religious minorities to participate fully in mainstream life—which they desired to do. Without these accommodations, the individuals would have had to "choose between" their participation in the workplace and, hence, the economic life of the community, and their religion. The goal of the pluralist interpretation is to try to avoid forcing such choices. In short, Lee asked to opt out of the common pool, while Sherbert and the others asked to be allowed in.

Similar judgments will have to be made concerning religious institutions. We have considered many eloquent arguments for a very extensive right to autonomy for religious institutions because they both create and sustain religious meanings. In Berger's words, they create the plausibility structures. Churches, of course, provide sources of meaning for both mainstream and marginal religious groups. They are particularly important in providing options to meet the religious needs of those who reject the wider society's culture and idiom. Judges will be asked to evaluate the importance of an institution's practices to its ability to sustain meanings for its members. This will be a difficult but not impossible task. I think it is possible for a judge to determine that church architecture is more crucial to conveying meanings than taxation of church-owned enterprises. Schools are crucial, but employment practices may be less so.

The case of *Southwestern Baptist Seminary*[43] helps illustrate my rather centrist approach on this point. In determining which employees were covered by Title VII protection, the appeals court attempted to fine tune the distinction between ministerial employees and other staff. Its reasoning was similar to what I have suggested; ministerial employees are intimately connected with the dissemination of religious meanings, while that connection is less immediate with respect to other employees. Such line drawing is always awkward and inelegant, but I think it makes for a decent compromise when several systems of values are overlaid upon each other. Neither the seminary's demands for administrative autonomy nor the state's interest in combating employment discrimination are absolute when we think of religious institutions as existing as part of the collage of overlapping social commitments.

The case of *Jimmy Swaggart Ministries v Board of Equalization of California*[44] illustrates the difference between my pluralist principle and that advocated by McConnell. In this case, the Supreme Court held that a general sales tax as applied to religious marketing does not violate the Free Exercise Clause. As I see it, the ministry is simply being required to participate in the shared burden of revenue collection; there is no threat to religious identities, meanings, or citizenship by being required to pay sales taxes on religious articles. It is true, of course, that the economic burden of taxation will deprive some individuals or churches of other opportunities to exercise religious choices and, in that sense, will diminish their heterogeneity. However, in contrast to McConnell, I find the common obligations of citizenship a sufficient justification for these economic costs. Sharing the common economic burdens of citizenship does not seem to pose any constitutional burden on religious diversity.

While recognizing the importance of religious institutions, I believe that some of the arguments for church autonomy excessively romanticize many institutional functions. Moreover, and more importantly, they reflect a vision of society more fragmented than my pluralistic one. My goal has been to present a means for society to encourage multiple sources of meaning, but not exclusive ones. To encourage a multiplicity of private institutions is to foster a social mosaic, but not a fragmented society. In short, institutional autonomy is valued as instrumental in a society of multiple sources of meaning, but it is not a constitutional right in the abstract. I cannot agree that religious institutions have a constitutional right to create vacuums for themselves. Especially when institutions participate in the wider society in acculturated ways, they may not selectively demand dispensations from the commitments of the wider culture.[45] Hence, the commitment to racial equality does encompass Bob Jones University when it acts as a university. Likewise, the prohibitions against discrimination, I believe, should have applied to the Mormon Church when it engaged in ordinary acculturated behavior as an employer and as the proprietor of a public gymnasium. These groups and their members are not insular; they operate religiously in the parlance of the wider culture; hence, it seems disingenuous to demand selective separation from it. Because insular groups—those who wish to protect the autonomy, insularity, or exclusiveness of their meaning systems—raise particularly difficult problems for the pluralist principle, they merit special attention, which they will be given later in this chapter.

The focus on meanings enables us to appreciate the importance of religious identities. Deprecating a person's religious identity or depriving a person of the symbols of that identity or of the right to develop an identity harms both religious meanings and equal citizenship. The protection of religious identity illustrates both the scope and limits of the pluralist principle. Separate religious identities are constitutionally protected, but my argument does not guarantee a right to an *exclusive* identity.

THE HARD CASES: RELIGIONS THAT SEEK UNIFIED MEANINGS

The pluralist vision runs contrary to another powerful vision of American life, which I have characterized as the fundamentalist one. Fundamentalism vigorously rejects the fragmentation of modern life and desires, above all, a unified pattern of identity and value. Whereas my approach celebrates overlapping identities, the fundamentalist one seeks a seamless one. Therefore, constitutional controversies raised by individuals or groups seeking to create for themselves a seamless system of religious and public meanings pose the most difficult problem for my approach. While my theory does a reasonable job of protecting fundamentalist religions, it will not do so in an overall framework that their adherents are likely to find appealing. As we shall see, the pluralist account creates serious problems for persons seeking a seamless life of clearly defined loyalties. Neither insular groups nor those committed to societal "redemption" will be entirely satisfied with the resulting constitutional policy.

The most difficult problem for my approach is posed by religious groups who reject the pluralist vision. The mosaic of overlapping meanings, structures, and institutions that pluralists find attractive is a source of pain and a symptom of pathology to those who seek a seamless social reality. Sociologist of religion Frank Lechner, describing all kinds of religious fundamentalism, notes that a common theme is the critique of the differentiated society. "The threat of modernity lies not so much in a new kind of theology, but rather in institutional differentiation, compartmentalization, and cultural pluralism — social life becomes horribly complex, and there no longer seems to be one true common culture. Thus, . . . the response to this threat is to revitalize the true faith and to dedifferentiate — to make all institutions operate on sound value principles, to implement the sacred world view across the board and to deprivatize religion."[46]

Two kinds of religious communities who pose the greatest problems for my moderate pluralism are insular communities, which seek to create and maintain their own integrated *nomos*, and redemptive communities, which seek to transform the wider one. The Amish, the Hasidim, and various Native American religious groups exemplify the first; the second includes a wide range of visionary groups from the conservative activist Christian fundamentalists who are enjoying political ascendance as these words are written. Both kinds of groups challenge the moderate pluralism of my theory — the first by demanding a much stronger pluralism, and the second, by seeking to proclaim unified meanings for the society as a whole.

In Chapter 8, we considered four related cases centered on religion and education: *Wisconsin v Yoder*,[47] *Bob Jones University v United States*,[48] *Mozert et al. v Hawkins County Board of Education*,[49] and *Board of Education of Kiryas Joel Village School District v Grumet*.[50] Juxtaposing these cases again will be helpful in exploring the concept of insularity and its implications for religious liberty. The Amish in *Yoder* and the Satmar Hasidim in *Kiryas Joel* are both insular in the sense that they live in separate communities, and maintain cultures dramatically different from the mainstream. Both found the public educational system culturally and religiously invasive. Neither Bob Jones University nor the parents who brought the case in *Mozert* were insular in the same way. As a university, Bob Jones was engaging the wider culture, except that it was actively sectarian and it scrupulously refused government support in order to avoid the accompanying requirements. Parents in *Mozert* would not be described as insular except insofar as they rejected many prevalent cultural values and sought to preserve more traditional ones.

The constitutional demands made by the four petitioners were quite different as well. The Amish asked that their teenagers by exempt from state compulsory education requirements; they asked to be left alone. The Hasidim, who privately educated most of their children, wanted their own public school district so that their disabled children could be educated at public expense in an insular cultural setting. Bob Jones University wanted to maintain its religiously motivated policy regarding the sexual separation of the races, while still enjoying the financial advantage of tax exemptions. And the parents in *Mozert* wanted the school system to accommodate their religious needs by altering the public school curriculum.

Crudely speaking, all these cases involved religious groups who rejected state demands that would have dragged them into the mainstream culture. In accordance with the method of "reflective equilibrium," I begin my analysis with my feeling that all four cases were decided correctly but with a lingering suspicion that they cannot be reconciled.[51] What is the difference between the *Yoder* and *Bob Jones* cases other than the fact that, like most commentators, I have a certain sentimental sympathy for the Amish and a personal distaste for the politics of Bob Jones? All four cases involve conflicts between the state's legitimate role as a creator of public values and religious groups who reject the values being promoted. This educative and value-creating function is an important one for the state, one Plato thought the most important. In both *Bob Jones* and *Yoder* constitutional litigation forced the state to consider its commitment to the specific values it had chosen to promote. In *Yoder* the state properly defended its role as educator, but the compelling state interest test required a certain humility by requiring the state to demonstrate that no less burdensome method was available to assure that students were prepared for adult life. The majority reasoned that compulsory education to age sixteen was simply not the only appropriate way in which that function might be fulfilled. Amish vocational training (or private schools or home schooling) could also fulfill that function. Michael McConnell understands the *Yoder* decision as a commitment to protect genuinely insular communities: "The Supreme Court held unanimously that the Amish have a constitutional right to protection from being 'assimilated into society at large. . . .' The legal system can accept the proposition that a religious community is a self contained unit with the right to set its own norms, so long as—in the Court's words in *Yoder*—it 'interferes with no rights or interests of others.' "[52]

Can we reconcile *Yoder* with the *Kiryas Joel* decision? Like the Amish, the Satmar Hasidim of Kiryas Joel are an insular community seeking a seamless way of life. The citizens of Kiryas Joel, of course, have an undeniable constitutional right to educate their children in private religious schools; equally, they have a right to public funds for special education of children with special needs. But to insist on receiving those funds on their own terms in order to preserve their insularity seems to ask for fragmentation and exclusivity rather than the citizenship within a pluralistic society. Still, the heart of the conflict is not the community's desire for public moneys. What the Establishment Clause prohibits is religious "gerrymandering." The Court majority ruled that public school district lines could not be drawn along religious lines in order to accommodate the needs of a religious community. Lines that today may be drawn benevolently may later be drawn maliciously. Moreover, and more importantly, reinforcing lines of separation by making congruent religious and governmental boundaries violates the pluralist commitment to overlapping patterns of community and cleavage.

The problem in *Bob Jones* occurs in a less insular setting: a private, religiously affiliated university that did not receive public funds but was a tax-exempt charitable institution. Based upon its founder's religious beliefs, it prohibited interracial dating or marriage. The government had determined that racial integration was a value to be pursued by a wide variety of public tools, including the Internal Revenue Code. In this case, the Internal Revenue Service had adopted a ruling that denied tax-exempt status to institutions practicing race discrimination. The university's constitutional challenge to that denial required the government to examine its commitment to the goal of racial equality. The Supreme Court decision upholding the IRS's ruling illustrates the occasions when government does exercise to the fullest its role as a meaning source, even to the point of denying financial advantages to those who pursue a contrary vision. And yet, there is the troubling sacrifice of genuine diversity in this decision. Justice Powell's concurring opinion describes it well:

[The majority] ignores the important role played by tax exemptions in encouraging diverse, indeed often sharply conflicting, activities and viewpoints. As Justice Brennan has observed, private, nonprofit groups receive tax exemptions because "each group contributes to the diversity of association, viewpoint, and enterprise essential to a vigorous, pluralistic society." Far from representing an effort to reinforce any perceived "common community conscience," the provision of tax exemptions to nonprofit groups is one indispensable means of limiting the influence of governmental orthodoxy on important areas of community life.[53]

Cases such as *Bob Jones* therefore force the state to confront its own certainty and commitment. As a matter of personal conviction, I believe that such bitter confrontations should be few and far between. The sacrifice of alternate meanings is a heavy price to pay in a pluralist society; yet, there may be rare occasions when the normative commitments to plurality and inclusion override the autonomy of a group with a contrary vision, so long as purely private options (not involving state support) remain available. Because guaranteeing an inclusive common citizenship is one of the most important duties of the pluralist state, and in light of the special history of racial exclusion, I believe that this goal was a truly compelling one.

The defenders of Bob Jones University and of Kiryas Joel may well object to the value I have placed on overlapping meanings in the social mosaic. Their vision of a unified life is surely an attractive one, perhaps ultimately preferable to the plural one. However, such a vision is ultimately not consistent with the American cultural and political heritage. Whether one thinks it is better or not, it is simply not *ours*.

The *Mozert* case stretches the notion of insularity—perhaps to a breaking point. But the issue raised in this case is similar to those discussed in the earlier ones. Here, too, a community wished to protect its religiously inspired way of life against state encroachment. Indeed, the values these people wanted to preserve are perhaps not very different from those in the other three cases. Yet, as I have suggested previously, I find their case the weakest of the four. They ask not for private space to pursue alternative meanings, they ask for public acquiescence to their values. In that sense, their mission is redemptive rather than insular.

My theory has surprisingly little support for redemptive communities.[54] For the most part, the Establishment Clause is at the heart of our constitutional protection against groups who seek to convert the society to their vision. The old and often repeated insight is still largely true: the Establishment Clause is a protection against majoritarian dangers to religion (or those who would impose their religious values on the majority), while the Free Exercise Clause is a protection for religious minorities. The two clauses overlap, however, when religious groups claim a Free Exercise right to redesign the public square. Our overriding commitment to plural and overlapping meanings confirms that the Free Exercise Clause offers no constitutional comfort to those who want to use the mechanisms of the state as tools of redemptive transformation—however noble the goals.

CONCLUSION

I have offered no bright-line solutions to Free Exercise conflicts. The pluralist principle will itself provide many sources of conflict. Yet, the very untidiness of the principle is its strength. It is messy because the social reality surrounding it is messy. Our world is replete with overlapping realities and webs of social meanings. Any attempt to impose an order on them—to suggest a hierarchy of values—would be a mistake both empirically and normatively. Empirically, we are a pluralist society, not only religiously but also in terms of overlapping patterns of consensus and cleavage. Normatively, the value commitment underlying my entire argument is a commitment to preserving that social mosaic. A polity committed to fostering alternate sources of meaning is not an entirely comfortable one, but it should ultimately be one that fosters an inclusive respect and civility.

NOTES

INTRODUCTION

1. The First Amendment reads, "Congress shall make no law respecting an establishment of religion, or prohibiting the free exercise thereof; or abridging the freedom of speech, or of the press, or the right of the people peaceably to assemble, and to petition the Government for a redress of grievances."

2. I have capitalized "Free Exercise" when I am referring specifically to the clause in the Constitution—in the way one would capitalize "First Amendment." When speaking in general of religious freedom, I use the lower case "free exercise."

3. The Free Exercise Clause was incorporated into the Fourteenth Amendment and hence is held applicable to the states, in the case of *Cantwell v Connecticut*, 310 US 296 (1940). In the mid-1980s, Federal District Court Judge Brevard Hand handed down some rather idiosyncratic rulings denying that the First Amendment applied to the states. See his decisions in *Wallace v Jaffree*, 472 US 38 (1985), and in *Smith v Board of School Commissioners of Mobile County*, 655 F. Supp. 939 (S. Dist. Ala. 937) (1986). These decisions were quickly overruled.

4. *Reynolds v United States*, 98 US 145 (1878).

5. *Cantwell v Connecticut*, 310 US 296 (1940); *Jones v Opelika*, 316 US 584 (1942), overruled in *Murdock v Pennsylvania*, 319 US 105 (1943); *Minersville School District v Gobitis*, 310 US 586 (1940), overruled in *West Virginia State Board of Education v Barnette*, 319 US 624 (1943); *Cox v New Hampshire*, 312 US 569 (1941); *Prince v Massachusetts*, 321 US 158 (1944). Not all of these cases represented victories for the Jehovah's Witnesses.

6. *Sherbert v Verner*, 374 US 398 (1963).

7. *Engel v Vitale*, 370 US 421 (1962); *Abington Township School District v Schempp*, 374 US 203 (1963).

8. *Wisconsin v Yoder*, 406 US 205 (1972). This approach is consistent with the strict scrutiny given to "fundamental freedoms" under the preferred freedoms approach in

general. Justice Murphy made a case for a preferred position of religious freedom in his dissent in *Jones v Opelika*, 584.

9. *United States v Seeger*, 380 US 163 (1965); *Welsh v United States*, 398 US 333 (1970).

10. *NLRB v Catholic Bishop of Chicago*, 440 US 490 (1979); *Corporation of Presiding Bishop of the Church of Jesus Christ of Latter-Day Saints v Amos*, 483 US 327 (1987).

11. For a discussion of this trend during the 1980s, see Bette Novit Evans, "Contradictory Demands on the First Amendment Religion Clauses: Having it Both Ways," *Journal of Church and State* 30 (1988): 463.

12. *The Williamsburg Charter* (Washington, D.C.: Williamsburg Charter Foundation, 1988).

13. *Employment Division, Department of Human Resources of Oregon v Smith*, 494 US 872 (1990).

14. *City of Boerne v Flores*, No. 95-2074 (decided June 25, 1997).

15. An exceptionally creative attempt to situate jurisprudence to concepts of religion is the analysis of *Lynch v Donnelly* in Winnifred Fallers Sullivan, *Paying the Words Extra* (Cambridge: Harvard University Press, 1994).

16. The *Oxford English Dictionary* speculates that the English word "religion" comes from *religare*, to bind, as to bind oneself to a vow or community. Michael Perry has used this insight to define religion as a "binding vision." See Michael Perry, *The Constitution, the Courts, and Human Rights* (New Haven: Yale University Press, 1982), 97.

17. The split between traditional, conservative communal religions and individualist, "secular" perspectives is the theme of those who observe "culture wars" dividing American religious culture. See, for example, James Davison Hunter, *Culture Wars: The Struggle to Define America* (New York: Basic Books, 1991).

18. Frederick Mark Gedicks, *The Rhetoric of Church and State* (Durham: Duke University Press, 1995), 11–12.

19. Mark Tushnet makes this point especially well in "The Constitution of Religion," *Connecticut Law Review* 18 (1986): 701.

20. Philip Kurland, *Religion and the Law* (Chicago: Aldine, 1961).

21. The statement is from Justice William O. Douglas's majority opinion in *Zorach v Clauson*, 343 US 306 (1952).

22. Ronald Dworkin, "Hard Cases," in *Taking Rights Seriously* (Cambridge: Harvard University Press, 1977), and "How Law is Like Literature," in *A Matter of Principle* (Cambridge: Harvard University Press, 1985).

CHAPTER 1

1. Advocates of originalism insist that the intentions of the authors, or at least the understanding of the founding generation, should be authoritative sources for constitutional interpretation. Among the many scholarly advocates of originalism, see Edwin Meese, "The Supreme Court of the United States: Bulwark of a Limited Constitution," *South Texas Law Journal* 27 (1986): 455; Edwin Meese, "Construing the Constitution," *University of California at Davis Law Review* 19 (1985): 22; Robert Bork, "Neutral Principles and Some First Amendment Problems," *Indiana Law Journal* 47 (1971): 1; Robert Bork, *The Tempting of America* (New York: Free Press, 1990); William Rehnquist, "The Notion of a Living Constitution," *Texas Law Review* 54 (1976): 693; and Peter Berger,

"Original Intention in Historical Perspective," *George Washington Law Review* 54 (1986): 296. For scholarship on the original understanding of the religion clauses, see M. Malbin, *Religion and Politics: The Intentions of the Authors of the First Amendment* (Washington, D.C.: American Enterprise Institute for Public Policy Research, 1978); Robert Cord, *Separation of Church and State: Historical Fact and Current Fiction* (New York: Lambeth Press, 1982); Leonard Levy, "The Original Meaning of the Establishment Clause of the First Amendment," in *Religion and the State: Essays in Honor of Leo Pfeffer*, ed. James E. Wood Jr. (Waco, Tex.: Baylor University Press, 1985); Michael McConnell, "The Origins and Historical Understanding of Free Exercise of Religion," *Harvard Law Review* 103 (1990): 1409; Thomas Curry, *The First Freedoms: Church and State in America to the Passage of the First Amendment* (New York: Oxford University Press, 1986); and Derek Davis, *Original Intent: Chief Justice Rehnquist and the Course of American Church/State Relations* (Buffalo, N.Y.: Prometheus Books, 1991).

Members of the Supreme Court have themselves often engaged in this debate. Among many such arguments, see Justice Black (for the Court) and Justice Rutledge (dissenting) in *Everson v Board of Education*, 330 US 1 (1947), and Justice O'Connor's concurring opinion and Chief Justice Rehnquist's dissenting opinion in *Wallace v Jaffree*, 472 US 38 (1985).

2. Steven Smith, *Foreordained Failure: The Quest for a Constitutional Principle of Religious Freedom* (New York: Oxford University Press, 1995).

3. For some of the most persuasive critiques of originalism, see Paul Brest, "The Misconceived Quest for the Original Understanding," *Boston University Law Review* 60 (1983): 204; William Brennan, "The Constitution of the United States: Contemporary Ratification," *South Texas Law Journal* 27 (1986): 433; Larry Simon, "The Authority of the Framers of the Constitution: Can Originalist Interpretation Be Justified," 73 *California Law Review* 73 (1985): 1482; and Lawrence Tribe, "Why Should Mere Intentions Matter?" *Constitutional Choices* 4 (1985).

4. Ronald Dworkin, "Interpretive Concepts," in *Law's Empire* (Cambridge: Harvard University Press, 1986), 52. See the entire chapter for the development of this argument.

5. This theory is worked out in detail and defended in Ronald Dworkin, "How Law is Like Literature," in *A Matter of Principle* (Cambridge: Harvard University Press, 1985), 147–66. See the entire chapter for the development of these ideas, and in particular, for his critique of originalism as an interpretive method.

6. This and other objections to Dworkin's interpretive method are developed by Stanley Fish in "Working on the Chain Gang: Interpretation in Law and Literature." Dworkin describes his method in "Law as Interpretation" and refutes Fish in "My Reply to Stanley Fish (and Walter Benn Michaels): Please Don't Talk About Objectivity Anymore." All three articles are collected in W. J. T. Mitchell, ed., *The Politics of Interpretation* (Chicago: University of Chicago Press, 1982).

7. Smith, *Foreordained Failure*, 68 (footnote omitted).

8. See Smith's objections to this method, particularly 88–98.

9. Franklin Gamwell, *The Meaning of Religious Freedom* (Albany: State University of New York Press, 1995).

10. Robert Cover, "The Supreme Court 1982 Term: Forward: Nomos and Narrative," *Harvard Law Review* 97 (1983): 4–5 (hereafter cited as "Nomos and Narrative"). Cover's analysis is particularly significant for religious clause interpretation. Cover argues that

each community creates its own law, which is as authoritative as that of the official legal system. His understanding of the "jurisgenerative" nature of communities creates a powerful argument for the autonomy of religious institutions (see particularly pp. 28–33). My position is sympathetic to Cover's approach, but it does not adopt his controversial "nonstatist premise"—that the interpretations offered by judges are "not superior" to those of a community with its own "normative boundaries" and to the "sacred narratives that ground the understanding of law they offer." (See Chapter 5.)

11. John Rawls, *A Theory of Justice* (Cambridge: Harvard University Press, 1977), 20.

12. *Wallace v Jaffree*, 472 US 38 (1985).

13. *Cantwell v Connecticut*, 310 US 296, 303 (1940).

14. *Abington Township School District v Schempp*, 374 US 203 (1963).

15. *Sherbert v Verner*, 374 US 398 (1963).

16. Rawls, *A Theory of Justice*, 560, 563. See also ch. 63. "The Definition of Good for Plans of Life": . . . [A] person's plan of life is rational if, and only if (1) it is one of the plans that is consistent with the principles of rational choice when these are applied to all relevant features of his situation, and (2) it is that plan among those meeting this condition which would be chosen by him with full deliberative rationality, that is, with full awareness of the relevant facts and after a careful consideration of the consequences" (408).

17. David Richards, *Toleration and the Constitution* (New York: Oxford University Press, 1986). See also Gail Merel, "The Protection of Individual Choice: A Consistent Understanding of Religion under the First Amendment," *University of Chicago Law Review* 45 (1978): 805.

18. The classic study of denominational affiliation is Will Herberg, *Protestant-Catholic-Jew* (Garden City, N.Y.: Anchor, 1955), in which he argues that denominations provide Americans with a crucial sense of identity. In the 1970s, Andrew Greeley found denominational affiliation equally crucial to the structure of American religion. See his *The Denominational Society* (Glenview, Ill.: Scott, Foresman, 1992).

19. See Andrew Greeley, *Religious Change in America* (Cambridge: Harvard University Press, 1989), 122.

20. Thomas Luckmann, *The Invisible Religion* (New York: Macmillan, 1967), 102; see also George Armstrong Kelly, "Politics and American Religious Consciousness," in *Religion and America*, ed. Mary Douglas and Steven Tipton (Boston: Beacon Press, 1982), 207.

21. Roger Finke and Rodney Stark, *The Churching of America, 1776–1990: Winners and Losers in Our Religious Economy* (New Brunswick, N.J.: Rutgers University Press, 1992). The authors, using demographic data, conclude that churches that are more demanding of sacrifice from their members are more attractive and thus ultimately more successful in attaining "market share."

22. Ibid., 205.

23. *Lee v Weisman*, 505 US 577 (1992). Justices Blackmun and Souter, each concurring separately, insisted that the absence of coercion is not the measure of Establishment Clause requirements. Justice Scalia, dissenting for himself and Justices Rehnquist, White, and Thomas found nothing coercive in the exercise.

24. The outstanding spokesman for this position is Richard Delgado. Among his works, see "When Religious Exercise is Not Free: Deprogramming and the Constitutional Status of Coercively Induced Belief," *Vanderbilt Law Review* 37 (1984); 1071. Delgado's works, and those of his critics, are discussed at length in Chapter 3.

25. Michael Sandel, ed., *Liberalism and Its Critics* (New York: New York University Press, 1984), 5–6.

26. Ibid., 6. See also on this point Alistair MacIntyre, "The Virtues, the Unity of a Human Life, and the Concept of a Tradition," in *After Virtue* (Notre Dame: Notre Dame University Press, 1981).

27. For example, *Ohio Civil Rights Commission v Dayton Christian Schools*, 477 US 619 (1986), involving sex discrimination by a religious school, posed a conflict between choices of a religious institution and those of a dissenting individual. I explore this problem in depth in Chapter 5.

28. See, for example, Frederick Mark Gedicks, "Toward a Constitutional Jurisprudence of Religious Group Rights," *Wisconsin Law Review* (1989): 99.

29. Mark Tushnet, "The Constitution of Religion," *Connecticut Law Review* 18 (1986): 701, 734.

30. Douglas Laycock, "The Remnants of Free Exercise," *Supreme Court Review* (1990): 1, 11.

31. Stephen Carter, *The Culture of Disbelief* (New York: Basic Books, 1993), 14–15.

32. James Madison, *Memorial and Remonstrance Against Religious Assessments*, vol. 8 of *The Papers of James Madison*, edited by W. Hutchinson and W. Rachal (New York: Oxford University Press, 1986), 298–305.

33. Richards, *Toleration and the Constitution*, ch. 4 and its accompanying notes are particularly helpful on this point.

34. Michael McConnell, "God is Dead and We Have Killed Him: Freedom of Religion in the Post Modern Age," *Brigham Young University Law Review* (1993): 163, 170.

35. Virginia Statute of Religious Liberty 1 (1786) as quoted by McConnell, "God is Dead," 170.

36. See, for example, *American Friends Service Committee v Thornburgh*, 718 F. Supp. 820 (C.D. Cal, 1989).

37. *United States v Kauten*, 133 F.2d 703, 708 (2d Cir. 1943).

38. Brief Amicus Curias in support of Petitioner for Writ of Certiorari on Behalf of Church of God in Christ, Mennonite, at 3–4, *Bob Jones University* (no. 81–83), quoted by Cover, "Nomos and Narrative," 27.

39. Michael Sandel, ed., "Religious Liberty—Freedom of Conscience or Freedom of Choice," *Utah Law Review* (1989): 597.

40. *Sherbert v Verner*, 374 US 398 (1963).

41. *Goldman v Weinberger*, 475 US 503 (1986). See Sandel's discussion of this case in "Religious Liberty."

42. Steven Gey, "Why is Religion Special?: Reconsidering the Accommodation of Religion under the Religion Clauses of the First Amendment," *University of Pittsburg Law Review* 52 (1990): 75. His work relies on a definition proposed by Stanley Ingber, "Religion or Ideology: A Needed Clarification of the Religion Clauses," *Stanford Law Review* 41 (1989): 233.

43. *Lyng v Northwest Indian Cemetery Protective Association*, 485 US 439 (1988).

44. 493 US 378 (1990).

45. Douglas Laycock, "The Remnants of Free Exercise," *Supreme Court Review* (1990): 1, 24–26. Laycock goes on to cite recent lower court decisions that have relied on this kind of reasoning.

46. McConnell, "The Origins of Free Exercise," 1409, 1490 (citations omitted).

47. *The Williamsburg Charter* (Washington, D.C.: Williamsburg Charter Foundation, 1988). Perhaps the most important American Catholic spokesman for religious freedom, John Courtney Murray, understood the principle in exactly the same terms; see his *We Hold These Truths* (New York: Sheed and Ward, 1960).

48. John Locke, *A Letter Concerning Toleration*, ed. John Horton and Susan Mendus (London: Routledge, 1991).

49. For an anthology entirely devoted to interreligious conflict in the United States, see Robert Bellah and Frederick Greenspahn, eds., *Uncivil Religion* (New York: Crossroad, 1987). See also William P. Marshall, "The Public Square and the Other Side of Religion," *Hastings Law Journal* 44 (1993): 843, Lawrence Solum, "Faith and Justice," *DePaul Law Review* 39 (1990): 1083, and Edward McGlynn Gaffney Jr., "Hostility to Religion, American Style," 42 *De Paul Law Review* 42 (1992): 263.

50. The best general account of the origins of the Establishment Clause is Leonard Levy, *The Establishment Clause: Religion and the First Amendment* (New York: Mac-Millan, 1986). In addition, see Robert Cord, *Separation of Church and State: Historical Fact and Current Fiction* (New York: Lambeth, 1982), and McConnell, "The Origins Free Exercise."

51. The Supreme Court rejected this reasoning and struck down the law in *McDaniel v Paty*, 435 US 618 (1978).

52. Michael McConnell recounts that the 1669 Fundamental Constitutions of the Carolina Colony, which John Locke helped to draft, established the Church of England but protected the right of any group of people to form their own church and practice their religion freely. There was no protection, however, for unchurched persons; membership in some church was required. See McConnell, "Origins of Free Exercise," 1428–29.

53. See James Beckford, "Religion and Power," in Thomas Robbins and Dick Anthony, *In Gods We Trust: New Patterns of Religious Pluralism in America*, 2nd ed. (New Brunswick, N.J.: Transaction Books, 1990), 43–60.

54. *Lemon v Kurtzman*, 403 US 602 (1971).

55. *Lemon v Kurtzman*, 622. The fear of sectarian conflict has been a frequent theme in Supreme Court opinions. In *Grand Rapids School District v Ball*, 473 US 373 (1985), for example, the Court noted that religion "can serve powerfully to divide societies."

56. *Everson v Board of Education*, 330 US 1 at 53–54 (Rutledge, J., dissenting).

57. *Meek v Pittinger*, 421 US 349 (1975).

58. *Board of Education v Allen*, 392 US 236, 254 (1968) (Black dissenting). Also see Brennan, dissenting in *Marsh v Chambers*, 463 US 783, 819 n. 39 (1983).

59. *Wolman v Walters*, 433 US 229 at 264 (1977).

60. The most influential article is Edward McGlynn Gaffney, "Political Divisiveness Along Religious Lines: The Entanglement of the Court in Sloppy History and Bad Public Policy," *St. Louis University Law Journal* 24 (1980): 205.

61. *Bowen v Kendrick*, 487 US 589 (1988). In this case, the Court upheld the Adolescent Family Life Act, which authorized federal grants to public and private organizations to promote chastity, to counsel adolescents on sexuality and preventing pregnancy, and to discourage abortions. The allocation of funds to religious institutions was challenged as a violation of the Establishment Clause.

62. 483 US 327 (1987).

63. 440 US 490 (1979).

64. Such a political interpretation might lead one to ponder why Catholic and Mormon employers fare well in labor law conflicts and why a controversial one, the Tony and Susan Alamo Foundation, was unsuccessful in its attempt to seek exceptions to the Fair Labor Standards Act. See *Tony and Susan Alamo Foundation v Secretary of Labor,* 471 US 290 (1985).

65. *Employment Division, Department of Human Resources of Oregon v Smith,* 494 US 872 (1990).

66. This view reconciles Scalia's apparently accommodationist dissenting opinion in *Jimmy Swaggart Ministries* and his apparently hostile majority one in *Smith.*

67. Ira Lupu, "Reconstructing the Establishment Clause: The Case Against Discretionary Accommodation of Religion," *Pennsylvania Law Review* 140 (1991): 555, and esp. 587–611.

68. Kathleen Sullivan, "Religion and Liberal Democracy," *University of Chicago Law Review* 59 (1992): 195, 216.

69. Jean-Jacques Rousseau, "On Civic Religion," in *Of the Social Contract,* trans. Charles N. Sherover (New York: Harper and Row, 1984). John Locke himself seemed to have accepted this position early in his life. In his 1680 unpublished manuscript, *Two Tracts on Government,* he espouses the argument that religious conflict could be reduced by enforced unity. See McConnell, "Origins of Free Exercise," 1432.

70. Sidney E. Mead, *The Lively Experiment: The Shaping of Christianity in America* (New York: Harper and Row, 1963), 60.

71. See McConnell, "The Origins of Free Exercise," 1432 (citations omitted).

72. Quoted by McConnell, "The Origins of Free Exercise," 1432.

73. Ralph Hancock, "Religion and the Limits of Limited Government," *The Review of Politics* 50 (1988): 682.

74. Richard John Neuhaus, *The Naked Public Square* (Grand Rapids, Mich.: Eerdmans, 1984).

75. Alexis de Tocqueville, *Democracy in America,* 2 vols., ed. Phillips Bradley (New York: Vintage, 1945). For a contemporary formulation, see the works of Paul Hirst, including "Associational Democracy," in *Prospects for Democracy: North, South, East, West,* ed. David Held (Cambridge: Polity Press, 1993), and his introduction to *The Pluralist Theory of the State,* ed. Paul Hirst (London: Routledge, 1989).

76. Carter, *The Culture of Disbelief,* 36–37.

77. See Dean Kelley, "Confronting the Danger," *Church, State, and Public Policy,* ed. Jay Melching (Washington, D.C.: American Enterprise Institute for Public Policy Research, 1978), 15.

78. *Bowen v Kendrick,* 487 US 589 (1988).

79. Cover, "Nomos and Narrative," 33–34.

80. 871 F.2d 1436 (9th Cir. 1989), 883 F.2d 662 (CA 9 Ariz. 1989).

81. 752 F. Supp. 1505 (D. Ariz. 1990).

82. 461 US 574 (1983).

83. 406 US 205 (1972).

84. 827 F.2d 684 (11th Cir. 1987).

85. 512 US 687 (1994).

86. Religious sociologist James Beckford notices that his discipline has tended to ignore

this aspect of religion. The dominant focus on religion as a meaning system has tended to obscure the ways in which religion exerts social power. Beckford identifies and explains the power of religion to confront, to confound, to convince, to contest, to control, and to cultivate. See Beckford, "Religion and Power," 43–60. See also Richard Fenn, *Liturgies and Trials* (Oxford: Blackwell, 1981).

87. The theoretical section of the next several pages owes much to the early sociological works of Peter Berger, especially his 1967 sociology of religion, *The Sacred Canopy* (Garden City, N.Y.: Doubleday, 1967). See also Peter Berger, "Afterward," in *Articles of Faith, Articles of Peace*, ed. Davison Hunter and Os Guinness (Washington D.C.: Brookings, 1990), 114–21. Interestingly, Stephen Carter uses the same phrase in *The Culture of Disbelief*, 40–41.

88. Berger, *Sacred Canopy*, 42.

89. George Orwell, *1984* (1948; San Diego: Harcourt Brace Jovanovich, 1977). In Thomas Hobbes, *The Leviathan*, ed. C. B. Macpherson (1651; London: Penguin, 1981), one of the attributes of sovereignty is the power to specify meanings. Sheldon Wolin has pointed out the immense political significance of the political power of specifying meanings. See Sheldon Wolin, *Politics and Vision* (Boston: Little, Brown, 1960), 257–62.

90. Sociologist Milton Yinger, for example, defines religion as a system of beliefs and practices by which a group of people struggles with the ultimate problems of human life. See Milton Yinger, *The Scientific Study of Religion* (New York: Macmillan, 1970). Anthropologist Clifford Geertz emphasizes religious symbols that help one interpret the meaning of life itself within a cosmology. See Clifford Geertz, "Religion as a Cultural System," in *Anthropological Approaches to the Study of Religion*, ed. Michael Banton (London: Tavistock, 1966), 1–46.

91. Berger, *Sacred Canopy*, 26, 28, 35–36. But recall James Beckford's criticism described in the preceding section. Beckford accuses Berger and his followers of focusing so much attention on religion as sources of meaning that sociologists have neglected religion as a source of power. See Beckford, "Religion and Power," 43.

92. Franklin Gamwell, *The Meaning of Religions Freedom* (Albany: SUNY Press, 1995), 30.

93. See Peter Berger and Richard John Neuhaus, *To Empower People: The Role of Mediating Structures in Public Policy* (Washington, D.C.: American Enterprise Institute for Public Policy Research, 1977), 30.

94. On this point, see Carl Esbeck, "Religion and a Neutral State: Imperative or Impossibility?" *Cumberland Law Review* 15 (1984–85): 67.

95. Mark DeWolfe Howe, *The Garden and the Wilderness* (Chicago: University of Chicago Press, 1965), 7–8.

96. The original statement of this argument appeared in Berger and Neuhaus, *To Empower People*. In 1978 the American Enterprise Institute sponsored a conference on mediating institutions; one of the results was a book entirely dedicated to church and state issues from this perspective: Melching, *Church, State, and Public Policy*.

97. Melching, *Church, State, and Public Policy*, 1–2; quotations from Berger and Neuhaus, *To Empower People*.

98. Melching, *Church, State, and Public Policy*, 1.

99. Berger and Neuhaus, *To Empower People*, 3. Dean Kelley reminds us that however important may be the other social functions of religious institutions, serving as sources

of meaning remains their most important (Dean Kelley, "Confronting the Danger," in Melching, *Church, State, and Public Policy*, 19).

100. Cover, "Nomos and Narrative," 28.

101. Ibid., 33–34.

102. Michael Walzer, "Civil Society Argument," in *Dimensions of Radical Democracy: Pluralism, Citizenship and Democracy*, ed. Chantal Mouffe (London: Verso, 1992), 98.

103. See, for example, *Mozert et al. v Hawkins County Board of Education*, 827 F.2d 1058 (6th Cir. Tenn. 1987). This issue is discussed at length in Chapter 3.

104. Berger, *Sacred Canopy*, 46–47.

CHAPTER 2

1. J. E. Barnhart, *The Study of Religion and its Meaning: New Explorations in Light of Karl Popper and Emile Durkheim* (The Hague: Mouton Publishers, 1977). For a discussion of various definitions of religion, see Rodney Stark and William Sims Bainbridge, *A Theory of Religion* (New York: Peter Lang, 1987).

2. See *Sheldon v Fannin*, 221 F. Supp. 766, 775 (D. Ariz. 1963), in which is stated that "religion in the establishment clause looks to the majority's concept, while 'religion' in the Free Exercise clause looks to the minority's concept." This point is particularly well made by Marc Galanter, "Religious Freedom in the United States: A Turning Point?" *Wisconsin Law Review* (1966): 266–67.

3. Kent Greenawalt, "Religion as a Concept in Constitutional Law," *California Law Review* 72 (1984): 753. (Greenawalt's argument is developed later in this chapter in the section entitled "Indicia and Analogies.") Lawrence Tribe, in the first (1978) edition of his monumental treatise *American Constitutional Law,* proposed a dual definition solution but rejected that argument in the second (1988) edition. See Lawrence Tribe, *American Constitutional Law* (Mineola, N.Y.: Foundation Press, 1988), 1186.

4. See Jesse Choper, *Securing Religious Liberty* (Chicago: University of Chicago Press, 1995). Choper's definition is discussed under "Obligations of Conscience," below.

5. *Malnak v Yogi*, 592 F.2d 197, 200 (3d Cir. N.J. 1979) (Adams, J., concurring).

6. *Everson v Board of Education*, 330 US 1 at 32 (1947) (Rutledge, dissenting).

7. Hobbes, *The Leviathan*. See Sheldon Wolin, *Politics and Vision* (Boston: Little, Brown, 1960), 257–62, on this point.

8. James Madison, *A Memorial and Remonstrance of the Religious Rights of Man*, in *James Madison on Religious Liberty*, ed. Robert Alley (Buffalo, N.Y.: Prometheus Books, 1985).

9. *Davis v Beason*, 133 US 333, 342 (1890).

10. The 1922 Georgia Supreme Court case of *Wilkerson v Rome* quoted in Philip E. Hammond, "The Courts and Secular Humanism," in *Church State Relations: Tensions and Transitions*, ed. Thomas Robbins and Roland Robertson (New Brunswick, N.J.: Transaction Books, 1987), 98–99.

11. *United States v Macintosh*, 283 US 605, 612 (1931). Chief Justice Hughes's dissent focuses on the obligations of conscience as the heart of religion.

12. 367 US 488 (1961).

13. The footnote to this statement adds, "Among religions in this country which do not teach what would generally be considered a belief in the existence of God are Buddhism,

Taoism, Ethical Culture, Secular Humanism, and others." These words have come back to haunt the Court more than once, most recently in the "secular humanist" cases discussed in Chapter 3.

14. A more cross-cultural belief-type definition was offered in 1873 by Edward Tylor, who defined religion as belief in "spiritual beings." This concept could include both ancestor worship as well as belief in spirits who did not have "supreme" powers. See Edward Tylor, *Primitive Culture*, vol. 2 (1873; New York: Harper and Row, 1958).

15. Rudolpf Otto, *The Idea of the Holy*, trans. J. Harvey (London: Oxford University Press, 1950).

16. Emile Durkheim, *The Elementary Forms of the Religious Life*, trans. Joseph Swain (New York: Free Press, 1965).

17. Mircea Eliade, *The Sacred and the Profane*, trans. Willard Trask (New York: Harcourt, Brace & World, 1959).

18. Paul Tillich, *What is Religion?* (New York: Harper and Row, 1969).

19. See Peter Berger, *The Sacred Canopy* (Garden City, N.Y.: Doubleday, 1967).

20. Clifford Geertz, *Islam Observed* (New Haven: Yale University Press, 1968).

21. John Haught, *What is Religion?* (Mahwah, N.J.: Paulist Press, 1990), 6–7.

22. Franklin Gamwell, *The Meaning of Religious Freedom* (Albany: SUNY Press, 1995).

23. The example that comes to mind here is Moses encountering the burning bush and hearing God tell him to remove his sandals because he was standing on holy ground (Exodus 3:2–6).

24. Timothy Hall, "The Sacred and the Profane," *Texas Law Review* 61 (1982): 139. See also Stanley Ingber, "Religion or Ideology: A Needed Clarification of the Religion Clauses," *Stanford Law Rev* 41 (1989): 233.

25. Eliade, *The Sacred and the Profane*, 20.

26. Jesse H. Choper, *Securing Religious Liberty* (Chicago: University of Chicago Press, 1995), 74–80. An earlier version of this definition, without the limiting context, was offered in Jesse Choper, "Defining Religion in the First Amendment," *University of Illinois Law Review* (1982): 597.

27. Milton Yinger, *The Scientific Study of Religion* (New York: MacMillan, 1970), 11.

28. Michael Sandel, "Religious Liberty—Freedom of Conscience or Freedom of Choice," *Utah Law Review* (1989): 597.

29. *United States v Macintosh*, 283 US 605, 633–34 (1931) (Hughes, C. J., dissenting)

30. Ben Clements, "Defining Religion in the First Amendment: A Functional Approach," *Cornell Law Review* 74 (1989): 532.

31. Steven Gey, "Why is Religion Special?: Reconsidering the Accommodation of Religion under the Religion Clauses of the First Amendment," *University of Pittsburgh Law Review* 52 (1990): 75, 167.

32. Gey, "Why is Religion Special?," 168. Interestingly, while Gey finds the conflict of obligations to be the only persuasive justification for accommodation, he goes on to deny a constitutional right even to behavior motivated by authoritative religious commands (180–85). I will return to his argument on this point in Chapter 8.

33. *Lyng v Northwest Indian Cemetery Protective Association*, 485 US 439 (1988).

34. *Jimmy Swaggart Ministries v Board of Equalization of California*, 493 US 378 (1990). See discussion of this point in Douglas Laycock, "The Remnants of Free Exercise,"

Supreme Court Review (1990): 1, 23–26. See also Frederick Mark Gedicks, "Toward a Constitutional Jurisprudence of Religious Group Rights," *Wisconsin Law Review* (1989): 99.

35. Tillich's works include *Systemic Theology* (Chicago: University of Chicago Press, 1951), *The Shaking of the Foundations* (New York: Charles Scribner's Sons, 1948), *The Courage to Be* (New Haven: Yale University Press, 1952), *Dynamics of Faith* (New York: Harper and Row, 1956), and *What is Religion?* (New York: Harper and Row, 1969). See James McBride, "Paul Tillich and The Supreme Court: Tillich's 'Ultimate Concern' as a Standard in Judicial Interpretation," *Journal of Church and State* 30 (1988): 245.

36. *United States v Macintosh*, 283 US 605 (1931).

37. *United States v Kauten*, 133 F.2d 703, 708 (2d Cir. 1943).

38. *United States v Seeger*, 380 US 163 (1965).

39. 325 F.2d 409 (1963).

40. Tillich, *The Shaking of the Foundations*, 57. However, critics argue that the Court misunderstood Tillich by failing to appreciate that the essential characteristic of religion is belief in transcendence. See James McBride, "Tillich in an Alice in Wonderland World," *Christian Century* 104 (1987): 519.

41. *Welsh v United States*, 398 US 333 (1970).

42. Greenawalt, "Religion as a Concept," 808–10.

43. James McBride, "Paul Tillich and The Supreme Court," 269.

44. Gamwell, *The Meaning of Religious Freedom*, 30.

45. Milton Yinger, *Religion, Society, and the Individual* (New York: Macmillan, 1957), 9.

46. Clifford Geertz, "Religion as a Cultural System," in *Anthropological Approaches to the Study of Religion*, ed. Michael Banton (London: Tavistock, 1966), 4.

47. On May 6, 1991, *Time Magazine* ran an extremely critical article on Scientology by Richard Beher entitled "The Cult of Greed."

48. *Founding Church of Scientology of Washington, D.C. v United States*, 409 F.2d 1146 (D.C. Cir. 1969). But in 1977, in *Missouri Church of Scientology v State Tax Commission*, 560 S.W.2d 837 (Mo. 1977), a Missouri court applied a belief in a Supreme Being test and disqualified Scientology from receiving state tax exemptions accorded to religious organizations. For discussion, see Marjorie Heins, "Other People's Faiths: The Scientology Litigation and the Justiciability of Religious Fraud," *Hastings Constitutional Law Quarterly* 9 (1981): 153.

49. *Africa v Pennsylvania*, 662 F.2d 1025 (3d Cir. 1981).

50. See David Little and Sumner Twiss, *Comparative Religious Ethics* (San Francisco: Harper and Row, 1978), 45–56.

51. See John Whitehead and John Conlan, "The Establishment of the Religion of Secular Humanism and its First Amendment Implications," *Texas Tech Law Review* 10 (1978): 1. See also "Secular Humanism and the Definition of Religion: Extending the Modified 'Ultimate Concern' Test to *Mozert et al. v Hawkins County Board of Education* and *Smith v Board of School Commissioners*," *Washington Law Review* 63 (1988): 445. For a critique of this view, see David McKenzie, "The Supreme Court, Fundamentalist Logic, and the Term 'Religion,'" *Journal of Church and State* 33 (1991): 731. McKenzie argues that the Fundamentalists "make a basic error in logic by confusing neutrality with disavowal" (741).

52. *Smith v Board of School Commissioners of Mobile County*, 827 F.2d 684 (11th Cir. Ala. 1987). This case is discussed in greater detail later in this chapter and again in Chapter 3.

53. See Durkheim, *The Elementary Forms of Religious Life*.

54. Ibid., 62.

55. Ibid., 59.

56. Yinger, *Religion, Society and the Individual*, 9 (emphasis added).

57. Stephen Carter, *The Culture of Disbelief* (New York: Basic Books, 1993), 17.

58. 489 US 829 (1989).

59. Ludwig Wittgenstein, *Philosophical Investigations*, trans. G. E. M. Anscombe (New York: Macmillan, 1953).

60. Ninian Smart, *Philosophers and Religious Truth*, 2nd ed. (London: SCM Press, 1969).

61. Greenawalt, "Religion as a Concept," 767–68 (citations omitted). See also George C. Freeman, "The Misguided Search for a Constitutional Definition of Religion," *Georgetown Law Journal* 7 (1983): 1519. Lawrence Tribe, arguing for a bifurcated definition, proposed that everything "arguably religious" should count as religious for Free Exercise purposes, but anything "arguably nonreligious" should be considered nonreligious for Establishment Clause purposes. See Lawrence Tribe, *American Constitutional Law* (Mineola, N.Y.: Foundation Press, 1978).

62. *Malnak v Yogi*, 592 F.2d 197 (3d Cir. N.J. 1979) (footnotes omitted). See also "Note: Transcendental Meditation and the Meaning of Religion Under the Establishment Clause," *Minnesota Law Review* 62 (1978): 887; Jesse Choper, "Defining Religion in the First Amendment," *University of Illinois Law Review* 41 (1982): 579; "Note: Defining Religion," *University of Chicago Law Review* 32 (1965): 533; "Defining Religion in Operational and Institutional Terms," *University of Pennsylvania Law Review* 116 (1968): 479; "Note: The Sacred and the Profane: A First Amendment Definition of Religion," *University of Texas Law Review* 61 (1982): 139; and "Note: Toward a Constitutional Definition of Religion," *Harvard Law Review* 91 (1978): 1056.

63. *Africa v Pennsylvania*, 662 F.2d 1025, 1035 (3d Cir. Pa. 1981). See also *Church of the Chosen People v United States*, 548 F. Supp. 1247 (D. Minn. 1982). This seems to be precisely Greenawalt's concern in warning against use of external indicators.

64. *Smith v Board of School Commissioners of Mobile County*, 655 F. Supp. 939 (S. Dist. Ala. 939) (1986), overruled 827 F.2d 684 (11th Cir. 1987). The conclusions Judge Hand drew in this case reaffirm the method's shortcomings. While the language suggests an effort to protect nontraditional religions, the actual definition was used to protect traditional fundamentalist Christianity against the "establishment" of the "religion" of humanism. By a sleight of hand, Judge Hand took language of free exercise and, without so much as a transition, turned it into an establishment argument, finding that secular humanism constituted a religion according to the above definition and its tenets could not be espoused, or espoused exclusively, in the public school curriculum. It is not surprising that the decision that incorporated this definition was in short time reversed.

65. See Greenawalt, "Religion as a Concept," 769.

66. For a general discussion, see Stephen Senn, "The Prosecution of Religious Fraud," *Florida State University Law Review* 17 (1990): 325.

67. See *Renners v Brewer*, 361 F. Supp. 537 (S.D. Iowa, 1973), and *Theriault v Silber*, 495 F.2d 390 (5th Cir. 1974).

68. See *Philbrook v Ansonia Board of Education*, 757 F.2d 476 (2d Cir. 1985).

69. *Davis v Beason*, 133 US 333 (1890).

70. *New v United States*, 245 F. 710 (9th Cir. 1917).

71. 322 US 78 (1944). On this case and on the issue of sincerity in general, see John Noonan, "How Sincere Do You Have to Be to Be Religious?" *University of Illinois Law Review* (1988): 713.

72. 322 US 578 (1944).

73. 409 F.2d 1146 (D.C. Cir. 1969). On this issue in general, see Marjorie Heins, "Other People's Faiths: The Scientology Litigation and the Justiciability of Religious Fraud," *Hastings Constitutional Law Quarterly* 9 (1981): 153.

74. 535 F. Supp. 1125 (D. Mass. 1982).

75. 61 Cal. 2d 716, 40 Cal. Rptr 69, 394 P.2d 813 (1964).

76. 267 N.C. 599, 48 S.D. 2d 565 (1966).

77. 383 F.2d 851 (5th Cir. 1967), *rev'd on other grounds*, 395 US 6 (1969).

78. *United States v Kuch*, 288 Fed. Supp 439 (D.D.C. 1968). The ministers were called "Boo Hoos"; the symbol was a three-eyed toad; the bulletin was the "Divine Toad Sweat"; the church key was a bottle opener; the official songs were "Puff the Magic Dragon" and "Row, Row, Row Your Boat"; and the church motto was "Victory over Horseshit."

79. See *Frazee v Illinois Department of Employment Security*, 489 US 829 (1989).

80. See *Thomas v Review Board of the Indiana Employment Security Division*, 450 US 707 (1981).

81. Contrast *Dobkin v District of Columbia*, 194 A.2d 657 (D.C. 1963), with *Philbrook v Ansonia Board of Education*, 757 F.2d 476 (2d Cir. 1985).

82. See *Hobbie v Unemployment Appeals Commission of Florida*, 480 US 136 (1987).

83. See *Sheldon v Fannin*, 221 F. Supp. 766 (D. Ariz. 1963).

84. Steven Smith, *Foreordained Failure* (New York: Oxford University Press, 1995).

85. Kent Greenawalt makes this argument in "Religion as a Concept in Constitutional Law," 753, 769. See also Gianella, "Religious Liberty, Nonestablishment, and Doctrinal Development Part I: The Religious Liberty Clause," *Harvard Law Review* 80 (1967): 1381, 1426.

86. These examples come from provocative comments by Angela Carmella, "A Theological Critique of Free Exercise Jurisprudence," *George Washington Law Review* 60 (1992): 782.

CHAPTER 3

1. *Reynolds v United States*, 98 US 145 (1878).

2. *Cantwell v Connecticut*, 310 US 296 (1940).

3. Among the constitutional commentators, only one seriously and intelligently advocates a view that the Free Exercise Clause protects only religious beliefs and their profession but not other actions stemming from them. See Steven Gey, "Why is Religion Special?: Reconsidering the Accommodation of Religion Under the Religion Clauses of the First Amendment," *University of Pittsburgh Law Review* 52 (1990): 75.

4. *Employment Division, Department of Human Resources of Oregon v Smith*, 494 US 872 (1990).

5. The statement reads thus: "He is bound by his own act; bound, I say to obey it, but not bound to believe it; for men's beliefs, and interior cognitions, are not subject to the commands, but only to the operation of God" (Thomas Hobbes, *The Leviathan*, ed. C. B. Macpherson [1651; London: Penguin, 1981], 332).

6. Leo Pfeffer, *God, Caesar, and the Constitution* (Boston: Beacon Press, 1974), 31. Tribe makes the same point in *American Constitutional Law* (Mineola, N.Y.: Foundation Press, 1978), 838 n. 13.

7. *Torcaso v Watkins*, 367 US 488 (1961).

8. *Minersville School District v Gobitis*, 310 US 586 (1940).

9. *West Virginia State Board of Education v Barnette*, 319 US 624 (1943).

10. *Wooley v Maryland*, 430 US 705 (1977).

11. *Society for Separationists, Inc. v Herman*, 939 F.2d 1207 (5th Cir. 1991). The court's reasoning was based in part on the "hybrid religion-plus-speech" dictum enunciated by Justice Scalia in *Employment Division, Department of Human Resources of Oregon v Smith*. See also *Gordon v Idaho*, 778 F.2d 1397 (9th Cir. 1985). For an excellent discussion, see Johnathan Belcher, "Religion Plus Speech: The Constitutionality of Oaths and Affirmations Under the First Amendment," *William and Mary Law Review* 34 (1992): 287.

12. *Lee v Weisman*, 505 US 577 (1992). The Court left open the possibility that student-initiated prayers might be constitutional.

13. See Charles L. Glenn Jr. *The Myth of the Common School* (Amherst: University of Massachusetts Press, 1988), and Diane Ravitch, *The Great School Wars, New York City 1805–1973: A History of the Public School as a Battlefield of Social Change* (New York: Basic Books, 1974).

14. See James Casper and Thomas Hurt, *Religious Schooling in America* (Birmingham, Ala.: Religious Education Press, 1984), and Eugene Provenzo Jr. *Religious Fundamentalism and American Education: The Battle for Public Schools* (Albany: SUNY Press, 1990). The Free Exercise controversies involving private religious schools will be discussed in Chapter 5.

15. See Ira Lupu, "Home Education, Religious Liberty, and the Separation of Powers," *Boston University Law Review* 67 (1986): 739, and William Gordon, Charles Russo, and Albert Miles, *The Law of Home Schooling* (Topeka, Kans.: National Organization on Legal Problems of Education, 1994).

16. See George Dent Jr. "Religious Children, Secular Schools," *Southern California Law Review* 61 (1988): 863; Stanley Ingber, "Religion or Ideology: A needed clarification of the Religion Clauses," *Stanford Law Review* 41 (1989): 233; Mary H. Mitchell, "Secularism in Public Education: The Constitutional Issues," *Boston University Law Review* 67 (1987): 603; and Wendell R. Bird, "Note: Freedom of Religion and Science Instruction in Public Schools," *Yale Law Journal* 87 (1978): 515.

17. *Stone v Graham*, 449 US 39 (1980).

18. *Edwards v Aguillard*, 482 US 578 (1987).

19. *Wallace v Jaffree*, 472 US 38 (1985).

20. In 1984, Congress passed the Equal Access Act, 20 USC 4071(a), which made it unlawful for "any public secondary school which receives Federal financial assistance and which has a limited open forum to deny equal access or a fair opportunity to, or discrimi-

nating against, any students who wish to conduct a meeting within that limited open forum on the basis of the religious, political, philosophical, or other content of the speech at such meetings." The Supreme Court upheld this law against an Establishment Clause challenge in *Board of Westside Community Schools v Mergens*, 497 US 226 (1990).

21. *Brown v Board of Education*, 347 US 483 (1954). See also Don Welch, "The State as a Purveyor of Morality," *George Washington Law Review* 56 (1988): 540. See, however, Arons and Lawrence, "The Manipulation of Consciousness: A First Amendment Critique of Schooling," *Harvard Civil Rights–Civil Liberties Law Review* 15 (1980): 309.

22. *Meyer v Nebraska*, 262 US 390 (1923); *Pierce v Society of Sisters*, 268 US 510 (1923), ruling that parental liberty to direct upbringing of children precluded the state from requiring all children to attend public schools; *West Virginia State Board of Education v Barnette*, 319 US 624 (1943), ruling that children whose religious beliefs prevented them from saluting the flag in a school-required ceremony could not be expelled from public school system; *Wisconsin v Yoder*, 406 US 205 (1972), holding that the Free Exercise Clause does not permit the state to compel Amish parents to send their children to public school past the age of fourteen in violation of their religious faith. See also Philip Kurland, "The Supreme Court, Compulsory Education, and the First Amendment's Religion Clauses," *West Virginia Review* 75 (1973): 213, Ellis West, "The Supreme Court and Religious Liberty in the Public Schools," *Journal of Church and State* 25 (1983): 87, Christopher Tully, "Public School Curricula, Secular Humanism and the Religion Clause," *Journal of Law and Policy* 10 (1994): 413, and Colin Mangrem, "Family Rights and Compulsory School Laws," *Creighton Law Review* 21 (1988): 1019.

23. *Hardwick v Fruitridge Board of School Trustees*, 205 P. 49, 54 Cal. App. 696 (1921).

24. *Spence v Bailey*, 325 F. Supp. 601 (1971).

25. *Moody v Cronin*, 484 F. Supp. 270 (C.D. Ill.) (1979).

26. *Davis v Page*, 385 F. Supp 395, 404–5 (D.N.H. 1974).

27. 753 F.2d 1528 (9th Cir. 1985).

28. 647 F. Supp. 1194 (E. Tenn. 1986); 827 F.2d 1058 (7th Cir. 1987). For an excellent argument on the issues raised in these cases, see Ellis West, "The Supreme Court and Religious Liberty in the Public Schools," *Journal of Church and State* 25 (1983): 87. Among the excellent commentaries on these cases, see Ingber, "Religion or Ideology: A Needed Clarification of the Religion Clauses," 233.

29. 827 F.2d 684 (11th Cir. 1987).

30. *Mozert et al. v Hawkins County Board of Education*, 647 F. Supp. 1194 (E.D. Tenn. 1986). This decision was overturned by the Sixth Circuit in August 1987, and the U.S. Supreme Court denied certiorari in February 1988. Compare this decision also with *Cornwell v State Board of Education*, 428 F.2d 471 (4th Cir.), in which the court ruled that teaching sex education in public school does not violate either Free Exercise or Establishment.

31. *Grove v Mead School District No. 354*, 753 F.2d 1528 (9th Cir. 1985).

32. *Smith v Board of School Commissioners of Mobile County*, 827 F.2d 684 (11th Cir. 1987). This case grew out of the original litigation challenging the moment of silence laws in *Wallace v Jaffree* but was separated early in the litigation. Many of the arguments upon which *Smith* was based were made prior to the case itself. See, for example, John Whitehead and John Conlan, "The Establishment of the Religion of Secular Humanism and its First Amendment Implications," *Texas Tech Law Review* 10 (1978): 1, and

Nadine Strossen, "Secular Humanism and Scientific Creationism: Proposed Standards for Reviewing Curricular Decisions Affecting Students' Religious Freedom," *Ohio State Law Journal* 47 (1986): 333. See also "Note: The Establishment Clause, Secondary Religious Effects, and Humanistic Education," *Yale Law Journal* 92 (1982): 1196; and "Note: Humanistic Values in the Public School Curriculum: Problems in Defining an Appropriate Wall of Separation," *Northwestern University Law Review* 62 (1966): 795.

33. 592 F.2d 197 (3d Cir. 1979). Indeed, one of the arguments against Judge Adams's *indicia* approach to defining religion is the eccentric use to which Judge Hand put it in the *Smith* case.

34. 827 F.2d 1058 (6th Cir. 1987).

35. 647 F. Supp. 1194 (E.D. Tenn. 1986); 827 F.2d 1058 (6th Cir. 1987). See James Harkins, "Of Textbooks and Tenets: *Mozert et al. v Hawkins County Board of Education* and the Free Exercise of Religion," *American University Law Review* 37 (1988): 985, and Hugh Bryer, "Cinderella, The Horse God and the Wizard of Oz: *Mozert et al. v Hawkins County Public Schools," Journal of Law and Education* 20 (1991): 63.

36. This claim is quite different from the claims of Jews, for example, who oppose using *The Merchant of Venice* in public schools because its characterization of Jews exposes their children to the disrespect of their classmates. This argument was made and rejected in *Rosenberg v Board of Education of New York City* (1949) cited by James Wood Jr. in "Religious Fundamentalists and the Public Schools," *Journal of Church and State* 28 (1987): 9.

37. *Wisconsin v Yoder*, 406 US 205 at 242–46 (1972) (concurring in part and dissenting in part).

38. His opinion specifically rejected the analogy with such cases as *Sherbert v Verner*, *Thomas v Review Board of the Indiana Employment Security Division*, and *Hobbie v Unemployment Appeals Commission of Florida*, in which a religious exemption was required. All of these cases involved "governmental compulsion to engage in conduct that violated the plaintiff's religious convictions," whereas there was no such violation in this case.

39. 319 US 624 (1943).

40. 393 US 97 (1968).

41. Robert Cover, "Supreme Court 1982 Term: Forward: Nomos and Narrative," *Harvard Law Review* 97 (1983): 60–62.

42. See Don Welch, "The State as Purveyor of Morality," *George Washington Law Review* 56 (1988): 540.

43. Among the vast literature on this phenomenon, see Thomas Robbins, William Shepherd, and James McBride, eds., *Cults, Culture and the Law: Perspectives on New Religious Movements* (American Academy of Religion) (Chico, Calif.: Scholars Press, 1985), Charles Harper and Brian LeBeau, "The Social Adaptation of Marginal Religious Movements in America," *Sociology of Religion* 54 (1993): 171, and Marcia Rudin, "The Cult Phenomenon: Fad or Fact?" *NYU Review of Law and Social Change* 9 (1980): 17. See also Marc Galantar, ed., *Cults and Religious Movements* (Washington, D.C.: American Psychiatric Association, 1989), and Marc Galantar, *Cults* (New York: Oxford University Press, 1989).

44. Thomas Robbins, "New Religious Movements on the Frontier of Church and State," in Robbins, Sheppard, and McBride, eds., *Cults, Culture, and the Law*, 1.

45. Thomas Robbins and Dick Anthony, "Deprogramming, Brainwashing and the Medicalization of Deviant Religious Groups," *Social Problems* 29 (1982): 3.

46. Richard Delgado, "When Religious Exercise is Not So Free: Deprogramming and the Constitutional Status of Coercively Induced Belief," *Vanderbilt Law Review* 37 (1984): 1075.

47. Delgado, "When Religious Exercise is Not So Free," 1076; see also Richard Delgado, "Religious Totalism: Gentle and Ungentle Persuasion under the First Amendment," *Southern California Law Review* 51 (1977): 1, and "Religious Totalism as Slavery," *New York Review Law and Social Change* 9 (1979–80): 58.

48. Richard Delgado, "Cults and Conversions: The Case for Informed Consent," *Georgia Law Review* 16 (1982): 533.

49. Delgado, "When Religious Exercise is Not So Free," 1086.

50. Robert Shapiro, "Mind Control or Intensity of Faith: The Constitutional Protection of Religious Beliefs," 13 *Harvard Civil Rights-Civil Liberties Law Review* 13 (1978): 751.

51. Dick Anthony and Thomas Robbins, "Law, Social Science, and the 'Brainwashing' Exception to the First Amendment," *Behavioral Sciences and the Law* 10 (1992): 5, 9.

52. Robert J. Lifton, *Thought Reform and the Psychology of Totalism: A Study of "Brainwashing" in China* (New York: Norton, 1961).

53. Edgar Schrin, *Coercive Persuasion: A Socio-Psychological Analysis of the "Brainwashing" of American Civilian Prisoners by the Chinese Communists* (New York: Norton, 1961).

54. See Robert J. Lifton, "Cult Processes, Religious Totalism, and Civil Liberties," in Robbins, Shepherd, and McBride, eds., *Cults, Culture, and the Law*, 59.

55. See, for example, David Bromley and J. Richardson, eds., *The Brainwashing/Deprogramming Controversy* (Lewiston, N.Y.: Edwin Mellon Press, 1983).

56. See Eli Shapiro, "Destructive Cultism," *American Family Physician* 15 (1977).

57. See, for example, Margaret Singer, "Thought Reform Programs and the Production of Psychiatric Casualties," *Psychiatric Annals* 20 (1990): 188–93.

58. The standard for admissibility of expert testimony is the "Frye rule," holding that evidence is admissible only if there is general agreement within the relevant scientific community concerning conclusions being offered (*Frye v US*, 294 F. 10114 [D.C. Cir., 1923]). See also Anthony and Robbins, "Law, Social Science, and Brainwashing."

59. Anthony and Robbins, "Law, Social Science, and Brainwashing."

60. For a discussion of the cultural conceptions of autonomy as they impact on this issue, see James Beckford, "Politics and the Anticult Movement," *Annual Review of the Social Sciences of Religion* 3 (1979). See also Robert Shapiro, "Indoctrination, Personhood, and Religious Beliefs," in Robbins, Shepherd, and McBride, eds., *Cults, Culture, and the Law*, 129–60.

61. Herbert Fingarette, "Coercion, Coercive Persuasion, and the Law," in Robbins, Shepherd and McBride, eds., *Cults, Culture, and the Law*, 81, 90.

62. Anthony and Robbins, "Law, Social Science, Brainwashing," 14.

63. See Shapiro, "Mind Control or Intensity of Faith, 751.

64. The most famous deprogrammer is Ted Patrick; he describes his career in T. Patrick and T. Dulack, *Let Our Children Go* (New York: Ballantine Books, 1976). See also Jeremiah Gutman, "Constitutional and Legal Aspects of Deprogramming," in *Deprogram-*

ming: Documenting the Issue (New York: American Civil Liberty Union, 1977); K. Pierce, "Cults, Deprogrammers and the Necessity Defense," *Michigan Law Review* 80 (1980): 271; W. Shepherd, *To Secure the Blessings of Liberty: American Constitutional Law and New Religious Movements* (Baltimore: Scholars Press, 1985); Thomas Robbins and Dick Anthony, "Deprogramming," in J. Childress and J. Macquarrie, eds., *The Westminster Dictionary of Christian Ethics* (Philadelphia: Westminster, 1986); Anson Shupe and David Bromley, *The New Vigilantes: Deprogrammers, Anticultists and the New Religious Movements* (Beverly Hills, Calif.: Sage, 1980); and J. Lemoult, "Deprogramming Members of Religious Sects," *Fordham Law Review* 46 (1978): 599.

65. Douglas H. Cook, "Tort Liability for Cult Deprogramming" (case note) *Ohio State Law Journal* 43 (1982): 465; John D. Ensley, "Civil Rights: A Civil Remedy for Religious Deprogramming Victim under 42 USC 1985(3)," *Washburn Law Journal* 21 (Spring 1982): 663; and Michael F. Coyns, "Federal Regulation of Intra-Family Deprogramming Conspiracies under the Ku Klux Klan Act of 1971" (case note), *Boston College Law Review* 23 (1982): 789. See also E. Babbit, "The Deprogramming of Religious Sect Members: A Private Right of Action under Section 1950(3)," *Northwestern Law Review* 74 (1979): 229, and Nancy Grim, "Religious Cult Members and Deprogramming Attempts," *University of Akron Law Review* 15 (1981): 165.

66. *Ward v Connor*, 657 F.2d 45 (4th Cir. 1981).

67. 299 N.W. 2d 123 (Minn. 1980). See Cook, "Tort Liability for Cult Deprogramming," 454.

68. On the other hand, in the subsequent case *Eilers v Coy* a federal district court judge refused to rely on apparent temporary consent to authorize abduction and deprogramming. In this case, damages were awarded to a plaintiff against deprogrammers for false imprisonment (*Eilers v Coy*, 582 F. Supp. 1093 [1984]). The jury in this case awarded only $10,000 in compensatory damages and no punitive damages because they were not convinced that the deprogrammers had acted with animosity toward religious beliefs.

69. See Kit Pierson, "Cults, Deprogrammers, and the Necessity Defense," *Michigan Law Review* 80 (1980): 271.

70. See D. Aronin, "Cults, Deprogramming, and Guardianship: A Model Legislative Proposal," *Columbia Journal of Law and Social Problems* 17 (1982): 163. See also Michael Bernick, "To Keep Them Out of Harm's Way: Temporary Conservatorship and Religious Sects," *California Law Review* 66 (1978): 845.

71. *Katz v Superior Court*, 73 Cal. App. 3d 952, 141 Cal Rptr. 234, modified, 74 Cal. App. 3d 582, (1977).

72. 322 US 78 (1944).

73. Anson Shupe, Roger Speilmann, and Sam Stigall, "Deprogramming: The New Exorcism," *American Behavioral Scientist* 20 (1977): 941. A great deal of literature developed in opposition to deprogramming. See, for example, Robert Shapiro, "Of Robots, Persons, and the Protection of Religious Beliefs," *S. California Law Review* 56 (1983): 1277, Shupe and Bromley, *The New Vigilantes*, Bromley and Richardson, *The Brainwashing/Deprogramming Controversy*, and Lee Coleman, "New Religions and 'Deprogramming': Who's Brainwashing Whom?" in Robbins, Sheppard, and McBride, eds., *Cults, Culture, and the Law*, 70.

74. 762 P.2d 46 (Cal. 1988). Contrast this result with *Meroni v Holy Spirit Association*, 506 N.Y.S. 2d 1914 (App. Div. 1986), which ruled that church recruitment methods

(chanting, cloistering, fasting, etc.) were neither so different from those used by other organizations nor so outrageous as to constitute a tort.

75. 962 Cal. Reptr. 219 (Ct. App. 1989). This case is described in detail in James T. Richardson, "Cult/Brainwashing Cases and Freedom of Religion," *Journal of Church and State* 33 (1991): 56.

76. 571 N.E. 2d 340 (Mass. 1990).

77. Delgado, "When Religious Belief is Not So Free."

CHAPTER 4

1. *Employment Division, Department of Human Resources of Oregon v Smith*, 494 US 872 (1990).

2. Robert Michaelsen, "Civil Rights, Indian Rights," in *Church-State Relations: Tensions and Transitions*, ed. Thomas Robbins and Roland Robertson (New Brunswick, N.J.: Transaction Books, 1987), 130.

3. *Lyng v Northwest Indian Cemetery Protective Association*, 485 US 439 (1988). Justice Brennan, writing in dissent, would have retained the concept of centrality but left claimants, "the arbiters of which practice are central to their faith, subject only to the normal requirements that their claims be genuine and sincere."

4. Peter Berger, *The Sacred Canopy* (Garden City, N.Y.: Doubleday, 1967).

5. Bruce Bagni, "Discrimination in the Name of the Lord: A Critical Examination of Discrimination by Religious Organizations," *Columbia Law Review* 79 (1979): 1514.

6. "A religious system" is "a symbolic cultural system of ritual acts accompanied by an extensive and largely shared conceptual scheme that includes culturally postulated superhuman agents" (E. Thomas Lawson and Robert N. McCauley, *Rethinking Religion: Connecting Cognition and Culture* [New York: Cambridge University Press, 1990], 5–6).

7. Howard Friedman, "Rethinking Free Exercise: Rediscovering Religious Community and Ritual," *Seton Hall Law Review* 24 (1994): 1800, 1819.

8. Steven Gey, "Why is Religion Special?: Reconsidering the Accommodation of Religion under the Religion Clauses of the First Amendment," *University of Pittsburg Law Review* 52 (1990): 75.

9. *Lawson v Commonwealth*, 291 Ky. 437, 164 S.W.2d 972 (1942). See also *Accord, Harden v State*, 188 Tenn. 17, 216 S.W.2d 708 (1948), upholding a statute criminalizing the display of a poisonous snake.

10. *State ex rel Swann v Pack*, Supreme Court of Tennessee, 1975, 527 S.W.2d 99 (Tenn. 1975), and *State v Massey*, 229 N.C. 734, 51 SE 2d 179 (1949).

11. *Employment Division, Department of Human Resources Oregon v Smith*, 494 US 872 (1990). Other aspects of this case are discussed at greater length in the last three chapters.

12. 394 P.2d 813, 61 Cal. 2d 716. 40 Cal. Rptr. 69 (1964).

13. In a passage reminiscent of Justice Burger's description of the Amish in *Wisconsin v Yoder*, 406 US 205 (1972), the dissenters emphasize the positive contribution of peyotist religion. They conclude that "the values and interests of those seeking a religious exemption in this case are congruent, to a great degree with those the State seeks to promote through its drug laws. Not only does the Church's doctrine forbid non-religious use

of peyote; it also generally advocates self-reliance, familial responsibility, and absence from alcohol" (494 US 872 [1990] at 921).

14. 113 S.Ct. 2217 (1993).

15. From Mircea Eliade, *The Encyclopedia of Religion*, vol. 13 (New York: Macmillan, 1987), as quoted in Justice Kennedy's majority opinion. See also Joseph M. Murphy, *Santeria: An African Religion in America* (Boston: Beacon Press, 1988).

16. As a Jew whose holy scriptures are replete with graphic references to animal sacrifices that are "pleasing to God," I find the community's reaction a bit strange. Even more difficult to understand is the abhorrence of a Christian community whose most important religious ceremony is the symbolic eating of the flesh and blood of the deity.

17. 28 CFR Ch. V § 548.12.

18. 405 US 319 (1972).

19. 482 US 342 (1987). The Court relied heavily on another First Amendment prisoners' rights case, *Turner v Safley*, 482 US 78 (1987), decided the same term.

20. *O'Lone v Estate of Shabbaz*, 482 US 342 (1987), Justice Brennan dissenting.

21. 830 F.2d 779 (7th Cir. 1987).

22. 743 F.2d 408 (6th Cir. 1984).

23. For a general discussion, see Louis Holscher, "Sweat Lodges and Headbands: An Introduction to the Rights of Native American Prisoners," *New England Journal of Criminal and Civil Confinement* 18 (1992): 33.

24. 42 USCA § 1996 (1978).

25. See *McKinney v Maynard*, 952 F.2d 350 (10th Cir. 1991).

26. 827 F.2d 563 (9th Cir. 1987).

27. 852 F.2d 462 (8th Cir. 1988).

28. *Malnak v Yogi*, 595 F.2d at 208–9 (concurring). Interestingly, Judge Adams denied just such a claim in *Africa v Pennsylvania*, 662 F.2d 1025 (3d Cir. 1981).

29. See, for example, *Application of President and Directors of Georgetown College, Inc.*, 331 F.2d 1000 (D.C. Cir. 1964).

30. The courts relied on this reasoning in *John F. Kennedy Memorial Hospital v Heston*, 58 N.J. 576, 279 A. 2d 670 (971); *Crouse Irving Memorial Hospital v Paddock*, 127 Misc. 2d 101, 485 N.Y.S. 2d 443 (Sup. Ct. 1985); and *United States v George*, 239 F. Supp. 752 (D. Conn. 1965). These cases are cited and discussed in "To Live or Die: A Qualified Right for Parents?" *Stetson Law Review* 17 (1987): 250.

31. See Jane E. Probst, "The Conflict between Child's Medical Needs and the Parent's Religious Beliefs," *American Journal of Family Law* 4 (1990): 175. See also Judith Inglis Scheiderer, "When Children Die as a Result of Religious Practice," *Ohio State Law Journal* 51 (1990): 1429; John T. Gathings Jr. "When Rights Clash: The Conflict Between a Parent's Right to Free Exercise of Religion versus his Child's Right to Life," *Cumberland Law Review* 19 (1989): 585; Donna Gwynn Lutz, "To Live or Die: A Qualified Right for Parents?" (case note) *Stetson Law Review* 17 (1987): 249; James T. Richardson and John Dewitt, "Christian Science Spiritual Healing, the Law, and Public Opinion," *Journal of Church and State* 34 (1992): 549; Wayne Alecha, "Note: Faith Healing Exemptions to Child Protection Laws: Keeping the Faith versus Medical Care of Children," *Journal of Legislation* 12 (1985): 243; "California Prayer Healing Dilemma," *Hastings Constitutional Law Quarterly* 14 (1987): 395; and "State Interference with Religious Motivated Decisions on Medical Treatment," *Dickinson Law Review* 93 (1988): 31.

32. 47 Cal. 3d 112 (1988); 763 P. 2d 852 (Cal). Similarly, in *Hermanson v State*, 570 So. 2d 322 (Fla. Dist. Ct. App. 2d Dist., 1990), Florida parents were convicted of felony child abuse and third-degree murder when their daughter died from diabetes while receiving spiritual healing. Florida also had a spiritual healing accommodation in its child abuse statutes, but as in the California case, this statute was ruled to be overridden by criminal statutes. Ultimately, the conviction was overruled on procedural grounds. See also *Minnesota v McKown*, 461 NW 2d 720 (1990), in which statutory accommodation of religion was not a defense against second-degree manslaughter in the death of a son; however, the charges were dropped on due process grounds since the statute did not give adequate notice of potential criminal liability.

33. See Matthew Blischak, "The State of Prisoners Religious Free Exercise Rights" (case note) *American University Law Review* 37 (1988): 53, and Barbara Knight, "Religion in Prison: Balancing the Free Exercise, No Establishment and Equal Protection Clauses," *Journal of Church and State* 26 (1984): 437.

34. 912 F.2d 328 (9th Cir. Ariz. 1990). See Abraham Abromovski, "First Amendment Rights of Jewish Prisoners: Kosher Food, Skullcaps, and Beards," *American Journal of Criminal Law* 21 (1994): 241.

35. See *Pollock v Marshall*, 845 F.2d 656 (6th Cir. 1988). A demand for headbands met the same result in *Standing Deer v Carlson*, 831 F.2d 1525 (9th Cir. 1987).

36. 662 F.2d 1025 (3d Cir. 1981). See Chapter 3 on this point.

37. See, for example, *Kahane v Carlson*, 527 F.2d 492 (2d Cir. 1975), holding that a Jewish prisoner must be provided with a healthy diet consistent with his religious restrictions.

38. 475 US 503 (1986). In this case, the Court paid particular deference to the fact that the challenged regulation was a *military* one. See Justice O'Connor's dissent on this point.

39. 683 F.2d 1030 (7th Cir. Ill. 1982).

40. *Moody v Cronin*, 484 F. Supp. 270 (C.D. Ill. 1979).

41. *United States v Board of Education of Philadelphia*, 911 F.2d 822 (3rd Cir. Pa. 1990).

42. See *You Van Yang v Sturner*, 728 F. Supp. 845 (D.R.I. 1990).

43. 374 US 398 (1963). See the next chapter for further analysis of denial of benefits at stake in the unemployment compensation cases.

44. Ibid.

45. 480 US 136 (1987).

46. 450 US 707 (1981).

47. 489 US 829 (1989).

48. *Employment Division, Department of Human Resources of Oregon v Smith*, 494 US 872 (1990).

49. 42 USC 200e(j) (1972).

50. *Trans World Airlines v Hardison*, 432 US 63 (1977).

51. *Ansonia Board of Education v Philbrook*, 479 US 60 (1986).

52. *Kern v Dynalectron Corp*, 577 F. Supp 1196 (N.D. Tex. 1983).

53. *Abrams v Baylor College of Medicine*, 805 F.2d 528 (5th Cir. 1986).

54. 472 US 703 (1985).

55. The Free Exercise rights of religious institutions in employment issues will be discussed at length in Chapter 5.

56. *Townley Engineering and Manufacturing Company v EEOC*, 859 F.2d 610 (9th Cir.

1988). See David Gregory, "The Role of Religion in the Secular Workplace," *Notre Dame Journal of Law, Ethics, and Public Policy* 4 (1990): 749.

57. 321 US 148 (1944).

58. *Brock v Wendell's Woodworks, Inc.*, 867 F.2d 196 (4th Cir. 1989).

59. *Quaring v Peterson*, 728 F.2d 1121 (8th Cir. 1984). *Jensen v Quaring*, 472 US 478 (per curium) (affirmed by an equally divided court).

60. *Bowen v Roy*, 476 US 693 (1986). The Court split five to four, and there were five separate opinions.

61. *Swanner v Anchorage Equal Rights Commission*, 874 P. 2d 274 (Alaska, 1994).

62. *State v French*, 460 N.W. 2d 2 (Minn. 1990). In the post-*Smith* legal environment, the state court explicitly relied on state constitutional protection of religion.

63. Mark Tushnet, "The Constitution of Religion," *Connecticut Law Review* 18 (1986): 701, 723–24.

64. See Chapter 8 for a discussion of this standard.

CHAPTER 5

1. *Santa Clara County v Southern Pacific Railroad Co.*, 118 US 394 (1886). See "Note: Constitutional Rights of the Corporate Person," *Yale Law Journal* 91 (1982): 1641; Ronald Garet, "Communality and Existence: The Rights of Groups," *S. California Law Review* 56 (1983): 1001; and for a general discussion, see Meir Dan-Cohen, *Rights, Persons, and Organizations* (Berkeley: University of California Press, 1986).

2. Speaking of free speech rights under the First Amendment, the Court said that "if the 'nature, history, and purpose' of a constitutional guarantee indicates that it was 'purely personal,' an organization cannot assert the right on its own behalf" (*First National Bank of Boston v Belotti*, 435 US 7765 [1978]). The complex relationship between individual and group rights is raised by affirmative action programs and particularly in the controversy under the Voting Rights Act regarding proportional representation by race.

3. Ira Lupu makes this point in "Where Rights Begin: The Problem of Burdens on the Free Exercise of Religion," *Harvard Law Review* 102 (1989): 933.

4. See *Church of Scientology v Cazares*, 638 F.2d 1272 (5th Cir. 1981). These institutions must meet rather stringent requirements for institutional standing. For example, in *Harris v McRae*, 448 US 297 (1980), the Women's Division of the Board of Global Ministries of the United Methodist Church was denied representational standing to challenge the Hyde Amendment on Free Exercise grounds. The standing issue is discussed briefly in "Developments in the Law: Religion and the State," *Harvard Law Review* 100 (1987): 1616, 1743–45.

5. Brief for respondent, at 21 *Yoder* (No. 70–110), quoted by Robert Cover, "Supreme Court 1982 Term: Forward: Nomos and Narrative," *Harvard Law Review* 97 (1983): 29.

6. Alisdair MacIntyre, *After Virtue* (Notre Dame: Notre Dame University Press, 1981); Michael Sandel, ed., *Liberalism and Its Critics* (New York: New York University Press, 1984), introduction. See especially "Note, Reinterpreting the Religion Clauses: Constitutional Construction and the Conception of the Self," *Harvard Law Review* 97 (1984): 1468.

7. Robert Bellah et al., *Habits of the Heart* (Berkley: University of California Press, 1985).

8. Emile Durkheim, *The Elementary Forms of Religions Life*, trans. Joseph Ward Swain (New York: Free Press, 1965), 59.

9. Peter Berger, *The Sacred Canopy* (Garden City, N.Y.: Doubleday, 1967), 46–47. Berger's theory is explained at greater length in Chapter 1.

10. 344 US 94 (1952). See Mark Howe, "Forward: Political Theory and the Nature of Liberty: The Supreme Court, 1952 Term," *Harvard Law Review* 67 (1953): 91. The case will be discussed in the section on church civil conflicts, below.

11. Douglas Laycock, "Toward a General Theory of the Religion Clauses: The Case of Church Labor Relations and the Right to Church Autonomy," *Columbia Law Review* 81 (1981): 1378.

12. Cover, "Nomos and Narrative," 32 n. 94.

13. Dean Kelley, ed., *Government Intervention in Religious Affairs*, vols. 1 and 2 (New York: Pilgrim Press, 1982).

14. The proceedings from this conference are published in James Wood and Derek Davis, eds., *The Role of Government in Monitoring and Regulating Religion in Public Life* (Waco, Tex.: Dawson Institute, 1992).

15. The philosophical argument is made eloquently and powerfully by Frederick Mark Gedicks, "Toward a Constitutional Jurisprudence of Religious Group Rights," *Wisconsin Law Review* (1989): 99. See also Lawrence Tribe, "Church and State in the Constitution," in *Government Intervention*, ed. Dean Kelley, 31; Michael McConnell, "Accommodation of Religion," *Supreme Court Review* (1985): 1; Mary Ann Glendon and Raul F. Yanes, "Structural Free Exercise," *Michigan Law Review* 90 (1991): 477; and Howard Freedman, "Rethinking Free Exercise: Rediscovering Religious Community and Ritual," *Seton Hall Law Review* 24 (1994): 1800. Similar arguments are made by Thomas Robbins, "Church State Tensions and Marginal Movements in the United States," in *Church State Relations: Tensions and Transitions*, ed. Thomas Robbins and Rolland Robertson (New Brunswick, N.J.: Transaction Books, 1987).

16. See Thomas Robbins, "Government Regulatory Powers and Church Autonomy: Deviant Groups and Test Cases," *Journal for the Scientific Study of Religion* 24 (1985): 237–52.

17. Angela Carmella, "A Theological Critique of Free Exercise Jurisprudence," *George Washington Law Review* 60 (1992): 782.

18. See Reinhold Niebuhr, *Christ and Culture* (New York: Harper and Row, 1951).

19. Angela Carmella, "The Religion Clauses and Acculturated Religious Conduct: Boundaries for the Regulation of Religion," in Wood and Davis, eds., *The Role of Government*, 21–49.

20. Carmella, "Religion Clauses and Acculturated Religious Conduct," 38–39.

21. 397 US 664 (1970).

22. 402 US 602 (1971).

23. Ira Lupu, "Free Exercise Exemptions and Religious Institutions: The Case of Employment Discrimination," *Boston University Law Review* 67 (1987): 319, 422.

24. Ibid. On associational rights, see *NAACP v Alabama*, 357 US 449 (1958).

25. Ira Lupu, "Keeping the Faith: Religion, Equality, and Speech in the U.S. Consti-

tution," *Connecticut Law Review* 18 (1986): 739, 765–66. Religious exemptions will be discussed in depth in Chapter 8.

26. A classic example of this problem is the case of *Rusk v Espinosa*, 456 US 951 (1982), in which the Supreme Court affirmed the invalidation of a city charitable solicitation ordinance that had distinguished between secular and religious solicitation, thus necessitating a decision of whether a program of the Seventh-Day Adventist Church was secular or religious.

27. Carmella, "Religion Clauses and Acculturated Religious Conduct," 25.

28. For a general discussion, see Carl Esbeck, "Governmental Regulation of Religiously Based Social Services: The First Amendment Considerations," *Hastings Law Quarterly* 19 (1992): 344.

29. *Needham Pastoral Counseling Center v Board of Appeals*, 560 N.E. 2d 121 (Mass. 1990). This case is discussed in Carmella, "A Theological Critique," and is her leading example of an acculturated religious activity. See also Angela Carmella, "Liberty and Equality: Paradigms for the Protection of Religious Property Uses," *Journal of Church and State* 37 (1995): 572.

30. *Lutheran Social Services v United States*, 758 F.2d 1283 (8th Cir. 1985).

31. Bruce Bagni, "Discrimination in the Name of the Lord: A Critical Evaluation of Discrimination by Religious Organizations," *Columbia Law Review* 79 (1984): 1514, 1539–40.

32. Laycock, "Toward a General Theory of the Religion Clauses"; Lawrence Tribe, *American Constitutional Law*, 2nd ed. (Mineola, N.Y.: Foundation Press, 1988), 1236; Paul Kauper, "Church Autonomy and the First Amendment," in *Church and State: The Supreme Court and the First Amendment*, ed. Philip Kurland (Chicago: University of Chicago Press, 1975).

33. 438 US 327 (1987). The religious discrimination aspects of this case will be discussed in the appropriate section of this chapter.

34. See Susan Rose, *Keeping Them out of the Hands of Satan: Evangelical Schooling in America* (New York: Routledge, 1988), and James Casper and Thomas Hunt, *Religious Schooling in America* (Birmingham, Ala.: Religious Education Press, 1984).

35. For a general discussion, see Neal Devins, "Fundamentalist Christian Educators versus the State: An Inevitable Compromise," *George Washington Law Review* 60 (1992): 818.

36. *State ex rel. Douglas v Faith Baptist Church*, 301 N.W. 2d 571 207 Neb. 802 (1981). See also *Meyerkorth v State*, 173 Neb. 889, 115 N.W. 2d 585 (1962). In the Nebraska case, the state supreme court, using a compelling interest test, found that whereas the state had a compelling interest in educational quality, the requirement that teachers hold a baccalaureate degree was not sufficiently related to that interest to withstand strict scrutiny. Ultimately, a legislative compromise was reached satisfactory both to the state and to the school. See Richard E. Shugrue, "An Approach to Mutual Respect: The Christian Schools Controversy," *Creighton Law Review* 18 (1985): 219.

37. 589 S.W.2d 877 (Ky. 1979).

38. *North Carolina v Columbus Christian Academy*, No. 111, N.C. Supreme Court, 1979.

39. See Cover, "Nomos and Narrative," 60. See also Paul R. Marr, "Constitutional Law: Religious Schools, Public Policy, and the Constitution" (case note), *North Carolina Law*

Review 62 (1984): 1051, Matthew B. Durrant, "Accrediting Church Related Schools: A First Amendment Analysis," *Arkansas Law Review* 38 (1985): 398, and William Marshall and Douglas Blomgren, "Regulating Religious Organizations under the Establishment Cause," *Ohio State Law Journal* 47 (1986): 293.

40. 440 US 490 (1979). See Laycock, "Toward a General Theory of the Religion Clauses," 1378.

41. See Mark Kohler, "Equal Employment or Excessive Entanglement: The Application of Employment Discrimination Statutes to Religiously Affiliated Organizations," *Connecticut Law Review* 18 (1986): 381 n. 62, for a discussion of this point.

42. 471 US 290 (1985).

43. A fascinating variation of this problem was raised in the case of *Brock v Wendell's Woodworks, Inc.*, 867 F.2d 196 (4th Cir. 1989), which is discussed in Chapter 4. Based on their religious beliefs, these church members apprenticed their children in the businesses of co-religionists, who employed them in violation of child labor and minimum wage laws. The Fourth Circuit rejected their Free Exercise defense in light of the dangers to the children and the importance of abolishing the evils of child labor.

44. 899 F.2d 1389 (4th Cir.).

45. 42 USC § 20003 (1976).

46. 78 Stat 255, as amended 42 USC § 2000e–1.

47. Among the many sources on these issues, see Carolyn Parmeter, "EEOC Jurisdiction over Churches: How Far Does it Go?" (case note), *Loyola Law Review* 28 (1982): 332; Michael McConnell, "Special Hiring Protection for Churches Upheld: The Impact of the Amos Decision," *Quarterly (Critical Legal Studies)* 8 (1987): 22; and Bruce Burleson, "The Applicability of Title VII to Sectarian Schools" (case note), *Baylor Law Review* 33 (1981): 381. For the general topic of the dilemma posed by voluntary associations in a democracy, the classic source is Robert Dahl, *Dilemmas of Pluralist Democracy* (New Haven: Yale University Press, 1982).

48. The institution must, however, be a genuinely religious one. This issue arose in *EEOC v Kamehameha Schools/Bishop Estate*, 990 F.2d 458 (9th Cir. 1993), challenging a requirement, designated by the founder of a private school, that it hire only Protestants as teachers. Because the school was not operated as a religious school, this requirement was not enforceable and treated as nothing more than a preference of the founder.

49. 479 US 1052 (1987).

50. Gedicks, "Toward a Constitutional Jurisprudence of Religious Group Rights," 114.

51. Steven Gey, "Why is Religion Special?: Reconsidering the Accommodation of Religion Under the Religion Clauses of the First Amendment," *University of Pittsburgh Law Review* 52 (1990): 75, 94–95. This outcome seems to confirm David Gregory's observation: "The Supreme Court has consistently demonstrated inordinate judicial deference to institutional employer interests. This has occurred at the expense of the employee's constitutional right to the free exercise of religion in the workplace, and of the statutory right not to be discriminated against in employment on the basis of religion." See David Gregory, "Government Regulation of Religion through Labor and Employment Discrimination Laws," in Wood and Davis, eds., *The Role of Government*, 123.

52. Gey, "Why is Religion Special?," 92.

53. For a general discussion, see "Equal Employment or Excessive Entanglement," 581.

54. *McClure v Salvation Army*, 460 F.2d 553 (5th Cir. 1972). But several years later,

in *EEOC v Pacific Press Publishing Company*, 676 F.2d 1272 (9th Cir. 1982), the Ninth Circuit had no difficulty holding a religious publishing company for sex discrimination against a female editorial secretary. Unlike in *McClure*, she was not a minister, and a religious publishing house was not a church.

55. *EEOC v Mississippi College*, 626 F.2d 477 (5th Cir. 1980).

56. Subsequently, the other five seminaries agreed to submit the form "under protest" pending the outcome of the litigation.

57. 485 F. Supp. 255, (N.D. Tex. 1980), review in part 651 F.2d 177 (5th Cir. 1981). See also Robert F. Salvia, "The Applicability of Title VII to Sectarian Schools: *EEOC v Mississippi College*, 626 F.2d 417 (5 Cir. 1980)," *New York Law School Law Review* 26 (1981): 915; Burleson, "The Applicability of Title VII to Sectarian Schools" (case note); and Carolyn Parmeter, "EEOC Jurisdiction over Churches: *Southwestern Baptist Theological Seminary*," *Loyola Law Review* 28 (1982): 332.

58. 477 US 619 (1986), rev'g 766 F.2d 932 (6th Cir. 1985), rev'g 578 F. Supp. 1004 (S.D. Ohio 1984).

59. Gedicks, "Toward a Constitutional Jurisprudence of Religious Group Rights," 102.

60. Ibid., 112.

61. *Madsen v Erwin*, 395 Mass. 715, 481 N.E. 2d 1160 (1985).

62. 536 F.2d 1 (Nov. 20, 1987). See Richard F. Duncan, "Who Wants to Stop the Church: Homosexual Rights Legislation, Public Policy, and Religious Freedom," *Notre Dame Law Review* 69 (1994): 393.

63. 26 USC 501(c)(3) (1986).

64. 397 US 664 (1970).

65. See R. Colin Mangrum, "Naming Religion (and Eligible Cognates) in Tax Exemption Cases," *Creighton Law Review* 19 (1986): 821. See also Sharon L. Worthing, "'Religion' and 'Religious Institutions' under the First Amendment," *Pepperdine Law Review* 7 (1980): 313–53; Terry Slye, "Rendering Unto Caesar: Defining 'Religion' for Purposes of Administering Religion-Based Tax Exemptions," *Harvard Journal of Law and Public Policy* 6 (1983): 219.

66. See Charles M. Whelan, "Church in the Internal Revenue Code: The Definitional Problems," *Fordham Law Review* 45 (1977): 885.

67. Treasury Regulation § 1.511–2(a)(3)(ii). Quoted by Stanley Weithorn and Douglas Allen, "Taxation and the Advocacy Role of the Churches in Public Affairs," in Wood and Davis, eds., *The Role of Government*, 55.

68. See Brian Petkanics and Sandra Petkanics, "Mail Order Ministries, the Religious Purpose Exemption, and the Constitution," *Tax Law* 33 (1980): 959; Note: "I Know it When I See It: Mail Order Ministry Tax Fraud and the Problem of a Constitutionally Acceptable Definition of Religion," *Criminal Law Review* 25 (1987): 113.

69. See *Holy Spirit Association for the Unification of World Christianity v Tax Commission*, 44 N.Y. 2d 512 (1982).

70. *United States v Sun Myung Moon*, 718 F.2d 1210 (2d Cir. 1983).

71. Lawrence Tribe et al. (counsel for appellant) Brief for Appellant *U.S. v Sun Myung Moon*, 718 F.2d 1210 (2d Cir. 1983). Notice that this is essentially the same reasoning that the Supreme Court relied on in *Amos*, holding that the distinction between a religious and nonreligious activity of a church was itself a religious distinction, for which

the Courts must rely on the church's own judgment. It is worth noting that Moon's position was supported by the National Council of Churches and other mainline church institutions, who perceived that the Moon precedent could endanger all church economic autonomy. For a contrasting view, see Joey P. Moore, "Piercing the Religious Veil of the So-called Cults," *Pepperdine Law Review* 7 (1987): 655–710. For a general discussion, see Robbins, "Church State Tensions," 135–49.

72. *United States v Sun Myung Moon*, 718 F.2d 1210 (2d Cir. 1983).

73. See *Fogarty v United States*, 780 F.2d 1005 (D. C. 1986); *Schuster v Commissioner*, 800 F.2d 672 (7th Cir. 1986).

74. See Weithorn and Allen, "Taxation and the Advocacy Role," 51–64; Ellis West, "The Free Exercise Clause and the Internal Revenue Code's Restriction on Political Activity of Tax Exempt Organizations," *Wake Forest Law Review* 21 (1986): 395; Robert E. Trautmann, "Conflicts Between the First Amendment Religion Clauses and the Internal Revenue Code: Politically Active Religious Organizations and Racially Discriminatory Private Schools," *Washington University Law Quarterly* 61 (1983): 509; and Ann Bernell Carroll, "Religious Politics and the IRS: Defining the Limits of Tax Controls on Political Expression by Churches," *Marquette Law Review* 77 (1992): 213.

75. *Regan v Taxation with Representation*, 461 US 540 (1983). See the discussion of unconstitutional conditions in Chapter 7.

76. Weithorn and Allen, "Taxation and the Advocacy Role," 63.

77. 544 F. Supp. 471 (S.D. N.Y. 1982).

78. *Abortion Rights Mobilization v Baker* (*In re United States Catholic Conference*), 885 F.2d 1020 (2d Cir. 1989). See also *Abortion Rights Mobilization Inc. v United States Catholic Conference*, 495 US 918 (1990).

79. In *Christian Echoes National Ministry v United States*, 470 F.2d 849 (10th Cir. 1972), right-wing evangelist Billy James Hargis lost his exemptions after compiling an egregious record of political involvement.

80. 461 US 574 (1983). See Douglas Laycock, "Tax Exemptions for Racially Discriminatory Religious Schools," *Texas Law Review* 50 (1982): 259. For a splendid account of the political background of this case, see Louis Fisher and Neal Devins, *Political Dynamics of Constitutional Law* (St. Paul, Minn.: West, 1992), 52–67. On the university itself, see Quentin Schultze, "The Two Faces of Fundamentalist Higher Education," in Martin Marty and Scott Appleby, eds. *Fundamentalisms and Society* (Chicago: University of Chicago Press, 1993), 490–535.

81. In *Runyon v McCray*, 427 US 160 (1976), the Court had held that the Reconstruction era Civil Rights Act 42 § USC 1981 forbade racial discrimination in private schools, but the issue of private religious schools was not addressed. It is interesting to contrast this case with a much earlier one, *Berea College v Kentucky*, 211 US 45 (1911), in which a private religious college was punished for violating a state's law *requiring* racial segregation.

82. Before 1971 it had not admitted black persons at all; from 1971 until 1975 it enrolled only married blacks; beginning in 1975 it admitted both blacks and whites, subject to the restrictions on interracial dating and marriage.

83. Cover, "Nomos and Narrative," esp. 62–67.

84. Ibid., 66–67.

85. See Chapters 2 and 3 for further explanation.

86. 490 US 680 (1989). See Mark Geier, "What the Good Lord Giveth, Uncle Sam Taketh Away," *Hamline Law Review* 13 (1990): 433.

87. *Davis v United States*, 495 US 472 (1990).

88. Review Rul. 83–104 SFTR Vol. 3, 911690.446.

89. *Texas Monthly v Bullock*, 489 US 1 (1989).

90. *Jimmy Swaggart Ministries v Board of Equalization of California*, 493 US 378 (1990).

91. Cover, "Nomos and Narrative," 33.

92. *Bemis Pentecostal Church v State of Tennessee*, 731 SW 2d 897 (May 26, 1987). See Dwight Tays, "Church Participation in Referenda and the First Amendment," *Journal of Church and State* 32 (1990): 391.

93. On the Sanctuary Movement, see Robin Johansen and Kathleen Purcell, "Government Response to the Sanctuary Movement," in Wood and Davis, eds., *The Role of Government*, 161–78; Ann Crittenden, *Sanctuary: The Story of American Conscience and Law in Collision* (New York: Weidenfeld and Nicholson, 1988); "A Symposium on the Sanctuary Movement," *Hofstra Law Review* 15 (Fall 1986): 37; and Ignatius Bau, *This Ground is Holy* (New York: Paulist Press, 1985).

94. 871 F.2d 1436 (9th Cir. 1989). For a related issue, see *American Friends Service Committee v Thornburgh*, 718 F. Supp. 820 (C.D. Cal. 1989).

95. 752 F. Supp. 1505 (D. Ariz., 1990).

96. 13 Wall. 679 (1872). On this topic in general, see John Garvey, "Churches and the Free Exercise of Religion," *Notre Dame Journal of Law, Ethics and Public Policy* 4 (1990): 567.

97. *Kedroff v St. Nicholas Cathedral of the Russian Orthodox Church*, 344 US 94 (1952).

98. *Serbian Eastern Orthodox Diocese v Milivojevich*, 426 US 696 (1976).

99. *Presbyterian Church v Mary Elizabeth Blue Hull Church*, 393 US 449 (1969).

100. 443 US 595 (1979).

101. See Thomas Robbins, "Government Regulatory Powers and Church Autonomy: Deviant Groups as Test Cases," *Journal for the Scientific Study of Religion* 24 (1985): 237, and Sharon Worthing, "The State Takes Over a Church," *Annals of the American Academy of Political and Social Science* 446 (1979): 136–48. See also Stephen Rader, "Government Protection of Church Assets from Fiscal Abuse: The Constitutionality of Attorney General Enforcement under the Religion Clauses of the First Amendment," *Southern California Law Review* 53 (1980): 1277.

102. For the vigorous autonomy argument, see Llyn R. Buzzard and Thomas Brandon, *Church Discipline and the Courts* (Wheaton, Ill.: Tyndale House Pub. Co., 1987).

103. 819 F.2d 875 (9th Cir. 1987). Of related interest are cases brought against the Church of Scientology by former members. See *Wollerstein v Church of Scientology*, 260 Cal. Rptr 331 (Ct. App 1989); *Van Schaick v Church of Scientology*, 535 F. Supp. 1125 (D. Mass 1982), and *Christofferson v Church of Scientology*, 644 P.2d 577 (Or. Ct. App. 1982).

104. 775 P.2d 766 (Okla. 1989).

105. Gedicks, "Religious Group Rights," 162.

106. The economic costs often lead affected institutions to challenge the designation under the Takings Clause as well as the First Amendment.

107. Angela Carmella, "Houses of Worship and Religious Liberty: Constitutional

Limits on Landmark Preservation and Architectural Review," *Villanova Law Review* 36 (1991): 401, 404–5. See also Thomas Pak, "Free Exercise, Free Expression and Landmark Preservation," *Columbia Law Review* 91 (1991): 1813.

108. 914 F.2d 348 (2d Cir. 1990).

109. 114 Wash. 2d 392, 787 P.2d 1352 (1990).

110. No. 87-3168, 87-4751, 87-6586, slip op. (Mass. Super. Ct. 1989).

111. *City of Boerne v Flores*, No. 95-2074 (decided June 25, 1997).

112. 321 US 158 (1944).

113. 316 US 584 (1942).

114. 319 US 105 (1943).

115. 452 US 640 (1981). Whereas the Minnesota Supreme Court had weighed only the costs of exempting ISKCON from the general policy and found in favor of ISKCON, the Supreme Court majority weighed the policy itself rather than the single exemption against the general policy. This kind of weighing is discussed in Chapter 8.

116. 456 US 228 (1982). Additionally, the case raised another issue, which was discussed in Chapter 2 — what constitutes a religion. The four dissenters would have denied standing to the Unification Church until their status as a religion had been fully litigated. The majority reasoned that the status was clear; had Unification not been considered a religion, the 50 percent requirement would not have been applied to them in the first place.

117. Lupu, "Keeping the Faith," 739.

118. *Wisconsin v Yoder*, 406 US 205, 234–36 (1972). This point is elaborated particularly well by Martha Minow, in "Pluralisms," *Connecticut Law Review* 21 (1989): 965.

119. 477 US 619 (1986).

120. 483 US 327 (1987).

121. Gedicks, "Religious Group Rights," 149–50.

122. See, for example, the difference in emphasis between the opinions of the majority and Justice Powell's concurring opinions in *Runyon v McCray*, 160, holding that the Civil Rights Act prohibits discrimination in nonsectarian private schools.

123. Lupu, "Keeping the Faith," 766.

124. *Jimmy Swaggart Ministries v Board of Equalization of California*, 493 US 378 (1990).

125. *Brown v Dade Christian Schools*, 556 F.2d 310 (5th Cir. 1978).

126. Laycock, "Toward a General Theory of the Religion Clauses," 1390–91.

127. Carmella, "The Religion Clauses and Acculturated Religious Conduct," 35.

128. Gedicks, "Religious Group Rights," 111.

129. See *Meek v Pittinger*, 421 US 349 (1975), and other parochial school aid cases. *Larsen v Valente*, 456 US 228 (1982).

130. 483 US 327 (1987).

131. 440 US 490 (1979). Such a political interpretation might lead one to ponder why Catholic and Mormon employees fare well in labor law conflicts, when a controversial one, like the Tony and Susan Alamo Foundation, was unsuccessful in its attempt to receive exemptions from the Fair Labor Standards Act. *Tony and Susan Alamo Foundation v Secretary of Labor*, 471 US 290 (1985).

132. *Employment Division, Department of Human Resources of Oregon v Smith*, 494 US 872 (1990). Judicial and legislative accommodation of religion will be discussed in depth in Chapter 8.

133. *Bob Jones University v United States,* 461 US 574 (1983).

134. Gedicks, "Religious Group Rights," 108–9.

135. Ibid., 144, 146 (citations omitted).

136. Cover, "Nomos and Narrative," 33.

137. Gedicks, "Religious Group Rights," 161 (citations omitted).

138. William Marshall and Douglas Blomgren, "Regulating Religious Organizations under the Establishment Clause," *Ohio State Law Journal* 47 (1986): 293, 309.

139. This formulation is similar to the argument made for individual autonomy by Jennifer Nedelsky in "Reconceiving Autonomy: Sources, Thoughts, and Possibilities," *Yale Journal of Law and Feminism* 90 (1987): 1.

CHAPTER 6

1. Emile Durkheim, *The Elementary Forms of Religious Life,* trans. Joseph Ward Swain (New York: Free Press, 1965).

2. Hans Mol, *Identity and the Sacred* (New York: Free Press, 1976), 1. Except where indicated, the remaining quotations in the following three paragraphs are from chapter 1 of Mol's book, pages 1–15.

3. Of course, the concept of identity is a problematic one. Mol's chapters 5 and 6 do an impressive job of surveying the literature on this elusive concept through the mid-1970s.

4. Mol, *Identity and the Sacred,* 55.

5. See Peter Berger, *The Sacred Canopy* (Garden City, N.Y.: Doubleday, 1967), and Peter Berger and Thomas Luckmann, *The Social Construction of Reality* (Garden City, N.Y.: Doubleday, 1966).

6. Clifford Geertz, "Religion as a Cultural System," in *Anthropological Approaches to the Study of Religion,* ed. Michael Banton (London: Tavistock, 1966), 4. Among the other sociological works emphasizing this theme, see Thomas Luckmann, *The Invisible Religion* (New York: Macmillan, 1967); Herve Carrier, *The Sociology of Religious Belonging* (New York: Herder and Herder, 1965). Consider meanings of the word identity. Eric Erickson's *Childhood and Society,* 2nd ed. (New York: Norton, 1963), for example, is useful here. See also Hans Mol, *Meaning and Place: An Introduction to the Social Scientific Study of Religion* (New York: Pilgrim Press, 1983).

7. Andrew Greeley, "Why Catholics Stay in the Church," *America* (Aug. 1–8, 1987).

8. The gendered noun is intentional here. The choosing self seems always to be a man. The discussion of free religious choice in Chapter 1 spells this theory out in more detail.

9. Michael Sandel, ed., *Liberalism and Its Critics* (New York: New York University Press, 1984), introduction, 5–6.

10. See, for example, Phillip E. Hammond and Kee Warner, "Religion and Ethnicity in Late Twentieth-Century America," *Annals of the American Academy of Political and Social Sciences* 527 (May 1993): 55.

11. See, for example, Roger Finke and Rodney Stark, *The Churching of America* (New Brunswick, N.J.: Rutgers University Press, 1992).

12. "Note, Reinterpreting the Religion Clauses: Constitutional Construction and Conceptions of the Self," *Harvard Law Review* 97 (1984): 1468.

13. Ibid., 1474.

14. Ibid., 1478.

15. Ibid., 1480–88.

16. Ibid., 1481–82.

17. For one perceptive argument on this theme, see Kenneth Karst, "The First Amendment, The Politics of Religion, and the Symbols of Government," *Harvard Civil Rights-Civil Liberties Law Review* 27 (1992): 503.

18. *Lynch v Donnelly*, 465 US at 688 and 692 (1984) (O'Connor concurring). The problem of government and religious symbolism continued in *County of Allegheny v ACLU*, 492 US 573 (1989), although with less elucidation. See in particular Justice Kennedy's refutation of O'Connor's endorsement test.

19. The school prayer and religious education cases often turn on this point. See most recently the dispute between Justice Kennedy's majority opinion and Justice Scalia's dissent on this point in *Lee v Weisman*, 505 US 577 (1992).

20. *Mozert et al. v Hawkins County Board of Education*, 827 F.2d 1058 (6th Cir. 1987); *Smith v Board of School Commissioners of Mobile County*, 827 F.2d 684 (11th Cir. 1987).

21. "Reinterpreting the Religion Clauses," 1478.

22. *Church of the Lukumi Babalu Aye, Inc., and Ernesto Pichado v City of Hialeah*, 508 US 520 (1993).

23. Kenneth Karst, "Religious Freedom and Citizenship," *Tulane Law Review* 69 (1994): 335, 352.

24. Ibid., 354.

25. 475 US 503 (1986).

26. See, for example, *Pollock v Marshall*, 845 F.2d 656 (6th Cir. 1988).

27. American Indian Religious Freedom Act, 42 USCA § 1996 (1978). See *Lyng v Northwest Indian Cemetery Protective Association*, 485 US 439 (1988). See also Fred Unmack, "Equality under the First Amendment: Protecting Native American Religious Practices on Public Lands," *The Public Land Law Review Annual* 18 (1987): 165; Erica Rosenberg, "Native American Access to Religious Sites: Underprotected under the Free Exercise Clause?" *Boston College Law Review* 26 (1985): 463; and Scott David Godshall, "Land Use Regulation and the Free Exercise Clause," *Columbia Law Review* 84 (1984): 1562.

28. See Mol, *Identity and the Sacred*.

29. Among many intelligent works on the concept of identity, my favorite is a series of cautionary and sometimes personal reflections by Leon Wieseltier in "Against Identity," *The New Republic*, Nov. 28, 1994, 24–32.

30. See Samuel C. Heilman, "The Jews: Schism or Division," in Thomas Robbins and Dick Anthony, *In Gods We Trust: New Patterns of Religious Pluralism in America*, 2nd ed. (New Brunswick, N.J.: Transaction Books, 1990), 185–98.

31. *Bowen v Roy*, 476 US 693 (1986).

32. "Reinterpreting the Religion Clauses," 1486.

33. After the research had been done for this book, I discovered two additional contributions to the jurisprudence of religious identity. See William Marshall, "Religion as Ideas: Religion as Identity," *Journal of Contemporary Legal Issues* 7 (1996): 385; and David B. Salmons, "Toward a Fuller Understanding of Religious Exercise: Recognizing the Identity-Generative and Expressive Nature of Religious Devotion," *University of Chicago Law Review* 62 (1995): 1243.

CHAPTER 7

1. 374 US 398 (1963).

2. See Ira Lupu, "Where Rights Begin: The Problem of Burdens on the Free Exercise of Religion," *Harvard Law Review* 102 (1989): 933.

3. Steven Smith, *Foreordained Failure* (New York: Oxford University Press, 1995), offers a devastating critique of Free Exercise jurisprudence based on this point.

4. *Employment Division, Department of Human Resources of Oregon v Smith*, 494 US 872 (1990).

5. *Sherbert v Verner*, 374 US 398 (1963).

6. Kathleen Sullivan, "Unconstitutional Conditions," *Harvard Law Review* 102 (1989): 1413, 1435.

7. *Sherbert v Verner*, 374 US 398 (1963).

8. *Hobbie v Unemployment Appeals Commission of Florida*, 480 US 136 (1987).

9. *Thomas v Review Board of the Indiana Employment Security Division*, 450 US 707 (1981).

10. *Frazee v Illinois Department of Employment Security*, 489 US 829 (1989). This and the preceding cases would appear to provide obvious precedents for the 1990 *Smith* case. The majority opinion, however, makes a peculiar use of this group of cases. Justice Scalia argues that unemployment compensation cases are the *only* ones in which the Courts have used the compelling state interest test, and then he goes on to treat *Smith* as though it were a criminal conviction instead of the unemployment compensation case it actually was.

11. 476 US 693 (1986). The Court split five to four, and there were five separate opinions.

12. 728 F.2d 1121 (8th Cir.1984). *Jensen v Quaring*, 472 US 478 (1985) (per curium) (affirmed by an equally divided Court).

13. 461 US 540 (1983). See Chapter 5 for a further discussion of taxation and religious institutions.

14. Sullivan, "Unconstitutional Conditions," 1415. Sullivan notes that while this view has "triumphed," it is nevertheless applied extremely inconsistently, and she cites numerous decisions to illustrate that fact.

15. Ibid., 1490.

16. Ibid., 1498.

17. Some situations are more ambivalent than the one I have depicted. In some instances, there was evidence that the patient wanted to live, was willing to have the treatment, but could not on religious grounds consent to it. Hence, having the treatment ordered without consent preserved the conscience of the patients while saving the life. See, for example, *Powell v Columbian Presbyterian Medical Center*, 49 Misc. 2d 215, 267 N.Y.S. 2d 459 (Sup. Ct. 1965); *United States v George*, 239 F. Supp. 752 (D. Conn. 1965); and *Application of President and Directors of Georgetown College, Inc.*, 331 F.2d 1000 (D.C. Cir. 1964). A slightly different twist was presented in the 1991 case of *Munn v Algee*, 924 F.2d 568 (5th Cir., 1991): A woman was fatally injured in an automobile accident in which the other driver admitted fault. The injured woman had refused a blood transfusion, and the defendant driver's insurance company successfully argued that she was responsible for her own death.

18. 485 US 439 (1988).

19. See *Sequoia v TVA*, 620 F.2d 1159 (6th Cir. 1980); *Badoni v Higginson*, 638 F.2d 172 (10th Cir. 1980); *Wilson v Block*, 708 F.2d 735 (D.C. Cir. 1983); *Fools Crow v Gullet*, 706 F.2d 856 (8th Cir. 1983). Among the many works on this subject, see "Note: American Indians and the First Amendment: Site Specific Religion and Public Land Management," *Utah Law Review* 1987 (1987): 673; "Note: American Indian Sacred Religious Sites and Government Development: A Conventional Analysis in an Unconventional Setting," *Michigan Law Review* 85 (1987): 771; "Note: Indian Religious Freedom and Governmental Development of Public Lands," *Yale Law Journal* 94 (1985): 1447; Robert Michaelson, "American Indian Religious Freedom and Litigation: Promise and Perils," *Journal of Law and Religion* 3 (1987): 47; Fred Unback, "Equality under the First Amendment: Protecting Native American Religious Practices on Public Lands," *Public Land Law Review Annual* 8 (1987): 165; and Scott David Godshall, "Land Use Regulation and the Free Exercise Clause," *Columbia Law Review* 84 (1984): 1562.

20. *Lyng v Northwest Indian Cemetery Protective Association*, 485 US 439 (1988).

21. 476 US 693 (1986).

22. 485 US 439 (1988).

23. Justice Brennan continues, pointing out that the majority's decision relies on a distinction between government actions that "compel affirmative conduct inconsistent with religious beliefs" and those government actions that "prevent" conduct consistent with religious beliefs. He then notes that one of the dictionary definitions of "prohibit" is "to prevent from doing something." *Id.* at 1334–35, note 4.

24. 435 US 618 (1978).

25. 456 US 228 (1982).

26. *Mozert et al. v Hawkins County Board of Education*, 827 F.2d 1058 (6th Cir. Tenn. 1987).

27. 508 US 520 (1993).

28. *Church of the Lukumi Babalu Aye, Inc., and Ernesto Pichado v City of Hialeah*, 723 F. Supp. 1467, 1483–83 (S.D. Fla. 1989).

29. *Church of the Lukumi Babalu Aye, Inc., and Ernesto Pichado v City of Hialeah*, 936 F.2d 586 (1991).

30. *Church of the Lukumi Babalu Aye, Inc., and Ernesto Pichado v City of Hialeah*, 508 US 520 (1993).

31. Justice Scalia, concurring, draws a distinction between lack of neutrality and lack of general applicability—although he notices that the distinction is not necessary in this case. Lack of neutrality for Scalia applies to laws that "by their terms impose disabilities on religion . . . whereas the defect of lack of general applicability applies primarily to those laws which, though neutral in their terms, through their design construction, or enforcement target the practices of a religion for discriminatory treatment."

32. See, for example, *Mobile v Bouldon*, 446 US 55 (1980).

33. This seems to be the position advocated by Jesse Choper in *Securing Religious Liberty* (Chicago: University of Chicago Press, 1995), 41–55.

34. Blackmun's concurring opinion was joined by O'Connor. In addition to the Blackmun-O'Connor opinion, Justice Souter wrote a concurring opinion calling for the reconsideration of the *Smith* distinction between laws specifically targeting religion and laws of general applicability.

35. See Michael McConnell, "Coercion: The Lost Element of Establishment," *William and Mary Law Review* 27 (1986): 933. See also Jesse Choper, "The Religion Clauses of the First Amendment: Reconciling the Conflict," *University of Pittsburgh Law Review* 41 (1980): 673. His position is elaborated more thoroughly in *Securing Religious Liberty*.

36. 492 US 573 (1989). Kennedy continues: "There is no suggestion here that the government's power to coerce has been used to further the interests of Christianity or Judaism in any way. No one is compelled to observe or participate in any religious ceremony or activity" (492 US 573 [Justice Kennedy, concurring in part and dissenting in part, at 659–62] [1989]).

37. *Lee v Weisman*, 505 US 577 (1992). The U.S. government amicus brief in this case advanced the theory that only practices that coerce religious belief or observance should be held to violate the Establishment Clause.

38. 485 US 439 (1988).

39. Sullivan, "Unconstitutional Conditions," 1446. On defining coercion, see Richard A. Epstein, "Unconstitutional Conditions, State Power, and the Limits of Consent," *Harvard Law Review* 193 (1988): 4; Peter Westen, "Freedom and Coercion—Virtue Words and Vice Words," *Duke Law Journal* (1985): 541; and Jeffrie Murphy, "Consent, Coercion, and Hard Choices," *Virginia Law Review* 67 (1981): 79.

40. Robert Nozick, "Coercion," in *Philosophy, Science, and Method*, ed. Sidney Morgenbresser, Patrick Suppes, and Morton White (New York: St. Martin's Press, 1969), 440.

41. Seth Kreimer, "Allocational Rights: The Problem of Negative Rights in a Positive State," *University of Pennsylvania Law Review* 123 (1984): 1293, cited by Sullivan, "Unconstitutional Conditions," 1450.

42. See Anthony Kronman, "Contract Law and Distributive Justice," *Yale Law Journal* 89 (1980): 472, cited by Sullivan, "Unconstitutional Conditions," 1449.

43. See Herbert Fingarette, "Coercion, Coercive Persuasion, and the Law," in *Cults, Culture, and the Law*, ed. Thomas Robbins, W. Sheppard, and J. McBride (American Academy of Religion, 1985), 81.

44. This dispute parallels the issues raised by Justice O'Connor's "dispassionate observer" test of "endorsement." See *Lynch v Donnelly*, 465 US 668 (1984), and *Allegheny County v ACLU*, 492 US 573 (1989).

45. *Reynolds v United States*, 98 US 145 (1879).

46. 435 US 618 (1978). In his concurring opinion in that case, Justice Brennan suggested that laws that classify and impose burdens along religious lines demand higher constitutional scrutiny than those that only incidentally burden religious exercises.

47. 456 US 228 (1982). See also *Fowler v Rhode Island*, 345 US 67 (1953), invalidating a law against public preaching aimed specifically at Jehovah's Witnesses.

48. 475 US 503, 512–13 (1986) (Stevens, J. concurring).

49. 494 US 872 (1990).

50. Ibid. (O'Connor, concurring).

51. Michael McConnell, "Free Exercise Revisionism and the *Smith* Decision," *University of Chicago Law Review* 57 (1990): 1136 (citations omitted). McConnell illustrates this point with the example of *Stanbury v Marks*, 2 US 213 (1793), in which a Jew was fined by the Pennsylvania courts for refusal to be sworn as a witness in court on a Saturday. In those days, courts were regularly open on Saturdays but closed on Sundays. The intent was not to disadvantage Jews; the religious impact was simply inadvertent. See Justice

Souter's concurring opinion in *Church of Babalu Lukumi Aye* for further explication of this point.

52. Douglas Laycock, "The Remnants of Free Exercise," *Supreme Court Review* (1990): 1, and "Text, Intent, and the Religion Clauses," *Notre Dame Journal of Law, Ethics, and Public Policy* 4 (1990): 683. One is reminded of the famous (perhaps apocryphal) comment about famed Notre Dame coach Vince Lombardi: "Coach treated all players equally—like dogs."

53. Laycock, "The Remnants of Free Exercise," 13.

54. McConnell, "Free Exercise Revisionism," 1139.

55. See Kenneth Karst, "Religious Freedom and Equal Citizenship: Reflections on *Lukumi*," *Tulane Law Review* 69 (1994): 335.

CHAPTER 8

1. 508 US 520 2217 (1993). See also *Larson v Valente*, 456 US 228 (1982).

2. The classic description of this process is still Robert Dahl's *Who Governs* (New Haven: Yale University Press, 1961).

3. *Employment Division, Department of Human Resources of Oregon v Smith*, 494 US 872 (1990). Among the enormous commentary on this case, the following are of particular note: Michael McConnell, "Free Exercise Revisionism and the *Smith* Decision," *University of Chicago Law Review* 57 (1990): 1109; Douglas Laycock, "The Remnants of Free Exercise," *Supreme Court Review* (1990): 1; James Gordon III, "Free Exercise on the Mountaintop," *California Law Review* 79 (1991): 91; and William Marshall, "In Defense of *Smith* and Free Exercise Revisionism," *University of Chicago Law Review* 58 (1991): 308.

4. Religious Freedom Restoration Act of 1993. Pub. L. No. 103–41, 197 Stat. 1480.

5. Advocates on all sides have appealed to the historical record for the intent of the framers of the Constitution. Michael McConnell reads the record as suggesting (although not proving) an intent to include religion-based exemptions; see Michael McConnell, "The Origins and Historical Understanding of Free Exercise of Religion," *Harvard Law Review* 103 (1990): 1410. Ellis West and Michael Malbin conclude that such exemptions were not intended. See Ellis West, "The Case Against a Right to Religion-Based Exemptions," *Notre Dame Journal of Law, Ethics, and Public Policy* 4 (1990): 591, and "The Right to Religion-Based Exemptions in Early America: The Case of Conscientious Objectors to Conscription," *Journal of Law and Religion* 10 (1993): 363; and Michael Malbin, *Religion and Politics: The Intentions of the Authors of the First Amendment* (Washington, D.C.: American Enterprise Institute, 1978). Since my approach does not take intent as authoritative, my survey does not include either argument.

6. Michael McConnell is the leading academic advocate of this view. Among his voluminous writings, see "Accommodation of Religion," *Supreme Court Review* (1985): 1; "Accommodation of Religion: An Update and a Response to the Critics," *George Washington Law Review* 60 (1992): 685; "Free Exercise Revisionism and the Smith Decision," 1109; "Neutrality Under the Religion Clauses," *Northwestern University Law Review* 81 (1986): 146; and "The Origins and Historical Understanding of the Free Exercise of Religion," 1409.

7. The classic statement of this position is made by Philip Kurland, "Of Church and

State and the Supreme Court," *University of Chicago Law Review* 29 (1961): 1. See also Steven Gey, "Why is Religion Special?: Reconsidering the Accommodation of Religion under the Religion Clauses of the First Amendment," *University of Pittsburgh Law Review* 52 (1990): 75.

8. See William Marshall, "The Case Against Constitutionally Compelled Free Exercise Exemptions," *Case Western Reserve Law Review* 40 (1989–90): 357. See also West, "The Case Against a Right to Religion-Based Exemptions," 591.

9. Ira Lupu, "Reconstructing the Religion Clauses," *University of Pennsylvania Law Review* 140 (1991): 555.

10. See Bette Novit Evans, "Contradictory Demands on the First Amendment Religion Clauses: Having it Both Ways," *Journal of Church and State* 30 (1988): 463.

11. Christopher Eisgruber and Lawrence Sager, "The Vulnerability of Conscience: The Constitutional Basis for Protecting Religious Conduct," *University of Chicago Law Review* 61 (1994): 1245, 1280.

12. *Goldman v Weinberger*, 475 US 503 (1986). The military had accommodated Sikhs by permitting turbans between the 1940s and 1960s, but the practice ceased when the military feared it would have to accommodate other kinds of religious garb.

13. P.L. 100–180, 101 Stat. 1086–87m S 508 (1987).

14. P.L. 104–41, 1993.

15. *Zorach v Clauson*, 343 US 306 at 313–14 (1952).

16. Among the arguments of this sort, see Jesse Choper, "The Free Exercise Clause: A Structural Overview and an Appraisal of Recent Developments," *William and Mary Law Review* 27 (1985–86): 943.

17. 472 US 703 (1985).

18. 483 US 327 (1987). This case is discussed at length in Chapter 5.

19. The classic statement is his "Accommodation of Religion," *Supreme Court Review* (1985): 1. But see Mark Tushnet's partial critique in "The Emerging Principle of Accommodation of Religion (Dubitante)," 76 Geo. L. J. 1691 (1988). McConnell's interpretation became the core of the Reagan administration Justice Department's understanding of Establishment, and it also found its way into the dissenting opinions in *Wallace v Jaffree*, 427 US 38 (1985).

20. Richard John Neuhaus, "A New Order for the Ages," *George Washington Law Review* 60 (1992): 620.

21. 482 US 578 (1987).

22. 489 US 1 (1989).

23. *Employment Division, Department of Human Resources of Oregon v Smith*, 494 US 872 (1990).

24. Lupu, "Reconstructing the Religion Clauses," 555. On the idea of equal liberty, he relies on Rawls's theory of justice, Dworkin's *Taking Rights Seriously*, and Richards's *Toleration and the Constitution*. The structure of Lupu's argument is strikingly reminiscent of Dworkin's distinction between a principle and a policy.

25. *Board of Education of Kiryas Joel Village School District v Grumet*, 512 US 687 (1994).

26. See *Aguilar v Felton*, 473 US 402 (1985), and *Grand Rapids School District v Ball*, 473 US 373 (1985).

27. On the advantages of multiple structures, see Robert Cover, "The Uses of Jurisdic-

tional Redundancy: Interest, Ideology, and Innovation," *William and Mary Law Review* 22 (1981): 629, and Martha Minow, "Pluralisms," *Connecticut Law Review* 21 (1989): 965.

28. 374 US 398 (1963).

29. 450 US 707 (1981).

30. 480 US 136 (1987).

31. 489 US 289 (1989).

32. *Wisconsin v Yoder*, 406 US 205 (1972).

33. 319 US 624 (1943).

34. 430 US 705 (1977). New Hampshire license plates carry the motto "Live Free or Die." Maynard was arrested for covering that message, which he found to be religiously and politically objectionable.

35. 472 US 478 (1985).

36. 471 US 290 (1985).

37. 475 US 503 (1986).

38. 455 US 252 (1982).

39. 461 US 540 (1983).

40. 482 US 342 (1987).

41. 493 US 378 (1990).

42. Philip Kurland, *Religion and the Law* (Chicago: Aldine, 1961), and "The Irrelevance of the Constitution: The Religion Clauses of the First Amendment and the Supreme Court," *Villanova Law Review* 24 (1978): 3, 24.

43. See, for example, Justice Black's classic statement in *Everson v Board of Education*, 330 US 1, 18 (1947): "[The First] Amendment requires the state to be neutral in its relations with groups of religious believers and nonbelievers; . . . State power is no more to be used so as to handicap religions, than it is to favor them."

44. West, "The Case Against a Right to Religion-Based Exemptions," 591. West notes that both Chief Justice Rehnquist and Justice Stephens have adopted this position.

45. Ibid., 600–601.

46. William Marshall, "The Free Exercise Dilemma: Free Exercise as Expression," *Minnesota Law Review* 67 (1983): 545, and "The Case Against the Constitutionally Compelled Free Exercise Exemption," 357.

47. Gey, "Why is Religion Special?," esp. 172–87.

48. Ibid., 180 (citations omitted).

49. In effect, as Douglas Laycock has noted, this reasoning understands the Free Exercise Clause as merely an adjunct to the equal protection guarantee. Religion may not be treated more disfavorably than any other activity. See Douglas Laycock, "The Remnants of Free Exercise," *Supreme Court Review* (1990): 1.

50. Scalia's critics note that in support of his argument he relies heavily both on discredited doctrines, such as *Reynolds v United States'* distinction between beliefs and actions, and long overruled decisions, such as *Minersville School District v Gobitis*. Furthermore, critics point out that the compelling state interest doctrine *has* in fact been given at least lip service most of the time—although it is true that except in unemployment compensation cases, courts have almost always found the burden met by the state.

51. This was the underlying logic of the Jewish merchant's arguments in *Braunfeld v Brown*, 366 US 420 (1961). Notice the sharp contrast with Justice Scalia's approach to minority religions in *Smith*.

52. Stephen Pepper, "Conflicting Paradigms of Religious Freedom: Liberty versus Equality," *Brigham Young University Law Review* (1993): 7, 41.

53. "The Vulnerability of Conscience: The Constitutional Basis for Protecting Religious Conduct," *University of Chicago Law Review* 61 (1994): 1245.

54. Eisgruber and Sager, "The Vulnerability of Conscience," 1283–84.

55. Ibid., 1281.

56. *Flores v City of Boerne*, 73 F.3d 1352 (5th Cir. 1996).

57. Michael McConnell, "Accommodation of Religion: An Update and A Response to the Critics," *George Washington Law Review* 60 (1992): 700.

58. See Thomas Robbins, "New Religious Movements on the Frontier of Church and State," in *Cults, Culture, and the Law*, ed. Thomas Robbins, W. Sheppard, and J. McBride (American Academy of Religion, 1985).

59. McConnell, "Accommodation of Religion: An Update," 703.

60. Ronald Dworkin, *Taking Rights Seriously* (Cambridge: Harvard University Press, 1977).

61. Consider *Jensen v Quaring*, 472 US 478 (1985), in which a woman with religious objections to personal images sought an exemption from the requirement of having her picture on her driver's license. If her claim had been weighed against the general interest of the state in photo-identified driver's licenses, she would not have had much chance to prevail. However, when courts weighed her claim against the anticipated problems caused by granting her an exemption and not the general policy, she had a far easier case. See also *Bowen v Roy*, 476 US 693 (1986). In both cases, U.S. solicitor general submitted briefs arguing that the state need only support its general policy against the claimant's rights rather than the state's interests in not granting the injunction. As Stephen Pepper points out, this argument put Solicitor General Charles Fried in an awkward position because Fried's argument to the contrary had been a classic in balancing-of-interests controversies. See Charles Fried, "Two Concepts of Interests," *Harvard Law Review* 76 (1963): 755, and Pepper's critique in Stephen Pepper, "*Reynolds, Yoder,* and Beyond: Alternatives for the Free Exercise Clause," *Utah Law Review* (1981): 309.

62. *United States v Carolene Products*, 304 US 144 n.4 (1938). The most thorough and persuasive argument on this approach is found in John Hart Ely, *Democracy and Distrust* (Cambridge: Harvard University Press, 1980).

63. 374 US 398 (1963).

64. 406 US 205 (1972).

65. *Employment Division, Department of Human Resources of Oregon v Smith*, 494 US 872 (1990), quoting *Reynolds v United States*, 98 US 145 (1878).

66. O'Connor quotes both *Wisconsin v Yoder* and *Bowen v Roy* as if to emphasize her point that the compelling state interest test is not an anomaly.

67. Pub. L. No. 103–44; 107 Stat. 1480.

68. *City of Boerne v Flores*, No. 95-2074 (decided June 25, 1997).

69. "Countermainstream" would be a better term in view of my argument that policy making is a matter of minority coalitions rather than majorities. However, the term is awkward, while "countermajoritarian" is widely understood.

CHAPTER 9

1. Franklin Gamwell, *The Meaning of Religious Freedom* (Albany: State University of New York Press, 1995).

2. Plato, *The Republic*, trans. G. A. Grube (Indianapolis: Hackett, 1974).

3. John Courtney Murray, who so strongly influenced Vatican II thinking on religious freedom, spoke from the American experience. Murray argued for broad religious freedom within a society committed to civility. However, he believed that very civility depended upon broad acceptance of a natural law that bound all persons and governments. Religious freedom in no way has constrained government from promoting and supporting theocratic faith in a nonsectarian way. See Murray, ed., *Religious Liberty: An End and a Beginning* (New York: Macmillan, 1966).

4. Michael Sandel, "The Procedural Republica and the Unencumbered Self," *Political Theory* 12 (1984): 1, and *Democracy's Discontent* (Cambridge: Harvard University Press, 1996).

5. Alasdair MacIntyre, *After Virtue*, 2nd ed. (Notre Dame, Ind.: University of Notre Dame Press, 1984).

6. Charles Taylor, *Multiculturalism and The Politics of Recognition* (Princeton, N.J.: Princeton University Press, 1992).

7. See Ronald Dworkin's "Liberalism," in *A Matter of Principle* (Cambridge: Harvard University Press, 1985).

8. Avigail Eisenberg, *Reconstructing Political Pluralism* (Albany, N.Y.: State University of New York Press, 1995), 16. See also Nancy Rosenbaum, "Pluralism and Self Defense," in *Liberalism and the Moral Life* (Cambridge, Mass.: Harvard University Press, 1989).

9. See, for example, Marilyn Friedman, "Feminism and Modern Friendship," in *Communitarianism and Individualism*, ed. Shlomo Avineri and Avner de-Shalit (New York: Oxford University Press, 1992).

10. John Figgis, *Churches in the Modern State*, 2nd ed. (New York: Russell and Russell, 1914). See also a collection of readings from G. D. H. Cole, John Figgis, and Harold Laski in *The Pluralist Theory of the State*, ed. Paul Q. Hirst (New York: Routledge, 1989).

11. Jacques Maritan, *Man and the State* (Chicago: University of Chicago Press, 1951), and *The Person and the Common Good*, trans. John J. Fitzgerald (Notre Dame: Notre Dame University Press, 1966).

12. See, for example, Abraham Kuyper, *The Problem of Poverty*, ed. James Skillen (Grand Rapids, Mich.: Baker, 1991).

13. Peter Berger and Richard John Neuhaus, *To Empower People: The Role of Mediating Structures in Public Policy* (Washington, D.C.: American Enterprise Institute for Public Policy Research, 1977).

14. One good example of this approach is Stephen Monsma's argument for the quasi sovereignty of religious communities and associations based on the stronger European and Christian pluralist theories. See Stephen Monsma, *Positive Neutrality* (Westport, Conn.: Greenwood Press, 1993). In a different context, see Chief Justice Rehnquist's defense of associational autonomy in "The Adversarial Society," *Miami Law Review* 33 (1978): 1.

15. Kenneth Karst, "Paths to Belonging: The Constitution and Cultural Identity," *North Carolina Law Review* 64 (1986): 303.

16. James Madison, "Federalist Number 10," in Alexander Hamilton et al., *The Federalist Papers* (1787–88; New York: Bantam, 1982), 46. Political scientist James Pieper has formalized the conditions for Madisonian pluralism in a dissertation entitled "Democracy, Equality and the Law: The Problem of Political Equality in the United States" (Ph.D. diss., Duke University, 1996).

17. James Madison, "Federalist 51," in Hamilton et al., *Federalist Papers*, 261–64.

18. These conditions for representative democracy have been worked out by several thinkers. Two that have influenced me are Elaine Spitz, *Majority Rule* (Chatham, N.J.: Chatham House, 1984), and Dahl, *Polyarchy*.

19. Arthur Bentley, *The Process of Government* (Chicago: University of Chicago Press, 1908).

20. David Truman, *The Governmental Process* (New York: Alfred A. Knopf, 1951).

21. Among Dahl's works, see especially *A Preface to Democratic Theory* (Chicago: University of Chicago Press, 1956), *Who Governs* (New Haven: Yale University Press, 1961), *Polyarchy* (New Haven: Yale University Press, 1971), and *Dilemmas of Pluralist Democracy* (New Haven: Yale University Press, 1982). For commentaries of Dahl's contributions, see David Held, *Models of Democracy* (Stanford: Stanford University Press, 1987); Carol Gould, *Rethinking Democracy* (Cambridge: Cambridge University Press, 1988); and Iris Marion Young, *Justice and the Politics of Difference* (Princeton: Princeton University Press, 1990).

22. Dahl's later work takes a more critical view of pluralism, showing particular concern for the effect of unequal resources. See, for example, *Democracy and Its Critics* (New Haven: Yale University Press, 1989). For another criticism in this tradition, see Theodore Lowi, *The End of Liberalism*, 2nd. ed. (New York: W. W. Norton, 1979).

23. The most articulate spokesman for the representation-enhancing view of judicial review is John Hart Ely, *Democracy and Distrust* (Cambridge: Harvard University Press, 1980).

24. This point is made particularly strongly by Eisenberg, *Restructuring Political Pluralism*, ch. 6, 130–70.

25. Michael Waltzer, *Spheres of Justice* (New York: Basic Books, 1983).

26. Eisenberg, *Restructuring Political Pluralism*, 178.

27. Ibid., 180.

28. Ibid.

29. John Rawls, *Political Liberalism* (New York: Columbia University Press, 1993). This consensus, in turn, presumes that people's comprehensive philosophical, religious, or moral systems can accommodate a commitment to basic toleration and civility. Clearly, not all religious and philosophical doctrines are included in this characterization. Thus, while Rawls's system is inclusive, it is not infinitely so; to be exact, his freedom of religion would not include religions that themselves cannot accept the principle of toleration.

30. James Davison Hunter, *Culture Wars: The Struggle to Define America* (New York: Basic Books, 1991).

31. Eisenberg, *Restructuring Political Pluralism*, 5. See also Young, *Justice and the Politics of Difference*, on this point. But this view has its critics as well. M. M. Slaughter has raised a provocative critique of this vision, noting that "pluralism diminishes the power of differences by treating all differences as equal when in terms of positionality, they are not." The point is that some of these differences convey power or its absence, and that

is a difference that makes a difference. See M. M. Slaughter, "The Multicultural Self: Questions of Subjectivity, Questions of Power," in *Constitutionalism Identity, Difference, and Legitimacy*, ed. Michael Rosenfeld (Durham: Duke University Press, 1994), 369–80, esp. 378.

32. Karst, "Paths to Belonging," 306.

33. Michael McConnell, "Religious Freedom at a Crossroads," in *The Bill of Rights in the Modern State*, ed. Geoffrey Stone, Richard Epstein, and Cass Sunstein (Chicago: University of Chicago Press, 1992), 115–94, 169.

34. Michael McConnell, "Christ, Culture, and Courts: A Niebuhrian Examination of First Amendment Jurisprudence," *De Paul Law Review* 42 (1992): 191, 211.

35. 283 US 605 (1931).

36. Among the many excellent discussions of religious discrimination, see Christopher Eisgruber and Lawrence Sager, "The Vulnerability of Conscience: The Constitutional Basis for Protecting Religious Conduct," *University of Chicago Law Review* 61 (1994): 1245; and Kenneth Karst, "The First Amendment, the Politics of Religion, and the Symbols of Government," *Harvard Civil Rights-Civil Liberties Law Review* 27 (1992): 503, and "Religious Freedom and Citizenship," *Tulane Law Review* 69 (1994): 355.

37. *Lynch v Donnelly*, 465 US 668, 688 (1984) (O'Connor concurring). She continues developing this point in her concurring opinions in *Wallace v Jaffree*, 472 US 38 (1985), and in *County of Allegheny v A.C.L.U.*, 492 US 573 (1989). See a particularly striking analysis of Justice O'Connor's view of religion in Winnifred Fallers Sullivan, *Paying the Words Extra* (Cambridge: Harvard University Press, 1994).

38. 592 F.2d 197 (3d Cir. 1979).

39. See *Mozert et al. v Hawkins County Board of Education*, 827 F.2d 1058 (6th Cir. 1987); *Smith v Board of School Commissioners of Mobile County*, 827 F.2d 684 (11th Cir. 1987); and *Grove v Mead School District No. 354*, 753 F.2d 1528 (9th Cir. 1985).

40. 406 US 205 (1972).

41. 455 US 242 (1982).

42. See *Sherbert v Verner*, 374 US 398 (1963); *Thomas v Review Board of the Indiana Employment Security Division*, 450 US 707 (1981); *Hobbie v Unemployment Appeals Commission of Florida*, 480 US 136 (1987); and *Frazee v Illinois Department of Employment Security*, 489 US 829 (1989).

43. *Equal Employment Opportunity Commission v Southwestern Baptist Theological Seminary*, 651 F.2d 177 (5th Cir. 1981).

44. 493 US 378 (1990). Here again, one might argue that the payment of sales taxes deprived the ministry of economic opportunities to pursue its religious mission — and thus the effect of the tax is to foster uniformity. I am not persuaded by this reasoning.

45. Here I rely on Angela Carmella's language and concept but reach a conclusion that I believe would differ from hers. See Carmella, "A Theological Critique of Free Exercise Jurisprudence," *George Washington Law Review* 60 (1992): 782.

46. Frank Lechner, "Fundamentalism Revisited," in *In Gods We Trust*, 2d ed., ed. Thomas Robbins and Dick Anthony (New Brunswick, N.J.: Transaction Books, 1990), 77, 80.

47. 406 US 205 (1972).

48. 461 US 574 (1983).

49. 827 F.2d 1058 (6th Cir. 1987).

50. 512 US 687 (1994).

51. See Mayer Freed and Daniel Polsby, "Race, Religion, and Public Policy: *Bob Jones University v US," Supreme Court Review* (1983): 1, arguing that *Bob Jones* is irreconcilable with *Yoder*. See also Douglas Laycock, "Tax Exemptions for Racially Discriminatory Schools," *Texas Law Review* 60 (1982): 259, criticizing the *Bob Jones* decision.

52. McConnell, "Christ, Culture, and Courts," 191, 196.

53. *Bob Jones University v United States,* 461 US 574 (1983) at 609.

54. This conclusion is surprising to me because my strongest sympathies are with the "redemptive" elements of liberal Judaism, the "peace and justice" activists of the Catholic Church, and the old Protestant civil rights coalition. Still, I find no way to privilege the redemptive agendas of these groups without applying the same principles to groups whose redemptive agendas I find abhorrent.

INDEX